HTML 4 For Dummies,
2nd Edition

Cheat Sheet

W9-BEW-063

Global Structure

`<!DOCTYPE>`	Document type
`<ADDRESS> ... </ADDRESS>`	Address
`<BODY> ... </BODY>`	Body
`<DIV> ... </DIV>`	Logical divisions
`<H1> ... </H1>`	Level 1 head
`<H2> ... </H2>`	Level 2 head
`<H3> ... </H3>`	Level 3 head
`<H4> ... </H4>`	Level 4 head
`<H5> ... </H5>`	Level 5 head
`<H6> ... </H6>`	Level 6 head
`<HEAD> ... </HEAD>`	Head
`<HTML> ... </HTML>`	HTML document
`<META>`	Meta information
`<SPAN> ... </SPAN>`	Span
`<TITLE> ... </TITLE>`	Document title
`<!- ... ->`	Comment

Lists

`<DD>`	Definition description
`<DIR> ... </DIR>`	Directory list
`<DL> ... </DL>`	Definition list
`<DT>`	Definition term
`<LI>`	List item
`<MENU> ... </MENU>`	Menu list
`<OL> ... </OL>`	Ordered list
`<UL> ... </UL>`	Unordered list

Tables

`<CAPTION> ... </CAPTION>`	Table caption
`<COL>`	Columns
`<COLGROUP>`	Column group properties
`<TABLE> ... </TABLE>`	Table
`<TBODY> ... </TBODY>`	Table body
`<TD> ... </TD>`	Table cell
`<TFOOT> ... </TFOOT>`	Table footer
`<TH> ... </TH>`	Table head
`<THEAD> ... </THEAD>`	Table head
`<TR> ... </TR>`	Table row

...For Dummies®: Bestselling Book Series for Beginners

HTML 4 For Dummies,® 2nd Edition

Cheat Sheet

Text Tags

`<ABBR> ... </ABBR>`	Abbreviation
`<BLOCKQUOTE> ... </BLOCKQUOTE>`	Blockquote
` `	Line break
`<CITE> ... </CITE>`	Short citation
`<CODE> ... </CODE>`	Code
`<DEL> ... </DEL>`	Deleted section
`<DFN> ... </DFN>`	Defined term
`<EM> ... </EM>`	Emphasis
`<INS> ... </INS>`	Inserted section
`<KBD> ... </KBD>`	Keyboard text
`<P> ... </P>`	Paragraph
`<PRE> ... </PRE>`	Preformatted text
`<Q> ... </Q>`	Short quotation
`<SAMP> ... </SAMP>`	Sample text
`<STRONG> ... </STRONG>`	Strong emphasis
`<SUB> ... </SUB>`	Subscript
`<SUP> ... </SUP>`	Superscript
`<VAR> ... </VAR>`	Variable text

Presentation Controls

`<B> ... </B>`	Boldface
`<BASEFONT>`	Base font
`<BIG> ... </BIG>`	Big text
`<CENTER> ... </CENTER>`	Center
`<FONT> ... </FONT>`	Font appearance
`<HR>`	Horizontal rule
`<I> ... </I>`	Italic
`<S> ... </S>`	Strike through
`<SMALL> ... </SMALL>`	Small text
`<STRIKE> ... </STRIKE>`	Strike through
`<TT> ... </TT>`	Teletype text
`<U> ... </U>`	Underlined text

IDG BOOKS WORLDWIDE

...For Dummies®: Bestselling Book Series for Beginners

™

BESTSELLING BOOK SERIES

References for the Rest of Us!®

Are you intimidated and confused by computers? Do you find that traditional manuals are overloaded with technical details you'll never use? Do your friends and family always call you to fix simple problems on their PCs? Then the *...For Dummies*® computer book series from IDG Books Worldwide is for you.

...For Dummies books are written for those frustrated computer users who know they aren't really dumb but find that PC hardware, software, and indeed the unique vocabulary of computing make them feel helpless. *...For Dummies* books use a lighthearted approach, a down-to-earth style, and even cartoons and humorous icons to dispel computer novices' fears and build their confidence. Lighthearted but not lightweight, these books are a perfect survival guide for anyone forced to use a computer.

> *"I like my copy so much I told friends; now they bought copies."*
>
> — Irene C., Orwell, Ohio

> *"Quick, concise, nontechnical, and humorous."*
>
> — Jay A., Elburn, Illinois

> *"Thanks, I needed this book. Now I can sleep at night."*
>
> — Robin F., British Columbia, Canada

Already, millions of satisfied readers agree. They have made *...For Dummies* books the #1 introductory level computer book series and have written asking for more. So, if you're looking for the most fun and easy way to learn about computers, look to *...For Dummies* books to give you a helping hand.

IDG BOOKS WORLDWIDE®

1/99

HTML 4
FOR
DUMMIES®
2ND EDITION

HTML 4 FOR DUMMIES®

2ND EDITION

by Ed Tittel
&
Natanya Pitts

IDG Books Worldwide, Inc.
An International Data Group Company

Foster City, CA ◆ Chicago, IL ◆ Indianapolis, IN ◆ New York, NY

HTML 4 For Dummies®, 2nd Edition

Published by
IDG Books Worldwide, Inc.
An International Data Group Company
919 E. Hillsdale Blvd.
Suite 400
Foster City, CA 94404
www.idgbooks.com (IDG Books Worldwide Web site)
www.dummies.com (Dummies Press Web site)

Library of Congress Catalog Card No.: 99-63190

ISBN: 0-7645-0572-6

Printed in the United States of America

10 9 8 7 6 5 4

2B/QR/RR/ZZ/IN

Distributed in the United States by IDG Books Worldwide, Inc.

Distributed by CDG Books Canada Inc. for Canada; by Transworld Publishers Limited in the United Kingdom; by IDG Norge Books for Norway; by IDG Sweden Books for Sweden; by IDG Books Australia Publishing Corporation Pty. Ltd. for Australia and New Zealand; by TransQuest Publishers Pte Ltd. for Singapore, Malaysia, Thailand, Indonesia, and Hong Kong; by Gotop Information Inc. for Taiwan; by ICG Muse, Inc. for Japan; by Intersoft for South Africa; by Eyrolles for France; by International Thomson Publishing for Germany, Austria and Switzerland; by Distribuidora Cuspide for Argentina; by LR International for Brazil; by Galileo Libros for Chile; by Ediciones ZETA S.C.R. Ltda. for Peru; by WS Computer Publishing Corporation, Inc., for the Philippines; by Contemporanea de Ediciones for Venezuela; by Express Computer Distributors for the Caribbean and West Indies; by Micronesia Media Distributor, Inc. for Micronesia; by Chips Computadoras S.A. de C.V. for Mexico; by Editorial Norma de Panama S.A. for Panama; by American Bookshops for Finland.

For general information on IDG Books Worldwide's books in the U.S., please call our Consumer Customer Service department at 800-762-2974. For reseller information, including discounts and premium sales, please call our Reseller Customer Service department at 800-434-3422.

For information on where to purchase IDG Books Worldwide's books outside the U.S., please contact our International Sales department at 317-596-5530 or fax 317-596-5692.

For consumer information on foreign language translations, please contact our Customer Service department at 1-800-434-3422, fax 317-596-5692, or e-mail rights@idgbooks.com.

For information on licensing foreign or domestic rights, please phone +1-650-655-3109.

For sales inquiries and special prices for bulk quantities, please contact our Sales department at 650-655-3200 or write to the address above.

For information on using IDG Books Worldwide's books in the classroom or for ordering examination copies, please contact our Educational Sales department at 800-434-2086 or fax 317-596-5499.

For press review copies, author interviews, or other publicity information, please contact our Public Relations at 650-655-3000 or fax 650-655-3299.

For authorization to photocopy items for corporate, personal, or educational use, please contact Copyright Clearance Center, 222 Rosewood Drive, Danvers, MA 01923, or fax 978-750-4470.

About the Authors

Ed Tittel is a full-time writer/trainer who manages a small gang of technoids at LANWrights, his company in Austin, TX. Ed has been writing for the trade press since 1986, and has worked on nearly 100 books. In addition to this title, Ed has worked on nearly 30 books for IDG Books Worldwide, *including Networking Windows NT Server For Dummies, XML For Dummies,* and *Networking with NetWare For Dummies.*

Ed teaches for Austin Community College, NetWorld + Interop, and the Internet Security Conference. He also trains on and writes about the Novell and Microsoft certification curriculum and exams. When he's not busy doing all that work stuff, Ed likes to travel, shoot pool, and wrestle with his indefatigable Labrador retriever, Blackie.

Contact Ed Tittel by e-mail at etittel@lanw.com.

Natanya Pitts is a writer, trainer, and Web guru in Austin, Texas. She recently joined Pervasive Software's Educational Services group as a courseware developer. Her primary activities are development and maintenance of customer Web sites and consulting with organizations about the development of their Web presences and Web based training efforts. She also teaches Web page development and electronic commerce classes in the Austin Community College Webmaster Certification program.

Natanya has authored, co-authored, or contributed to more than a dozen Web and Internet related titles; the most recent include *The Dynamic HTML Black Book, The XML Black Book,* and *XML In Record Time.* Her current projects include developing, maintaining, and administering Web-based versions of her Web-related classes for Austin Community College.

Ms. Pitts has taught classes on HTML, Dynamic HTML, and XML at several national conferences (including MacWorld, Networld + Interop, and HP World), as well as at the NASA Ames Research Center.

Contact Natanya Pitts at natanya@lanw.com or natanyap@yahoo.com.

ABOUT IDG BOOKS WORLDWIDE

Welcome to the world of IDG Books Worldwide.

IDG Books Worldwide, Inc., is a subsidiary of International Data Group, the world's largest publisher of computer-related information and the leading global provider of information services on information technology. IDG was founded more than 30 years ago by Patrick J. McGovern and now employs more than 9,000 people worldwide. IDG publishes more than 290 computer publications in over 75 countries. More than 90 million people read one or more IDG publications each month.

Launched in 1990, IDG Books Worldwide is today the #1 publisher of best-selling computer books in the United States. We are proud to have received eight awards from the Computer Press Association in recognition of editorial excellence and three from Computer Currents' First Annual Readers' Choice Awards. Our best-selling *...For Dummies®* series has more than 50 million copies in print with translations in 31 languages. IDG Books Worldwide, through a joint venture with IDG's Hi-Tech Beijing, became the first U.S. publisher to publish a computer book in the People's Republic of China. In record time, IDG Books Worldwide has become the first choice for millions of readers around the world who want to learn how to better manage their businesses.

Our mission is simple: Every one of our books is designed to bring extra value and skill-building instructions to the reader. Our books are written by experts who understand and care about our readers. The knowledge base of our editorial staff comes from years of experience in publishing, education, and journalism — experience we use to produce books to carry us into the new millennium. In short, we care about books, so we attract the best people. We devote special attention to details such as audience, interior design, use of icons, and illustrations. And because we use an efficient process of authoring, editing, and desktop publishing our books electronically, we can spend more time ensuring superior content and less time on the technicalities of making books.

You can count on our commitment to deliver high-quality books at competitive prices on topics you want to read about. At IDG Books Worldwide, we continue in the IDG tradition of delivering quality for more than 30 years. You'll find no better book on a subject than one from IDG Books Worldwide.

John Kilcullen
Chairman and CEO
IDG Books Worldwide, Inc.

Steven Berkowitz
President and Publisher
IDG Books Worldwide, Inc.

Eighth Annual Computer Press Awards ≥ 1992

Ninth Annual Computer Press Awards ≥ 1993

Tenth Annual Computer Press Awards ≥ 1994

Eleventh Annual Computer Press Awards ≥ 1995

IDG is the world's leading IT media, research and exposition company. Founded in 1964, IDG had 1997 revenues of $2.05 billion and has more than 9,000 employees worldwide. IDG offers the widest range of media options that reach IT buyers in 75 countries representing 95% of worldwide IT spending. IDG's diverse product and services portfolio spans six key areas including print publishing, online publishing, expositions and conferences, market research, education and training, and global marketing services. More than 90 million people read one or more of IDG's 290 magazines and newspapers, including IDG's leading global brands — Computerworld, PC World, Network World, Macworld and the Channel World family of publications. IDG Books Worldwide is one of the fastest-growing computer book publishers in the world, with more than 700 titles in 36 languages. The "...For Dummies®" series alone has more than 50 million copies in print. IDG offers online users the largest network of technology-specific Web sites around the world through IDG.net (http://www.idg.net), which comprises more than 225 targeted Web sites in 55 countries worldwide. International Data Corporation (IDC) is the world's largest provider of information technology data, analysis and consulting, with research centers in over 41 countries and more than 400 research analysts worldwide. IDG World Expo is a leading producer of more than 168 globally branded conferences and expositions in 35 countries including E3 (Electronic Entertainment Expo), Macworld Expo, ComNet, Windows World Expo, ICE (Internet Commerce Expo), Agenda, DEMO, and Spotlight. IDG's training subsidiary, ExecuTrain, is the world's largest computer training company, with more than 230 locations worldwide and 785 training courses. IDG Marketing Services helps industry-leading IT companies build international brand recognition by developing global integrated marketing programs via IDG's print, online and exposition products worldwide. Further information about the company can be found at www.idg.com.   1/24/99

Authors' Acknowledgments

Because this is the fifth iteration of *HTML For Dummies*, I'd like to start by thanking our many readers for making this book such a success. I'd also like to thank them and the IDG editorial team for the feedback that has led to the continuing improvement of this book's contents. Please, don't stop now — tell us what you want to do with HTML, and what you don't like about this book.

Let me go on by thanking my sterling co-author, Natanya Pitts, for her efforts on this revision (and on previous ones). I am eternally grateful for your ideas, your hard work, and your experience in reaching the audience of budding Web experts. It's a pleasure to finally put your name on this book's cover. Likewise, thanks to Stephen N. James for his contributions to this book over the years.

Next, I'd like to thank the great teams at LANWrights and IDG for their efforts on this title. At LANWrights, my fervent thanks go to Kyle Findlay, for his services and his time spent on this book. I'd also like to thank Bill Brogden for his outstanding programming efforts on the HTML tool you'll find on the CD that accompanies this book. I'd also like to thank Dawn Rader, Mary Burmeister, and Chelsea Valentine for their help and their great attitudes. At IDG, I must thank Pat O'Brien for his outstanding efforts, and Barry Childs-Helton for his marvelous way with our words. Other folks we need to thank include Shawn Aylsworth and His Fabulous PLTs for their artful page layouts, Jesper Rasmussen for his painstaking trials, and Heather Dismore and the Heather Dismore Media Chorus for their CD production expertise. IDG's Steve Hayes demonstrated extraordinary insight and taste by hiring us again for this edition.

Finally, I'd like to thank my parents, Al and Ceil, for all the great things they did for me, and my sister, Kat, and her family for keeping me plugged into the family side of life. I must also thank my faithful sidekick, Blackie, who's always ready to pull me away from the keyboard — sometimes literally — to explore the great outdoors.

Ed Tittel

First and foremost I'd like to thank my co-author Ed Tittel for giving me the opportunity to work on this book. It's been fun! In addition to being a great co-author you've been a great friend. Special thanks to my beloved husband Robby. All things are easier because you are a part of my life. Thanks to my parents, Charles and Swanya, for always believing in me and supporting me. And finally thanks to my furry fuzzball Gandalf for keeping me company while I work.

Natanya Pitts

Publisher's Acknowledgments

We're proud of this book; please register your comments through our IDG Books Worldwide Online Registration Form located at http://my2cents.dummies.com.

Some of the people who helped bring this book to market include the following:

Acquisitions, Editorial, and Media Development

Project Editor: Pat O'Brien

Acquisitions Editor: Steven Hayes

Copy Editor: Barry Childs-Helton

Technical Editor: Jesper Rasmussen

Media Development Editor: Marita Ellixson

Media Development Coordinator: Megan Roney

Associate Permissions Editor: Carmen Krikorian

Media Development Manager: Heather Heath Dismore

Editorial Manager: Rev Mengle

Editorial Assistant: Jamila Pree

Production

Project Coordinator: E. Shawn Aylsworth

Layout and Graphics: Angela F. Hunckler, Dave McKelvey, Brent Savage, Jacque Schneider, Rashell Smith, Michael A. Sullivan, Dan Whetstine

Proofreaders: Christine Berman, Brian Massey, Marianne Santy, Rebecca Senninger

Indexer: Ty Koontz

General and Administrative

IDG Books Worldwide, Inc.: John Kilcullen, CEO; Steven Berkowitz, President and Publisher

IDG Books Technology Publishing Group: Richard Swadley, Senior Vice President and Publisher; Walter Bruce III, Vice President and Associate Publisher; Joseph Wikert, Associate Publisher; Mary Bednarek, Branded Product Development Director; Mary Corder, Editorial Director; Barry Pruett, Publishing Manager; Michelle Baxter, Publishing Manager

IDG Books Consumer Publishing Group: Roland Elgey, Senior Vice President and Publisher; Kathleen A. Welton, Vice President and Publisher; Kevin Thornton, Acquisitions Manager; Kristin A. Cocks, Editorial Director

IDG Books Internet Publishing Group: Brenda McLaughlin, Senior Vice President and Publisher; Diane Graves Steele, Vice President and Associate Publisher; Sofia Marchant, Online Marketing Manager

IDG Books Production for Dummies Press: Debbie Stailey, Associate Director of Production; Cindy L. Phipps, Manager of Project Coordination, Production Proofreading, and Indexing; Tony Augsburger, Manager of Prepress, Reprints, and Systems; Laura Carpenter, Production Control Manager; Shelley Lea, Supervisor of Graphics and Design; Debbie J. Gates, Production Systems Specialist; Robert Springer, Supervisor of Proofreading; Kathie Schutte, Production Supervisor

Dummies Packaging and Book Design: Patty Page, Manager, Promotions Marketing

◆

The publisher would like to give special thanks to Patrick J. McGovern, without whom this book would not have been possible.

Contents at a Glance

Cartoons at a Glance

By Rich Tennant

Fax: 978-546-7747 • E-mail: the5wave@tiac.net

Table of Contents

Introduction

● ●

*W*elcome to the wild, wacky, and wonderful possibilities inherent in the World Wide Web. In this book, we introduce you to the mysteries of the HyperText Markup Language used to build Web pages, and initiate you into the still-select, but rapidly growing, community of Web authors.

If you've tried to build your own Web pages before but found it too forbidding, now you can relax. If you can dial a telephone or find your keys in the morning, you too can become an HTML author. (No kidding!)

When we first wrote this book, we took a straightforward approach to the basics of authoring documents for the World Wide Web. In this edition for a new generation of Web page designers, we went after the best of old and new. We've kept the amount of technobabble to a minimum and stuck with plain English as much as possible. Besides plain talk about hypertext, HTML, and the Web, we include lots of examples, plus tag-by-tag instructions to help you build your very own Web pages with minimum muss and fuss.

We also include with this book a peachy CD that contains each and every HTML example in usable form — plus a number of interesting widgets that you can use to embellish your own documents and astound your friends. For this edition, we've added discussions of important topics that have come increasingly to the fore (though not yet to the putting green) in the last few years. Finally, the CD also includes the magnificent and bedazzling source materials for the *HTML 4 For Dummies,* 2nd Edition, Web pages, which you might find a source of inspiration and raw material for your own use! And we carry on a time-honored tradition upheld by the computer industry generally and IDG Books Worldwide in particular:

Anything silly you might read herein is *a feature, not a bug.*

About This Book

Think of this book as a friendly, approachable guide to taking up the tools of HTML and building readable, attractive pages for the World Wide Web. Although HTML isn't hard to learn, it does pack a plethora of details; you'll need to wrestle with them some while you build your Web pages. Some sample topics you find in this book include

- ✔ Designing and building Web pages
- ✔ Uploading and publishing Web pages for the world to see
- ✔ Creating interesting page layouts
- ✔ Testing and debugging your Web pages

Although at first glance it might seem that building Web pages requires years of arduous training, advanced aesthetic capabilities, and ritual ablutions in ice-cold streams, take heart: It just ain't so. If you can tell somebody how to drive across town to your house, you can certainly build a Web document that does what you want it to. The purpose of this book isn't to turn you into a rocket scientist (or, for that matter, a rocket scientist into a Web site); it's to show you all the design and technical elements you need to build a good-looking, readable Web page, and give you the know-how and confidence to do it!

How to Use This Book

This book tells you how to use HTML 4 to get your page up and running on the World Wide Web. We tell you what's involved in designing and building effective Web documents that can bring your ideas and information to the whole online world — if that's what you want to do — and maybe have some high-tech fun communicating them.

All HTML code appears in monospaced type like this:

```
<head><title>What's in a Title?</title></head>...
```

When you type in HTML tags or other related information, be sure to copy the information exactly as you see it between the angle brackets (< and >) because that's part of the magic that makes HTML work. Other than that, you find out how to marshal and manage the content that makes your pages special, and we tell you exactly what you need to do to mix the elements of HTML with your own work.

The margins of a book don't give us the same room as the vast reaches of cyberspace. Therefore some long lines of HTML markup, or designations of World Wide Web sites (called *URLs*, for *Uniform Resource Locators*), may wrap to the next line when we present them here. Remember that your computer shows such wrapped lines as a *single line of HTML*, or as a single URL — so if you're typing in that hunk of code, keep it as one line. Don't insert a hard return if you see one of these wrapped lines. We'll clue you in that it's supposed to be all one line by breaking the line at a slash (to imply "but wait, there's more!") and slightly indenting the overage, as in the following silly example:

```
http://www.infocadabra.transylvania.com/nexus/plexus/lexus/
praxis/okay/this/is/a/make-believe/URL/but/some/real/ones/
are/SERIOUSLY/long.html
```

 HTML doesn't care if you type tag text in uppercase, lowercase, or both (except for character entities, which must be typed exactly as indicated in Chapter 7 of this book). To make your own work look like ours as much as possible, enter all HTML tag text in lowercase only. Those of you who own previous editions of the book may see this as a complete reversal of earlier instructions. That it is! But the makers of HTML, the World Wide Web Consortium (or W3C), have changed the rules of this game, so we changed our instructions to follow their lead.

Three Presumptuous Assumptions

They say that making assumptions makes a fool out of the person who makes them and the person who is subject to those assumptions (and just who are *They,* anyway? We *assume* we know, but . . . never mind). Even so, practicality demands that we make a few assumptions about you, our gentle reader:

- ✔ You can turn your computer on and off.
- ✔ You know how to use a mouse and a keyboard.
- ✔ You want to build your own Web pages for fun, for profit, or because it's part of your job.

In addition, we assume you already have a working connection to the Internet, and one of the many fine Web browsers available by hook, by crook, by download from that same Internet, or from the attached CD. You don't need to be a master logician or a wizard in the arcane arts of programming, nor do you need a Ph.D. in computer science. You don't even need a detailed sense of what's going on in the innards of your computer to deal with the material in this book.

If you can write a sentence and know the difference between a heading and a paragraph, then you're better off than nine out of ten playground bullies — *and* you can build and publish your own documents on the World Wide Web. If you have an active imagination and the ability to communicate what's important to you, even better — you've already mastered the key ingredients necessary to build useful, attractive Web pages. The rest is details, and we help you with those!

How This Book Is Organized

This book contains seven major parts, arranged like Russian nesting dolls: All these parts contain three or more chapters, and each chapter contains several modular sections. Any time you need help or information, pick up the book and start anywhere you like, or use the Table of Contents and Index to locate specific topics or key words.

Here is a breakdown of the parts and what you find in each one.

Part I: Getting Started with HTML

This part sets the stage and includes an overview of and introduction to the World Wide Web and the software that people use to mine its treasures. It also explains how the Web works, including the HyperText Markup Language to which this book is devoted, and the server-side software and services that deliver information to end-users (as all of us are when we're not doing battle with the logical innards of our systems).

HTML documents, also called *Web pages,* are the fundamental units of information organization and delivery on the Web. Here, you also discover what HTML is about and how hypertext can enrich ordinary text. Next, you take a walk on the Web side and build your very first HTML document.

Part II: Cranking Out Pages

HTML mixes ordinary text with special strings of characters, called *markup,* used to instruct browsers how to display HTML documents. In this part of the book, you find out about markup in general and HTML in particular. This includes an overview of HTML tags and how they work. Then, we tell you all about HTML text pages to help you understand how to include and manage text on a Web page. After that, you find out how to mix graphics in with the text, and how to create pages that can make a good impression on their readers.

By the time you finish Part II, expect to have a good overall idea of what HTML is, what it can do, and how you can use it yourself.

Part III: Formatting Your Data

Part III takes the elements covered in Part II and explains them in far greater detail to help you design and build commercial-grade HTML documents. This includes working with HTML tag syntax and structures, plus working with the kind of presentation controls you need to build complex Web pages. After that, you find out how to make the most of HTML style tags and structures, how to build a variety of lists, and how to include all kinds of keen symbols in the text that appears on screen in your Web pages.

Part IV: Shaping Your Design

Part IV adds sophistication and elegance to the basics covered in Part III. By the time you read these chapters, you can build complex Web pages of many different kinds. You also find out about how to organize textual and graphical data into a variety of tables, how to create and use clickable images called image maps for navigating on your Web site, and how to break your display into individual on-screen areas called frames to improve your readers' access to Web document contents and functions.

Part V: The Bleeding Edge

In this Part, you go a little beyond the built-in capabilities that HTML 4.0 delivers to its users, to examine some interesting new developments that sometimes show up in Web pages. This includes working with HTML forms to solicit and deliver user input, and working with separate HTML style sheets to control document fonts, formats, and element positioning. Part V concludes with a discussion of Dynamic HTML, sometimes known as DHTML, which adds all kinds of interesting possibilities for user interaction and documents that change as users read them, to the basic layout and information presentation that ordinary HTML can deliver.

Part VI: The Part of Tens

In the concluding part of the book, we sum up and distill the very essence of what you now know about the mystic secrets of HTML. Here, you have a chance to review the top do's and don'ts for HTML markup, to rethink document design, and to catch and kill potential bugs and errors in your pages before anybody else sees them.

Part VII: Appendixes

The last part of this book ends with a set of Appendices designed to sum up and further expand on the book's contents. Appendix A is an alphabetical list of HTML tags, designed for easy access and reference. Appendix B is a Glossary of the technical terms that appear in this book. Appendix C is a list of HTML-related software tools that your authors think you might find useful. Finally, Appendix D lists the details about what's on the *HTML 4 For Dummies*

CD-ROM, including a snazzy Java-based HTML lookup tool we built for your use our very own selves. As noted in this Appendix, the materials on the CD-ROM are organized into modules that correspond to the organization of the book to make it easy for you to find URLs and examples referenced therein.

By the time you make it through all the materials in the book and on the CD, you should be pretty well-equipped to build your own Web documents and perhaps even ready to roll out your own Web site!

Icons Used in This Book

This icon signals technical details that are informative and interesting, but not critical to writing HTML. Skip these if you want (but please, come back and read them later).

This icon flags useful information that makes HTML markup, Web page design, or other important stuff even less complicated than you feared it might be.

This icon points out information you shouldn't pass by — don't overlook these gentle reminders (the life, sanity, or page you save could be your own).

Be cautious when you see this icon. It warns you of things you shouldn't do; the bomb is meant to emphasize that the consequences of ignoring these bits of wisdom can be severe.

When you see this spiderweb symbol, it flags the presence of Web-based resources that you can go out and investigate further. You can also find all these references on the Jump Pages on the CD-ROM that comes with this book!

This icon tells you that some additional related information is elsewhere in this book.

Text marked with this icon contains information about something that's on this book's CD-ROM.

Where to Go from Here

This is the part where you pick a direction and hit the road! *HTML 4 For Dummies* is a lot like the parable of the six blind men and the elephant: It almost doesn't matter where you start out; you'll look at lots of different parts as you prepare yourself to build your own Web pages — and each part has a distinctive nature, but the whole is something else again. Don't worry. You'll get it handled. Who cares if anybody else thinks you're just goofing around? We know you're getting ready to have the time of your life.

Enjoy!

Part I

Getting Started
with HTML

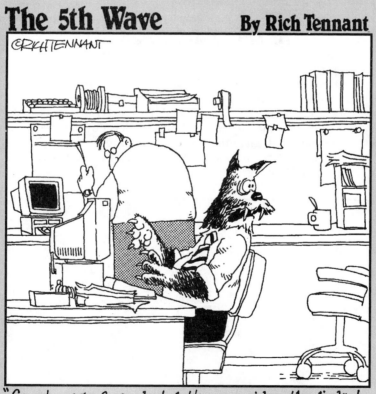

The 5th Wave   By Rich Tennant

"Great page, Sue – but let's reconsider the link to
www.lycanthropy.com."

In this part . . .

This part includes an introduction to the HyperTextMarkup Language, explaining a bit of its history and the software that people use to make it sing. We cover the basic principles behind the way HTML works, including the markup to which this book is devoted. We take you on a behind-the-scenes guided tour of a typical Web page. Then you find out how to design and build your very first Web page.

Chapter 1

Okay, What's HTML?

- -

- -

*T*he real secret behind the HyperText Markup Language is that there is no secret: Everything's out in the open, just waiting for the right interpretation. The beauty of HTML is its simple content (it's just a stream of plain characters, which makes virtually any text editor a potential HTML generator). The challenge of using HTML is working within its boundaries.

Simple as it is, HTML is finicky about the order in which characters occur and the way they're used — to produce the right results, you have to humor it. The reason is sheer practicality — *some* browsers might forgive the omission or misstatement of *certain* HTML elements, but the readers of your Web page could be using who-knows-what for a browser. The only reliable way to get consistent Web page appearance and behavior (short of magic) is to know the rules for creating HTML documents.

This chapter presents the brass tacks: fundamental ideas behind HTML, concepts and operation of hypertext, and some basic principles of building well-structured, readable Web pages. Your mission, should you decide to accept it, is to develop that knack — and use it to your readers' advantage!

HTML Basics

"What's in a name?" HTML's moniker contains the two concepts that make it work (and make the World Wide Web a phenomenal resource):

- ✔ **Hypertext:** The term may sound like science fiction — and you *can* do amazing things with it. Hypertext is a way of creating multimedia documents — and of forging links within or between them.

- ✔ **Markup language:** A method of embedding special tags that describe the structure as well as the behavior of a document. (The language you use when a preschooler scrawls on your wall is something else again.)

The simplicity and power of HTML markup can enable just about anyone to concoct Web documents for private or public use — anyone who plays by the rules, that is.

Of Links and Sausages

When a Web-head talks excitedly about links, it isn't about breakfast, though it does mean some sizzling fast transitions between Web locations — whether within the same document or to different data elements elsewhere on the Web. You can do it because HTML offers built-in support for *multimedia links* and *document* links. Both types of links work the same way; when you've used one link, you know how to use the others to get around.

Tags are the pieces of code that you use to create links — a simple concept at the heart of the incredible breadth and versatility of the Web. Put the correct HTML tags around text or graphics to create an *active* (linked) area, and you've already added an intriguing capability: When readers visit your Web site and click on the active area, the link transports them to another spot within the same file, to another document in the same Web site, or off to some other Web site. Figure 1-1 shows links to several resources on the *...For Dummies* Web site. Each of these links connects to a valuable source of information.

Different browsers use different methods to denote links, but all browsers provide a visual clue that you've selected an active area on the screen. You may see text underlined in a bright color, notice a font change to boldface, or be grabbed by a graphic outlined in a contrasting color. In these and similar cases, you're looking at a portal to another world — or at least another part of the Web.

Your browser's way of saying *Congratulations! You found the link!* may be an *image map* — in which case, your only visual cues are the changing coordinates in the browser's status line (these correspond to the location of your cursor on screen). Using this kind of link is like playing an adventure game: You're not always sure where you're going, what you'll find after you get there, or whether you just triggered a rolling boulder.

Jumping around inside documents

One variety of link connects points within the same document; these are called *internal anchors*. Webmasters often use this kind of link to move readers from a table of contents (at the top of an HTML file) to related sections throughout a document. Also, you can use this method to jump directly to the start of the document from its end — this beats the heck out of scrolling up through a long file!

Jumping around is the characteristic advantage of hypertext — circumventing the linear nature of the paper documents we've been used to since Gutenberg. The rapid, obvious (well, *modern*) way to navigate within or among documents is to travel by link. Sure, you can do the same thing with the table of contents or the index of a paper book by looking up what you want and flipping the pages yourself — a bit of a chore if the book is more than a few measly hundred pages. Hypertext not only automates this task for you, it makes the jump from page 1 to page 1000 — or to that key document in Kalamazoo — as effortless as the jump to page 10. Links are a snap to use (a click, actually), and almost as easy to create.

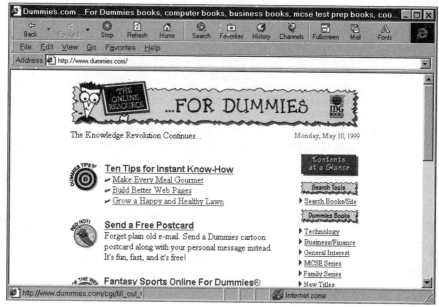

Figure 1-1:
A simple
HTML link
example.

Jumping across documents (and services)

When you've put together your page the way you want it, you can also use HTML as a kind of cyberglue to link your page to other Web pages, no matter where they reside on the Web. It's a quick way to boost the capabilities of your Web pages and enhance your readers' experience by using a combination of links and *Uniform Resource Locators (URLs)* — the standardized addresses that tell the browser where to go (so politely that it actually goes there).

The same hypertext technology that lets you jump around inside a document also gives you the reach to touch any other resource available through the Web — so long as you know its exact URL (address) — and to send your reader there, so to speak. Actually, HTML's simple text-tagging technique erases the practical difference between *here* and *there*. With a single click of the mouse or selection of the active text field, you *are there,* or the information *is here,* or . . . you get it.

Whenever you create a link to a particular URL in an HTML document, visit the site that the URL refers to, and then use cut-and-paste to copy the URL from a browser address window if possible. This is good practice for three reasons: (1) You've checked the site and know it's still there, (2) you save typing time — some URLs can get pretty long — and (3) even better, you get the reference right. (For an additional check, test the URL with a browser to make sure that it's still valid after you copy it.)

The Web as we know it today springs from the work of individual Web weavers who include links to other documents from their Web sites. URLs can point to — and get you to — a variety of protocols and services on the Internet, not just other HTML files. You can link through telnet, WAIS, Gopher, FTP, Usenet newsgroups, or even e-mail. Individual documents may represent the *content* of the Web, but hyperlinks are the heart of the Web's true nature: They are the strands that make up the Web itself, tying people, ideas, and locations together.

The World Wide Web has more users now than ever before, but not all of them agree on whether to refer to a Uniform Resource Locator as *a URL* ("a yew-are-ell") or *an URL* ("an earl"). Just so you know, we're not taking sides; this book uses *a URL* ("a yew-are-ell"), strictly for the sake of technical clarity. (Well, okay, somebody *might* read it aloud in the House of Lords . . . .)

You've Used Hypertext without Knowing It

If you're like most folks who consider new things, you may be wondering *What is this hypertext stuff and am I normal if I use it?* Although hypertext may seem strange and exotic, you're probably much more familiar with it than you think. Your own desktop computer undoubtedly contains several hypertext applications that you use regularly.

For example, if you use Microsoft Windows, then you use a hypertext application every time you run the Windows Help utility. In addition, as Figure 1-2 shows, Microsoft Word for Windows offers hypertext links to technical support options.

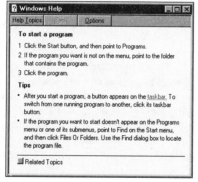

Figure 1-2: The Microsoft Windows Help engine is a well-known example of hypertext.

Notice the three buttons on the upper portion of the screen shot: `Help Topics`, `Back`, and `Options`. These buttons work like the navigation tools for a Web browser; their labels tell whether they take you forward to a list of available links within a document (`Help Topics` and `Options`) or back to where you've been (logically enough, `Back`). The underlined phrases (such as `taskbar`) identify links to text within the help system. They work much like the HTML links you encounter with your browser.

Hypertext applications have concepts in common with the Web, including some kind of home page (starting point), various navigation tools (shaped arrows and specific commands), multimedia data, and plenty of links to select. Each of the examples given here, however, offers support only to specific kinds of links; they can't navigate the Web. Only the capabilities of the Web itself can enable users to jump across the Internet and follow links to other Web documents and servers. Enabling this ability is exactly what gives HTML its unique value — and helps make the Web so popular.

Believe it or not, HTML is unfazed by ancient rivalries between operating systems. Microsoft is in the process of switching its help system over to use HTML directly; UNIX users familiar with FrameMaker or multimedia authoring can find common ground with the Web's hypertext capabilities. And Macintosh users who identified HyperCard and SuperCard as hypertext applications are *absolutely right* (extra credit on that one — hey, it's free — but no points if you guessed "games of chance").

Beyond Text and Into Multimedia

You're traveling to a wondrous land whose boundaries are . . . oops, wrong medium, though multimedia capabilities can produce some out-there effects. If you do include nontext files (such as sound, graphics, and video) in your Web pages, you must employ a certain amount of alchemy. Shipping Web information in *MIME* (Multipurpose Internet Mail Extensions) format means you can bundle attachments within individual e-mail files — giving even a mild-mannered Web server the power to deliver multiple forms of data to your browser in a single transfer.

When a MIME file with attachments shows up at your workstation, additional processing begins immediately. The text portion of the message file arrives first. It contains a text-only HTML page description that lets the browser get right to work building and displaying the text portions of the page. Because the text arrives first, you may see placeholders or icons for graphics when you catch your first glimpse of a Web page. Eventually, graphics or other forms of data replace these placeholders as their related attachments arrive.

While you watch the Web page being built — making good use of the time by reading the text or wishing for a faster modem — the browser receives attachments in the background. As they arrive, the browser identifies these attachments by file type, or by the descriptive information contained in an attachment tag (as specified by the MIME format or its associated Internet Media Type). Once the browser knows what kind of file is attached, it can handle playback or display. Table 1-1 lists some common file types used on the Web, including the inevitable alphabet soup (now fortified with explanations!) of filename extensions.

Table 1-1	Common Sound, Graphics, and Motion-Video Formats on the Web	
Extension	*Format*	*Explanation*
Sound Formats		
.RA	RealAudio	Used with RealAudio Web Server and RealAudio Player add-on for browsers.

Extension	Format	Explanation
.SBI	Sound Blaster Instrument	Used for a single instrument with Sound Blaster cards (multi-instrument: .IBK).
.SND, .AU	8KHz mulaw	Voice-grade sound format used on workstations (such as Sun, NeXT, HP9000, and so on).
.WAV	Microsoft Waveform	Sound format used in Windows for event notification.
Still-Video (Graphics) Formats		
.GIF	Graphics Interchange Format	Compressed graphics format commonly used on CompuServe; easy to render multiplatform. Can be *interleaved* (displayed gradually) or not, depending on how image is created.
.JPEG, .JPG	Joint Photographic Experts Group	Highly compressed format for still images, widely used for multi-platform graphics.
.PDF	Portable Document Format	Adobe's format for multiplatform document access through its Acrobat software.
.PS	PostScript	Adobe's type description language, used to deliver complex documents over the Internet.
Motion-Video Formats		
.AVI	Audio Video Interleaved	Microsoft Video for Windows standard format; found on many CD-ROMs.
.DVI	Digital Video Interactive	Another motion-video format, also found on CD-ROMs.
.FLI	Flick	Autodesk Animator motion-video format.
.MOV	QuickTime	Apple's motion-video and audio format; originated on the Macintosh, but also available for Windows.

(continued)

Table 1-1 *(continued)*

Extension	Format	Explanation
.DCR	Director	A "shocked" (animated) version of a Macromedia Director multimedia file.
.MPEG, .MPG	Motion Picture Experts Group	Full-motion video standard using frame format similar to .JPEG with variable compression capabilities.

Many Web sites contain large amounts of information on file formats and programs; here are two of the best that we turned up by searching on the string "common Internet file formats" at www.excite.com:

✔ **Common Internet File Formats:** An annotated list of audio, graphic, and multimedia file formats with links to related applications, compiled by Eric Perlman and Ian Kallen for Internet Literacy Consultants. This site hasn't been updated since December 1995, but it remains quite useful.

    www.matisse.net/files/formats.html

✔ **GRAPHICS:** Maintained by Martin Reddy at the University of Edinburgh, this site contains "everything you ever wanted to know" about graphics and links to additional resources.

    www.dcs.ed.ac.uk/%7Emxr/gfx/

Hyperhelpers: Useful "helper" applications

When referenced by a Web page, non-text data shows up as attachments to an HTML file. Sometimes the browser itself handles playback or display, as in the case of simple, two-dimensional graphics (including .GIF and .JPEG files). Even so, other applications may handle these (especially for character-mode Web browsers such as Lynx).

When other kinds of files need special handling (beyond the scope of most browsers), the browser hands off these files to other applications for playback or display. Such *helper* or *plug-in* applications have the built-in smarts to handle the formats and the processing needed to deliver on demand the contents of a specialized file.

The process normally works something like this:

1. The browser builds a page display that includes an active region (underlined or outlined in some way) to indicate the attachment of a sound, video, or animation playback.

2. If the user selects the active region (the link), the browser calls on another application or plug-in to handle playback or display.

3. The helper or plug-in takes over and plays back or displays the file.

4. After the helper completes display or playback, the browser reasserts control, and the user can continue on.

A standard part of browser configuration supplies the names and locations of helper programs, or configures specially tailored add-ons called *plug-ins,* to assist the browser when such data arrives. If the browser can't find a helper application or plug-in, it simply won't respond to an attempt to display or play back the requested information. For plug-ins, however, most browsers can recognize what they're missing, and some (like Navigator or IE) will ask you if you want to add the missing plug-in to your current configuration.

For example, RealAudio is a common sound player plug-in for Web browsers, primarily for PCs running some flavor of Windows. As part of the configuration that occurs when you install a plug-in, associations between particular file types (like the .SBI and .WAV file extensions common on the PC) and the plug-in may be automatically established. Once this association is created, the browser automatically invokes the plug-in when it encounters files with those extensions. This causes the sounds to play (which, we assume, is a good thing!).

For comprehensive listings of PC, Mac, and UNIX plug-in or helper applications, and links to their sources, start your search at one of the following URLs:

```
browserwatch.iworld.com/
tucows.myriad.net/acc95.html
wwwhost.cc.utexas.edu/learn/use/helper.html
```

You should also check out both the Netscape and Microsoft sites for information about the latest plug-ins. (For example, Netscape has a link to a set of pages labeled "Plug-ins" in the "Software Download" section of its home page at `home.netscape.com`.)

Well, okay, helper applications might not send out for pizza or make you a decent cup of coffee, but we've found some useful Windows helpers (visit `www.shareware.com` for download locations):

- **For still graphics:** Lview is a good, small graphics viewer that can handle .GIF, .PCX, and .JPEG files. For the compulsively creative, Lview supports some intriguing image-editing capabilities.

- **For video:** The applications of choice for making your monitor act like a TV are QuickTime for Windows (which plays QuickTime movie-format files) or MPEGplay for .MPEG video files.

- **For PostScript viewing:** Ghostview for Windows works with a program called Ghostscript that allows users to view or print PostScript files from any source, including the Web. Because so many documents on the Internet use the PostScript format, Ghostview and Ghostscript are outrageously handy.

A good set of plug-ins or helper applications can make your browser even more effective at bringing the wonders of the Web to your desktop. With the right additions, your browser can play back, render, or establish friendly relations with just about any multimedia format that lands in your system.

The value of visuals

Without a doubt, graphics add impact and interest to Web pages, but that extra punch comes at a price. It's easy to get carried away by the appeal of pictures and plaster them all over your Web page. (And no, size doesn't matter — those innocuous little images that make such cool buttons and on-screen controls have BIG clutter potential if overdone.)

Yea, therefore, heed these caveats when using graphics:

- **Not everybody who reads your page can see the graphics.** Readers may not see graphics because they use character-mode browsers that can't display them, or because they switch off their graphics displays to improve response time (a common option on most Web browsers to conserve *bandwidth,* the capacity of a system to move data at faster-than-glacial speed).

- **Graphics files — even compressed ones — can be huge** — often ten or more times bigger than the HTML files to which they belong. Moving graphics takes time and consumes bandwidth. Also, it penalizes users with slower modems (usually the majority) far more than it penalizes those who have speedy (and expensive) direct connections to the Internet.

Sometimes graphics are essential — for example, a diagram or illustration may be the best and quickest way to explain your material — and certainly an appropriate degree of visual impact can be vital if your home page is where you make a first impression. You can make an even better long-term impression, however, if you are consistently sensitive to the different capabilities and bandwidths of your readers.

Here we humbly present some rules of thumb for using graphics effectively in your Web pages. (One more word to the wise: As you examine the work of others, notice what happens to your attitude when you find that they have violated some or all these rules.)

✔ Keep your graphics small and uncomplicated whenever possible. This reduces file sizes and keeps transfer times down.

✔ Keep file sizes smaller by using compressed formats (like .GIF and .JPEG) whenever you can.

✔ Create a small version (called a *thumbnail*) of a graphic to include on your Web page (an easy way to do this is by sizing your image on screen, and then taking a screen shot when you display it in the proper dimensions; usually 100 x 100 pixels or so). If you must use larger, more complex graphics, link thumbnails to full-sized versions of the graphics. This spares casual readers the impact of downloading large versions every time they access your page (and keeps Internet use under better control, making you a better *netizen*!).

✔ Keep the number of graphic elements on a page to a minimum. Practically speaking, this means *at most* a half-dozen graphic items per page. Most of these should be compact, icon-like navigation controls; any larger ones should be content-specific graphics, used sparingly. Here again, the goal is to limit page complexity and to speed transfer times.

Sometimes, the temptation to violate these rules can be nearly overwhelming. If you must break the rules, be sure to run your results past some disinterested (but not *un*interested!) third parties. Watch them read your pages, if possible, and take heed of their reactions. Listen carefully to any feedback you get, to gauge whether you've merely bent the rules of good graphics or pretty well smithereened 'em.

Remember, not everyone who accesses your pages can see your graphics. For readers who don't use graphical browsers, or who turn graphics off, try to think of ways to enhance their reading experience without graphics.

Mavens of multimedia

The rules for graphics go *double* for other forms of multimedia. If graphics files are large when compared to HTML text files, then sound and video files are *enormous.* They are also time-dependent; the longer they play, the bigger they are, *and* the longer the browser takes to download them to your computer. Although they're appealing and definitely increase the interest level for some topics, sound and video files are not germane to many topics on the Web. Use them sparingly or not at all, unless your Web site is an Internet radio show or movie theater.

With the advent of the smaller, faster display and interactivity tools for the Web (such as Java, VRML, and Shockwave), the Web employs more and more multimedia applications. Java *applets* work with Navigator, IE, and other browsers to allow quick display of animated graphics and other special effects. VRML (Virtual Reality Modeling Language) is similar to HTML but provides 3D viewing capabilities. Shockwave is the name of the Macromedia plug-in that allows Director movies to appear inside Web pages.

Before you go Hollywood in your Web page design, invest a little time in mastering the basics of HTML. Then, when you feel ready to rock with some video tools, check out these URLs for more information:

> ✔ **Java — Sun Microsystems:** `www.javasoft.com` or `java.sun.com`
>
> ✔ **VRML:** `www.vrml.org/`
>
> ✔ **Shockwave and Director — Macromedia:** `www.macromedia.com`

Once again, the trick is to make large files available *through links* instead of cramming them onto pages that everyone must download. Label these active regions with the size of the associated file, so that people know what they're in for if they choose to download the material. (For example: `Warning! This points to a 40K sound byte of a barking seal.`)

Bringing It All Together with the Web

Earth calling — come on back from multimedia hyperspace, assume a comfortable orbit in the cyberspace world of your future Web page, and stand by for a message. The following paragraph embodies (to the best of our knowledge and experience) the essence of all successful Web pages.

The three most important factors in building good Web pages are content, content, and content (Get the idea?). If content is well-organized, engaging, and contains links to interesting places, your Web site can become a potent tool for education and communication. If your Web site is all flash, sharing it can be an exercise in sheer frustration (and humiliation for the webmaster . . . that's you!). Therefore, if you put your energy into providing high-quality content and link your readers to other high-quality, content-filled pages, your Web site will be a howling success. If you don't, your site will become the electronic equivalent of a ghost town!

When you've had a chance to examine and practice these principles, you'll be well prepared to use — and build — documents for the Web. Step into our parlor for a look at what's in (and on) a Web page.

Chapter 2

What's in a Page?

*T*he knack for understanding and using HTML lies in knowing how to separate the two components of the HTML file. Here's the skinny on what makes them different:

✔ **Controls** give your page its glitzy capabilities; they're also known as *tags* or *markup* (as in *markup language* — coincidence? We think not . . .). If you look at an HTML source file and see some text that doesn't show up when your browser displays the page, look for the HTML bracket markers (< and >); they surround the tags that control how characters appear on your screen. If you flip through this book, you'll see plenty of examples.

✔ **Content** is what you want your page to actually *say* (whoa, what a concept!). You can stash most of your content in a plain text (ASCII) file with no tagging whatsoever — but tagging or no, it should be good stuff; once you're clear about the statement you want to make, the rest — however high-tech — is emphasis.

The really tricky — ah, *interesting* — parts of HTML are the possible combinations of markup and content, such as the commands used to give titles to pages or to specify guideposts to help clarify the text for the reader — headers, graphics, lists of elements, and so on. But the best place to start building a good Web page is to get really good at telling content apart from controls — to separate the guts from the glitz — so you can use both to best effect. Therefore this chapter gives you a guided tour of the components that make up a Web page, and offers some pointers on how to assemble them.

It's All in the Layout

The human eye and (especially) brain are marvelous instruments, capable of scanning incredible amounts of material and zeroing in on the things that are most important to the reader. As a Web-page designer, your quest is to find the best way to guide the reader to your page's best stuff quickly, efficiently, and appealingly. Nothing communicates this concern — or lack of it — more clearly than a document's layout.

Layout is the overall arrangement of the elements in a document. Layout isn't just scooting the individual text elements around the page till your eyes water. Instead, layout means putting in the time to make some decisions: how many elements you want, how to arrange them, and how much white space surrounds them.

The layout of a document — whether Web page, magazine ad, or résumé — can be a crucial stage of communication: that first impression nobody gets to make twice. Of course, some documents are mandatory to look at, whatever tedious mess is on the page (let's hear it for tax forms!) — but if you have to *attract* an audience, it pays to be layout-literate.

Here's a quick thought-experiment in contrasts: Think of the deadliest text-book you ever slogged (slept?) through — endless pages of text in big blocky paragraphs, maybe an anemic graphic or two wedged in as an afterthought, and just for fun, assume it was about a topic you like (or *used* to like . . .).

By comparison, think of a recent ad that reached out of a magazine or TV screen and *grabbed* you. Careful work went into the eye-catching images, appealing language, and the arresting combinations of elements. Which of these experiences was less torturous?

An inviting Web page can be as challenging to design as a hot ad (or, for that matter, a really good textbook). Pages that are all pizazz and no substance tend to disappear quickly — but pages that stress content at the expense of layout barely attract a yawn, let alone an audience. Even if you've discovered antigravity and want to trumpet it to the world, don't assume the world is automatically interested; your page — anyone's, for that matter — joins millions of other sites on the WWW in the age-old struggle for attention. A page that's pleasant to read, rich with content, and efficient about getting its point across is a standing invitation to users to visit often — and to link your site to theirs, which means the hits keep coming.

So Much to Say, So Much to Say

Whether you're just a Web-savvy average earthling with choice info to offer the world, or an organization with products and services to advertise, you're probably hearing a siren song that calls you to publish online ASAP. Some of that temptation comes from HTML itself; as markup languages go, it's simple and easy to learn — and yes, you *do* get to learn it in this book — but whoa, bucko, not just yet.

Remember that saying about what happens when a kid picks up a hammer ("everything starts to look like a nail")? Nearly everyone who picks up on HTML wants to charge right out and build "killer Web pages" on the fly — an easy way to kill a Web page before it even gets to fly. The usual mistake is to tack on too much of the wrong stuff. Trust us, it won't hurt to step back and do a little analysis and design work before you pick up that hammer.

Who's listening?

There's a reason it's called Web *publishing;* knowing your audience is critical to building a Web page that people can use, enjoy, and want to revisit. If you don't know who's going to visit your Web site, and why they should want to, why build it?

Of course, if you don't care who visits your site, you wouldn't be (exactly) alone; most personal pages on the Web are *vanity pages* with "content" that boils down to *Here's some stuff about me that you must be dying to know.* A few Web surfers might visit a typical vanity page — once — while everyone else remains blissfully unaware of its presence.

If you have a more (ahem) grown-up reason for building your Web site — and some substantial content to offer — you're two steps closer to a good page. Next question: Which potential visitors you want to reach, what messages are they likely to respond to, and how do you emphasize your message? If you aren't blessed with clairvoyance (or a big market-research budget), then you must base your Web document design on certain assumptions — educated guesses — about your audience.

Advertisements and encyclopedias are often designed to reach specific audiences. You could do worse than to shoot for the best of both worlds — the initial interest and impact of an advertisement, but enough depth of content that your audience is likely to react with *Wow — really?* or *I didn't know that!* or (okay, so much for grown-up) *Awesome!*

How can you get to know your audience? Think of it as a form of hunting and gathering: Identify your target group and then start visiting their haunts, whether in cyberspace or in the real world, to learn their ways and habits. Watch and listen to them. Gather enough information to imagine the world from their point of view, as best you can.

When you recognize their interests, you also get a sense of their needs and wants. How does your content speak to those needs? Is there a clear niche that it can fill? If so, can you hook them into your content by filling that niche in a way they haven't seen before? If you can — and you deliver solid, usable information to the people in your target group — then your site becomes a resource; they come back for more and spread the word about what you have to offer.

Thus we come back to the C-word — *content* — and here be dragons. No matter how long, short, convoluted, or simple your content, we can offer a basic principle to follow safely through the dragon's lair. It just happens to be our next heading.

Design springs from content; form follows function

In effect, we're just talking about good show and tell: If you have content to impart, a good design complements it; a bad design obscures it. As your page shapes up, keep in mind what you want it to do for you, and you can't go far wrong.

For starters, remember the audience you intend to reach. Once you've done your homework and developed a good working sense of your potential users' interests, you can speak to those interests by hitting the high points of what you've found out. Just knowing a lot is, however, no guarantee of success. Web pages built around long, sinuous documents with complex ideas take more forethought and struggle to design (big surprise . . . NOT), but size doesn't matter here, either. Even a short, single-concept document may not be easy to make into a good Web page.

To get your page to speak your users' language well enough for effective emphasis, you've got to be fairly fluent in *two* languages: your native tongue and HTML. Therefore let us call upon the fearsome writing skills laid before us long ago — and verily the first of these is to *Create an outline before you start writing* (or creating HTML, for that matter).

Outlining your content gives you a potent clue to establishing appropriate links — to your audience as well as to other sites. As you organize your information, consider these pointers:

- ✔ List the topics and major elements in your document.

- ✔ Identify the relationships between your main topics; make notes on what other information sources on the Web might enhance them.

- ✔ Experiment with the order of topics till you find the clearest and most engaging sequence.

- ✔ Assess possible uses for graphics, sound, or other multimedia; pare them down later to no more than the essentials.

- ✔ Consider what visual cues could help your users read and navigate your document (remember, go easy on the graphics where possible).

- ✔ Think of the outline as a blueprint you'll come back to as you construct the document.

What do I intend to put across?

The information you put into your Web page — and the way you arrange it — are both influenced by what you want your page to accomplish. Whether your intent is to inform, educate, persuade, or question — plays a major role in its design.

- ✔ **If your goal is to inform or educate**, then reduce the number of eye-catching displays (too many can be distracting) and make the highlights of your information easy (but not painfully so) to see.

- ✔ **If your goal is to persuade or sell,** then try to hook users' attention with compelling visuals and riveting testimonials; follow through with important details about the goods.

- ✔ **If your goal is to question** a political or social issue, then raise that issue early, make your case as succinctly as you can, and provide pointers to additional discussion and related information.

In each case, the goal behind a document strongly conditions its execution and delivery — which affects whether it attracts an audience. Identifying a clear goal and a conscious intent can be just as important as sticking to them.

Which messages do I want to stand out?

Your page should emphasize your message but stop short of giving the reader a headache. At the beginning of your document design process, you must answer the question "What are you trying to say?" Approach this task by outlining key ideas or messages that you seek to convey and put the most important ones first. Then follow each main idea with any relevant information to make your case, prove your point, or otherwise substantiate what you say.

If you follow this exercise carefully, much of the content will emerge gracefully from your outline. Important relationships among various elements of your document (and other documents) will also reveal themselves as you work through the outlining process.

How does my document direct the flow of information?

Information, like water, has a flow — and unless you direct where it's going, all you've got is a puddle. Fortunately, plumbing is available: Web designers customarily use some formal devices to communicate a document's organization, which can give a clueless reader some hope of navigating the information. The word that encompasses these devices is *superstructure*. Though it may sound like something you'd find on a submarine, actually the superstructure of a document includes some pretty handy elements:

- A table of contents
- A set of common controls
- An index
- A glossary of technical terms

Creating superstructure is like giving your readers a can opener so they can get at your content and be nourished by what they read or view. Not every document needs all the possible elements of superstructure, but most documents — especially longer ones — can benefit from at least some such plumbing. (Some documents cry out for superstructure — if you're an economist who does brain surgery for a hobby, your page just might.)

- **The TOC (table of contents):** After a lifetime of exposure to printed materials, we expect a table of contents at the beginning of a document (is that so wrong)? Your garden-variety TOC lays out the document's topics and coverage — but if you put hypertext in it, you can whisk users directly from any entry to the information it lists. Your TOC becomes not just a list of topics, not just an organizational map for your document, but a convenient navigation tool as well! *Now* how much would you pay?

- **Common controls for all screens:** Imagine a book in which every page was a different shape, size, or color, and had to be turned in a different direction. (Hurts, doesn't it?) To promote readability and familiarity within your Web site, have mercy — use *common controls* that work the same wherever your reader finds them: icons to click, text links to accommodate nongraphical browsers, labeled buttons that take the reader forward, back, or to familiar territory (the TOC or to your home page). A common look and feel for your pages helps your users navigate. (Consistency may be "the last refuge for the unimaginative," but it does have its uses — save the imagination for your content.)

✔ **Index or search engine?:** Helping users locate key words or individual topics helps them get the best use from your content. Another great thing about hypertext is that an old-fashioned index may be unnecessary. Because your content is online and accessible to the computer, you can often replace an index with a built-in search engine for your Web pages.

If you include a search tool for keywords in your Web site, make the tool accessible from any document.

Chapter 14 covers search engines, including tools to index your documents online.

✔ **A glossary helps manage specialized terms and language:** If you cover a subject that bristles with jargon, technical terms, or other arcane gibberish (beloved of experts and feared by newcomers), include a glossary with your Web pages. Fortunately, HTML includes a text style specifically built for defining terms, which, in turn, helps you to construct a glossary (beloved of beginners and feared by obfuscators) whenever you need one. You still have to come up with the definitions yourself — unless you can find a Web site with a glossary that you can link to your page — which is entirely possible (love that Web!).

Grabbing the audience's attention

Audience attention can be fickle, but myriad methods exist for capturing it (some more humane than others). Movie fans may recall a classic bigger-is-better example: the standard demonstration of the THX theater sound system. First, a simple "THX" graphic fills the entire screen, lingering as a sustained orchestral chord (overlaid with a powerful pipe-organ note) starts quietly, builds to a peak over 20 seconds, hits like a jet fighter taking off overhead at 200+ mph, then fades away on a low pedal-tone that seems to sway the entire theater. Having raised the audience nearly out of its seats, the demonstration states coyly, "The audience is listening." (Gee . . . ya think?)

If you're like some advertisers and entertainers, you might yearn to grab your audience with all the subtlety and charm of a hungry T. Rex. But a great effect in a theater may not be feasible — or desirable — on the Web. A grand *ta-daa*, even if technically possible, has two potential drawbacks: (1) Users may not appreciate what it does to their systems (speakers, screens, ears, whatever) and (2) It overwhelms your content (oh, yeah, that . . .).

In fact, your readers have offered you at least some of their attention the moment they get a glimpse of your page. A kinder, gentler grab, if you do it well, can get them interested, get them oriented, and intrigue them enough that they'll want to stay and look around.

Nothing does a civilized grab as effectively as a tasteful image coupled with a brief, compelling introduction. Include information that tells why your page is important, what it contains, and how to navigate it.

They're after the goods . . . don't get in the way!

Okay, you've got their attention — now it's up to you to help them find the real content. Make your superstructure visible enough to use but not so elaborate that it bogs down their interest. If you include pointers that direct your visitors to more detailed info, make them (1) few, (2) obvious, and (3) easy to distinguish from the rest of a page. Maze-of-the-month designs, layouts, or flow of information can hamper easy access to your content, and that can evaporate your visitors' interest.

This advice translates into some important rules, particularly for introductory materials. Keep your welcome (home) page simple and elegant. Use short, direct sentences. Keep your focus on the topic(s) at hand. Use the superstructure to emphasize your content. For a complex Web site, include a link to an "About This Site" page for those who want to understand the site's structure and function.

What should they remember?

As amazing as the human mind is, it's always filtering information because its storage space is limited. People exposed to new concepts generally remember *10 percent of what they're exposed to* — at best. (The wise Web page designer should remember 100 percent of *that* concept.)

Of course, paring down 100 ideas to 10 brilliant insights may not be all you need to do. Sad but true, most people also remember a limited amount of *detail.* If 10 percent of your concepts stick in your visitors' minds, don't assume they've absorbed 10 percent of your overall *content.* You've got the best chance of creating a striking Web page (with a memorable 10 percent) if you apply the following principle: *Strongly related concepts linger in memory far better than loosely linked or unrelated ones.*

Your audience is human, too. Give 'em a break. How many of us would remember the details of ten full pages out of a hundred in a document we'd never seen before, and had looked at for less than an hour? (Show of hands? Anyone?)

As you design your Web documents, keep asking yourself, *"Which 10 percent do I want my users to remember?"* Use this question as a way to focus on your most important ideas. Be hard-nosed; not all of them will make the grade. Then plan to direct your audience's attention to the winners, reinforcing them throughout your Web pages. As with so much else in life, maintaining your focus is the key to successful communication.

Meet the Elements of Page Design

When you've had a chance to get comfortable with the design concepts that build good Web pages, you're ready to examine and heft the parts of an HTML document. You may recognize some of these elements right away; they're integral parts of any well-written document. Other components that come with exotic names and concepts — like hypertext links — are relative newcomers. All are basic building blocks that make up Web pages. After a look at each one, we get into how they affect the flow of information and can influence your choice of design elements.

Tags — they're it

You can always tell an HTML text file apart from an ordinary ASCII file: You'll see some snippets of its text enclosed in angle brackets (< >). It isn't for decoration; those snippets are the *tags* that make HTML work — and most of them travel in pairs that aren't *quite* identical. For example, the code that creates a document heading is set apart by two tags: <head> to mark where it starts and </head> to mark where it ends. That slash character in the second tag identifies it as an *end tag*.

HTML, fussy language that it is, is case-sensitive about tags. If you see all caps between the angle brackets, the tag you're looking at identifies a chunk of code that creates an *element* — one of the major parts of your document's structure (such as headings). Only element tags get the all-caps treatment.

Once the elements are identified, you can use other tags that identify code chunks (called *attributes*) that help you tell your page how to do its job. For example, some attribute tags identify pointers that refer to data outside your Web page; others label information that has to be communicated back to a Web server. Still others label the code that specifies how to display an on-screen object (for example, the alignment or dimensions of a logo or headline).

Certain special-purpose attributes provide the endpoints for those nifty links that your visitors will be using to zip around within your site and across documents. These must-have attributes are called *link anchors* (or *anchors*, for short). They describe the relationship between two named locations in the Web — the source and destination — and tell the system *Yep, that's a link.* The endpoints can be in the same document, in different documents, or in different sites. (So far as we know, they do have to be on the same planet.)

In HTML, you indicate the destination of a link by including a *document reference* (if you're linking to some other document), a *location reference* (if the link is closer to home, inside the same document), or a combination of the two (for a specific point inside another document). Chapter 8 gives you a closer look at some examples: the <base>, <a> (anchor), and <link> tags.

HTML tags vary in how many — and which — attributes they demand before they'll work. Some require you to specify particular attributes, and only those; others can take on optional attributes and values; still others abstain from attributes altogether. We let you in on which is which for each element of document design we present in this book; to do less wouldn't be sportsmanlike.

Titles (when "this @*&# thing" just won't do)

A Web document isn't really finished till you call it something (preferably something printable) and can easily tell its parts, well, apart. That means a small exercise in creative writing: titles and labels.

Every self-respecting HTML document needs a *title* — not just to save it from anonymity, but also to serve some practical purposes on the Web:

- A title identifies the document to users. (You'd be surprised how easy it is to overlook the obvious; a title tells them what they're reading and where to begin.)

- A title identifies your document in hotlists, which makes it a navigation or selection tool for Web cruisers who use the lists.

- A title constitutes the brief document description grabbed and spirited away by prowling robots (automated Web-site search programs); a useful title makes the entries in search databases more accurate.

- A title helps you manage your documents, especially if they're complex and voluminous. Think of it as a small investment of time that will save you vast amounts of frustration later.

Once you've titled your Web document, at last it has something to put in the window's title bar when you open the document. As a sterling example, Figure 2-1 shows the window for an HTML Style Guide with the title `Style Guide for online hypertext` prominently displayed. (Well, okay, it may not be the most exciting title, but *Titanic* was taken.)

Labels plain and fancy

Labels are like small-scale, optional titles; though they aren't required, you may find that your document hangs together a lot better if you label its parts. Labeling sections or topic areas in a document is a courtesy to your visitors. In fact, you can go one better if you use labels for links. Suddenly a courtesy becomes an active navigation aid for users, which can help them feel welcome and encourage them to come back again.

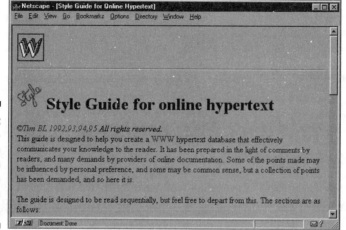

Figure 2-1:
The docu-
ment's title
shows up
on the
window's
title bar.

Making a label into a link is pretty straightforward: You'd use a label's `name`
`attribute` inside an anchor, which directs an HTML link to a named section
in your document — which could be the head of the document or another
labeled part. Consider the following example:

```
<a name="Mexican Dove">Linda Paloma</a>
```

If you wanted to link to the `Linda Paloma` area of the document in which it
appears, all you'd need to do is create an HTML link definition by using the
anchor's `name` (in this case, `"Mexican Dove"`). Using an anchor this way also
sends a signal to other browsers: *If you point to me, refer to me by my anchor's
NAME attribute.* Simple means and rich results.

Links: Text, hypertext, and hot

HTML was designed to keep certain vital operations simple — linking, for
example. Only one kind of link is available — a one-way association between a
source and a target. But you can use that one kind of link in four different ways:

- ✔ **Intradocument linking** moves you from one location to another inside
  the same document.
- ✔ **Interdocument linking** moves you from one document to another
  document.
- ✔ **Linking to an** *agent* **program** that acts on behalf of the Web server gives
  your HTML document a way to handle a query or provide a service
  (such as information gathering).
- ✔ **Linking to a nontext object** gives you a royal road to multimedia: graphics, sounds, video, or The Next Big Thing (maybe a hungry T. Rex?).

When you link HTML files to other types of data — say, sound, graphics, or motion video — suddenly you've done the next best thing to magic: You've enabled HTML's hypertext capabilities. (Shazam.) Before you know it, you're cooking up links all over the place — inside and outside your document, hooking up to agents, shooting out the electronic tendrils that are the look, feel, and power of the Web.

The world ain't flat; neither is text anymore

Hypertext is the kind of everyday wonder nobody would have imagined twenty years ago — but most people still think of *text* as inert words that just sit there, usually on paper, waiting to be read one page at a time. If you find it difficult to think about text in nonbook, nonmagazine, *nonpaper* terms, you're not alone. The worldwide legacy of linear text goes back thousands of years. The Web has been around for a whole lot less time.

Books in their familiar form still have highly appropriate uses — consider (ahem) the one you're reading — but Web document designers, whether they know it or not, have to fight a nearly overwhelming tendency to make their documents *read like* books. If you want a truly forceful page, you must discover the ways of the Web and exploit the hypertext capabilities of HTML.

If your Web pages use freshly evolved cybercapabilities — such as multimedia displays and link navigation — in appealing and useful ways, they'll not only meet the expectations of your users but also extend the reach and impact of your content (whoa, there's that word again).

In the sections that follow, as you examine some common techniques for organizing Web documents; you also encounter a species of creature that's never existed before: documents that can exist *only* on the Web.

Stringing pages together the old-fashioned way

Some pages demand to be read in sequence; many are narratives that build on previous elements (you know — letters, novels, certain congressional reports). Such material lends itself to being strung together in the time-honored page-by-page way, as shown in Figure 2-2. Documents that run to five pages or more — if you believe Tim Berners-Lee in his *Hypertext Online Style Guide* — should use a sequential structure anyway.

But hold on; here's where it gets intriguing. Hypertext gives you the option of chaining pages together forward *and* backward so that you can easily "turn" pages either way. Other links can make appropriate contributions to this basic structure (such as links to other HTML documents, a glossary, or other points inside your document) without disrupting that comfy booklike feel.

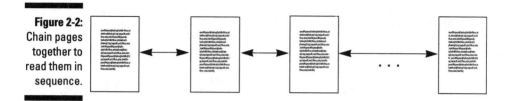

Figure 2-2:
Chain pages
together to
read them in
sequence.

Pulling rank in HTML hierarchies

If you use another ancient-but-serviceable tool and construct documents
from an outline, you may be immediately drawn to ranging your links in a
hierarchy. Most outlines start with major ideas, working their way down
through levels of divisions that refine and elaborate the details of the content
(aha! the C-word again) till at last you behold a complete plan of your work.
(Well, at least the *best* ones do it that way.) Figure 2-3 shows a four-level document hierarchy that organizes an entire set of documents — perhaps even a
whole Web site).

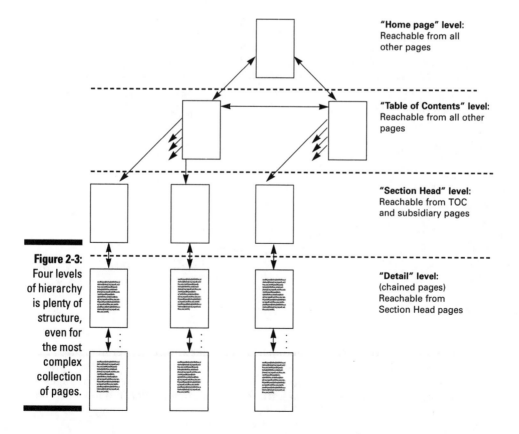

"Home page" level:
Reachable from all
other pages

"Table of Contents" level:
Reachable from all other
pages

"Section Head" level:
Reachable from TOC
and subsidiary pages

Figure 2-3:
Four levels
of hierarchy
is plenty of
structure,
even for
the most
complex
collection
of pages.

"Detail" level:
(chained pages)
Reachable from
Section Head pages

HTML itself places no limits on how many levels of hierarchies you can build; the only limit is how much complexity you (and your audience) feel ready and willing to handle. For both your sakes, keep it simple, Socrates.

Multiple tracks for multiple audiences

It's more common these days for Web page designers to build documents that encompass different kinds of information to meet the needs of different audiences. HTML makes such an approach possible; you can easily interlink basic introductory documents (such as a tutorial or technical overview) with in-depth reference materials. Your home page can point beginners to a tutorial and lead them through an overview so that they're prepared for the acceleration when you blast them off into the details of your "real" content.

This kind of organization, depicted in Figure 2-4, lets you notify experienced users how to bypass introductory materials and access your in-depth content directly. Such an approach lets you design for multiple audiences without taking on tons of extra work.

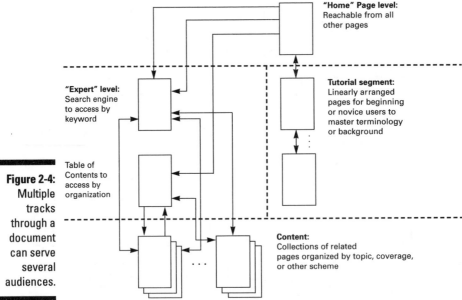

Figure 2-4: Multiple tracks through a document can serve several audiences.

"Home" Page level: Reachable from all other pages

"Expert" level: Search engine to access by keyword

Tutorial segment: Linearly arranged pages for beginning or novice users to master terminology or background

Table of Contents to access by organization

Content: Collections of related pages organized by topic, coverage, or other scheme

The organization in Figure 2-4 departs from that shown earlier in Figures 2-2 and 2-3 — and maybe from that used for the last 500-or-so years. It emphasizes links between related documents *more* than it does the flow of pages within those documents. In fact, the kind of document pictured in Figure 2-4 would probably combine a linear *and* a hierarchical structure in its page flow. Users would read the tutorial from front to back (or at least a chapter at a time), but they would consult the reference section by topic (and only rarely read all the way through). Welcome to the early future.

Web wonderland: "Hotlists" and "jump pages"

Some of the best resources we've located on the Web are *hotlists* (also called *jump pages*) that are nothing more than lists of annotated references to other documents — with, of course, HTML capabilities. These lists usually relate to one or more specific topics. You can see this kind of document structure in Figure 2-5, which shows a single page that points to multiple pages in various locations. In this example, the picture fails to do justice to the concept. For a better illustration, we'd say call up and look at a real Web page — and we just happen to have one handy (so to speak). Fire up your browser and check out the URL listed here — it's a stellar example of what a good hotlist can do!

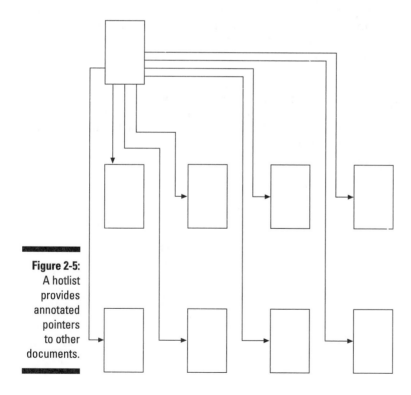

Figure 2-5:
A hotlist provides annotated pointers to other documents.

 You can find more good hotlists on the Web than you can shake a stick at. Dan Kegel's collection of ISDN references is one of the true "seven wonders" of the Web: www.alumni.caltech.edu/~dank/isdn/.

Welcome back, my friends, to the page that never ends

A type of page that would be unlikely to survive outside the Web solicits input from users, who help to create an open-ended document. Users contribute comments, additional text, and hypermedia, or they add to an ongoing narrative. The structure of such a document is hard to predict and, therefore, hard to *depict*. Suffice it to say that this kind of Web document can grow like a coral colony, more by accretion than by organization or design. But hey, it's an *organic* experience.

For an example of this kind of living, ongoing document, consult the following URL: `bug.village.virginia.edu/`.

WAXweb is a hypermedia implementation of a feature-length, independent film, *WAX or the discovery of television among the bees* (David Blair, 85:00, 1991). WAXweb is a large hypermedia database available over the Internet. It features an authoring interface that lets users collaborate in adding onto the story. WAXweb includes thousands of individual elements, ranging from text to music, motion videos, and video transcriptions of motion picture clips. For users with VRML-capable browsers, WAXweb also offers a pretty nifty three-dimensional VRML implementation, as well.

The only limitations on how you structure a document are those imposed by your need to communicate effectively with your audience. The rest is plumbing — the page-flow and organizational techniques we've outlined here. Once you're familiar with how to use them to best effect, it's time to boldly go forth into the world of markup languages.

Chapter 3

Your First HTML Page

- -

In This Chapter

▶ Getting the right tool for the job

▶ Cranking up the Edit-Review cycle

▶ Tinkering with templates

▶ Bracing for what comes next (just kidding)

- -

*T*he deeper you get into the details and capabilities of HTML, the more you may be itching to go out and build a page of your own. Rest assured, such a response is normal; this chapter helps you scratch that itch: It unwraps the mechanics of putting together a minimal, but working, HTML page.

An HTML file is basically a plain ASCII text file with a secret identity; its powers come from special character sequences called *markup* that separate the content (you know, the stuff you want to impart to your audience) from the controls (the guides that tell your browser how to display that content). To review the basics of HTML, spin through Chapter 1.

Building good Web pages means understanding how they're put together in the first place and maintained thereafter. So we describe creating the text, viewing it in a Web browser, making corrections or changes, and so on — a process we call the *Edit-Review cycle*. You don't need toe clips to use this particular cycle, but it *is* (to crank the metaphor) strictly hands-on. The exercises in this chapter should give you a good grip on the process.

Get the Right Tool for the Job

Although you can find a myriad of tools built specifically to help you create and manage HTML pages, we think that a plain text editor does the job pretty well. That's why we recommend that you include a favorite text editor in your HTML toolbox, even if you use other tools. Even if you decide to use an HTML editor like HoTMetaL, HotDog, FrontPage, or some other HTML-savvy piece of software to create pages, nothing beats a plain vanilla text editor for rapid postcreation tweaking or maintenance tasks. Even though we have lots of options available to us for building HTML pages, we still use a plain text editor as our tool of choice for most circumstances.

For more discussion of HTML tools of all kinds, please consult Appendix C, Tools of the Trade. (You find a general tool discussion there, along with discussions of our personal favorites, plus separate sections for PC, Macintosh, and UNIX users.)

For Mac users, SimpleText works pretty well; for UNIX-heads, an ordinary text editor like *vi* is more than adequate for the task. For PC users, a text editor like NotePad (or its burly cousin WordPad) does the job quite nicely. We base the examples we show in this chapter on the version of Notepad that ships with Windows 95/98 and Windows NT.

If you absolutely must use a word processor (such as Microsoft Word), be aware that most such programs do not produce plain text files by default. That's why you have to remember to save any HTML files you create within your program as "text only" or "plain text" with a .html or .htm extension. And no fair using the built-in "Convert to HTML" option, either. Word processors were not built to be HTML editors, and the code that they generate can be — to put it nicely — sloppy and icky. Better to use your handy-dandy text editor and your own HTML knowledge instead.

The Edit-Review Cycle

The process of building an HTML file is actually cyclical; it starts when you type in some HTML markup and some plain old text, save the file, and then open the saved file within a Web browser. But if you're like most of us, it doesn't end there when you see what you've wrought. To err is human; to edit, even more so — whatever you may have missed, misspelled, or just plain don't like in your page-to-be, you can refine it in three simple steps:

1. **Make some changes in the text editor.**

2. **Save the changes in the text editor.**

3. **Open (or refresh) the file in a Web browser to check your work.**

Repeat as often as needed — or until the dinner bell, or till wild horses drag you away from your work. Think we're kidding? (Well, yes, but this activity *is* habit-forming.)

Time has no meaning when you build or tweak Web pages. Be prepared to lose hours, days, and sometimes even months of your life!

Oh, well, at least the first one's free: Behold! We bring forth the basic text that any well-formed Web page needs to make it both viewable and legal. Type the following characters into your favorite text editor, and save the resulting file as test.htm or test.html:

```
<html>
<head>
<title>My very first Web Page!</title>
</head>
<body>
<h2>Daisy's Phone List</h2>

<ul>
      <li>Micky<br>
          555-2290<br><br>
      <li>Minnie<br>
          555-1230<br><br>
      <li>Donald<br>
          555-4476<br><br>
      <li>Goofy<br>
          555-4455<br><br>
</ul>

</body>
</html>
```

After you type this material and save the file as **test.html**, open your Web browser and look in the File menu for an entry that says something like Open (in Internet Explorer you can point at a file on your hard drive from this entry) or Open File (Netscape Navigator accepts a local filename here). Figure 3-1 shows what test.html looks like from Internet Explorer.

Figure 3-1:
Our first
HTML
efforts
create a
ducky
phone list.

Though the text that shows up in the browser's display window is just a simple phone list, don't let its simplicity fool you; a number of classic HTML features are visible. First, notice that the text between the <title> and </title> tags appears in the title bar at the top of the Internet Explorer window. Also, notice that one of the buttons on that toolbar is labeled "Refresh." From here on out, the Edit-Review cycle works like this:

1. **Switch to the text editor, enter some text.**

2. **Save the file in the text editor.**

3. **Switch to your Web browser, and hit the Refresh button.**

4. **Check your most recent efforts; if further changes are necessary, go back to Step 1!**

Trust us, this process will become very familiar, very soon. Even so, two of its steps are often overlooked: (a) saving the file after making changes in the text editor and (b) remembering to refresh the browser display so that it shows the most recent version of the file. If you remember to do these things every time, the Edit-Review cycle becomes practically second nature as you create and maintain your Web pages.

Now to create a creature with a bit more substance, Igor. Return to your text editor, open up a fresh document, and operate upon your document till it looks like this one:

```
<html>
<head>
<title>Home Page: The Institute of Silly Research</title>
</head>
<body>
<h1>Welcome to the ISR!</h1>
The ISR is the world's best-known repository of truly
trifling and insignificant research results. Visit our
pages regularly to keep up with the exciting efforts of
our team of talented scholars, and their magnificent
efforts to extend the boundaries of science and
technology to ever more meaningless ends.
<h2>The ISR Staff</h2>
Dr. Maury Singleton-Smith, PhD, Director<br>
Dr. Gwyneth Gastropolis, PhD, Chief of Research<br>
Dr. Simon Schuster, MD, PhD, Head, Impracticality Dept.<br>
<h2>ISR's Current Projects</h2>
Beyond Charm and Strangeness: The Nerdon<br>
Lukewarm Fusion<br>
Harnessing the Power of Stilton Cheese<br>
The Dancing Louie Louie Masters<br>
<hr>
For more information about the ISR, please contact
<a href=mailto:NERDBOY@ISR.ORG>Dr. Singleton-Smith</a>.
All financial contributions are cheerfully accepted.
</body>
</html>
```

As you enter this text, you may find yourself dealing with HTML mistakes (remember to enclose all tags with ‹ and ›, and to precede the text for closing tags with a /). You may also find yourself dealing with typos, omissions, and other kinds of content errors as well. Just remember: *Each time you find an error, shift back into your text editor to make the necessary changes.* Then, save the file as `isr.html`. When you return to your Web browser, refresh the page, and you may then contemplate the results of your latest efforts. Keep editing and reviewing, and soon you shall have a page every bit as insignificant and meaningless as the one shown in Figure 3-2.

(Hey, who said practice can't be fun?) The real point behind the exercise, of course, is to familiarize yourself with creating and editing an HTML document as you build a page to include on a Web site. As you get more adept at it, you can let good habits take care of these operational issues; then you're free to concentrate on the description and (oh yeah) content of your documents. By the time you create a few pages, this process should feel nearly as natural as working on paper.

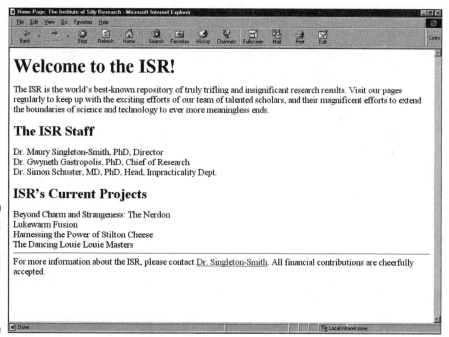

Figure 3-2:
The full-blown home page for the ISR is overwhelming in its triviality!

Working with Templates

Nothing is so simple that it can't benefit from a few well-chosen shortcuts. Building a Web page may not quite be like falling off a log, but we've put some *template files* on this book's CD-ROM to help you get your feet wet. (You'll find a collection of these ready-made files in the /Template directory on the disc.) Try using one as a starting point for your own Web page design. Simply copy it to your hard drive, give it a few tweaks to reflect your own interests, and then edit it to kick-start the Edit-Review cycle. A couple trips around the block on that cycle and your file will soon look like a Web page!

Whenever you want to use a template as a point of departure for your work, *save it under a different name* as soon as you open it in your text editor. That way, you won't have to recopy the files from the CD-ROM each time you want to reuse the same template.

Part II
Cranking Out Pages

The 5th Wave   By Rich Tennant

"It's a user-coercive search engine. When the user clicks the siphon icon, it installs a proprietary browser and collects the registration fee. Patching into the user's 401(k) was Bill's idea."

In this part . . .

In this part of the book, we describe the markup that makes Web pages possible. Next, we show you how ordinary text can be enriched and enlivened in a attractive Web-based presentation. Then, we explain how to add graphics to your pages for more visual interest. Finally, we take you through some high-impact Web pages to show you just how hot HTML can sizzle!

Chapter 4

Cracking the Code

●●

In This Chapter

▶ Scrutinizing HTML tags

▶ Categorizing HTML tags

●●

*I*f you're looking for more of a no-holds-barred look at HTML markup, you've come to the right place, Pilgrim (you just have to imagine a John Wayne .WAV file here). In this chapter, we talk some serious turkey about HTML syntax to make sure you can keep up with all the gory details. We also establish some categories for what HTML can do and group the markup tags in meaningful categories (to make them easier to learn and use). The remainder of the chapter is a reference tool, where we describe all the HTML tags in alphabetical order for easy access.

Buckle up, and let's go!

HTML Tags at a Glance

As we discuss in Part I, *HTML tags* are code words that tell a computer program, such as a Web browser or a word processor, how to format the rest of the text in an HTML document. When a Web browser or a word processor reads an HTML document, the program finds the formatting by watching for specific words and punctuation — the program assumes everything else is the actual text of your document.

Browsers and word processors assume that you follow the rules of HTML syntax, such as these:

✔ Tags are enclosed in left and right angle brackets, like this:

```
<HEAD>
```

✔ Tags usually come in *pairs*. For example, <HEAD> marks the beginning of a document heading block, and </HEAD> marks the end.

Your browser considers all the text that occurs between opening and closing tags the focus of that tag and handles the text appropriately. Because the majority of HTML tags work this way, we flag all the possible exceptions when we introduce them.

✔ HTML has no requirement for uppercase or lowercase.

Future versions of HTML may require tags in lowercase. For future compatibility, we encourage you to write code in lowercase.

✔ Tags can sometimes take attributes to

• Define data sources or destinations

• Specify URLs

• Further specify the characteristics of the text to which a tag will be applied.

For example, the <IMG> tag for placing graphics can use the following attributes to specify the source and placement of an image on a page:

• SRC = source for image (usually a URL).

• ALT = text to display if browser doesn't show graphics.

• ALIGN indicates placement of a graphic.

• ISMAP indicates that the graphic is a clickable image map with one or more links to other locations built onto the image. If it's absent, the image is not a map.

Some attributes take on values — in this case, SRC, ALT, and ALIGN all require at least one value — whereas others, like ISMAP, do not. Attributes that don't require values are usually true ("turned on") if present and false ("turned off") when omitted. Also, tags may have default values for required attributes that are omitted, so make sure that you check the HTML specification to determine how such defaults are handled.

At this point, you may already know quite a bit about HTML syntax and layout. But you need to know quite a bit of additional stuff, some of which we had to use in our discussion in the preceding bullet item. Discussions of this additional stuff contain some goofy characters that aren't part of HTML itself but are necessary to explain it formally.

Syntax conventions are no party!

While we're providing formal definitions of the various HTML commands, we use typographical notation in an equally formal way. What this means (in plain language) is that you better pay attention to how we write some things down because we intend for the notation to describe how you should combine, construct, and use terms.

Describing a formal syntax means using certain characters in a special way to talk about how to treat elements that appear in conjunction with these characters. This is nearly identical to these HTML notions:

- ✔ Angle brackets surround a tag (`<HEAD>`).
- ✔ A forward slash following the left angle bracket denotes a closing tag (`</HEAD>`).
- ✔ An ampersand leads off a character entity, and a semicolon closes it (`&egrave;`).

These special characters clue us (and our browser software) into the need for special handling. Chapter 12 provides in-depth information about character entities and their special formatting, while we focus on the HTML tags in this chapter.

HTML rules! (or at least bosses)

In addition to the formal syntax for HTML that we use throughout the book (for HTML is a very finicky language), the markup language itself has some general properties that are worth covering before you encounter the tags directly.

No embedded blanks, please!

All HTML tags require that the characters in a name be contiguous. You can't insert extra blanks within a tag or its surrounding markup without causing that tag to be ignored (which is what browsers do with tags they can't recognize).

This requirement means that `</HEAD>` is a valid closing tag for a document heading, but that none of the following is legal:

```
< /HEAD>
</ HEAD>
</H EAD>
</HE AD>
</HEA D>
</HEAD >
```

We hope that you get the idea: Don't use blanks inside tags, except where you use a blank deliberately to separate a tag name from an attribute name (for example, `<IMG SRC="sample.gif">` is legal, but `<IMGSRC="sample.gif">` is not).

When assigning values to attributes, however, spaces are okay. Therefore, all four of the following variants for this `SRC` assignment are legal:

```
<IMG SRC="sample.gif">
<!- Previous line: no spaces before or after = sign ->
<IMG SRC = "sample.gif">
<!- Previous line: spaces before and after = sign ->
<IMG SRC= "sample.gif">
<!- Previous line: no space before, one after = sign ->
<IMG SRC ="sample.gif">
<!- Previous line: one space before, none after = sign ->
```

Where one space is legal, multiple spaces are legal. Don't get carried away with what's legal or not, though — try to make your HTML documents as readable as possible and everything else should flow naturally.

We sneaked more HTML markup into the preceding example. After each `<IMG>` tag line, we inserted readable HTML comments to describe what occurred on the preceding line. This lets you infer that the HTML markup to open a comment is the string `<!-` and the string `->` ends the comment. As you go through the markup section later on, we cover some style guidelines for using comments effectively and correctly.

What's the default?

If a tag can support an attribute, what does it mean when the attribute isn't present? For `ISMAP` on the `<IMG>` tag, for example, you already know that when the `ISMAP` attribute is present, it means *the image is a clickable map*. If `ISMAP` is absent, this means *the image is not a clickable map*.

This is a way of introducing the concept of a *default,* which is not a way of assigning blame but rather a way of deciding what to assume when an attribute is not supplied for a particular tag. For `ISMAP`, the default is absent; that is, an image is only assumed to be a clickable map when the `ISMAP` attribute is explicitly supplied.

But how do images get displayed if the `ALIGN` attribute isn't defined? As a quick bit of experimentation shows you, the default for most graphical browsers is to insert the graphic at the left-hand margin. These kinds of defaults are important, too, and we'll try to tell you what to expect from them as well.

The nesting instinct

Sometimes it's necessary to insert one set of markup tags within another. You might want a few words within a sentence already marked for special emphasis to be the trigger for a hyperlink. For example, the entire heading "Other Important Numbers: Emergency Phone Numbers" will draw the readers' attention if it is rendered in boldface, but you only want the words *Emergency Phone Numbers* to be clickable and lead to another HTML document listing relevant emergency numbers.

Enclosing one set of markup within another is called *nesting*. When the nesting instinct strikes you, the best rule is to close first what you opened most recently. For example, the text tags `<A HREF="ephone.html">` . . . `</A>` provide a way of bracketing text linking to another HTML document. If this occurred within strongly emphasized text, `<STRONG>` . . . `</STRONG>`, the proper way to handle the hyperlink is like this:

```
<STRONG>Other Important Numbers:
<A HREF:"ephone.html">Emergency Phone Numbers</A></STRONG>
```

That way, you close the nested `<A>` tag with its mate before you close out the `<STRONG>` heading. Some browsers may let you violate this rule, but others may behave unpredictably if you don't open and close tags in the right order. Figure 4-1 shows what this combination of tags looks like. (Notice that the words *Emergency Phone Numbers* appear in heavier type than the rest of the heading.)

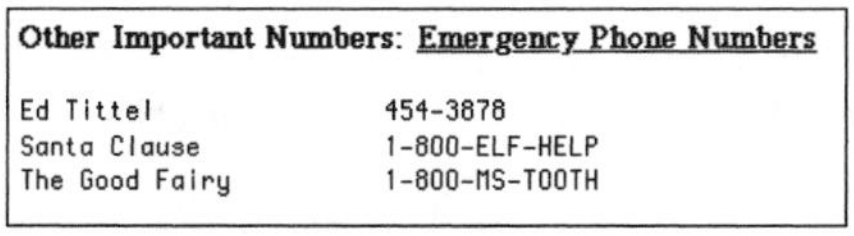

Figure 4-1:
Using nested tags to create a hyperlink within strongly emphasized text.

```
Other Important Numbers: Emergency Phone Numbers

Ed Tittel          454-3878
Santa Clause       1-800-ELF-HELP
The Good Fairy     1-800-MS-TOOTH
```

Nesting just doesn't make sense for some tags. For instance, within `<TITLE>` . . . `</TITLE>`, you deal with information that shows up only on a window title, rather than on a particular Web page. Text and layout controls clearly do not apply here (and are cheerfully ignored by some browsers, while making others curl up and die).

Always look back to the left as you start closing tags you already opened. Close the closest one first, then the next closest, and so on. Check the tag details (later on in this chapter) to find out which tags you can nest within your outermost open tag. If the tag you want to use doesn't appear on the okay list, then don't try to nest that tag inside the current open ones. Close out what you have open and then open the tag you need.

Keeping your tags in the right nests keeps your readers' browsers from getting confused! It also makes sure that you hatch only good-looking Web pages.

Okay, you want to know about all these tags we keep twittering about. Gotcha covered:

✔ In most of the following chapters of this book, the chapter begins by introducing you to a group of tags; the rest of that chapter shows you how to spin them. If you read straight through from here to the end of the book, you'll cover the basic everyday stuff first, then the tricky stuff.

✔ Appendix B lists all the standard HTML tags in alphabetical order. For each tag, we tell you what it does and which chapter shows you how to do it.

HTML Categories

Before we take you through the HTML tags in alphabetical order, we'd like to introduce them to you grouped by category. These categories help to explain how and when you can use the tags, and what functions the tags provide.

✔ **Text tags:** Text tags provide a logical structure for content. This structure may or may not alter that content's display properties.

✔ **Lists:** You use list tags to define a variety of different lists.

✔ **Tables:** Table tags define the structure and layout of tables. Tables can be used to arrange data or to aid page layout and design.

✔ **Links:** Link tags create connections, such as hyperlinks, image links, and links to style sheets, between Web resources.

✔ **Inclusions:** You use these tags to include non-HTML objects, such as Java applets and multimedia files, within Web documents.

✔ **Style sheet tags:** These HTML elements define how content is rendered in the browser.

✔ **Presentation controls:** Presentation tags alter the display of content by affecting properties such as font styles and horizontal rules.

✔ **Frames:** Frame tags define and control frames within the display area of a browser.

> ✔ **Forms:** Form tags control the input of data from a user and transmission of that data to a background CGI or similar application.
>
> ✔ **Scripts:** You use these tags to embed programming language scripts into Web documents.

HTML tags give you power over your document at various levels, from managing its structure to controlling the look and feel of its text. In the next section, we take apart some HTML tags and lay them out on the workbench.

HTML Tags

A complete list is never quite possible. Many browser builders are adding extensions to HTML for their own use. And it's virtually guaranteed that future standards will introduce significant changes and enhancements to HTML. Progress marches on (except on the Web, where it's wearing rocket Rollerblades).

This book emphasizes the state of the art in HTML coding. For futuristic HTML stuff that you can't use today, consult the World Wide Web Consortium Web site at `www.w3.org/`.

The rundown on attributes

In HTML, attributes typically take one of two forms within a tag:

> ✔ `ATTRIBUTE`: Where the name itself provides information about how the tag should behave (for example, `ISMAP` in `<IMG>` indicates that the graphic is a clickable map).
>
> ✔ `ATTRIBUTE="value"`: Where `value` is typically enclosed in quotes (`" "`) and may be one of the following kinds of elements:
>
>> • URL: A uniform resource locator
>>
>> • Name: A user-supplied name, probably for an input field
>>
>> • Number: A user-supplied numeric value
>>
>> • Text: User-supplied text
>>
>> • Server: Server-dependent name (for example, page name defaults)
>>
>> • (X|Y|Z): One member of a set of fixed values
>>
>> • #rrggbb: Hexadecimal color notation

As we discuss attributes for individual tags, you see them in a section under the tag name. For each one we provide a definition. We also indicate choices for predefined sets of values or provide an example for open-ended value assignments.

Common attributes

You'll find six attributes listed for more than 85 percent of the tags. We list them here, along with a brief description, to save a few trees and avoid being redundant. All these attributes have *implied values,* which means that you don't have to actually list them in your tags unless you want to change their values. For example, the implied value for the DIR attribute is ltr, which stands for "left to right," the direction the tag and its contents will be read. If for some reason you wanted to change the value to rtl ("right to left"), then you would need to include the attribute and its value.

- ✔ ID="name": A document-wide identifier that you can use to give an HTML element a unique identifier within a document.

- ✔ CLASS="text": A comma-separated list of class names, which indicates that the element belongs to a specific class or classes of style definitions.

- ✔ STYLE="text": Provides rendering information specific to this element, such as the color, size, and font specifics.

- ✔ TITLE="text": Defines an advisory title that will display additional help. Balloon text around hyperlinks and graphics are generated using this attribute.

- ✔ DIR="(LTR|RTL)": Indicates the direction the text will be read in, left to right or right to left.

- ✔ LANG="name": Specifies the language that the element and its contents are written in.

Intrinsic events

The designers of HTML 4.0 included numerous intricacy event triggers to support programming and scripting mechanisms. Basically, one of several intrinsic events, like an onmouseover, when tied to an HTML tag, causes a script to run without needing a hyperlink. The user simply performs the event, such as moving a mouse over a tag with the onmouseover attribute, and the script is automatically called.

Because you see intrinsic events listed for many of the tags, we want to warn you ahead of time that they are scripting related. A quick look at intrinsic events shows that

✔ You can use the `onreset, onsubmit` intrinsic events with the following markup tag: `<FORM>`.

✔ You can use the `onload, onunload` intrinsic events with the following markup tags: `<FRAMESET>` and `<BODY>`.

✔ You can use the `onchange, onselect` intrinsic events with the following markup tags: `<INPUT>`, `<SELECT>`, and `<TEXTAREA>`.

✔ You can use the `onblur, onfocus` intrinsic events with the following markup tags: `<BUTTON>`, `<INPUT>`, `<LABEL>`, `<SELECT>`, and `<TEXTAREA>`.

✔ You can use the `onclick, ondblclick, onkeydown, onkeypress, onkeyup, onmousedown, onmousemove, onmouseout, onmouseover, onmouseup` intrinsic events with the following markup tags: `<A>`, `<ABBR>`, `<ADDRESS>`, `<B>`, `<BIG>`, `<BLOCKQUOTE>`, `<BODY>`, `<BUTTON>`, `<CAPTION>`, `<CENTER>`, `<CITE>`, `<CODE>`, `<COL>`, `<COLGROUP>`, `<DD>`, `<DEL>`, `<DFN>`, `<DIR>`, `<DIV>`, `<DL>`, `<DT>`, `<EM>`, `<FIELDSET>`, `<FORM>`, `<H*>`, `<HR>`, `<I>`, `<IMG>`, `<INPUT>`, `<INS>`, `<KBD>`, `<LABEL>`, `<LEGEND>`, `<LI>`, `<LINK>`, `<MENU>`, `<OBJECT>`, `<OL>`, `<OPTION>`, `<P>`, `<PRE>`, `<Q>`, `<S>`, `<SAMP>`, `<SELECT>`, `<SMALL>`, `<SPAN>`, `<STRIKE>`, `<STRONG>`, `<SUB>`, `<SUP>`, `<TABLE>`, `<TBODY>`, `<TD>`, `<TEXTAREA>`, `<TFOOT>`, `<TH>`, `<THEAD>`, `<TR>`, `<TT>`, `<U>`, `<UL>`, and `<VAR>`.

When you know that much about intrinsic events, it keeps you busy for awhile. This way cool technology adds interactivity to Web pages in a relatively simple way and is well worth exploring after you get your feet firmly planted in HTML land.

As you examine HTML tags, including attributes, you find that some (the ALIGN attribute, for example) are *deprecated* — earmarked to be left for dead by future versions of HTML. Coders will have to use style sheet properties, which are covered in Chapter 13. As always, obsolescence is the cruel-but-just law of the cyberjungle.

```
<A>, <ABBR>, <ADDRESS>, <APPLET>, <B>, <BDO>, <BIG>,
<BLOQUOTE>, <BODY>, <BUTTON>, <CAPTION>, <CENTER>, <CITE>,
<CODE>, <DD>, <DEL>, <DFN>, <DIV>, <DT>, <EM>, <FIELDSET>,
<FONT>, <FORM>, <H*>, <I>, <IFRAME>, <INS>, <KBD>, <LABEL>,
<LEGEND>, <LI>, <NOFRAMES>, <NOSCRIPT>, <OBJECT>, <P>, <Q>,
<S>, <SAMP>, <SMALL>, <SPAN>, <STRIKE>, <STRONG>, <SUB>,
<SUP>, <TD>, <TH>, <TT>, <U>, <VAR>
```

Rather than include code snippets and screen shots, we thought you might like to see HTML at work for yourself. So we included some sample code for every tag, and for attributes where possible, on the CD-ROM. Using your browser, just open the file list under the "Examples" section to see how tag information is rendered. To view the HTML, choose View Source in your browser or open the .HTM file with a text editor. See file /html4Fd2/examples/ch04/img.HTM.

Chapter 5

Tried and True Text Pages

. . . .

In This Chapter

▶ Tooling up a document for the first time

▶ Putting templates to work for you

▶ Starting page layout at the top

▶ Writing titles and headings with a purpose

▶ Building better bodies for your pages

▶ Fortifying your paragraphs

▶ Giving your lists the proper structures

▶ Linking to your Web site and beyond

. . . .

*B*uilding your first Web page is exciting if you keep this thought firmly in mind: *You can change anything at any time; good Web pages always evolve.* Change is just a keystroke away; nothing is cast in concrete (good thing, too — concrete is murder on a keyboard).

The pressure's off; you can build your own simple, but complete, Web page. Think of it as a prototype for future pages. You can always go back to it later and add bells, whistles, or hungry T. Rexes, whatever's needed to make your Web page the one you want — whether for a business, an academic institution, or a government agency.

Your *look and feel,* which is the way the page looks to the user, combined with your king-sized content, is how your site creates its all-important first impression; the first time a user visits an ugly page with little or no useful content, may also be the last time. This is one place where looks and guts matter — fortunately, HTML gives you a way to describe your content so that it looks great in any Web browser.

Remember that the Web itself is a confusing concept to many users. Your Web pages can be pleasing to the eye — and an oasis of clarity — if you follow the KISS approach (Keep It Simple, Sweetheart!). Everything you can do to make your page "intuitively obvious" to a visitor — and keep it that way — makes your viewers happier and keeps them coming back for more.

Chapter 2 presents the basic concepts for a good Web page. It emphasizes efficient form and (especially) worthwhile content over sheer HTML prowess — and it never hurts to brush up on page layout and information flow before you forge ahead into the nuts and bolts of HTML. If you used Chapter 3 to create a quickie Web page, revisit your creation with an eye toward using what you discover in this chapter to improve it.

The basics of good Web page design are content, layout, first impression, and KISS (Keep It Simple, Sweetheart!). Be ye mindful of them, and yea, they shall bring you contentment and your visitors enlightenment.

Templates as Strong Bones

After you've nosed around the Web long enough to get a look at some actual Web pages, you'll probably notice two things about them right away:

- ✔ Most well-constructed examples of the species contain the following elements in some form: *title, heading, body,* and *footer.*

- ✔ Web pages that lack one or more of those basic elements have an uncanny way of frustrating the visitor and inviting a quick departure.

Centuries of print media have predisposed us to look for certain familiar elements of good construction; Web pages that lack them are neither pleasing to the eye nor intuitive to use. Don't let that happen to your work — use this basic template for each HTML document you produce:

```
<HTML>
   <HEAD>
      <TITLE>Your Title</TITLE>
   </HEAD>

   <BODY>

   <P>
      Your headings and wonderful text and graphics
      go here.
   </P>

   <ADDRESS>
      Copyright  &copy; 1998,  Your Name <BR>
      Revised — Revision Date <BR>
      URL: <A HREF = "http://this.page's.url.here">

   </ADDRESS>

</BODY>
</HTML>
```

Starting down the path of enlightenment is really that simple: This template actually works. Figure 5-1 shows what it looks like when viewed with Netscape Navigator.

Figure 5-1:
The basic
Web page
template
viewed with
Navigator.

Figure 5-1 shows how this particular bit of HTML looks in Netscape Navigator on a PC running Windows 98 with particular settings. It may look a little different in Navigator on another PC running Windows 98 because no two users' settings are exactly the same.

The bottom line is that no Web page is ever displayed in *exactly* the same way from browser to browser and computer to computer. The browser type and version, operating system, and particular user settings all affect the final display of the HTML in the Web browser. This means you, as the page designer, never have total control over the final look and feel of your Web page for each individual user.

Don't panic! Remember that HTML is a markup language, not a formatting language, and as long as you use it correctly and consistently, your pages will look good in any browser. Coincidentally — NOT! — this book teaches you all you need to know to create pages that look great anywhere.

In case you might need a discreet refresher, here's how to view local pages with your browser:

✔ Launch your Web browser.

✔ Choose Open, Open Page, or something similar from the browser's File menu.

✔ Navigate through the folders and files on your hard drive until you find the HTML page you want to view. To make it easy to find your HTML files — especially if your hard drives are as full and cluttered as ours — we recommend that you save all your Web documents in one top-level folder called "Web Docs," "HTML Pages," or some other intuitive title.

> ✔ If you use Navigator, remember to set memory and disk caches to zero so that Navigator reloads each new version of your file from the disk, instead of loading from its cache. Other browsers cache pages, too, so be sure you read what you edited — not some older version!

As you can see, this home page is plain and simple — sturdy bones, but not much plumage. It may not cause folks to flock to see it, but that's where your own killer text and understated-but-elegant graphics come in. Although the browsers that most Web surfers use have some form of graphical user interface (GUI), have one more look at Chapter 2 before you stick in that way-cool animated pterodactyl — first and foremost, put your creative energy into high-quality *content*. Once you've got that, Chapter 6 covers how to add graphics to your Web page (animated flying things optional).

Page Layout Top to Bottom

Now that you have a basic template, you can start to change it. To begin the fun, make sure that your first Web page doesn't occupy more than a single screen. This size limit makes a page much easier to edit and test. You can get more than enough information on a single screen and help your audience avoid unnecessary scrolling.

A *single screen* seems like an easy concept, but is it? A single screen is how much information a browser can display on a monitor without scrolling. This amount varies because not all browsers — or monitors — are created equal. Your users may be running quite a menagerie of equipment. Though this doesn't mean you have to design for lowest-common-denominator capabilities, we *can* tell you how to avoid one monster mistake: *Don't assume that your users can see your page the same way you see it in your browser.*

Testing your pages at a relatively low resolution (640 x 480 pixels) with several different browsers can help you see your pages through your users' eyes. Getting this view is well worth taking the extra time! Each operating system has a specific way to set monitor resolution. To find out how to set yours, consult your OS help file or manual.

You may find it helpful to sketch your design ideas on paper first, or to use a drawing program to create a model of your layout and components. Figure 5-2 offers one such model, showing not only the spatial relationships on the page but also the amounts and locations of the ever-important breathing room that page designers call *white space*. Although you can leave too much white space on a page, most designers err in the other direction and wind up with far too little, which makes their pages appear cramped and cluttered.

Title
  Heading

  | Text and/or Main Graphic here. |

  Body

  | Explanation of page purpose. |

  | Information and primary links.
  Most important graphics, but only
  a couple of large or 3-4 small ones. |

  | Secondary links.
  Less important graphics. |

  Footer

  | Author, Date revised, Link to Home
  Page if this isn't, or another page,
  copyright notice if you desire & URL. |

Figure 5-2:
A sketch of
basic Web
page layout,
complete
with white
space.

Organize your page so that your viewers can scan through its content quickly and easily.

> ✔ Start with the most important information near the top, in large type, surrounded by plenty of white space.

> ✔ Follow with the less earth-shaking items.

Good page design isn't a space-stuffing contest. You're trying to hit the highlights and invite closer examination — usually of no more than one topic per page. If you have lots of material or more topics to cover, you can easily make more pages and link them to this one. One good rule comes from professional presenters: *A single slide (or, in this case, screen) should try to convey no more than three to five pieces of related information.*

Rarely will you create a stand-alone Web page, but instead you'll create a group of pages that — when combined — create an entire Web site. Links are the glue that connects that collection of Web pages. Find out more about links in Chapter 13.

What's in a Name? That's Up to You

You normally don't see Web pages titled "Untitled" (or "The page formerly known as . . .," which is almost as bad) for a reason. HTML files use their titles to give search engines (Yahoo!, Excite, AltaVista, and so on) something to grab and put in an index. For indexing purposes, your title should contain the most important information a user needs to know about your Web site, distilled to short-but-sweet. Once the title has piqued your visitors' interest and ushered them into your Web site, document headings show them around.

HTML styles, or the users' browser settings, determine the font, page size, and length of line your users see on-screen. Despite the range of possible browsers and monitors, you still have some say-so over the first impression your page makes. With appropriate content and layout, you can make your pages' titles and headings attractive and informative.

To find out all you ever wanted to know — and more — about the markup associated with titles and headings, look to Chapter 8.

Titles — bait the hook with something juicy

Think of your Web page's title as a sort of electronic fishing lure. Many Web indexing search engines — the software robots that relentlessly cruise the Web in search of information — use titles to create index records in *their* databases, pointing the way to *your* pages. Also, most browsers use titles in the name fields of their *hotlist* or *bookmark* sections, which collect URLs that users want to revisit. That means they use your titles to figure out what's on your pages.

Because you want people to find and read your pages, make your titles as *concisely descriptive* as possible. Try to fit your title on no more than a single line; it should be an arresting arrangement of keywords that describe the contents of your page (it helps to know your content thoroughly).

Start with the simple stuff: Type a short list of keywords that best describe your page. Then use them in a sentence. Next, delete all conjunctions, adverbs, and unnecessary adjectives. With a little rearranging, what's left should be a pretty good title. Here's an example of constructing a title:

- **Words:** George, classical guitar player, bicycle racing.
- **Sentence:** George is a classical guitarist who races bicycles.
- **Title:** George's classical guitar and bike racing page.

The following shows what this title looks like with some markup around it to describe it as a title:

```
<HTML>
    <HEAD>
       <TITLE>George's classical guitar and bike racing
             page</TITLE>
    </HEAD>
...
</HTML>
```

This title should fit on one line when viewed by most browsers. Test it with several browsers to see how it looks. If it's too long, shorten it!

Web browsers display the content between the `<title>...</title>` tags in the window's title bar, not at the top of the page as you may expect. Don't panic when you add a title to your document and don't see it appear automatically on the page. Look to the top of your browser window to see it instead.

Headings — right this way to the info

Headings are actually a family of specialized critters, some more immediately visible than others. Every Web page needs a *heading section* after its title and various *paragraph headings* within the body of the document. In the print world — for example, in this book — headings take the form of emphasized text that appears just before particular paragraphs. So while we're at it, a closer look at them is in order.

Headings, along with the title, are the most important text in your Web page. They are the first text that users notice. If headings aren't attractive and instantly informative, users may jump to another page with a single click. Well-written headings hook readers and make them want more.

As with the other parts of your Web page, concentrate on content first. Your headings should exhibit consistent, meaningful ties to the paragraphs they introduce, and they should do that throughout your pages. As you mull and you analyze your content, ideas for headings should arise naturally. If they don't, then a fresh outline of your content may be just what the doctor ordered.

The neutron-bomb test

A good, strong heading should paraphrase an important concept that you are about to present. If you were to blast all other text out of your document, leaving only the headings, you should be left with a good outline or a detailed table of contents. (Coincidence? We think not.)

If the situation permits, headings can be humorous and/or refer to a common theme to help catch users' eyes and interest. Try the neutron-bomb test here, too: It's okay if the outline you're left with is entertaining, but does it still do its job? (Well, okay, we admit to using this approach with the headings in this book; it's one ambitious goal of the whole ...*For Dummies* series.)

A time-honored principle applies here: *Dying is easy; comedy is hard.* Your visitors may have a wide range of funny bones; not all of them may be jogged by the same stuff. Whether zingers or not, your headings will fly if you *use your imagination but keep your audience in mind.*

As a quick and (ahem) modest example, Table 5-1 shows some of the headings from this book in "plain" and "humorous/theme" forms.

Table 5-1	Headings: Plain versus Extra-Crunchy
Plain	*A Bit More Interesting*
Building Documents	Building Better Document Bodies
Building Paragraphs	Building Strong Paragraphs Six Ways
Logos and Icons	Eye-Catchers: Logos, Icons, and Other Gems

Web pages give you some creative space, but not an unlimited amount. You have only a few headings per screen or page; make them count. Keep the structure (and the outline level) of similar headings consistent throughout your pages to help keep your users oriented. Although most browsers recognize at least four levels of headings, most well-constructed Web pages use no more than three levels, even for long documents. (Three is a classic "just-right" number — ever hear of a story called *Goldilocks and the Five Bears?* We haven't, either.)

The design-versus-information squabble

As you create your headings and assign them levels of importance, you run into two schools of thought about the best way to use them:

✔ **The information school** pontificates that *heading tags should be used in increments or decrements of one and always start with* <h1>. This approach gives your content an ordered, standardized structure and makes it easy for Web crawlers to pick out headings for their indexes. A practical, logical, dependable approach.

✔ **The design school** takes one look at the practical approach and screams, "BORING!" Design advocates want to *use headings to draw attention to content. Putting an* <h1> *next to an* <h3> *or an* <h4> *creates visual interest.* A wild-eyed, iconoclastic approach. And maybe a breath of fresh air.

As with most design decisions, the choice is yours. Experiment with heading tags till you arrive at a combination that looks good, tells it like it is, and accurately reflects the mood and purpose of your page.

Too much emphasized text diminishes the overall effect. Use it sparingly — emphasis works better when it remains exceptional. Using too many headings is like crying *Wolf! And look, there's another one! And another one! . . .*

Building Better Document Bodies

The *body* of an HTML document is the core of a Web page. It stands between the header and the footer. What you put in the body (its *content*) depends on the type and amount of information you want to put online — and on the audience you want to reach.

Personal Web pages are generally quite different from their business, academic, or government cousins. The most striking differences are in the content and form of their bodies, although the layout for each type may be strikingly similar. The bodies of most personal Web pages contain text for, or pointers to, the following elements:

- **Résumé:** mostly dense text with a picture
- **Personal history:** mostly plain text
- **Favorite sports or hobbies:** text with an occasional picture and links to sports or hobby sites
- **Favorite Web sites:** lists of links to Web sites

Pretty good, as far as it goes. But if you want to do business with that page, it needs some judicious editing and restructuring with the market in mind. Take, for example, the body of a commercial artist's Web pages:

- **Pictures, pictures, pictures:** usually small thumbnail-size pictures that link to much larger versions
- **Credentials:** a page containing a résumé or a list of shows and exhibits, awards, and other professional activities
- **Professional references:** links to online samples of work on other pages around the Net

Government pages are yet another species, often using text in a characteristic fashion (think of an anaconda that's swallowed an elephant). Many of these documents are simply HTML reproductions of long text originals. Some are 100 screens long or more. (Who knows? We may yet see a Virtual Paperwork Reduction Act . . . well, maybe next century.)

Fortunately, you won't need a 200-year life span to download what you need of these pages. Some government webmasters provide a brief description of their text files along with FTP hyperlinks so you can easily download these monsters without having to read through them on-screen

The more scrolling required, the slower the experience of reading your Web page becomes. Lots and lots of scrolling means *too much text, already!* and your users may fly away to less wordy climates.

So, how much text is enough, not too much, to put in the body of your page? The answer, my friend, is blowin' in the minds of your viewers. The better you know their needs and interests (not to say attention spans), the more closely you can gauge how much text to offer them.

How much text is okay?

If you've ever transcribed someone else's dictation, you know that even five minutes' worth of speaking equals quite a stack of paper. If you can feel the white space shrinking as you work on your Web page, beware: When most Web surfers want to read pages and pages of dense text, they buy the book or download the file and print it. They don't hang around online with the meter running.

Online reading, almost by definition, means keeping your online writing succinct. Many users (especially those who dial in with slower connections) view great globs of text as a waste of bandwidth. Not that your Web pages have to be as hit-and-run as those 30-second video bites that sell beer during the Super Bowl. But a little realism can't hurt: At the current level of Web development, most users are looking for fast ways to find the information they want. They aren't going to dig down through too many strata of text to find it. Your job is to give your readers the fast track to the gist, within the body of your pages. Help them cut to the chase by using an appropriate page layout; lean, informative text; and a considered use of tools such as indexes with hypermedia links.

Composition as balancing act

The Web-page equivalent of the body beautiful should contain three to five short, well-written paragraphs. Now imagine, if you will, these paragraphs interspersed with moderate-sized headings, enough white space for breathing room, and small graphics to add visual interest. *Readers will probably scan them in their entirety.* And love it.

Judicious use of separators and numerous links to other (relevant!) pages can also give your page design more bang for the buck. The idea is to have nothing in your page that doesn't belong there; the result should be a page that's between one and three full screens long. More may be technically possible, but that doesn't always mean *commonly* possible. Hardly anybody has a 33-inch, high-resolution monitor (or a flying car) yet, and both are likely to stay scarce for quite a while.

Pruning those long pages

Web page benchmark: For any given page, you should be able to count the screens of text on the fingers of one hand. A page that runs to more than five screens of text (or, for that matter, five screens of URL link lists) can bog down your reader's attention. Split it into multiple pages. If your content ferociously resists being served in short pages, you can still make a long page readable. Try linking a table of contents (TOC) to each section of the page and providing a link back to the beginning of the page from each section. (If your visitor can travel conveniently, the distance won't seem as long.)

This linking structure does add some structural complexity (it's similar to splitting a page into multiple files), but it also offers two considerable advantages:

✔ Your readers can capture the document as a single file.

✔ The HTML file becomes easier to edit.

You want to balance your convenience (as the page's creator) against the penalty (from the user's point of view) of moving a single large chunk of data — moving it takes a long time! Links can add to the usability of your page, but (as with all the parts of a Web page) don't overdo them.

Once again, dear friends, we've reached that risky borderland between content controls (links to other pages can count as both, especially if you're laying out a relatively long Web page). When you have lots of content, make it easily approachable by including effective controls, and only the essential ones. If you want your page to rock, *content is King* (thank ya vurry much).

The bottom line on page bodies

The rules for creating great Web page bodies are simple and wondrous to behold:

✔ Keep layouts consistent to provide continuity for users.

✔ Provide plenty of white space and headings for easy scanning.

✔ Write short paragraphs and use them sparingly.

✔ Use meaningful graphics, but only when absolutely necessary.

> ✔ Make liberal use of hypertext links to additional pages, instead of making your audience scroll, scroll, scroll.
>
> ✔ Vary the placement of hyperlink words to provide more visual contrast on the page.
>
> ✔ Write meaningful hyperlink text, not *Click here.* (When confronted with a *Click here,* have you ever thought *Oh, yeah? Why should I?* More about this later.)

Building Strong Paragraphs Eight Ways

Web users demand the clearest and most concise text you can muster. Alas, not everyone on the Web is an English professor. For many folks, grammar was a heavy and dolorous subject (and English class was like doing pull-ups in concrete sneakers). Many have never heard of *The Elements of Style,* a slim volume by William Strunk, Jr., and E. B. White that has eased the pain of writing for generations of students. Two timeless Strunk and White prescriptions are especially healthful for Web page text:

> ✔ **Omit needless words.** This doesn't mean getting rid of all the details. Just scrutinize your paragraphs and ask, *What can I throw out?*
>
> ✔ **Make the paragraph the unit of composition.** Writing one paragraph at a time means not getting stuck on a particular sentence or struggling to turn out a whole page at a time. Often a single paragraph is easier to subdue.

All Web surfers must read *some* language — whether Sanskrit, Mandarin, or High Computerese — and clarity promotes accurate communication, whatever the lingo. To this end, follow these eight steps to build better paragraphs:

1. **Create an outline for your information. Check out Chapter 2 for more information on outlines.**

2. **Write one paragraph for each significant point, keeping the sentences short, direct, and to the point.**

3. **Edit your text mercilessly, omitting all needless words and sentences.**

4. **Proofread and spell-check.**

5. **Check your page on a variety of different hardware and software setups.**

6. **Ask a few volunteers to evaluate your work.**

7. **Revise your text and edit it again as you revise it.**

8. **Solicit comments when you publish online.**

   To find out all you ever wanted to know about soliciting reader response, turn to Chapter 17.

Listward, Ho! Using a List Structure

Provided you don't lose them, lists can be useful (laundry, grocery, mailing) or entertaining (how about those droll "top ten lists" on late-night TV?). They're also a simple, effective way to call your viewer's attention to specific items on your Web page.

The most commonly used list structure, the *unordered list*, is actually a lot more ordered than a jumble of vaguely related facts. It implies that several ideas are related without having to assign them a rank or a rigid level of priority (as *numbered lists* normally do). You may know the unordered list by its other name, the *bulleted list*.

A bulleted list is handy for emphasizing several short lines of information. The following shows HTML markup for an unordered list (displayed with Navigator in Figure 5-3).

```
<ul>
<li> This is noticed.
<li> So is this.
<li> And so is this.
</ul>
```

Figure 5-3:
An
unordered
list viewed
with
Navigator.

The following HTML fragment shows the tags for an unordered list in a Web page body. The list serves to emphasize and separate the text lines.

```
You have reached the <i>HTML for Dummies</i> Web Pages,
a charming, and hopefully helpful, addition to the WWW
universe. These pages are designed to aid you in three
key areas:<br>
<ul>
```

(continued)

(continued)

```
<li> To help you find current information on the Web
     about HTML

<li> To provide working examples and code for all the
     Web tricks in the book

<li> To introduce <i>HTML for Dummies</i> - your
     friendliest resource for HTML material offline!
</ul>
```

Figure 5-4 shows how this displays in Internet Explorer. The bulleted list definitely emphasizes the body and adds to the visual appeal of the page.

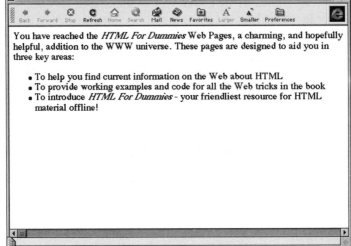

Figure 5-4:
HTML
document
with a
bulleted list
viewed
with IE.

Although the cardinal rule of page layout is still *Keep It Simple, Sweetheart,* some information is simply clearer as a list — even a *nested list* (which produces outline formatting, as we explain in Chapter 11). If you use such structures intelligently and sparingly, that's the impression they'll make.

If you're feeling the symptoms of list-o-mania, Chapter 11 presents the different types of HTML list tags you can use to relieve the urge.

Hooking Up Your Pages

Hypermedia links within the body of your pages bring out the power of the Web. To many users, surfing the Web is the ultimate video game. Following links just to see where they go can be interesting and informative.

As a Web page designer and Web weaver, you want users to like your pages well enough to tell others, who tell others, and so on. Therefore, you must provide good links within your own pages and to other Internet resources.

Links come in two flavors — *relative* and *absolute* (also called *full*). They do their work in two distinct places — respectively, inside your Web site and out on the wider Web.

Relative links (to pages within your Web site)

A typical *relative link* in its native habitat looks like this:

```
<a href="ftpstuff.htm">Click here to jump straight
   to the FTP page!</a>
```

You can use a link like this one to get around (or show your visitors around) inside your Web site.

How does it do that?

The URL refers to the directory that contains the Web page itself (which, in turn, calls the reference). In this case, the Web page calls a file (ftpstuff.htm) in the same directory as the current HTML file (whose address is the current URL). Same Web site, same folder; a relative link keeps you close to home (you know, the place where your relatives are).

In jargonese, we'd say it this way: "The reference is relative to the server's document root plus the path in the file system where the current URL is stored." Got that? (We'd never use such language to order a cappuccino.)

The tension of extensions

Normally, when you create links to HTML documents, you'd use the .html extension — all four letters. However, some servers only accept three character extensions, so you can't use .html even if you want to.

Regardless of the number of characters you use in your extensions, remember that file.htm and file.html are *not* the same file but are instead two different files. Always double-check the extension on a file that you're linking to and make sure the link to it matches the exact filename.

As a bit of a heads up, here are some typical cross-platform sticky wickets:

✔ If the page resides on a DOS machine that requires the ancient and venerable three-character extension, then the server's usual habit is to ignore the fourth letter (the 1). This is okay unless you're moving your pages back and forth from a DOS machine to another computer that supports four-character extensions. If this is the case, just standardize on .htm and save yourself the grief.

✔ If you upload .htm files from a DOS or Windows computer to a UNIX server, make sure some kindly technical wizard has taught your server to recognize files that end in .htm as valid HTML files).

✔ Simple Macintosh text editors (such as SimpleText) don't place default .htm or .html extensions after a filename. Take heed, Mac webmasters — always add an .html or .htm extension onto each and every Web page you create.

In the past, Web servers required the full four-letter html extension, not only for filenames but also for the links that called them. Today (ah, progress!), you can use either a four- or three-letter extension (html or htm) as long as your naming scheme is *consistent*. But before you dash off to change all your extensions, ask your webmasters or system administrators about how your server really works, and what extensions it can see and use.

A bit of advice regarding overuse of links: Use them only when they convey needed information; use each specific link only once per page. Users can get irritable if each occurrence of a particular word or phrase on a single page turns out to be a link — especially if all those links take them to exactly the same place.

Absolute links (to the world outside your Web site)

As useful as relative links can be within a page, the whole point of the Web is to establish connections with those realms beyond your own immediate machine. Hence the evolution of the *absolute* (or *full*) link that gives the entire HTTP URL address. A representative of the species looks like this:

```
<a href = "http://www.lanw.com/html4dum/html4dum.htm">
```

You can use absolute URLs for all your links without any noticeable difference in speed, even on a local server. But relative links are shorter to type (which may improve your overall productivity enough so that you can go get that cappuccino). Whether it's better to use relative or absolute links is a debate for the newsgroups or your local UNIX users' group. Might be worth bothering your webmaster about, though; who wants to put all that work into a link that doesn't?

When including absolute URLs for links, we strongly recommend that you go on a little hunting trip first: *Link to the resource and capture its URL with your browser.* Then copy and paste this URL into your HTML file. Where URLs are concerned, this technique can stop typographical errors before they happen.

The links in your HTML document are what makes your site Web-ready. As you create them, you are primarily concerned with (1) the content of the links within your Web site, (2) their relationships to one another, and (3) their contribution — not only to your own Web site, but also to the wider Web out there.

Chapter 15 gets fancy with Web links, roping such evolved critters as image maps into the fray.

Choose your hyperlinks with care

Your home page may have links similar to those shown in Figure 5-5 (from the *HTML For Dummies* home page). Notice which words in the sentence are included in the hyperlink text (highlighted and/or underlined). You must click on these words to open the link.

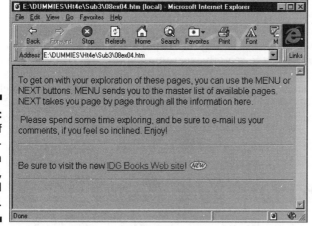

Figure 5-5:
Portion of
HTML docu-
ment with a
hyperlink,
viewed
with IE.

The following HTML document fragment shows the tags that make up the innards of the hyperlink in Figure 5-5.

```
<p>
To get on with your exploration of these pages, you can
use the MENU or NEXT buttons. MENU sends you to the
master list of available pages. NEXT takes you page by
page through all the information here.
</p>

<p>
Please spend some time exploring, and
be sure to e-mail us your comments, if you feel
so inclined. Enjoy!
</p>

<hr>

<p>
<br>Be sure to visit the new
    <a href="http://www.idgbooks.com/">
    IDG Books Web site!</A><br>
<img src="new.gif" height=17 width=32 align=top>

<hr>
```

Choose your link text and images carefully. Keep the text short and the graphics small. And never, ever use the phrase *click here* by itself for link text. ("Why?" you ask. Because your readers may imagine you too lazy, uncaring, or boorish to write more helpful text for the link. Mustn't have that.)

Well-chosen hyperlinks let your users quickly scan hyperlink text and choose links without having to read the surrounding text. (Surrounding text is usually included only to provide readers with clarification of the link anyway.) Remember, users are in a hurry to scan your pages and quickly pick out the important links; unique wording or graphics can aid this process. Make this job easy by using meaningful hyperlinks, and the overall impression left in the reader's mind is *Nice cyberhospitality. I could come here again.*

Footers Complete Your Pages

Unlike an HTML header and body, a footer is not defined by a specific set of markup tags. By convention, a footer is simply the bottom portion of the page body. Of course, that doesn't mean we can't be authoritative about it. The *Yale C/AIM Web Style Guide* provides a concise statement about the use of footers on your Web pages (info.med.yale.edu/caim/manual/index.html):

Page footers should always carry basic information about the origin and age of the page. Every Web page needs to bear this basic information, but this repetitive and prosaic information often does not deserve the prominence of being placed at the top of the page.

(**Hint:** Readers may be "reading aloud" in their minds, in which case seeing *My Fantastic Web Site, June 1999, Version 17.2* at the top of every page is at best redundant and at worst an interest-killer.)

Footers may seem pedestrian, but they provide the pedigree of your pages by attributing authorship, contact information, legal status, version/revision information, and a link to your home page. Each footer should contain some or all of the elements listed here:

- ✔ Institution or company
- ✔ Phone number
- ✔ E-mail address
- ✔ Postal mailing address
- ✔ Copyright notice
- ✔ Date of page's last revision
- ✔ Links to the page's URL
- ✔ Legal disclaimer or language designating the page as the official communication of the company or institution
- ✔ Official company or institutional seal, logo, or other graphic mark
- ✔ Hypertext link(s) to home page or to other pages
- ✔ Hypertext link(s) to other sections of this page

Your basic home page HTML document already contains the minimum suggested footer information for a home page:

```
<address>
    Copyright  &copy; 1999,  Your Name <br>
    Revised — Revision Date <br>
    URL: <a href = "http://this.page's.url.here">

</address>
```

Even though this document is a home page, it contains a link to itself in the URL line. All other local pages in your Web must also contain a link in the footer to a full home-page URL, as in the sterling example just shown. Why? We're glad you asked: If a user saves your page as an HTML file and later wants to know its location, there it is on the bottom of the page, both visible and as a link. Don't you wish everyone did this?

The name of your home page file depends on your Web server software. Some servers require a specific name and extension, such as `index.html`. Check with your ISP to determine the requirements of the server that houses your Web site. Most likely, one of these formats works:

```
<a href="http://www.servername.net/yourdirectory">
  <!- least desirable ->
<a href="http://www.servername.net/yourdirectory/">
  <!- better ->
<a href="http://www.servername.net/yourdirectory /index.html">
  <!- most desirable ->
```

Government agencies and other public institutions are notorious for big footers because the who and what of their creation has some public importance. So they often include what seems like their entire staff directory and departmental history in their footers. (At least they're at the bottom of the page.) If you must use a long footer, put a home page link above it so that users don't have to scroll as far to find it!

Figure 5-6 illustrates a well-balanced footer for a business-style home page, from the LANWrights home page (ours, as it happens). This footer contains all important footer information (notice the separate contact icon in the upper right of the figure). This footer *doesn't* contain a phone number or snail-mail address, for some practical reasons:

- On the Net, e-mail rules! Sometimes phone and snail-mail aren't necessary or relevant.

- For whatever reason (say, your mailroom isn't set up to handle mass quantities of envelopes) you may not want hordes of casual visitors to your page calling you or writing letters to you.

- In our case, the contact page already includes all this information.

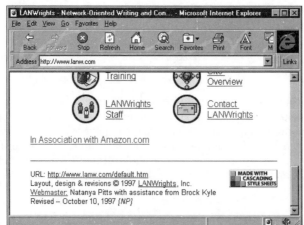

Figure 5-6:
Footer of the LANWrights home page, viewed with IE.

Instead of placing all footer information directly in each page, you may want to put some of it in a page of its own and put a link to that information in the footer instead. The bigger the footer, the handier the link — especially if your information requires a legal disclaimer or other complex language. (Check with your legal representative concerning the fine points of using disclaimers on the Web.)

Copyright

Copyright law hasn't quite caught up with the explosion in electronic publishing on the Web. While you're waiting, it won't hurt you or your organization to put a copyright notice at the bottom of any Web page that you don't want freely copied without being attributed to you or without your permission.

The copyright notice shown in Figure 5-6 is standard text except for the copyright symbol. Most browsers can display the copyright symbol © if you use the character entity ©. Otherwise, simulate it with (C) or (c).

For the complete rundown on entities, check out Chapter 12.

Counting coup — versions, dates, times

One of the greatest values of publishing on the Web is the ability to change your pages quickly — but why should you even bother to note when you change them? Well, it *is* a courtesy to your users, especially if any of them are the *Been there, done that* type. Not only do your users need to know what's up, you need to keep track of which version you're publishing so that you can be certain to update the old stuff when newer versions are ready.

This (or next?) year's model

If it's appropriate, you may want to use *version numbers* in addition to a revision date. This enables you to refer to a particular page as version 12B, for example, rather than the second revision from December. It's less ambiguous, more direct, and shorter, too!

Placing a revision date in the footer of each page keeps track of its chronology. The format should be January 02, 1999, to avoid confusion. In the United States, this date would be abbreviated 01/02/99. In Europe, this would be read as the 1st of February, 1999. The international ISO 8601 standard date notation is YYYY-MM-DD (year, month, day), which would result in 1999-01-02. Use that format for dates if you want to be globally correct.

If, for some reason, you don't want to show a revision date on the page, you'll be happier in the long run if you use HTML comment tags and hide the revision date inside them.

What (or which) time is it?

You may add the time to the date for time-sensitive information. Because users from all over the world can view your information at any time, 24-hour, *UTC* (*Universal Time,* which used to be called GMT — Greenwich Mean Time) is the appropriate format, expressed as hh:mm:ss (which is *hour:minute:second,* using two characters for each).

Make sure you note the time as UTC — that is, 18:30:00 UTC or 18:30:00Z for 6:30 p.m. (The *Z* stands for *Zulu* in the NATO radio alphabet and refers to the Zulu or Zero meridian of longitude used for measurement. Now, *there's* an obscure tidbit for *Jeopardy!*)

Hungry for Feedback?

Every well-constructed home page has some way for users to give feedback to a page's developer or owner. To make it happen, you can choose between an *e-mail link* and a *form.* (Your choice may depend on which of these options your Web service provider makes available.) Of the two, e-mail is simplest, and most generally used on personal home pages. Businesses tend to use forms, fill-in-the-blank screens that prompt the user for specific information.

Most custom business forms seek to turn users into paying customers. For more about these specialized tools, see Chapter 17.

One common e-mail approach is to include a special hyperlink (called a mailto: *link*) in the Web page itself so that users can send e-mail to the page owner. The link works by starting the browser's e-mail program or another one on the user's computer; keep in mind that not all Web browser software supports this capability.

If a mailto: link is an available option for you, go for it. The standard approach is to provide an e-mail address as text inside the <address>... </address> tags. Consider the following modest example:

```
E-mail: <a href="mailto:html4dum@/anw.com">
    HTML For Dummies at html4dum@/anw.com</a>
```

Steady — that's HTML code, all right, but it's translatable. The actual hyperlink is mailto:html4dum@/anw.com. For readers who aren't equipped to use a mailto: URL, a second instance of the e-mail address occurs in HTML For Dummies at html4dum@/anw.com to highlight the e-mail address on the page. That way a user can easily print it out or jot it down (on parchment, clay tablets, whatever).

Outside the actual address portion of the link (`<a href = "mailto :html4dum@/anw.com">...</A>`), you can customize the wording to your heart's content. You can also put text in front of it — say, `Send kudos or wisecracks to:` (or the more demure `E-mail:` shown in the example, taken from our very own *HTML For Dummies* Web pages).

Comments for Posterity (And Sanity)

Do yourself a big favor and *comment* on your HTML documents, overtly and often, by including text in the file that does nothing more than sit there and explain (to the programmer, editor, or tech-support stalwart) what a particular hunk of the page is supposed to do or why it's there. Comments can also explain the relevance of links or identify information that needs updating. Fast-forward to the future: That joyous noise in the background is you, thanking yourself many times over for this valuable resource.

Most newer browsers ignore comments inside HTML documents, a trend that is likely to continue. HTML comment lines are formatted like this:

```
<! —comment text— >
```

A comment line starts with `<!—` and ends with `—>`. As a general rule, place comments on a line apart from other HTML text. This way you won't interrupt HTML text (because browsers *also* ignore any extra spaces [over one] between HTML tags).

Chapter 6

Warning, Graphic Language

- -

In This Chapter

▶ Adding logos, icons, and other little gems

▶ Building high-impact graphic pages

▶ Transforming graphics into hyperlinks

- -

The Web is both a cooperative and a competitive environment; it depends on interdependence, but it's impatient with boredom. Web sites come and go all the time; many sink without a ripple. Yours can remain afloat and well visited for as long as it makes a lasting and positive impression on visitors. This chapter offers some handy hints for keeping your page fresh and vital through the careful and informed use of graphics.

Eye-Catchers: Logos, Icons, and Other Gems

Graphics add color and impact to Web pages for users with GUI browsers, but for most of us, they aren't the main point. Unless your Web page focuses primarily on computer graphics as its content, the watchwords are *small, relevant, and tasteful*, and use them only where they add value. Why small? Well, half that answer is technical (the larger a graphic, the slower it loads) and half is human nature (the only speed acceptable to computer users is instantaneous). That's why small is beautiful!

Speaking of small, fast-loading graphics (and subtle segues), here's where we add some sparkle to the plain-vanilla home page we built in Chapter 5 (you might want to flip back there for a refresher).

So far, the Chapter 5 page has nice-looking headings and simple black bullets next to the list lines (steal a quick look back at Figure 5-4). Because the basic layout is well-established, all you need is a few splashes of color in appropriate locations to really spice things up.

Hitting the (red) spot with an ⟨img⟩ *tag*

Let's pick on that harmless-looking bullet point and turn it red. Adding an image to your HTML document is as simple as inserting a line using the ⟨IMG⟩ tag:

```
<IMG SRC="graphics/dotred.gif">
```

This line contains a *reference* (URL) for a .GIF file named dotred.gif. In this case, it's a relative reference that points to a file that the Web server expects to find in a subdirectory named graphics — skulking directly beneath the directory where the current page (the page from which the link is called) resides.

Using this particular relative URL to create the red dot causes the server to look for a file with the following absolute path:

```
http://www.lanw.com/html4dum/graphics/dotred.gif
```

If your situation (and preferences) mandate the use of absolute URLs, you may use the following image tag with the full URL to link to the red dot:

```
<IMG SRC="http://www.lanw.com/html4dum/
          graphics/dotred.gif">
```

Snagging an image from far away

If you wanted to link to an image file of a red dot (dotred.gif) located on another Web site, you'd have to use an absolute URL (sometimes called a *full URL*) in the ⟨img⟩ tag, like this:

```
<img src="http://www.someothersite.net/icons/dotred.gif">
```

If you use a full URL to a faraway site in a link on your page, then every time a user loads the image, the browser that hosts the Web page actually links to the other remote Web server to retrieve the graphic. This increases the time needed for the browser to load the file (not a kindly gesture). If the remote location is not online, the browser can't load the image at all (an even unkindlier gesture). Therefore, it usually works better if you keep your graphics in the same place on your own server and thus avoid getting the unkindliest gesture of all — mass exodus of your visitors.

Some ISPs charge their users for the amount of data — HTML, images, and any other data sent via the Internet — that visitors to their site download on a weekly or monthly basis. If you link to a graphic stored on someone else's Web page then you'll add to the amount of information that their site sends out each time *your* Web page is loaded. This is unfair — to say the very least — and just plain ol' bad form. If you're going to use graphics from someone else's Web site, do the right thing and save a copy to your own Web server and reference it locally.

Absolute URLs do require judicious, careful, and limited use, though that doesn't mean you have to avoid them on pain of cyberwarts. If your site can benefit from links to remote images that change over time (such as a weather map, clock, or Webcam picture), or from a large, complex image in a file too big to park on your server, you might want to try such a link. In the first case, the other site maintains the changing image and your users see it directly from their sites, included in your page. In the second case, you save on server disk space by pointing to a remote location for a multimegabyte picture. (Of course, you may want to warn your users about what they're getting into before you encourage them to click.)

Bottom line: An absolute URL might be good if you're linking to a storm update, but it's too much hassle if all you want is a red dot. So the first principle of linking to graphics is *Whenever possible, keep 'em small, simple, and handy.*

Chasing small, defenseless graphics around

For a detailed practical example, we invite you to observe how several small graphic elements are used to navigate the LANWrights Web site. The portion of its HTML document shown in Figure 6-1 uses nine different small graphic elements — *navigation icons* that take the visitor to other locations throughout the site. Each of these graphics is less than 1K in size, so they download and display quickly.

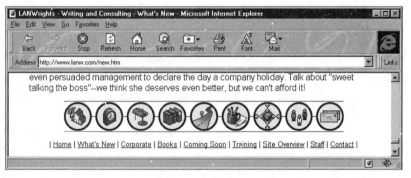

Figure 6-1:
A view of the LANWrights navigation icons.

Reusing the same graphics on a single Web page doesn't add significant time or disk storage requirements when a user's browser *caches* them (or stores previously viewed images in memory). Therefore, using the same graphical elements repeatedly helps keep load and display times for these images to a minimum. Recycling images makes as much sense for Web pages as it does for the environment!

Horizontal rules — but colors reign

Separating sections with a colored line graphic can add an additional touch of color to a page. You could accomplish this separation using a simple HTML *horizontal rule tag* that goes by the name of <HR>. However, because <HR>'s only display is as a 3-D line (gray, black, and white to give the 3-D effect), you don't get the same visual impact that a brightly colored line provides.

Using a colored line to bracket an announcement just above footer information sets it apart from surrounding text and makes a grab for the user's attention. When used this way, colored ruler lines are perfect for segmenting pages into eye-pleasing information blocks. You can make these lines with most "paint" programs in any length, thickness, and color combination imaginable (except, maybe, neon paisley, but give it a few years). If you don't mind chasing rainbows, you can actually *find* some on public-access graphic Web sites where they are available for your use, generally with no strings attached. (In fact, feel free to use ours any way you like! You'll find a rainbow image on the CD-ROM in the /html4Fd2/graphics directory, named rainbow.gif).

To see a colored line (or two or three) at work in the real Web world, check out another page on the LANWrights site, shown in Figure 6-2. This page uses a burgundy hard rule in a couple of different places to divide the page contents up — separating header and footer information from the rest of the document's guts.

Rather than list any of the thousands of sites with .GIFs and .JPEGs available for download here, we suggest that you search for GIF archives or JPEG archives on one of the many Web search engines such as www.altavista.com, www.excite.com, or www.yahoo.com.

It may be quicker and easier to click the HTML editor button that inserts the good old <HR> into your document than to type a link to the colored line image, especially if you have more than a few of them occurring over many pages. In this case, consider what works best — consistency or punch?

Some Web-searching spiders or agents use the <HR> tag to distinguish breaks in text for their indexes. They might not recognize the colored line image as a replacement for the <HR> tag. But as always, the spirit of experimentation is alive and well on the Web.

Bored with dots? Have a ball . . .

The standard structure of an HTML unordered list places black list dots (bullets) to the left its elements by default. Efficient, but tame. If you want to jazz up the look of your list, you can use small graphical elements for heightened visual appeal.

Figure 6-2:
Colored
hard rules
are both
functional
and fun.

It just so happens that we have some graphics on hand that use highlights and shadows to convey the impression of a three-dimensional ball. (What a lucky break . . . .) The redball.gif image in the /html4Fd2/graphics directory on the CD-ROM makes a catchy bullet point.

If you alternate shiny balls of different colors — say, red, white, and blue for a political Web page — you increase their eye-catching effects. Each line stands out from the line above it and the line below it. (If you want to try out this effect, look for files named whiball.gif and bluball.gif in the same directory on the CD-ROM where you'll find the red one.)

We generally reserve special effects such as these for home pages and other documents where looks are most important. As always, before you toss in some snazzy spheroids, rainbows, or pterodactyls (how'd they get in there?), study up on how such substitutions might affect your page's all-important relationship with the Web. Speaking of which . . . .

One word of caution about making changes such as replacing list bullets with colored dots: If you use your own images to create snappy lists, the list structure of your document won't fit the standard HTML model. The next section explains why that might matter to your Web page.

. . . But please don't confuse the spiders

If you blithely replace <hr> with rainbow lines or list bullets with festive balls throughout your document, you could run into a functional problem: An active spider or agent looking at your page might get confused and not know what to grab. It can deduce that an object following an <li> tag is part of the list it just entered (and can organize its gleanings accordingly), but it's still a pretty simple creature. A spider or agent cannot recognize an "imitation list" that uses colored dots as a list at all. If you're presenting a list of items that you want to show up as a list wherever it appears on the Web, use HTML list tags.

The HTML standard sets specs for unordered or bulleted lists for the sake of consistency — list items in nonsequential order are *supposed* to be set off by a preceding symbol. Style attributes in the HTML 4.0 specification let you set the way you want your numbers or bullets to appear in your lists, as long as they're "normal" bullets. Every browser that adheres to the HTML 4.0 standard should display these bullets in much the same way; they might be a little stodgier, but they'll be consistent. This can't be said about individual images of colored dots — so if you can't decide between the safe-but-plain way and a blatant disregard for HTML conformity, try it both ways and see which you like best. Just don't say we didn't *warn* you.

A solid example of this principle at work is the page on the LANWrights Web site that describes this book's predecessor, *HTML 4 For Dummies*, shown in Figure 6-3.

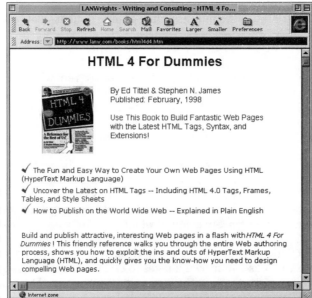

Figure 6-3:
A view
of the
LANWrights
navigation
icons.

Notice that the "list" of the book's features are all marked with graphical checkmarks. These little descriptors, although listed one after the other, won't suffer greatly if a spider or robot doesn't recognize them as a coherent list. The small graphical checkmarks add a splash of color to the page and mark each feature as a unique item. Once again graphics are both fun and functional. See, we really do try to practice what we preach when we build our own sites.

If you simply want to lighten up and add a little life to your home page with some visual hoopla — and don't mind confusing a few spiders — go for it. This act of rebellion — peppering a line of text with colored dots or other small graphics — is as simple as inserting tagged URLs in the text at the points where you want each graphic to appear. Consider, for example, the following HTML code snippet:

```
<img src="graphics/dotred.gif">
   To help you find current information on the Web
   about HTML<br>
```

It creates our familiar red dot with `<img src="graphics/dotred.gif">` and displays it right before `To help you...` on-screen. Notice the space between the `>` and the `To`. Although browsers generally ignore spaces, some of them (such as Netscape Navigator and Internet Explorer) may recognize a single space before or after text. Such a kindness can help you format sentences properly and keep images from crowding text.

But can you depend on the kindness of strangers? Many browsers ignore multiple spaces when they render text. Even so, when you're working in and around HTML tags, careful placement of spaces *while you're writing the code* can prevent painstaking reformatting work later on.

Navigation with icons — it's a .GIF

A few well-designed and carefully located icons can help your users quickly find their way around your Web pages. We use the term *icon* here to describe any small graphic image that you can substitute for a unit of text.

Icons stored as `.gif` files are usually small and load quickly. In most instances, adding an icon is painless: Simply put a standard image-tag with a source URL in the position where you want it to appear.

Most icons are so small that you don't need to align text next to them (we get to aligning larger images later in this chapter). The default for most browsers is to align the text with the bottom of an image.

The navigation bar we built to teach a Web-site management class is a convenient example. No, a *navigation bar* isn't a lounge with a nautical motif; it's a set of icons arranged along one side of a page in an HTML document, used for getting around the site. In the case of our class, we designed the icons to help our students jump easily to particular modules of the course, or to a set of navigation instructions. We added these icons to the HTML document by means of the following code:

```html
<html>
 <body bgcolor="#ffffff">
  <p>
   <a href="navigate.htm">
    <img vspace=1 align="center" border="0"
         src="graphics/nav.gif" alt="Navigation">
   </a>
  </p>

  <p>
   <a href="isp.htm">
    <img vspace=1 align="center" border="0"
         src="graphics/isp.gif" alt="isp">
   </a>
  </p>

  <p>
   <a href="track.htm">
    <img vspace=1 align="center" border="0"
         src="graphics/track.gif" ALT="Tracking">
   </a>
  </p>

  <p>
   <a href="search.htm">
    <img vspace=1 align="center" border="0"
         src="graphics/search.gif" alt="Searching">
   </a>
  </p>

 </body>
</html>
```

This particular set of magic words makes each icon a hyperlink. Click one of these icons and you go directly to the appropriate HTML document — a compact, simple navigation technique that's easy for users with graphical browsers to use. A full-blown implementation of this idea would include an equivalent set of text-based hyperlinks to accommodate a wider range of users, including

  ✔ Visually impaired users who normally magnify the text

  ✔ Users who keep graphics turned off to speed download time

The navigation bar appears on the right-hand side of Figure 6-4 (available at www.lanw.com/training/myw/myw.htm).

Figure 6-4:
The icons
on the right-
hand side of
the page
provide a
constant
source of
navigation
in this
example
site.

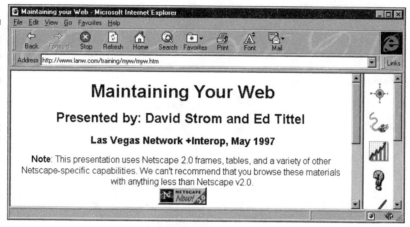

Figure 6-4:
The icons on the right-hand side of the page provide a constant source of navigation in this example site.

Hyperlinked logos and graphics

Logos are an art unto themselves. An image that imparts a positive sense of your organization to an audience in a *get-it-got-it-go* manner is a joy (and often a profit) to behold. It shouldn't overpower the Web page or overstimulate the user to the point of irritation. Go easy on the size and special effects — especially if you're expecting your logo to do double duty as a hyperlink.

Logos are special-use graphics. However cool it may look, a logo's first goal in life is to identify your business or institution in a memorable, pleasing, eye-catching way. Logos can vary from icon size to much larger — sometimes too large. Complex logos that take too long to load are nugatory on any Web page. Keep It Simple, Simon.

A moderate-size logo at the top of a home page is generally acceptable: big enough to look good, small enough to load fast. Using icon-sized logos in the footer of each Web page is equally acceptable. Remember that text-only browsers and GUI browsers with image loading turned off (for faster page loading) won't display your fantastic logos, anyway. (Yet another argument for good taste.)

Figures 6-5 and 6-6 illustrate the visual effects of using a moderate-size logo .GIF at the top of a page. The LANWrights logo file is only 4,930 bytes, so it loads in a few seconds. This second image, despite the increase in size, is still only 7,342 bytes.

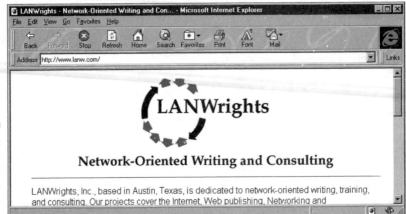

Figure 6-5:
The
LANWrights
logo on the
home page.

Figure 6-5's home page shows the logo used by itself; subsidiary pages combine the logo with an associated navigation icon. Voilá — a visual link between the topic and its related image, as shown in Figure 6-6.

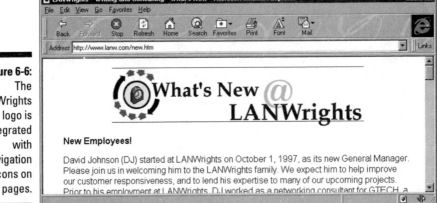

Figure 6-6:
The
LANWrights
logo is
integrated
with
navigation
icons on
other pages.

Now we get a little fancy, gathering navigation icons into a table under the LANWrights logo at the top of the home page (shown in Figure 6-7), illustrating the use of tabular graphics as hyperlinks.

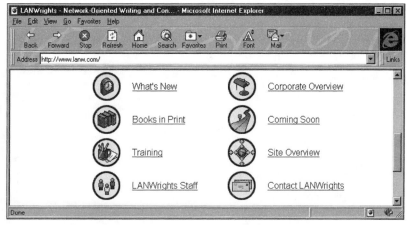

Figure 6-7:
LANWrights
uses navi-
gation
graphics as
hyperlinks.

Built according to code

Okay, let's open up this home page for a look at the code that makes it tick. The following lines from the HTML document produced the views you've just been gazing at so intently. (Well, we can hope.) The code is a compact illustration of how to nest an icon image within link-reference tags (between `<a href>` and `</a>`). It endows an icon with the powers of a hyperlink:

```
<center>
 <table width="90%" border="0" cellspacing="4"
        cellpadding="2">

  <tr>

   <td width="10%"><br></td>

   <td WIDTH="15%" HEIGHT="23">
   <center>
    <a href="new.htm">
     <img src="graphics/new.gif align="bottom"
         width="51" height="51" border="0"
         alt="What's New!">
    </a>
    </center>
   </td>

   <td width="30%">
    <a href="new.htm">What's New</a>
   </td>

   <td width="15%">
    <center>
     <a href="corporat.htm">
      <IMG SRC="graphics/corporat.gif" WIDTH="51"
```

(continued)

(continued)

```
          height="51" align="bottom" border="0"
          alt="Corporate Services">
    </a>
   </center>
  </td>

  <td width="30%">
   <a href="corporat.htm">Corporate Overview</a>
  </td>
</tr>

<tr>

  <td><br></td>

  <td height="23">
   <center>
    <a href="books.htm">
     <img src="graphics/books.gif" width="51" height="51"
          align="bottom" alt="Books in Print"
          border="0">
    </a>
   </center>
  </td>

  <TD>
   <A HREF="books.htm">Books in Print</A>
  </TD>

  <td>
   <center>
    <a href="topress.htm">
     <img src="graphics/comisoon.gif" width="51"
          height="51" align="bottom" alt="Coming Soon"
          border="0">
    </a>
   </center>
  </td>

  <td>
   <a href="topress.htm">Coming Soon</a>
  </td>
</tr>

<tr>
  <td><br></td>

  <td>
   <center>
    <a href="training.htm">
     <img src="graphics/training.gif" width="51"
          height="51" align="bottom" border="0"
```

```
          alt="Training">
     </a>
    </center>
   </td>
   <td>
    <a href="training.htm">Training</a>
   </td>

   <td>
    <center>
     <a href="overview.htm">
      <img src="graphics/wayfind.gif" width="51"
           height="51" align="bottom" alt="Wayfinder"
           border="0">
     </a>
    </center>
   </td>

   <td>
    <a href="overview.htm">Site Overview</a>
   </td>
</tr>

  <tr>
  <td><br></td>

  <td height="23">
   <center>
    <a href="lanwstaf.htm">
     <img src="graphics/staff.gif" width="51" height="51"
          align="bottom" alt="Staff"
          border="0">
    </a>
   </center>
  </td>

  <TD>
   <A HREF="lanwstaf.htm">LANWrights Staff</A>
  </TD>

  <td><
   <center>
    <a href="lanwcmmt.htm">
     <img src="graphics/contact.gif" width="51"
          height="51" align="bottom" alt="Contact"
          border="0">
    </a>
   </center>
  </td>

  <td>
   <a href="lanwcmmt.htm">Contact LanWrights</a>
```

(continued)

(continued)

```
   </td<
   /tr>

</table>
</center>
```

Fair-sized chunk of code, that, but we are talking about some major capabilities here. All the more reason not to leave your graphics-free visitors out in the cold. Funny you should mention that.

Text hyperlinks for the graphics-free user

Notice the use of the alternate text attribute, ALT="text" that appears within each image tag in the code example. If some of your users don't indulge in graphics, it's one way to cover your bases. This attribute tells text-only browsers to ignore the icon and display the associated "text" as a hyperlink instead. No problem.

Some graphic browsers are also equipped to use this handy substitution. If they're running with the image display function turned off, they simply display place-holders where the icons would be and use the alternate text as the hyperlink. Either way, you've politely provided any graphically challenged visitor to your site (whether speed-demon or DOS curmudgeon) with a way to use the navigation you've so painstakingly defined. For better looks (and, what the heck, greater clarity) we added explicit text definitions in the table cells next to each icon.

According to the official HTML 4.0 specification an HTML page isn't a valid — 100% correct — document if you don't have ALT= attributes for each and every graphic. Yet another argument for taking time out to make your pages accessible to all.

As we put together the LANWrights Web site, we found that a little creative use of icon images as hyperlinks to other pages in the site added not only visual interest but also convenience for our users. It's a twofer; if your Web pages are visually striking and easy to navigate, you get a double reward and then some: Your site stands out and is easy to remember as a nice place to visit.

Chapter 7

High-Impact Pages

In This Chapter

▶ The good

▶ The bad

▶ The ugly

*Y*ou know high style when you see an example of classic elegance — *rich results from simple means* — whether it's the understated curve of a sleek fender, a striking-but-simple color scheme, or a musical arrangement with just the right instruments.

Such creations pack a high sensory impact with no two-by-fours anywhere in sight. We encourage you to embark on a quest for Web pages that embody classic elegance — not to slavishly imitate or filch, but to learn.

Graphic Page Layout

At the LANWrights Web site (at `www.lanw.com`), we set out to practice what we preach. We can say, with some pride and a straight face, that the graphic layout of the Web pages you see in this chapter did not occur by accident. (Well, okay, maybe a million monkeys poking randomly at computers might have come up with it — but we had a deadline.) En route to the final layout, we made two discoveries: (1) The approach we used worked pretty well, and (2) no matter how practiced you get at it, layout is still a learn-by-doing process.

Here, not necessarily in chronological order, is what we learned:

✔ If yours is a business site, keep its mission in mind. (Ours focuses on informing visitors about LANWrights services, books, and capabilities.)

✔ Layout for a business page should shoot for an impression that's conservative enough to be reassuring but lively enough to be interesting. If you use a logo on your home page, make it easy to see right away.

✔ Add graphics sparingly to brighten the look and enhance visual contrast. Experiment till you find the best locations for them on your page.

✔ Choose graphics that are relevant, handy to link to, quick to load, and relatively simple. Use horizontal rules and highlighted hyperlinks (for example) to focus attention.

✔ Size your graphics to fit the layout and purpose of each page. (Only your home page should look like a home page; don't clone it.) Keep navigation icons small; give them a consistent look and location.

✔ Put additional thought into the design and layout of pages that use larger graphics — the bigger the image, the more thought that's required. Accommodate users of both GUI and text-only browsers so that each always has something interesting to look at, regardless of whether graphics are available or not.

If you follow the sage advice in this book (gathered at great pains and with your best interests at heart), you can do the same as we have — and much more — on your Web pages.

Grappling with graphics files

A picture may be worth a thousand words, but which picture? And which thousand words? On a Web page, pictures — the output of graphics files — work more like specialized building blocks. They are both a visual stimulus for your user and a structural element for your page (not to mention a possible navigational aid if you turn them into hyperlinks). To wrestle a graphics file into submission, you have to attack on two distinct levels: size and format. The prize is a visually sophisticated page layout that still supports optimum functionality (or, as the want ads might say of a car, "looks great, runs great").

Do I have to . . . do art?

To produce high-quality images for your Web pages, you don't really have to be an artist (besides, not everybody looks good in a beret). You needn't even become a world-beater at using graphics-manipulation programs such as Paint Shop Pro, GraphicConverter, Photo Styler, Graphics Workshop, Wingif, or LView Pro — or, for that matter, the newer programs that pop up almost weekly on the Web. If you plan to work with images regularly, however, we recommend getting fairly adept at one or more of these programs, or a commercial equivalent. We've learned two essential truths about these programs: (1) They can be a lot of engrossing fun, and (2) don't forget to eat.

Search for `graphics editor` on your favorite search engine and you can find links to many useful sites for freeware and shareware graphics tools.

Inspiration versus appropriation

Everyone needs influences and role models to help inspire original content. Exploring the Web for ideas is surfing with a purpose. When you see a Web page with a layout that you especially like, view the HTML source file to examine its formatting techniques. You can use your browser's Save As feature to save any HTML source to your own hard disk or you can print it, for later study.

At the same time, you can add especially arresting pages to your bookmark file so that you can find them again. Most browsers also let you save the images associated with a page to files on your hard disk. However, before you include somebody else's work on your pages, be aware of copyright restrictions — always get the author's permission *in writing* before you use the work of others. (If you're in doubt whether it's okay to reuse something, *don't do it!*)

Imitation may be the sincerest form of flattery, but stealing other authors' content — text and images — to use on your Web pages is illegal in most countries (and trying to pass off stolen creativity as original can be as hazardous as it is repugnant). However, discovering new techniques by appreciating and studying the work of others is the way most Web-weavers expand their horizons. Use these techniques to build your own pages, with your own content, in your own unique way.

You don't have to create in a vacuum; you can always e-mail other Web authors and request permission to use something of theirs in your page. Many independent Web authors are happy to help because others helped them find new Web tools and techniques. But it's common courtesy not to assume that someone else's creation is common property.

As e-commerce continues to forge ahead, most corporate Web sites are completely copyrighted, and they take a dim view of anyone who uses things from their site without permission, which they probably won't grant (nothing personal; it's strictly business).

The more commercialized and crowded the Web becomes, the more you need to know and respect the legal boundaries around Web property — others' and your own. Good manners, as well as good design, can be a civilizing influence.

On-screen and in the file — downsize and smile

A graphic image actually has *two* sizes — one visible to the user, one not. First, consider the *on-screen size* of the images themselves, and their impact on the complexity of your document's layout. Second, consider *the size of the graphics files (in bytes)* and how long it takes users to download them.

Modestly, we think you should have another look at our own business site, conveniently represented in Figure 7-1. The original logo file it illustrates — built in Adobe Illustrator — was a pretty big honker (over 1MB) that filled the entire screen. Problem: Even at today's chip and modem speeds, a megabyte of data can take several *minutes* (in Web terms, an Ice Age) to load over a slow link.

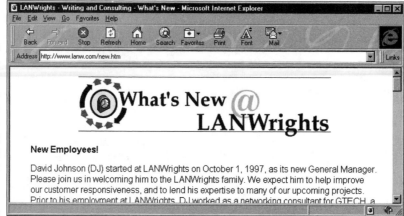

Careful cropping, resizing, and *resampling* (using fewer pixels per inch) brought the file size down to under 5,000 bytes. These changes gave us (to understate somewhat) a *dramatic* improvement in load time: A 5,000-byte file moves in seconds, even over a fairly slow modem. Problem solved.

If you like GUI, you'll love .GIF and .JPEG

Not all graphics files are created equal — and even some *formats* for graphics files are clearly "more equal than others" for use on the Web. Although the Web doesn't put much practical restriction on the types of graphic files you can use, two file formats are especially popular. You can recognize them by their distinctive filename extensions: .GIF and .JPEG.

Virtually all GUI browsers have built-in display capabilities that accommodate .GIF and .JPEG formats; most use external helper applications to display other file types. There's also an advantage when it comes to file transfer: Compressed .GIF and .JPEG files are the smallest (therefore fastest to load) of all commonly used graphics file types.

Most good shareware image-manipulation programs — such as those mentioned earlier — can load and save files produced in the .GIF and .JPEG formats.

The graphics programs we've mentioned also support a couple of more arcane formats: GIF87a and GIF89a (whether transparent or interlaced). If you're working on a Macintosh and are faced with interlaced .GIFs, use GifConverter to handle them. (If you're curious about *interlacing* and/or suspect it has nothing to do with hiking boots, take a peek up ahead at the handy sidebar we've devoted to it.)

Whenever you build any image in GIF89a format, however, be sure to test any interlaced images on multiple browsers. Some graphics lend themselves better to interlacing (and to transparency) than others. Here we're back to learning-by-doing; the process is much closer to old-fashioned trial-and-error than it is to an exact science. Testing your images across multiple browsers — on multiple platforms — is a must!

Actually, some graphics are pretty transparent

The GIF89 format also introduced the *transparent background* feature. This feature "turns off" one of the colors in an image displayed by a browser — and allowing whatever is behind the image to show through at every point where the color is transparent. Usually, what's back there is a background color, but you can lay images over other images or text as well. To users, your image appears to float on the browser's background instead of atop a square of some other color around the image.

Programs such as *giftrans* for UNIX and DOS, and Transparency for the Macintosh, create images with transparent backgrounds for browsers that support the GIF89 format. For Windows users, LView for Windows is also worth checking out. Transparent images really add to the visual richness and drama of a Web page.

A new pic's resolution . . .

. . . should be *"I will load fast and refrain from causing eyestrain in the people who look at me."* Lecturing your graphics file on New Year's Eve may not help, but giving it an appropriate *degree of resolution* will. As you might expect, you perform this miracle by manipulating numbers (that's the only way we post-moderns can *do* magic). The first of these numbers is a ratio: *bits per pixel:* How many bits does a particular format use to create one pixel?

The more-capable graphics programs give you the option of setting the bits-per-pixel ratio. It's a straightforward relationship:

- ✔ Using more bits to create one lowly pixel means you can depict subtler colors and outlines — which sharpens the image but balloons the file.

- ✔ Using fewer bits per pixel reduces the resolution (therefore the quality) of the images rendered by a browser but makes the file smaller and faster to load.

Of course, if you can possibly avoid it, you don't want to use more bits per pixel than most browsers can handle (they'll see the image, all right, but miss the subtlety, which is a waste of bandwidth). Besides, too much subtlety is lost on any Web site visitor who's in a hurry. We're not talking art for art's sake here. However artistic, your Web site graphics are not sitting there to be stared at — unless your visitors are confused, lost, or glazing over (and your page will be too well designed for that, right?).

So let's settle on a magic bits-per-pixel number for starters. Try storing images with 7 (or even 5) bits per pixel if you need to show a large image as quickly as possible. For other, smaller graphics, you can practice the balancing act outlined here to find the right mix of resolution and speed.

The second magic figure you can use to reduce the size of a graphic image is the *number of colors* in the picture. A computer "sees" color as information — in particular, instructions that tell it which of those pretty phosphors on the monitor screen to light up. If the file doesn't have to explain the difference between sagebrush green and chartreuse, the instructions are simpler *(just make it light green)* — and voilá! The file is smaller. Here's where the trade-off comes in. Either you can get the color you want *(Why did the logo designer have to make it fuchsia?)* or an image that most of your audience can see *(Neat shade of purple. Where's the info?)* showing up in their browsers. Sometimes practicality means settling for a little of both and all of neither.

Check your graphics program documentation to find out whether these techniques are in its arsenal.

A standard .GIF image requires 8 bits per pixel, which results in 256 colors. Seven bits of information per pixel produces 128 colors, 5 bits 32 colors, et cetera. Some programs, such as Paint Shop Pro (shareware) and Adobe Photoshop (commercial) allow a specific number of colors to be selected. For example, setting the number of colors to 43 results in 7 bits per pixel, but the remaining 85 empty color definitions are set at 0,0,0 (or undefined), which results in a smaller (and faster) graphic than you'd get if you set the resolution to 7 bits per pixel and left it at that. Most of these programs also tell you how many unique colors appear in an image and let you manipulate the number of colors until you can achieve the best compromise between size and fidelity.

Interlacing:
Slice and dice for better response time

What is an interlaced .GIF? you ask. (You *did* ask, right?) Well, call it a way to show order coming out of chaos. An interlaced .GIF stores graphics information in a .GIF file so that a browser can load a low-resolution image on the first of multiple passes, and then fill in the image to its normal resolution on subsequent passes. This method gives images a "Venetian blind" look as your browser draws them.

The load time for images remains the same whether images are interlaced or not, but some browsers load the text of the page with the first pass of the images. This lets users begin scrolling and reading while the browser completes additional image passes. Users get to your information faster, which generally results in happier users!

Rules for using graphics

Keep these rules in mind while you design your Web pages:

- ✔ Sketch your layout with and without graphics.
- ✔ Focus on overall page look and content.
- ✔ KISS your images . . . *Keep It Small and Simple.* (Do we sense a theme developing here?)
- ✔ Use compressed, interlaced .GIFs or .JPEGs.
- ✔ Link thumbnail versions of images to larger files instead of dumping megabyte-sized files on your unsuspecting users.
- ✔ Include the size of image files in the text that describes large images.
- ✔ Use graphics sparingly for maximum effect.
- ✔ Use images or graphics to enhance text information.

If you understand and can implement all the topics discussed in this chapter, congratulations — you're not an HTML ignoramus. You know enough to design and create well-balanced, attractive, user-friendly Web pages.

Keep right on going to find out even more fun things to add to your Web pages (sorry, no pterodactyls). The next chapter reveals how to master the intricacies of complex Web pages with élan, panache, and the occasional crêpe suzette. (Who knows? You may want to get that beret, after all!)

Part III
Formatting Your Data

The 5th Wave   By Rich Tennant

BOWZER

"... and when you click the fire hydrant, it marks your domain for you."

In this part . . .

Part III is where you roll up your sleeves, and get down and dirty with HTML. In other words, it's time to tackle several collections of HTML tags up close and personal. You begin with the global structure tags that give an HTML document its form, and that can describe its content. After that, you encounter the presentation tags that allow HTML to manage fonts and text styles.

From there, it's on to the HTML tags for character styles, including ways to label and present various kinds of content, and multiple methods to represent computer output and input. After that, you tackle the various ways of building lists using HTML, and explore some interesting and offbeat uses for this markup. Your next markup adventure involves the numeric and character entities that HTML recognizes, that allow you to include all kinds of special characters in your Web pages, including elements from alphabets of many kinds.

Chapter 8

HTML Document Structure

*B*uilding a well-formed Web page requires that you use certain HTML tags to describe a document's composition and structure and that you give a Web page a definite title. Certain tags advertise information about the document in which they appear, while others define the document's contents and structure. Even within the content, you can use a variety of HTML tags to further subdivide your material and help you organize that content thoroughly and professionally. In this chapter, we tell you about these structure tags and how you can use required tags with optional tags to improve on the bare minimum that HTML itself demands.

The Importance of Document Structure

Whether by design or by default, all HTML documents have a structure of one kind or another. Here, we tell you more about the tags that help you to create, manage, and identify a document's structure and syntax.

Some of these tags, which we call *global structure tags* because they define and control the structure that HTML documents can take, are necessary to meet basic syntax requirements for a valid, well-formed HTML document.

Other members of this tag set, though not strictly required, can add a lot to the way a document behaves and help you to keep your content better organized. Either way, structure tags define the basic building blocks for HTML documents and are well worth getting to know.

What browsers forgive, a validator may not!

Validators are a type of software program that performs basic quality control on your HTML documents. Validators check the syntax and structure of a document against a model for what the syntax and structure should be in order to help developers find and fix errors, omissions, and other gotchas.

Where HTML is concerned, such programs are sometimes called *HTML validators.* The ultimate HTML validator comes from — who else? — the World Wide Web Consortium, fondly abbreviated as the W3C. The name of their program is the HTML Validator Service, and you can use it through the Web page at `validator.w3.org` to check out your own HTML documents free of charge.

The interesting thing about going through the validator is that you discover that what a Web browser happily lets you get away with, the validator finds fault with — loudly and vociferously. In other words, most Web browsers are quite indifferent to the requirements built into HTML and cheerfully display so-called HTML documents that aren't worthy of the name!

Today, this is no big deal, because HTML itself doesn't follow a truly strict or regular syntax. (And we're not talking about a tax on booze or cigarettes here; we're talking about a regular, predictable way to describe what HTML markup is and how it works.) In fact, some of what HTML allows is hard for computers to check at all! But the W3C is busily engaged in building a next-generation HTML that will be more rigorously defined and extremely well-suited to mechanical validation. When that happens, all bets on current-generation pages will be off. Don't ever say we didn't warn you.

Computer geeks like to talk about code as being valid, which means that it passes through a validator program well-formed with no errors showing, following all the syntax rules for those elements that must be present in a program, as well as adhering to the rules whenever optional elements appear. Someday soon, you'll be able to apply the same standards to HTML, so why not start now?

The very model of a valid, well-formed HTML document

You will no doubt discover, if you try, that browsers let you omit almost all the required elements that make up a valid, well-formed HTML document. But because of the shape of things to come, and in the spirit of recommending only the best of practices to you, we present a model for a valid, well-formed HTML document. In our model, required elements appear in boldface and optional elements appear in plain text. We also try to include all the tags that appear in this chapter, just for grins!

```
<!DOCTYPE HTML PUBLIC
    "-//W3C//DTD HTML 4.0 Transitional//EN"
    "http://www.w3.org/TR/REC-html40/loose.dtd">
<html>
<head>
<title>The very model of a well-formed HTML
    document</title>
<base href="http://www.lanw.com">
<style>
body {background color:teal}
H1 {font:14pt Times bold}
P {font: 12 Times; text-align: justify;}
</style>
<meta http-equiv="Resource type" content="document">
<meta http-equiv="Copyright" content="LANWrights, Inc.
    1999">
</head> <!— ends header portion of the document —>
<body> <!— begins body portion of the document —>
</div>
<h1> A Level One Header</h1>
This is a section of the document.</div>
<div>This is another, longer section of the document.
<p>Notice, the font size does not drop from the default
until the first &lt;p&gt; tag.
Within this section, we can also add a span section. <p>
<span type = "text/css" style="font-size: 18pt">
The span text appears in a larger font.
</span>
This text will be back to the original font again, but
with no line break.
</div> <!— This ends the second division —>
</body> <!— This ends the body of the document —>
</html> <!— This ends the entire HTML document —>
```

The page that results from this HTML markup appears in Figure 8-1 and shows the effects of the various document divisions and so forth. The main thing you should notice is that, except for the title, none of the structure tags produces any stuff on a Web page. Because they work behind the scenes, that's why we call them structure tags!

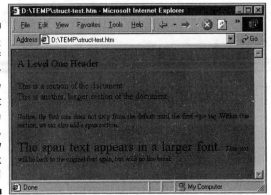

Figure 8-1:
The fruits of
all this labor
don't show
much, but
are quite
interesting,
if you know
what to look
for!

Now that you've seen all this apparent gibberish, let's take a look at these various tags. By the time you make your way through the next section, you should be better prepared to take these tags on in your own documents! At the end of the chapter, we explain the sample HTML file a little more fully.

<!— . . . —> Comments

The browser ignores the text between the brackets. Use this tag to document your HTML tags and page structures, to make notes for future reference, or to provide extra information for others who must read your HTML code.

You can use comments to temporarily hide sections of a document. Simply adding a comment tag pair around the text you wish to hide keeps it from showing up when you view the document through a Web browser.

<!— . . . —> is legal within all HTML tags.

Although the results won't appear on-screen, you can enclose any other HTML tags within a pair of comment tags: <!— . . . —>. As the preceding tip indicates, this results in "hiding" the enclosed information from your Web browser.

Examples: See file /html4Fd2/examples/ch08/comment.htm.

<!DOCTYPE> Document type

<!DOCTYPE> specifies the version of HTML used in the document through SGML declaration. All documents should contain a <!DOCTYPE> declaration to tell browsers, HTML validation tools like the W3C's HTML Validation Service, and other software exactly what version of HTML is used in that document.

✔ `<!DOCTYPE>` should be the first element within any HTML document. `<!DOCTYPE>` is not legal within any markup tag. It must appear before the `<HTML>` tag.

✔ `<!DOCTYPE>` is a required element in any syntactically valid HTML document. It can only be omitted because most browsers don't require this value to be supplied. (They assume a default value instead.) We recommend that you use this tag to help you get ready for the newer, stricter version of HTML that the W3C is working on right now.

✔ `<!DOCTYPE>` can't appear in any other markup tag, and no other tags can be used within `<!DOCTYPE>`.

DOCTYPE Attributes: `HTML PUBLIC "version name" "URL"`

HTML identifies the markup language as a version of HTML.

PUBLIC identifies the source of the markup language's definition as well-known and publicly accessible.

"version name" must reference a proper and complete HTML version name. The name of the most typical current English-language version of HTML 4.0 is "-//W3C//DTD HTML 4.0 Transitional//EN".

"URL" indicates where a PUBLIC definition resides, may either be "`http://www.w3.org/TR/REC-html40/loose.dtd`" for a pretty forgiving, but still official definition of HTML 4.0, or "`http://www.w3.org/TR/REC-html40/strict.dtd`" for a stricter, less forgiving, entirely official definition of HTML 4.0.

For more information about valid HTML version names and their associated URLs, please visit HTML Help's excellent overview of the `DOCTYPE` tag at:

`www.htmlhelp.com/reference/html40/html/doctype.html`

Technically, `DOCTYPE` is an SGML tag, not an HTML tag. But because it's required at the head of any valid HTML document, we cover it for that reason.

Examples: See file /html4Fd2/examples/ch08/doctype.htm.

<address> . . . </address>
Attribution information

`<address>` . . . `</address>` encloses credit and reference information about an HTML document, such as the author's name and address, signature files, and contact information. Most browsers display `<address>` items in an italics font. `<address>` imposes no major layout changes, but does act much like a character-level style, like the tags discussed in Chapter 10 of this book. But because it delivers important information about a Web document's creator, we cover it here in the discussion of global HTML document structure. <address> is not a required HTML document structure tag.

You can use the <address> tag where you want a footer; no <footer> markup tag exists in HTML 4.0. Include this tag at the end of any document to supply author contact information for questions or feedback.

Examples: See file /html4Fd2/examples/ch08/address.htm.

<base> Basis for relative addressing

Use the <base> tag to define a root-level URL for a collection of Web pages. As long as you put a <base> tag in the <head> section of an HTML document (which is the only area in which it may legally be placed), any URLs that occur within the <body> section of the document need include only as much information as is needed to navigate from the <base> definition. The <base> tag is not a required HTML structure tag.

<base> attributes

href="URL"

Establishes a base URL for the Web document and defines the basis for relative URLs that may appear elsewhere within the same document.

Example: <base href="http://www.lanw.com">

With the tag <base href="http://www.lanw.com"> in the <head> section of a document, any URL in the <body> of that document acts like it is appended to that base. URLs for files in the base directory can take the form href="file.ext", and files in a directory named graphics beneath the http://www.lanw.com base directory take the form href="graphics/file.ext". This technique is called *relative addressing*.

target="windowname"

Use this on framed Web pages to designate that links should be loaded into a window named windowname. We cover framed Web pages and use of the target attribute in Chapter 16.

Example: <base target="menu"> <!- loads linked reference into menu window ->

<body> . . . </body> Document body

<body> . . . </body> has only one use; it identifies the body of an HTML document, which is where the real document content resides. This explicit structure tag is required for strictly interpreted HTML.

All the individual attributes for the <body> tag are *deprecated,* which means that they won't be supported in future versions of HTML. All such information will be captured through a separate style sheet or in specific style tags within the document itself. You can safely omit any or all of these attributes, which we describe in the following text sections.

<body> attributes

alink = #RRGGBB **or** "colorname"

Sets the color for the active (currently selected) link; colors may be set using a six-digit RGB color code preceded by a pound sign or with a recognized color name; if omitted, the browser picks the color for this link.

Example: <body alink="teal"> Colors the active link using the color named teal.

background="URL"

Points to the URL where an image to be used as the (tiled) background of the document resides.

Example: <body background = "http://www.lanw.com/graphics/lanwlogo.fig">

bgcolor = #RRGGBB **or** "colorname"

Sets the background color, where colors may be set using a six-digit RGB color code preceded by a pound sign, or with the name of a recognized color; if omitted, the browser sets the color to white.

Example: <body bgcolor="black">

link=#RRGGBB **or** colorname

Sets the color for unvisited links, using a six-digit RGB code or a specific color name; if omitted, the browser sets the color (usually to blue).

Example: <body link=#009933>

text=#RRGGBB **or** colorname

Sets the Color used for textual data, using a six-digit RGB code or a specific color name; if omitted, the browser sets the color to black (#000000).

Example: `<body text="black">`

`vlink=#RRGGBB` **or** `colorname`

Sets the Color for links that have already been visited (since the last time the cache was refreshed); if omitted, the browser sets the color to purple (#0033FF).

Example: `<body vlink=#FFFF00> <!— pure red —>`

Examples: See file /html4Fd2/examples/ch08/body.htm.

<div> . . . </div> Logical division

`<div>...</div>` creates distinct divisions within an HTML document. Use this element to divide a document into separate sections, where each one can have separate style definitions, including alignment values, font choices, text colors, and so forth. Such assignments apply to everything between the opening `<div>` and the closing `</div>` tags.

<div> Attributes

`align=LEFT` *or* `CENTER` *or* `RIGHT` *or* `JUSTIFY`

Specifies the default horizontal alignment for the contents within the `<div>` element.

Example: `<div align="LEFT">`

`style="text"`

Supports all standard HTML style properties and values, as described in Chapter 18 of this book. When using the style attribute, you must also use the type attribute to identify the kind of style sheet language in use (the following example references the notation used for cascading style sheets, or CSS).

Example: `<div type="text/css" style="color:navy">`

Note that the align attribute in any element inside `<div>` overrides the align value for the `<div>` element itself. You can't use `<div>` in conjunction with `<p>`, because a `<div>` element terminates any preceding paragraph.

Examples: See file /html4Fd2/examples/ch08/div.htm.

<h> . . . </h*> Header levels*

Headers come in different styles and sizes to help you organize your content and make it easier to read. The size and display characteristics for any header level are determined by the browser. But by default, a level 1 heading `<h1>` is larger and more pronounced than a level 2 heading `<h2>`, and so on. Header tags are by no means required in a document, but they help to organize its contents. Header tags may be numbered from `<h1>` to `<h6>`, but you seldom find a document with more than three or four levels of headers in use.

<h> Attributes
`align=LEFT` *or* `CENTER` *or* `RIGHT` *or* `JUSTIFY`

Sets the alignment of header text on the Web page; `left` is the default.

Example: `<h1 align="CENTER">Test Header 1</h1> <!– centers this level 1 heading –>`

Using headings regularly and consistently helps add structure and divisions to your documents. Some experts recommend not using a subordinate header level unless you plan to use at least two of them beneath a parent level. In other words, don't use a single `<h3> . . . </h3>` after an `<h2> . . . </h2>` pair. This practice follows the outlining principle where you don't indent unless you have at least two subtopics under any particular topic. Although we think the occasional exception is okay, this is a good guideline for HTML documents.

Examples: See file /html4Fd2/examples/ch08/h.htm.

<head> . . . </head> Document head block

`<head> . . . </head>` creates a container for all kinds of information that describes an HTML document, including the document's title, search engine information, index information, a next page pointer, and even links to other HTML documents. `<head> . . . </head>` is required at the head of an HTML document. Even though many browsers can display documents without a `<head> . . . </head>` block at the beginning, including one is good practice, especially if you want to establish a base URL for relative page addressing should you have numerous graphics or hyperlinks to other local documents in your page. In fact, the `<head> . . . </head>` tag pair is required to create a valid, well-formed HTML document.

<head> Attributes

```
Profile="URL"
```

Defines the location for a metadictionary or profile where a set of applicable profile tags are defined.

Example: `<head profile="http://www.lanw.com/profile.txt">`

Examples: See file /html4Fd2/examples/ch08/head.htm.

<html> . . . </html> HTML document

The `<html>` . . . `</html>` tag pair should enclose any entire HTML document as the outermost layer of its overall structure. Its job is to denote where an HTML document begins, and where it ends. The `<html>` . . . `</html>` tag pair is required to create a valid, well-formed HTML document.

<html> Attributes

```
version="URL"
```

Specifies a URL for a document type definition to be used to interpret this document. This is usually the same URL that's included in the `<!DOCTYPE>` declaration. If you follow our recommendations for building valid, well-formed HTML, this attribute is unnecessary.

`<html>` . . . `</html>` is not legal within any other markup tags.

You can only use the following markup tags within `<html>` . . . `</html>`: `<body>`, `<frameset>`, and `<head>`.

Examples: See file /html4Fd2/examples/ch08/html.htm.

<meta> Meta-information

Use the `<meta>` tag within the `<head>` element to embed document meta-information (information about information in your document). Such information can be extracted by servers or clients and may be used to identify, index, or catalog specialized document meta-information. This is the kind of stuff that Web robots care about a lot, which means that this data is often used to categorize and label your Web pages on a search engine like Yahoo!, Excite, or AltaVista.

<meta> Attributes

`name="text"`

Used to name any of several document properties, including its author, publication date, and so on. If this attribute is left out, the name is assumed to be the value set for `http-equiv`.

Example: `<meta name="author" content="Natanya Pitts">`

`content="text"`

Used to supply a value for some named property, or for an `http-equiv` response header.

`http-equiv="text"`

This attribute binds the element to an HTTP response header that will be sent when a robot or browser queries the page for this information. If the HTTP response header format is known to its requester, its contents can be processed. HTTP header names are not case-sensitive. If `http-equiv` is absent, use the `name` attribute to identify this meta-information, but it won't show up within an HTTP response header when requested (that's why we recommend you use this attribute to label your site for public consumption).

Example: `<meta http-equiv="Copyright" content="LANWrights, Inc. — 1999">`

`scheme="schemename"`

Identifies the scheme to use to interpret a property's values. This attribute is necessary only when metadata requires interpretation to make sense.

`<meta>` is legal within the `<head>` markup tag. You can't use any markup tags within `<meta>`; it is a singleton tag.

Meta-information makes a site's contents more accessible to spiders and robots for automatic indexing. It also makes information more accessible to programs you use to manage a Web site. No universal `http-equiv` values exist; instead, document designers and robot/agent owners tend to stick to a limited vocabulary of terms. Thus, when a robot/agent declares its support for a specific `http-equiv` value, it quickly spreads around the Web. Some robots record all meta-information so that specialized or focused data searches can use that information, even it if it's not standardized. The Web Robots Pages at `info.webcrawler.com/mak/projects/robots/robots.html` can tell you more about how these software programs work and how to use the `<meta>` tag to make your site more accessible to them. Also, you can use the Platform for Internet Content Selection (PICS) through the `<meta>` tag to identify content, sign code, aid privacy, or identify intellectual property rights. Details are available at `www.w3.org/PICS/`.

Examples: See file /h4d5e/examples/ch08/meta.htm.

<span> . . . </span> Localized style formatting

This tag applies style information to text within a document on an arbitrary basis. (`<div>` actually requires dividing a document up into separate containers; `<span>` lets you select any chunk of HTML code to which you can apply styles.) Therefore, you should use `<span>` for localized text formatting using the `style` attribute.

<span> Attributes

`align=LEFT` *or* `CENTER` *or* `RIGHT` *or* `JUSTIFY`

Specifies the default horizontal alignment for contents of the `<span>` element.

`style="text"`

Supports all standard HTML style properties and values, as described in Chapter 18 of this book. When using the style attribute, you must also use the type attribute to identify the kind of style sheet language in use. (The following example references the notation used for cascading style sheets, or CSS.)

Example: `<span type="text/css" style="color:navy">`

`<span>` is an inline division element. It applies no changes to standard rendering to surrounded content without a `style` attribute definition. You can use `<span>` within paragraphs, unlike `<div>`, but you can't use it to group multiple elements together, as `<div>` can.

Examples: See file /html4Fd2/examples/ch08/span.htm.

<style> . . . </style> Style information

`<style>...</style>` provides a way to include rendering and display information in an HTML document using standard style sheet notation. Cascading Style Sheets (CSS1 and CSS2) are the most widely supported standard and most references to style sheets refer to CSS1. Information in the `<style>` tag works with a client's default configuration, as well as any externally referenced style sheets, to define the set of style rules that applies to a given Web page. This material is the subject of Chapter 18 in this book, so please look

there for specific examples of HTML markup that uses complex style definitions. The <style> tag is by no means required in an HTML document, but it
provides a powerful way to control how your documents look and behave.

<style> Attributes

type="text"

Specifies the type of style sheet in use. The type for CSS1 sheets is text/css;
for CSS2, it's text/css2.

media= screen *or* print *or* projection *or* braille *or* speech *or* all

Identifies the ideal environment in which the Web page should be conveyed.
The default is all, and screen is used in most cases because Web pages are
most often viewed on a computer screen. However, pages designed for presentations should use the projection value, whereas those meant to be
read by a text-to-speech reader should use the speech value. Currently, this
attribute provides information only and doesn't affect the way the style sheet
is interpreted or the page is rendered. You may include more than one media
type, where each is separated by a comma.

The <style> tag should contain only valid style statements in the language
indicated by the type attribute. Style sheets are now formally part of the
HTML 4.0 specification and are supported in full by Internet Explorer 4.0 and
Netscape Navigator 4.0, and newer versions. Older versions of browsers that
don't support style sheets ignore style markup.

Example: See file /html4Fd2/examples/ch08/style.htm.

<title> . . . </title> Document title

The <title> . . . </title> tags enclose the title for an HTML document, which normally appears in the title bar in the browser's window. By
default, the title is set to the HTML document's filename if a title is not specified. <title> . . . </title> is legal only within <head> . . .
</head>. Only plain text can be used within <title> . . . </title>,
because this text only displays on the title bar of the browser window. The
<title> tag also takes no attributes.

Try to come up with a useful title for every HTML document you write. An
accurate, descriptive title helps the many Web search engines and tools to
accurately identify or label your content.

Examples: See file /html4Fd2/examples/ch08/title.htm.

Back to the Future

Prior to the preceding section, we created an example HTML file that showed all the structure tags in this chapter. If you flip back to the preceding definitions as we explain this file line by line, you can form a pretty good picture of what's going on here.

```
<!DOCTYPE HTML PUBLIC
   "-//W3C//DTD HTML 4.0 Transitional//EN"
   "http://www.w3.org/TR/REC-html40/loose.dtd">
```

The DOCTYPE statement identifies that we're using a public HTML definition known as the transitional HTML 4.0 document type definition as defined by the W3C, which resides at the URL that appears in the last line above.

```
<html>
```

The <html> tag opens the HTML portion of the document and continues all the way to the end to the closing </html> tag.

```
<head>
```

The <head> tag opens the HTML document header, which contains all kinds of information that describes this document, as you see in the lines that follow up to the </head> tag.

```
<title>The very model of a well-formed HTML
   document</title>
```

The text between the two <title> . . . </title> tags defines the title for the resulting HTML document when viewed in a browser, as a quick jump back to Figure 8-1 confirms.

```
<base href="http://www.lanw.com">
```

This <base> tag identifies the root for all relative references in the body of the document as the LANWrights Web server at http://www.lanw.com.

```
<style>
body {background color:teal}
H1 {font:14pt Times bold}
P {font: 12 Times; text-align: justify;}
</style>
```

This section of code defines a set of styles for the entire body of the HTML document to follow. It sets the page background color to teal, requires level 1 heads to use 14-point Times boldface fonts, and indicates that all text following the first paragraph marker, <p>, should be in 12-point Times, and the text aligned for even right- and left-hand margins.

```
<meta http-equiv="Resource type" content="document">
<meta http-equiv="Copyright" content="LANWrights, Inc.
   1999">
```

These two `<meta>` tags are a subset of what you'd put on a typical Web page, but they indicate that this file contains an HTML document in the first line and provides a copyright notice for LANWrights, Inc., in the second line.

```
</head> <!— ends header portion of the document —>
```

This line closes the header portion of the document, followed by an HTML comment that reinforces this point.

```
<body>  <!— begins body portion of the document —>
```

The `<body>` tag opens the content portion of the document. Except for the text between the two `<title>` . . . `</title>` tags in the `<head>` section, only text in the `<body>` . . . `</body>` section of an HTML document shows up on screen.

```
<div>
```

This `<div>` tag opens the first division in the document, which includes the following header level 1 line and the text line after that.

```
<h1> A Level One Header</h1>
```

This is a level one header that identifies itself as such. In a more normal HTML document, you'd use header levels to identify various levels of structure within a document (or a division within that document).

```
This is a section of the document.</div>
```

The `</div>` tag at the end of this line marks the end of the first section of this document, and imposes a paragraph break after this line as a consequence.

```
<div>This is another, longer section of the document.
<p>Notice, the font size does not drop from the default
until the first &lt;p&gt; tag.
Within this section, we can also add a span section. <p>
```

The three preceding lines open up a new division within the document, and show the effects of the `<p>` paragraph style from the `<style>` section in the document header.

```
<span type = "text/css" style="font-size: 18pt">
The span text appears in a larger font.
</span>
```

Here, we begin a `<span>` section within a document division, marked by the larger text that appears immediately thereafter. As soon as the `</span>` tag appears to close this section, the font reverts to its original size setting. But because no paragraph break is implied when a `</span>` tag appears, the next line follows immediately, with no line break.

```
This text will be back to the original font again, but
with no line break.
</div>  <!- This ends the second division ->
```

The `</div>` tag closes out the second division of the document.

```
</body>  <!- This ends the body of the document ->
</html>  <!- This ends the entire HTML document ->
```

The `</body>` tag marks the end of the HTML document's body, and the `</html>` marks the end of the document itself. Notice that comments after the closing tag are perfectly valid (they're ignored by design).

The best way to understand the importance of HTML's structure tags is to recognize that they define the primary containers for text and other information in an HTML document.

- DOCTYPE identifies what is to follow.
- `<head>`, `<title>`, `<style>`, `<meta>`, and `<base>` tags set the style and the stage for what is to come.
- `<body>`, `<div>`, `<h1>` . . . `<h6>`, and `<span>` tags identify the containers within which you can place the document's content.

Chapter 9

Presentation Controls

● ●

In This Chapter

▶ Understanding document styles versus element controls

▶ Managing fonts by type, weight, style, and color

▶ Establishing text direction

▶ Ruling out your text boundaries

▶ Controlling character appearance

● ●

*H*TML includes a wide range of tags that permit you to manage the way that text appears on screen. Such tags govern font selection, text styles, colors, and so forth and let you control which way text flows on a page (from left to right, or vice versa, or from top to bottom, or vice versa). As a category, these tags permit you to manage what text in your document looks like, which is why we call them presentation controls. In this chapter, you'll encounter a variety of such tools.

Style versus Presentation

This chapter is chock-full of HTML tags that you can use to manage text. These tags allow you to manage everything from the kind of font you instruct the browser to use for your text — which might be something like Times New Roman, Courier, Arial, or some other well-known typeface — to the size and weight of the characters chosen from that font. It also includes a variety of controls for text styles (by which we mean settings like **bold** and *italic*), and other kinds of related items.

Sounds pretty good doesn't it? But before you take a spin through these tags, stop to consider this: Except for a single tag (<bdo>) that controls the language choice for a text section and the direction in which text displays, all tags in this chapter create text effects that you can control through styles instead.

In fact, many of the tags in this chapter are known as *deprecated* tags. In ordinary terms, the word "deprecated" refers to something that those in authority disapprove of strongly. In official HTML-speak, a deprecated tag is one that is headed for the scrap heap, and will probably be abandoned when the next release of HTML is ready.

Thus, even though these deprecated tags are perfectly legal today, and most browsers should display them perfectly, we don't recommend that you use them without pausing to consider that there may come a time when these tags won't work anymore. If your Web pages live only for a short while, or you plan to replace them with newer versions before the new millennium gets too old, you should be okay.

Just to keep you on the straight and narrow, Table 9-1 lists all the tags in this chapter that are deprecated. Surprisingly, this covers the bulk of the tags covered in this chapter.

Table 9-1   Deprecated Presentation Control Tags in HTML 4.0

Tag	What's Deprecated	Explanation
<b>	tag only	Bolds enclosed text
<basefont>	tag & attributes	Selects default font
<center>	tag	Centers enclosed text
<font>	all attributes	Selects typeface, size, color
<hr>	some attributes	Draws horizontal rule; size & width attributes are deprecated
<i>	tag	Italicizes enclosed text
<s>	tag	Strikes enclosed text through
<strike>	tag	Strikes enclosed text through
<u>	tag	Underlines enclosed text

Here's how to interpret the contents of this table:

✔ If the tag is deprecated, it is to be phased out with the next release of HTML. If that tag takes attributes, the same goes for them, too.

✔ If all attributes are deprecated, the tag will remain in effect, but the attributes are to be phased out with the next release of HTML.

✔ If some attributes are deprecated, the tag and its other attributes will remain in effect, but the designated attributes are to be phased out with the next release of HTML.

In addition to these deprecated tags (which comprise over half the tags covered in this chapter), we don't recommend you use the tags shown in Table 9-2 either. That's because they, too, produce no effects that can't be created more easily using style sheets or style markup in your HTML documents (remember, Chapter 18 is where you can find out about this style stuff in HTML). But because they're not deprecated, and we don't recommend their use, we call these tags "nugatory," which means they're trifling, insignificant, or of no worth.

Table 9-2	Nugatory Presentation Control Tags in HTML 4.0	
Tag	**What's Deprecated**	**Explanation**
<big>	tag	Increases font size for enclosed text
<small>	tag	Decreases font size for enclosed text
<tt>	tag	Uses a monospaced font to look like typewriter text

Because you're going to see these tags all over the place in HTML code, and because you may prefer to use these tags' quick-and-dirty capabilities from time to time, we have no choice but to tell you about them. Plus, better you should hear about them from us, than on the playground or in an alley somewhere.

But whether you succumb to your base desires to use these tags, or decide to use style-related markup instead, remember this: Instead of using these presentation control tags, you can use any of the following techniques:

- ✔ Reference an external style sheet. In such a style sheet, you can select default fonts, and manage font sizes, font styles, and even font colors to your heart's content. You can also control margins, spacing before and after text elements, and more.

- ✔ Create a <style> section in an HTML document's <head> section to define the same font characteristics for an entire Web document.

- ✔ Use the style attribute in most HTML tags to control relevant characteristics only for the text associated with the tag you're working on.

We think that managing text presentation in an HTML document is best done with style markup, using one of the techniques just described, but it's your HTML document and you can do whatever you like!

Presentation Control Tags

By the time you eliminate all the deprecated tags covered in Table 9-1 and the nugatory tags covered in Table 9-2, the only tag that's left is the `<bdo>` tag. If you've already decided to use style sheet markup with your HTML documents, you can skip straight to that tag in the text that follows. Then, when you're done with that tag, you're done with this chapter!

On the other hand, if you want to find out more about a collection of tags you're pretty likely to encounter in most HTML markup that you'll read in other people's Web pages, go ahead and plow through the other tags in this chapter. That way, you'll know what you're missing if you decide to take the style route, or you'll know what to look for, if you ever decide to go the other way.

`<b>` . . . `</b>` Bold text

Use of these tags indicates that the enclosed text should appear in boldface type. As such, the `<b>` . . . `</b>` tag pair may be used to provide specific focus or emphasis on words or phrases in paragraph or body text in an HTML document. But style sheets can match the same effects and can better manage character weight and font style. That's why we recommend that you "do it with style" rather than using this tag.

Example: `<b>Hello</b>` displays the word "Hello" in bold type.

Examples: See file /html4Fd2/examples/ch09/b.htm.

`<basefont>` Base font

Definition: Sets basic font parameters to be used as the default for any text on a Web page that is not otherwise formatted by a style sheet or by using the `<FONT>` element directly.

This tag and its attributes are deprecated in HTML 4.0 in favor of style sheet rules. Rather than using the `<basefont>` tag, use style settings to manage font selection within your documents.

`<basefont>` Attributes
`color=#RRGGBB` *or* "**colorname**"

Defines the color for the base font; colors may be set using a six-digit RGB color code preceded by a pound sign, or with a recognized color name; if this attribute is omitted, the browser picks the color for this font. You cannot use additional tags within `<BASEFONT>` because it is a singleton tag.

Example: `<basefont alink="teal">` sets the base font to the color named teal (RGB value #669999).

`face=`**"name"**

This attribute specifies the base font face; it should be a well-known font family name like Times New Roman, Courier, and so forth, or one of the generic CSS font families: serif, sans serif, monospace, cursive, or fantasy.

Example: `<face="Times New Roman">` sets the base font to the Times New Roman font; if this font is not available on a particular user's machine, the browser will substitute the nearest equivalent font face.

`size=`**"number"**

This attribute defines the size of the base font. The value of *number* can be between 1 and 7 inclusive; the default is 3, and 7 is the largest legal value. Relative font size settings (for example, `<FONT SIZE=+3>`) are set according to this value throughout the document.

Example: `<face size="5">` sets the default font size for the document two sizes larger than the normal default.

Examples: See file /html4Fd2/examples/ch09/basefont.htm.

<bdo> . . . </bdo> Bidirectional algorithm

These tags name the primary language in use on a document, and can establish, alter, or reverse the default algorithm used for display direction. For English and most other European languages, this algorithm is right to left and top to bottom; other languages, such as Japanese and Arabic, use a different algorithm.

<bdo> Attributes

`lang=`"language-code"

This attribute defines the primary language to be used in the HTML document where it appears. A list of primary language codes appears in ISO Standard 639a, which you can read online at:

```
www.oasis-open.org/cover/iso639-2a.html
```

Common language codes include "en" for English, "fr" for French, "de" for German, and so forth.

Example: `<bdo lang="fr">` sets the language to French.

dir=`"LTR"` *or* `"RTL"`

Specifies the direction of text interpretation for languages that are read from right to left, such as Hebrew, or for languages whose direction of viewing may be unclear. The default is left to right, so it's usually unnecessary to use this attribute except when including languages that don't adhere to this display direction.

Example: `<bdo lang="he" dir="RTL">` sets the language to Hebrew, and the direction to right to left.

Examples: See file /html4Fd2/examples/ch09/bdo.htm.

<big> . . . </big> Big text

These tags increase the text font for text enclosed between them to one size larger than the size set in the `<basefont>` tag. For the same reasons that we don't recommend use of the `<basefont>` tag, we also recommend against this tag pair — namely because you can handle these effects more transparently using style-related tags, if not an external style sheet. The `<big>` tag takes no attributes.

Example: The HTML markup `Mr. <big>Big</big>` causes "Mr." to appear at the default font size, but "Big" will be one size larger.

Examples: See file /html4Fd2/examples/ch09/big.htm.

<center> . . . </center> Centered text

As its name should suggest, the `<center>` . . . `</center>` tags center any text horizontally that occurs between them. The `<center>` tag breaks the current line of text and centers the text between it and the closing `</center>` tag on a new line, even if no other markup to control line breaks is used. The `<center>` tag takes no attributes.

The `<center>` tag is deprecated, and will not be supported in future versions of HTML. Use the `align="CENTER"` attribute that can be applied to many HTML tags, or use style sheets to impose centered alignment on specific tags instead.

Example: `<center>This text shows up centered.</center>` centers the text on a line by itself.

Examples: See file /html4Fd2/examples/ch09/center.htm.

<font> . . . </font> Font appearance

Definition: Sets the size, font, and color of text enclosed between the two tags.

All the individual attributes for the `<font>` tag are deprecated in HTML 4.0. Thus, we recommend that you use style sheet rules to achieve the same effects when possible. If you specify a particular font face (called a font family in Cascading Style Sheet terminology), remember that if users don't have that font installed on their machines, the browser will use a default font instead. For that reason, you should stick to well-known font faces, or reference generic fonts instead.

<font> Attributes
`color="#RRGGBB"` *or* `"colorname"`

Sets the font color; colors may be set using a six-digit RGB color code preceded by a pound sign, or with a recognized color name; if this attribute is omitted, the browser picks the color for this font.

Example: `<font color="teal">` sets the font to the color named teal (RGB value #669999).

`face=`**"name[, name2[, name3]]"**

Sets the font face. You can specify a list of font names, separated by commas. If the first font is available on the system, it is used; otherwise, the second is tried, and so on. If none of the named fonts is available, a default font is used instead.

Example: `<font face="Times, Times New Roman, Courier">` indicates that the browser should try to use a font named Times first, one named Times New Roman second, and one named Courier third.

`size=`**"number"**

Specifies a font size between 1 and 7 (where 7 is the largest legal value). A plus or minus sign before the number indicates a size relative to the current size setting. Relative font sizes are not cumulative, so using two `<font size="+1">` elements in a row does not increase relative size by 2.

Example: `<font size="+3">` increases the relative size of the font by three settings.

Examples: See file /html4Fd2/examples/ch09/font.htm.

<hr> Horizontal rule

This tag draws a horizontal line across the page, usually one or two pixels wide. Use it to separate body text from page footers, or to separate areas on a Web page. Note also that you can't use any tags within `<HR>`, because it is a singleton tag. Some Web browsers (for example, Internet Explorer) will accept `color` as an attribute to this tag.

<hr> Attributes

`align="LEFT"` *or* `"CENTER"` *or* `"RIGHT"`

Draws the horizontal rule left aligned, right aligned, or centered, depending on the align type assigned, which can be `LEFT`, `RIGHT`, or `CENTER`. The default is for the rule to be centered, but also for the width to be 100 percent, or the entire width of the display area, so you can't tell unless you mess with the size attribute (which is deprecated).

Example: `<hr align="LEFT" width="50%">` left-justifies the rule across half the page width.

`noshade`

Draws the outline of the rule without filling it in or providing any 3-D shading effects (which some browsers also do).

Example: `<hr noshade>` draws a horizontal rule without filling it in or shading it. This is most noticeable if you increase the size attribute to 10 or so.

`size="number"`

Sets the height of the rule in pixels. This attribute is deprecated in HTML 4.0.

Example: `<hr size="10">` creates a thick horizontal rule that is 10 pixels high.

`width="`**number**`"` *or* "**%**"

Sets the width of the rule in pixels or as a percentage of window width. To specify a percentage, the number must end with a percent (%) sign. This attribute is deprecated in HTML 4.0.

Example: `<hr width="50%">` centers a horizontal rule that covers half the page width.

Examples: See file /html4Fd2/examples/ch09/hr.htm.

<i> . . . </i> Italic text

This pair of tags italicizes all text enclosed between them. The `<i>` tag takes no attributes, and is deprecated for HTML 4.0. Use italics sparingly for emphasis or effect, remembering that their effectiveness fades quickly with overuse. If you are setting off a citation or quoting from a text resource in your document, use the `<cite>` ... `</cite>` tags instead of the italics tags.

Example: `<i>deprecated</i>` displays the word "deprecated" in italics.

Examples: See file /html4Fd2/examples/ch09/html.htm.

<s> . . . </s> Strikethrough

This pair of tags causes all enclosed text to appear with a strikethrough (a fine line, one pixel wide, will be drawn through the text). This tag causes the same effect as the `<strike>` tag, and both of these tags are deprecated in HTML 4.0, in favor of similar style sheet properties. Strikethrough text is difficult to read on a monitor, so use this tag sparingly. It's most commonly used to show text removed from earlier versions of a document. This tag takes no attributes.

Example: `Three <s>strikes</s> and you're out,` causes the word "strikes" to be stricken through.

Examples: See file /html4Fd2/examples/ch09/s.htm.

<small> . . . </small> Small text

Using these tags makes the text they enclose one size smaller than the base font size. Although this tag is not deprecated, you can use style sheet rules to achieve the same effects. This tag takes no attributes.

Example: The HTML markup `Mr. <small>Little</small>` shows "Mr." at the default font size, but "Little" at the next smaller font size.

Examples: See file /html4Fd2/examples/ch09/small.htm.

<strike> . . . </strike> Strikethrough

All text placed between this tag pair appears with a fine line, one pixel wide. This tag pair is functionally identical to the `<s> . . . </s>` tags, and likewise is deprecated. Strikethrough text is difficult to read on a monitor, so use this tag sparingly. It's most commonly used to show text removed from earlier versions of a document. This tag takes no attributes.

Example: `Three <strike>strikes</strike> and you're out,` causes the word "strikes" to be stricken through.

Examples: See file /html4Fd2/examples/ch09/strike.htm.

<tt> . . . </tt> Teletype text

Text enclosed with this tag pair appears in a monospaced (teletype) font, typically some variety of Courier or another sans serif font. Use these tags to set off monospaced text, where character position is important, or when trying to imitate the look of line-printer or typewriter output. Teletype is often used to indicate computer output. Two similar, but already obsolete HTML tag pairs of `<KBD> . . . <KBD>` and `<CODE> . . . <CODE>` are sometimes used to indicate user input or existing text, respectively.

Example: The HTML markup `Type <tt>route</tt> at the command line` displays all text except the word "route" in the default typeface, but displays "route" in a monospaced font.

Examples: See file /html4Fd2/examples/ch09/tt.htm.

<u> . . . </u> Underlined text

All text enclosed between this tag pair will be underlined. This tag pair is deprecated in HTML 4.0, in favor of similar style sheet properties. Try to avoid this tag, because most browsers use underlines to emphasize hyperlinks. Underlining can confuse your users, making them think they see hyperlinks that do not work.

Example: The HTML markup `Don't do <u>that</u>!` displays all text except the word "that" in the default typeface, but adds an underline to the word "that."

Examples: See file /html4Fd2/examples/ch09/u.htm.

Chapter 10

Text Controls

*H*TML includes an interesting assortment of tags that permit you to flag the way text appears in a document, based on its content or significance. Unlike the tags in Chapter 9, where you operate directly on how the text looks, in this chapter you operate on text to control how its readers will interpret its meaning.

Text control tags let you handle quotations from other sources, both long and short, and attribution of those sources, whether visible on the document or hidden in the HTML source code. They also let you apply varying degrees of emphasis to the text in your documents. You can even mark text in one version of a document as deleted from a prior version, or added since that prior version was published. Perhaps most confusing — but potentially most powerful — you can use HTML markup to distinguish text that originates from a variety of sources, or is destined to be used as input to a computer or other text-driven device. You not only find out how to use these tags, but when to use certain tags that might otherwise seem indistinguishable from one another.

Separating Form from Content

Although numerous tags in this chapter may produce the same visual effects as tags you can find in Chapter 9, it's important to understand that the tags in this chapter try to label the content they embrace, whereas the tags in Chapter 9 simply address the way the text they enclose appears on a Web page.

For instance, consider these two one-line fragments of HTML code:

```
Homer's <i>Iliad</i> recounts the Trojan War.
Homer's <cite>Iliad</cite> recounts the Trojan War.
```

Viewed inside a browser, both lines look exactly the same, as long as the defaults are left unchanged. But the meaning of the `<cite>` tag is quite different from that of the `<i>` tag — namely, `<cite>` indicates clearly that what follows next is a citation from a resource of some kind, whereas what follows the `<i>` could be anything forced into italic text. Humans and browsers can read significance into the `<cite>` tag and what follows next; the `<i>` tag carries no such weight of meaning for its readers.

The same is true for many of the other tags covered in this chapter. You can match their appearance quite easily (and perhaps even do so with fewer keystrokes) by using the presentation tags that match their look and feel, but you can't capture the same kind of information with the presentation tags that these text controls can provide.

Using style to emphasize content differences

Perhaps that's why we try to steer you clear of the vast majority of presentation tags in Chapter 9, but recommend the text control tags in this chapter both enthusiastically and forcefully. In fact, we recommend that when you must create documents that require the use of multiple kinds of text that you augment the meaning of these tags with additional changes in their appearance using style markup to underscore their differences.

For example, when creating an online manual for a computer program, you might want to distinguish among three or more kinds of text. It's easy to see, for instance, that users might need to be able to see and readily understand the differences between:

- ✔ Text produced by a program to solicit user input
- ✔ Text that the user needs to enter at the keyboard
- ✔ Reports that user input causes the program to emit
- ✔ Error messages that faulty or incomplete user input can provoke

By establishing the right kinds of "look and feel" for each of these kinds of text, you will be able to cue your readers about what they're seeing, and help them to separate what the program will show them from what they must input into that program. You'll also be able to help them better understand the kinds of information that the program can provide for them, and to help them recognize error messages, and take appropriate action to correct the mistakes that can sometimes cause such messages to appear.

About common attributes

For several of the tags in the following sections, you'll see the phrase "this tag takes no unique attributes." This doesn't mean the tag takes no attributes whatsoever, but rather, that the tag takes no attributes in addition to the six common attributes that appear in this list:

✔ id="name": A document-wide unique identifier that you can use to give an HTML element a unique name within a document.

✔ class="text": A comma-separated list of class names, which indicates that the element belongs to a specific class or classes of style definitions.

✔ style="text": Provides rendering information specific to this element, such as its size, color, and font specifics.

✔ title="text": Defines an advisory title that will display additional help. Balloon text around hyperlinks and graphics use this attribute.

✔ dir="LTR" _or_ "RTL": Indicates the direction in which text should flow, either left to right, or right to left.

✔ lang="name": Specifies the language, as per ISO639a's two-character language codes (see Chapter 9 for an online source of these codes).

Even those HTML tags that do take unique attributes may also support the foregoing list of common attributes. To check the status for any particular HTML tag, you can try it and see what happens, or consult the HTML 4.0 DTD at www.w3.org/TR/REC-html40/.

Text control tags

As you work your way through the text control tags in the sections that follow, try to associate each tag with a specific kind of information, or to appreciate the labels for information that using such a tag can deliver. Think of these tags as a way to inform readers about what the information they see means, and to separate your thoughts and data from information quoted from other sources. Likewise, some of these tags will permit you to clearly separate user input from program output, and even to create distinctions in each of those areas of computer activity as well.

<blockquote> . . . </blockquote> Quote style

Use `<blockquote>...</blockquote>` to set off large chunks of material quoted from external sources, publications, or other materials. When you quote from an external source (more than one line long), use `<blockquote>` to offset the text from both left and right margins. Always attribute your sources. Remember to use `<cite>` to highlight the actual publication, if applicable.

<blockquote> attributes
cite=**"text"**

This attribute provides information about the source of the quote between the <blockquote>...</blockquote> tags.

Example: <blockquote cite="The CGI Bible, pg. 115">This optional attribute specifies a URL for processing image events ...</blockquote> associates the page reference with information about the imagemap attribute for the now-obsolete HTML 3.0 <fig> tag.

Examples: See file /html4Fd2/examples/ch10/block.htm.

*
 Force line break*

The <br> tag forces a line break in HTML text, immediately after it occurs.
 is a singleton tag. This tag is useful for creating short lines of text, or for text that must be broken in specific places, such as verse.

*
 attributes:*
clear="LEFT" *or* "ALL" *or* "RIGHT" *or* "NONE"

LEFT inserts space that aligns the following text with the left margin directly below a left-aligned floating image. ALL places the following text past all floating images. RIGHT inserts space that aligns the following text with the right margin directly below a right-aligned floating image. NONE is the default, which does nothing.

Example: The HTML markup Go down, Moses<br clear="ALL"> breaks the line right after the word "Moses," and places any following text past all floating images on the page.

Examples: See file /html4Fd2/examples/ch10/br.htm.

<cite> . . . </cite> Citation emphasis

Use the <cite>...</cite> tags to highlight external resource citations for documents, publications, and so forth. The <cite> tag takes no unique attributes.

Example: The HTML markup Homer's <cite>Oddysey</cite> is the story of an epic journey. sets off the title of that work in a different text style (which most browsers render in italics), while the rest of the line appears in plain text.

Examples: See file /html4Fd2/examples/ch10/cite.htm.

<code> . . . </code> Program code text

`<code>...</code>` is used to enclose programs or samples of code to offset them from normal text. Most browsers use a monospaced font, like Courier, to set off such text. These tags provide a good way to set off programs, code fragments, or computer output within the body of an HTML document. The `<code>` tag takes no unique attributes.

Example: The HTML markup `Enter the string <code>route print 172*</code> into your batch file.` sets off the string "route print 172*" in a monospaced font. It does not break the line, however, either before the opening `<code>` tag, or after the closing `</code>` tag. To set such text off more emphatically, be sure to precede the opening tag with a `<br>` and follow the closing tag with another `<br>`.

Examples: See file /html4Fd2/examples/ch10/code.htm.

<del> . . . </del> Deleted text

Use this pair of tags to mark text as deleted, usually to show changes with respect to a previous version of the Web document in which this markup appears. This kind of tag is only likely to be used when multiple authors share a single document, and deletions must be explicitly marked for approval or feedback from all parties to the document. That's why the timing attributes are so inclusive and specific. Use the companion tag pair `<ins>...</ins>` to show where new text is inserted, if necessary.

<del> attributes
`cite="URL"`

Points to another document that describes why the text was deleted.

Example: The markup `The <del URL="http://www.lanw.com/doc/changes.html">Summary</del> References section contains the list of source materials.` shows the word "Summary" with a strikethrough line through the term. You must, however, examine the HTML source to read the contents of the `cite` and `datetime` attributes for this tag.

`datetime=YYYY-MM-DDThh:mm:ssTZD`

Marks the time when you changed the document. This attribute's value must use the specific format shown above to conform to the ISO8601 time/date specification. The abbreviations shown here match the following date and time information:

- ✔ YYYY = The year

- ✔ MM = The two-digit month — for example, "03" for March

- ✔ DD = The day

- ✔ T = Indicates the beginning of the time section

- ✔ hh = The hour, in military time (0–23 hours), without a.m. or p.m. specifications

- ✔ mm = The minute

- ✔ ss = The second

- ✔ TZD = The time zone

- ✔ Z = The Coordinated Universal Time (CUT)

- ✔ +hh:mm = The local time that is hours (hh) and minutes (mm) ahead of the CUT

- ✔ -hh:mm = The local time that is hours (hh) and minutes (mm) behind the CUT

Example: The markup The `<del datetime="1999-05-10T09:36:00-0600>Summary</del>` References section contains the list of source materials. sets the time of the deletion to May 10, 1999, at 9:36 in the morning, six hours behind Coordinated Universal Time (known in the United States as Central Daylight time).

Examples: See file /html4Fd2/examples/ch10/del.htm.

<dfn> . . . </dfn> Definition of a term

Use `<dfn> . . . </dfn>` to mark terms when they appear for the first time in a Web document. The text between these opening and closing tags usually appears in italics so users can identify the first occurrence of a term or key phrase. The `<dfn>` tag takes no unique attributes.

Example: The HTML markup A `<dfn>McGuffin</dfn>, according to Alfred Hitchcock, is the central object in a film, around which the plot revolves.` sets off the term "McGuffin" in italics in most browsers.

Examples: See file /hrml4Fd2/examples/ch10/dfn.htm.

<em> . . . </em> Emphasis

The `<em> . . . </em>` tag pair provides typographic emphasis, usually rendered as italics. Use this tag wherever you need to add mild emphasis to body text. Make certain to use sparingly, both in terms of the number of emphasized words and how often text emphasis occurs. The `<em>` tag takes no unique attributes.

Example: The HTML markup `Push the <em>button</em>, Mr. Chips!` sets off the word "button" in italics in most Web browsers.

Examples: See file /html4Fd2/examples/ch10/em.htm.

<ins> . . . </ins> Inserted text

Use this tag pair to mark text that's been added since the prior version of the Web document was published.

<ins> attributes
`cite="URL"`

Points to another document that describes why the text was inserted.

Example: The markup `The <ins URL="http://www.lanw.com/doc/changes.html">References</ins> section contains the list of source materials.` underlines the word "References" in that sentence. To read the contents of the `cite` and `datetime` attributes for this tag, you must examine the HTML source.

`datetime=YYYY-MM-DDThh:mm:ssTZD`

Marks the time when you changed the document. This attribute's value must use the specific format shown here to conform to the ISO8601 time/date specification. The abbreviations shown above match the following date and time information:

- ✔ YYYY = The year
- ✔ MM = The two-digit month — for example, "03" for March
- ✔ DD = The day
- ✔ T = Indicates the beginning of the time section
- ✔ hh = The hour, in military time (0–23 hours), without a.m. or p.m. specifications
- ✔ mm = The minute
- ✔ ss = The second
- ✔ TZD = The time zone
- ✔ Z = The Coordinated Universal Time (CUT)

✔ +hh:mm = The local time that is hours (hh) and minutes (mm) ahead of the CUT

✔ -hh:mm = The local time that is hours (hh) and minutes (mm) behind the CUT

Example: The markup The <ins datetime="1999-05-10T09:36:00-0600>References</ins> section contains the list of source materials. sets the time of insertion to May 10, 1999, at 9:36 in the morning, six hours behind Coordinated Universal Time (known in the United States as Central Daylight time).

Examples: See file /html4Fd2/examples/ch10/ins.htm.

<kbd> . . . </kbd> Keyboard text

This pair of tags indicates that enclosed text should be entered at a computer keyboard. <kbd> . . . </kbd> changes the type style for all the text it contains, typically into a monospaced font like that used in character-mode computer terminal displays. Whenever you want to set off text that the user needs to type in from the body text, use <kbd> . . . </kbd>. This is different from <code>, which indicates existing program text. This is also different from <tt>, which indicates computer output. The <kbd> tag takes no unique attributes.

Example: The HTML markup Enter <kbd>route print 172*</kbd> to show all routes related to networks that begin with 172. sets the text "route print 172*" in a monospaced font. As with the <code> tags, these tags do not force a line break either before the opening <kbd> or after the closing </kbd> tag. To set off keyboard copy more visibly, use a <br> before the opening tag, and another <br> after the closing tag.

Examples: See file /html4Fd2/examples/ch10/kbd.htm.

<p> . . . </p> Paragraph

The <p> tag defines paragraph boundaries for normal text. A line break and carriage return occurs where this tag is placed. The closing tag, <p> is not currently required in HTML 4.0 (it's optional), but may be required in the next version of HTML. If the closing tag is used, it causes another line break and carriage return to occur after the <p>. Use paragraphs to break the flow of ideas or information into related chunks. Each idea or concept should appear in its own paragraph for a good writing style.

<p> attributes:
align="LEFT" *or* "CENTER" *or* "RIGHT" *or* "JUSTIFY"

Sets the alignment of the paragraph. The align type can be LEFT, CENTER, RIGHT, or JUSTIFY. The default alignment is LEFT.

The align attribute is obsolete, and will not be supported in future versions of HTML. To achieve the same effects, use a separate style sheet, <style> markup in the document <head> section (will affect all uses of the <p> tag in the document), or in a specific <p> tag to control that paragraph separately.

Example: The HTML markup <p>My kingdom for a paragraph.</p> causes a carriage return and line feed at the beginning and end of the enclosed text.

Examples: See file /html4Fd2/examples/ch10/p.htm.

<pre> . . . </pre> Preformatted text

Enclosing text within a pair of <pre> . . . </pre> tags forces the browser to reproduce the same formatting, indentation, and white space that the original text contains. This can be useful when reproducing formatted tables or other text, such as code listings, especially when other alternatives (such as table-related tags) may not work for all users' browsers.

<pre> attributes

width="number"

The value set for width specifies the maximum number of characters per line and allows the browser to select appropriate font and indentation settings. Within a <pre> . . . </pre> block, you can break lines by pressing Enter, but try to keep line lengths at 80 characters or less, because <pre> text is typically set in a monospaced font. This tag is great for presenting text-only information, or for reproducing complicated formats where the information is already available in text-only form.

Example: To conserve space, we don't give any short examples here (preformatted text examples invariably span multiple lines); please consult the examples on the CD, as indicated here.

Examples: See file /html4Fd2/examples/ch10/pre.htm.

<q> . . . </q> Quotation markup

Text placed between <q> . . . </q> tags permits you to highlight short quotations from external resources. When you use a short quote from an external resource, place it within <q> . . . </q> tags. Always attribute your sources. Remember to use the <cite> tag to mention the actual publication, if you want that information to appear on your Web document (entries for the cite attribute for <q> appear only in the HTML source code).

<q> attributes:

<q> attributes:

cite="text"

This attribute provides information about the source of the quote, but that information is only visible in the HTML source code.

Example: The HTML markup `<q cite="Thomas Paine">"Give me liberty, or give me death!"</q>` is a worthy sentiment. does not change text appearance by default in most Web browsers; to add effects, you must use style markup to do so.

Examples: See file /html4Fd2/examples/ch10/q.htm.

<samp> . . . </samp> Sample output

Use `<samp> . . . </samp>` for sequences of literal characters or to represent output from a program, script, or other data source. The `<samp>` tag takes no unique attributes. In practice, it is sometimes hard to decide when to use `<samp>` rather than `<code>` or `<kbd>`. We find this tag largely superfluous on our Web pages, but you may decide to use it if you have to distinguish among a number of different kinds of output in a document.

Example: The HTML markup `During the show, the teleprompter read <samp> Kiss your telephones! </samp> at one point.` causes Salvador Dali's maxim to appear in a monospaced font as part of the body copy. For more separation, add `<br>` tags before and after the `<samp> . . . </samp>` tags. When using multiple kinds of output in an HTML document, consider using style tags to change font selections or text colors to help readers distinguish `<code>`, `<kbd>`, and `<samp>` tagged text.

Examples: See file /html4Fd2/examples/ch10/samp.htm.

<strong> . . . </strong> Strong emphasis

Use the `<strong> . . . </strong>` tags to place strong emphasis on key words or phrases within normal body text, lists, and other text elements. This tag is designed to up the emphasis above the `<em> . . . </em>` tags. The `<strong>` tags provide the heaviest degree of inline emphasis available in HTML. Remember that overuse blunts the effect, so use emphatic text controls sparingly. The `<strong>` tag takes no unique attributes.

Example: The HTML markup `Do it <strong>now</strong>, or I'll kill you.` puts strong emphasis on the word "now." By default this shows up as bold text (the `<em>` tags produce italics by default).

Examples: See file /html4Fd2/examples/ch10/strong.htm.

_{. . .} Subscript

Use these tags to render enclosed text as a subscript, slightly lower than the surrounding text. This will be most useful when reproducing scientific or mathematical notation. The <sub> tag takes no unique attributes.

Example: The HTML markup H₂O reproduces the chemical symbol for water quite nicely.

Examples: See file /html4Fd2/examples/ch10/sub.htm.

^{. . .} Superscript

Use these tags to render enclosed text as a superscript, slightly higher than the surrounding text. This is not only useful for mathematical or scientific notation, but also for footnotes, and when working with foreign languages or proper names. The <sup> tag takes no unique attributes.

Example: The HTML markup McGuffin moves the "c" in McGuffin up from the baseline for other lowercase characters in that line, and reduces character size by one level. It's also useful for numerical exponents such as 2⁴ to represent two raised to the fourth power, or the number 16.

Examples: See file /html4Fd2/examples/ch10/sup.htm.

<var> . . . </var> Variable text

Text enclosed between the <var> . . . </var> tags is meant to highlight variable names or arguments to computer commands. Use this markup to indicate a placeholder for a value the user supplies when entering text at the keyboard (see example).

Example: The HTML markup When prompted with the <tt>Ready:</tt> string, enter <var>your first name</var> to begin the logon process. uses monospace text for the <tt> prompt, and italics for the <var> text. You may want to play with styles to make these tags even more distinctive.

Examples: See file /html4Fd2/examples/ch10/var.htm.

Mastering Many Forms of Text On-screen

If you've read the preceding section, with its alphabetical list of text control tags, you've no doubt noticed that there are four types of tags that perform similar functions. In fact, three of these tags produce monospaced text that looks the same when default settings are left unchanged; only the <var> tag looks different — it uses italics by default. These four tags are:

✔ `<code>...</code>`: meant for display of programs and code fragments

✔ `<kbd>...</kbd>`: meant for display of keyboard input

✔ `<samp>...</samp>`: meant to display literal character sequence or computer output

✔ `<var>...</var>`: meant to display variable names or command arguments, which change with user identity or circumstances

If the content on your Web pages requires that you use two or more of these tags, you'd be well advised to use HTML styles to alter their appearance somewhat, to make them a bit easier to tell apart. This could be something as simple as using the nearly-ubiquitous style attribute when invoking both kinds of text, as this code example is meant to illustrate (please assume, for our sake if not for your own, that this HTML markup occurs within the context of a well-formed document):

```
During the logon process, the program prompts you
as follows<br>
<samp>Please enter your first name:</samp><p>
Please enter your first name, then strike the Enter
key to continue:<br>
<var>your first name<var><samp>[Enter]<samp><br>
For someone named Mary, this produces the following
output:<br>
<samp>Please enter your first name:</samp>
<kbd>Mary</kbd><br>
```

In a typical Web browser (this image comes from IE 5.0), this produces the display shown in Figure 10-1. Please notice how hard it is to separate the various types of text from one another in this display.

Figure 10-1:
Without
changing
defaults for
their
appearance,
`<samp>`
and `<kbd>`
look exactly
alike.

By adding the following markup to the `<head>` section of the preceding HTML markup, you see a big difference in the version of the same text that appears in Figure 10-2 following the markup.

```
<style>
samp {font-family:Courier;
      font-weight:900;
      font-size:14 pt}
var  {font-family:Arial;
      font-weight:bold;
      color:teal}
kbd  {font-family:Lineprinter;
      font-size:12 pt;
      font-style:italic;
      color:red}
</style>
```

Figure 10-2:
With styles
defined for
`<samp>`,
`<kbd>`, and
`<var>`, the
elements
are easier to
tell apart.

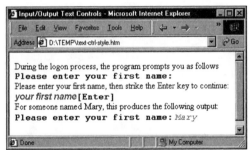

Here the `<samp>` elements appear in a heavy black Courier font at 14 points, the `<kbd>` elements appear in a 12-point Lineprinter font in red, and the `<var>` elements appear in bold Arial at the default font size in teal. All three elements are now easy to distinquish and even dense text with lots of usage is easy to follow.

The benefit of taking this approach — namely creating a `<style>` ... `</style>` section in the `<head>` of the document — comes from its application to all instances of the referenced tags in the `<body>` section. Thus, you can use all three tags as often as you like and the style definitions apply to each instance. You can investigate style markup further in Chapter 18 of this book, but hopefully this example helps explain why we keep pushing this concept!

Chapter 11

Listward Ho!

In This Chapter

▶ Writing list code

▶ Using lists effectively

*L*ists are a terrific way of delivering information concisely and distinctively. This chapter shows how to code lists and maximize their impact.

List Tags

Just like everything else in HTML, you have to know the secret words to create spiffy lists.

<dd> Definition description

<dd> denotes the descriptive or definition part of a definition list element. This element is displayed indented below the term it defines. The <dd> tag is a singleton tag, and takes no unique attributes. Use this tag for glossaries or other lists where a single term or line needs to be associated with a block of indented text.

Example: See the "Definition list" section later in this chapter.

Examples: See file /html4Fd2/examples/ch11/dd.htm.

<dir> . . . </dir> Directory list

Use these tags to enclose lists of short elements (usually shorter than 20 characters long), such as filenames or abbreviations. The <dir> tag is deprecated in HTML 4.0, and will probably not be continued in the next version of HTML 4.0. You can use the unordered list <ul> tags to do everything that <dir> can do. The <dir> tag takes no unique attributes.

Example: See the "Directory list" section later in this chapter.

Examples: See file /html4Fd2/examples/ch11/dir.htm.

<dl> . . . </dl> Definition list

Definition: <dl> encloses a collection of definition items in a definition list. You would usually use the <dd> tag for glossaries or other situations where short, left-aligned terms precede longer blocks of indented text. Browsers usually render definition lists with the term (<dt>) in the left margin and the definition (<dd>) on one or more lines indented to the right from the term. Use the <dl> . . . </dl> tags for lists where left-justified elements (for example, terms and definitions) precede longer, indented blocks of text, such as glossaries or a dictionary.

Do not use <DL> to create an indented section of text. This is syntactically invalid HTML and is not guaranteed to work.

<dl> attributes

compact

Renders a list as compactly as possible by reducing line leading and spacing. This attribute is deprecated in HTML 4.0, and may not be supported in future versions of HTML. However, HTML style markup permits control over line spacing, word spacing and even letter spacing, so this effect can easily be reproduced by associating the appropriate styles with the <dl> tag.

Example: See the "Definition list" section later in this chapter.

Examples: See file /html4Fd2/examples/ch11/dl.htm.

<dt> Definition term

<dt> denotes the term part of a definition entry. Use this tag in situations where left-justified, short entries pair up with longer blocks of indented text, such as glossaries or definition lists. The <dt> tag is a singleton tag, and takes no unique attributes.

Example: See the "Definition list" section later in this chapter.

Examples: See file /html4Fd2/examples/ch11/dt.htm.

<li> List item

The <li> denotes an element belonging to one of several HTML list styles. Such elements are treated in accordance with the list type tag within which they appear, which may be a directory list <dir>, a menu <menu>, an ordered list <ol>, or an unordered list <ul>.

<li> attributes

```
type="DISC" or "SQUARE" or "CIRCLE"
      or "1" or "a" or "A" or "i" or "I"
```

When an ordered list <ol> is used, the <li> element will be rendered with a number. You can control that number's appearance with the <type> attribute. Similarly, inside an unordered list <ul>, you can control the type of bullet displayed with <type>. You can't control <dir> and <menu> this way, because they are not required to be bulleted or numbered. In HTML 4.0, the closing </li> tag is optional, but you might want to get in the habit of using it because it may be required in the next version of HTML.

Shape types define a named shape for bullets:

- DISC uses a filled circular shape for a bullet.
- SQUARE uses a filled square shape for a bullet.
- CIRCLE uses a circular outline shape for a bullet.

Outline style types define the numbering or labeling scheme used, as they might be used in an outline:

- 1 Number using Arabic numerals (default starts with "1").
- a Enumerate using lowercase alpha characters (default starts with "a").
- A Enumerate using uppercase alpha characters (default starts with "A").
- i Enumerate using lowercase Roman numerals (default starts with "i").
- I Enumerate using uppercase Roman numerals (default starts with "I").

```
value="number"
```

Changes the count of ordered lists as they progress. Use this to re-set numbers or resequence parts of lists as needed.

Example: See the "Ordered Lists" and "Unordered Lists" sections later in this chapter.

Examples: See file /html4fd2/examples/ch11/li.htm.

<menu> . . . </menu> Menu list

These tags enclose a menu list in which each list element is typically a word or short phrase that fits on a single line. This list is rendered more compactly than most other list types. However, the <MENU> tag is deprecated in HTML 4.0, and may not be supported in future versions of HTML. By imposing length restrictions on an unordered list and using styles to force a more compact display, you can replace the functions of this tag without too much effort.

<menu> attributes

`compact`

Renders the list as compactly as possible by reducing line leading and spacing. Provides the most compact way to display information in short, simple lists. If you need to squeeze things in, use the `compact` attribute.

Example: See the "Menu list" section later in this chapter.

Examples: See file /html4fd2/examples/ch11/menu.htm.

<ol> . . . </ol> Ordered list

Creates an ordered list that numbers list elements in their order of appearance. The `type` attribute provides great flexibility in terms of how list elements may be numbered. Ordered lists work well for step-by-step instructions, or other situations where the order of presentation is important.

<ol> attributes

`type="1"` *or* `"a"` *or* `"A"` *or* `"i"` *or* `"I"`

Changes the style of the list, where:

- ✔ 1 Numbers using Arabic numerals (default starts with "1").
- ✔ a Enumerates using lowercase alpha characters (default starts with "a").
- ✔ A Enumerates using uppercase alpha characters (default starts with "A").
- ✔ i Enumerates using lowercase Roman numerals (default starts with "i").
- ✔ I Enumerates using uppercase Roman numerals (default starts with "I").

`compact`

Renders the list as compactly as possible by reducing line leading and spacing. This attribute is deprecated in HTML 4.0, and may not be supported in the next version of HTML. Use style tags to control line, word, and letter spacing, to achieve the same effects.

```
start="value"
```

Indicates the start value where list numbering or lettering should begin.

Example: See the "Ordered lists" section later in this chapter.

Examples: See file /html4Fd2/examples/ch11/ol.htm.

<ul> . . . </ul> Unordered list

These tags produce bulleted lists of items. The type attribute permits some control over bullet symbols; HTML styles support nearly any kind of bullet symbols to be used. Use bulleted lists when the order in which items appear is not important, or where sequencing plays no role.

<ul> attributes

```
compact
```

Renders the list as compactly as possible by reducing line leading and spacing. This attribute is deprecated in HTML 4.0, and may not be supported in the next version of HTML. Use style tags to control line, word, and letter spacing, to achieve the same effects.

```
type="DISC" or "SQUARE" or "CIRCLE"
```

Specify a bullet format using the type attribute. The three styles to choose from are "disc" for a closed circular bullet, "square" for an open square, and "circle" for an open bullet.

Example: See the "Unordered Lists" section later in this chapter.

Examples: See file /html4Fd2/examples/ch11/ul.htm.

Using List Structures

The preceding section presents the different types of HTML tags that can be used when building a variety of different list types. Now, we can show you a generic example of what it means to build a list structure in HTML.

Here's what's required, presented as a form of pseudo-HTML markup, to give you an idea of a simple, one-level list structure (once again, treat this as a fragment of a well-formed and complete HTML document):

```
<list-open tag: dir, dl, menu, ol, ul>
    <list element tag: li {for dir, menu, ol, ul}>
    <list element tag: dt for dl>
    <list element tag: repeat as needed>
<list-close tag: /dir, /dl, /menu, /ol, /ul>
```

Here's a verbal rendition of the set of rules that you could extract from this pseudo-HTML:

- All types of lists must begin with an opening list tag: `<dir>`, `<dl>`, `<menu>`, `<ol>`, or `<ul>`.

- Any valid list must have one or more list elements: `<dt>` for the `<dl>` list type; `<li>` for the other types: `<dir>`, `<menu>`, `<ol>`, and `<ul>`.

- All types of lists must end with a closing tag that corresponds to the opening tag: `</dir>`, `</dl>`, `</menu>`, `</ol>`, or `</ul>`.

What's more, you can mix and match list types, or nest multiple instances of the same type to create what are sometimes called "nested lists." Of course this simply means placing one list inside another, to model the multiple levels of hierarchy found in most outlines, action plans, or other multileveled lists.

In the sections that follow next, you learn about the various list types individually, after which you learn about a few interesting combinations.

Unordered lists

The unordered or bulleted list is handy for emphasizing several short lines of information. The following shows HTML markup for an unordered list with a few added bells and whistles (a change in typeface, and open circles instead of more traditional bullets). A screen shot of this code appears in Figure 11-1.

```
The following capabilities make unordered lists
peachy:
<font face="Arial">
<UL type="circle">
<LI> You can add as many elements as you need.
<LI> You can enter elements as they occur to you.
<LI> Some elements can be short.
<LI> Other elements can be long enough to become tiresome.
</UL>
```

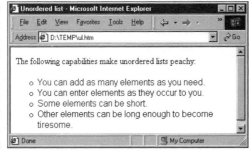

Figure 11-1:
An
unordered
list with a
bullet type
change and
a different
typeface.

Although you should keep page layouts simple, lists and even nested lists may be needed to display certain information. Use such structures intelligently and sparingly. Notice that a line break occurs when the list begins, as the ⟨ul⟩ tag is encountered. Each list item gets an automatic line break, and a paragraph break occurs (carriage return plus linefeed) when the ⟨/ul⟩ tag is identified.

The following HTML fragment shows the tags for an unordered list in a Web page body. The list serves to emphasize and separate the text lines.

```
You have reached the <I> HTML for Dummies</I> Web Pages, a
          charming, and hopefully helpful, addition to the
          WWW universe. These pages are designed to aid you
          in three key areas:<BR>
<UL>
<LI> To help you find current information on the Web about
          HTML
<LI> To provide working examples and code for all the Web
          tricks in the book
<LI> To introduce <I> HTML 4 for Dummies</I>, 2nd Edition -
          your friendliest resource for HTML material
          offline!
</UL><P>
```

Figure 11-2 shows how this appears in Internet Explorer. The bulleted list definitely emphasizes the body and adds to the visual appeal of the page.

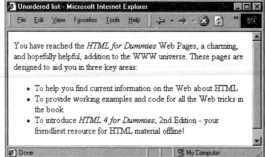

Ordered lists

An ordered or numbered list is just the thing for delivering step-by-step instructions, explaining an algorithm, or conveying other information where the order of instructions is significant. The following shows HTML markup for an ordered list with a few added bells and whistles (a change in typeface, and lowercase Roman numerals instead of more traditional Arabic numbers). A screen shot of this code appears in Figure 11-3.

```
The following attributes make ordered lists simply wonderful:
<font face="Arial">
<OL type="i">
<LI> Start at the beginning.
<LI> Make your way through the middle steps.
<LI> More middle elements are good.
<LI> Last things come last.
</UL>
```

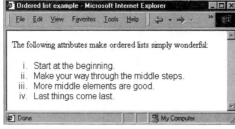

Directory list

A directory list is a format devised for lists of short elements. You'd normally use this for a list of filenames, a bill of materials, or some other list of items, components, or parts. The following HTML markup produces a list of files that also appears in Figure 11-4:

```
The following files normally appear in a Windows NT system
            directory:
<dir>
<li>boot.ini
<li>ntldr
<li>ntdetect.com
</dir>
```

Figure 11-4: HTML document with a representative directory list.

Remember that the `<dir>` . . . `</dir>` tags are deprecated in HTML 4.0. There's nothing special about this markup that you can't reproduce in exactly the same way, by substituting `<ul>` for `<dir>` and `</ul>` for `</dir>`.

Definition list

The definition list is the only list type that uses a different list element tag — namely, `<dt>` — rather than the `<li>` tag used in other list types. Otherwise, its construction is the same as the other list types, as shown in the following HTML markup that is also depicted in Figure 11-5.

```
Here's a brief glossary of list terms:
<dl>
<dt>opening list tag
<dd>the markup that begins a new list, or that indents another
            level in a nested list.
```

(continued)

(continued)

```
<dt>closing list tag
<dd>the markup that ends a simple single-level list, or that
         outdents to the previous level in a nested list.
<dt>list item
<dd>the markup that indicates a list element. Lists can
         contain an arbitrary number of such items.
</dl>
```

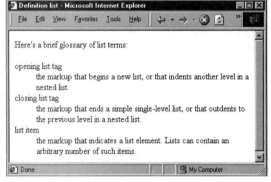

Figure 11-5:
HTML
document
with a
simple
definition
list.

Please note that the definition text associated with the `<dd>` tag is indented to the right of the left margin where the definition terms associated with the `<dt>` tag appear. Such lists provide a good way to create annotated lists of items of all kinds, where the items appear with `<dd>` tags, and the annotations with `<dt>` tags.

Menu tags

Create a list in which each element is a word or short phrase that usually fits on a single line. It is usually displayed in a more compact format than other list types. The following HTML markup is also depicted in Figure 11-6.

```
<h1>Common Edible Mollusks</h1>
<menu>
<li>Cherrystone clam
<li>Green Bearded Mussel
<li>Limpet
<li>Quohog
<li>Razor clam
</menu>
```

Remember that the `<menu>` . . . `</menu>` tags are deprecated in HTML 4.0. There's nothing special about this markup that you can't reproduce in exactly the same way, by substituting `<ul>` for `<menu>` and `</ul>` for `</menu>`.

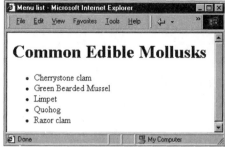

Figure 11-6:
HTML
document
with a
simple
menu list.

Nested lists

When it comes to representing hierarchical listings of information — such as tables of contents, outlines, and so forth — nesting lists within lists is just the technique to help you master such a job. Robin Cover's "SGML/XML Web Page" starts with a multilevel table of contents that helps keep its hundreds of entries well organized. A nice snippet of this information (which we've edited slightly to make it more compact) appears in Figure 11-7, after the corresponding HTML markup.

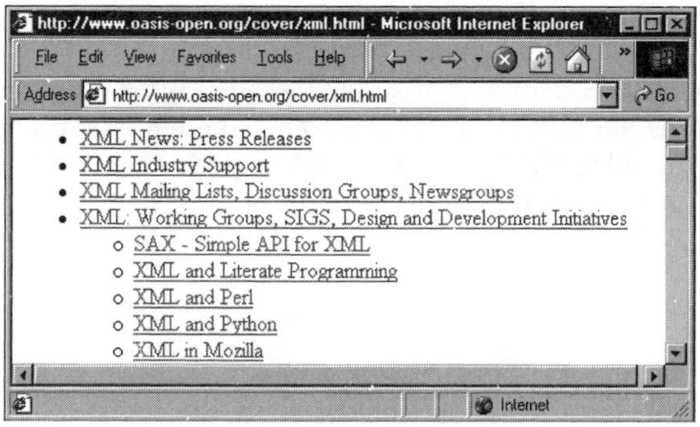

Figure 11-7:
A multi-level unordered list is a good way to organize a table of contents.

```
<li><a href="xmlNews.html">XML News: Press Releases</a></li>
<li><a href="xmlSupport.html">XML Industry Support</a></li>
<li><a href="#discussionLists">XML Mailing Lists, Discussion
        Groups, Newsgroups</a></li>
<li><a href="#techDesign">XML: Working Groups, SIGS, Design
        and Development Initiatives</a>
<ul>
```

(continued)

(continued)

```
<li><a href="#saxAPI">SAX - Simple API for XML</a></li>
<li><a href="#xmlLitProg">XML and Literate
          Programming</a></li>
<li><a href="#xmlAndPerl">XML and Perl</a></li>
<li><a href="#xmlAndPython">XML and Python</a></li>
<li><a href="#xmlInMozilla">XML in Mozilla</a></li>
</ul></li>
```

Because Mr. Cover is a proponent of valid, well-formed HTML and XML, he uses the optional ⟨/li⟩ tag to close out all list items. Notice also that this table of contents uses ⟨a⟩ . . . ⟨/a⟩ anchor tags to turn the table of contents listings into hyperlinks to the Web pages where the next layer of information resides.

When nesting lists, each sublist occurs within an outer list that's been started with its opening tag but whose closing tag is still pending. You can nest lists arbitrarily as far as HTML itself is concerned, but think about your readers when you start digging down more than three or four layers deep. Just as you will seldom need more than three or four header tags (⟨h1⟩, ⟨h2⟩, ⟨h3⟩, and ⟨h4⟩) you should seldom need to nest lists more than three or four levels deep.

But because they work equally well in older browsers as well as newer ones, and are guaranteed to accommodate readers with visual disabilities (pure text can always be turned into Braille or synthesized into speech), lists represent a powerful way to collect and organize large amounts of information. Especially for tables of contents, outlines, plans, and even textual "site maps" (a list of the titles of all the files in a Web site) nested tables offer a great way to represent and deliver the data to your readers.

Chapter 12

Character Actors

●●

In This Chapter

▶ Coloring outside the character boundaries

▶ Producing special characters

▶ Inspecting the ISO-Latin-1 character set

●●

*I*f you've seen the panoply of HTML tags and have gone through examples in Chapter 6 that included strange notations like < or °, maybe these odd locutions aren't as cryptic as they first appear. Hopefully, you now realize that they simply instruct the browser to look up these symbols and replace them with equivalent characters as the browser renders a document. The symbol < produces the less-than sign < on your computer screen, and the symbol ° produces the degree symbol °.

Entities Don't Have to Be an Alien Concept

Instructing a browser to look up entities such as the degree symbol with the string ° may leave you wondering why these contortions are necessary. Here are three important reasons:

✔ Entities let a browser represent characters that it may otherwise interpret as markup.

✔ Entities let a browser represent higher-order ASCII characters (those with codes over 127) without having to fully support higher-order ASCII or non-ASCII character types. Also, these codes support some characters that are even outside the ASCII character set altogether (as is the case with non-Roman alphabet character sets and some widely used diacritical marks).

✔ Entities increase portability of SGML documents.

Okay, so now you know what character and numeric entities are for — they let browsers display symbols that aren't part of the standard ASCII character set — like © — or display markup elements — like < and > — without the browser treating them as markup. In the end, entities let browsers represent a larger range of characters without expanding the actual character set used to write HTML. This helps browsers interpret and display pages faster, which is always a good thing.

As you travel into the land of HTML character and numeric entities, you encounter strange characters and symbols that you may never use. On the other hand, if your native language isn't English, you can probably recognize lots of diacritical marks, accents, and other character modifications that allow you to express yourself correctly!

Producing Entities

There are three special characters that are part of the code for each and every HTML entity:

- **Ampersand (&):** An & is the browser's first clue that what follows is a code for a character entity instead of an ordinary text.

- **Pound sign (#):** If the next character after & is #, then the browser knows that what follows next is a number that corresponds to the character code for a symbol to be produced on-screen. This kind of code is called a *numeric entity*.

  If the next character is anything other than the pound sign, this tells the browser that the string that follows is a symbol's name and must be looked up in a built-in table of equivalent character symbols. This is called a *character entity*. Some entities can be represented by both character and numeric entities. For example both © and © are codes for the copyright (©) symbol.

- **Semicolon (;):** When the browser sees a ; , it knows that it has come to the end of the entity. The browser then uses whatever characters or numbers that follow either the ampersand or the pound sign to perform the right kind of lookup operation and display the requested character symbol. If the browser doesn't recognize the information supplied, most browsers display a question mark (?) or some other odd character instead.

A couple of things about character and numeric entities may differ from your expectations based on what you know about HTML tags and what you may know about computer character sets:

✔ Numeric entities are case-sensitive. This means that À is different from à, so you need to reproduce character entities exactly as they appear in Tables 12-1 through 12-8. That's one reason we prefer using numeric entities — it's harder to make a mistake.

✔ Numeric codes for reproducing characters within HTML are not ASCII collating sequences; they come from the ISO-Latin-1 character set codes, as shown later in this chapter in Tables 12-1 through 12-8.

If you concentrate on reproducing characters as they appear in Tables 12-1 through 12-8 or copying the numbers that correspond to the ISO-Latin-1 numeric coding scheme, you can produce exactly the right effects on your readers' screens.

You may sometimes encounter problems when trying to represent some of the ISO-Latin-1 character codes in written or printed documentation, as we learned when creating the tables for this chapter in earlier versions of this book. Be prepared to obtain some oddball fonts or symbols to help you overcome this problem, especially for the Icelandic character codes! But what you see in this chapter should indeed be what shows up in your browser when you use the codes you see here. If not, please let us know.

Nothing Ancient about the ISO-Latin-1 HTML

The name of the character set that HTML uses is called ISO-Latin-1. The *ISO* part means that it comes from the International Standards Organization's body of official international standards — in fact, all ISO standards have corresponding numeric tags, so ISO-Latin-1 is also known as ISO 8859-1. The *Latin* part means that it comes from the Roman alphabet (A, B, C, and so on) commonly used worldwide to represent text in many different languages. The number *1* refers to the version number for this standard (in other words, this is the first version of this character set definition).

ISO-Latin-1 distinguishes between two types of entities for characters:

✔ **Character entities:** Collections of characters that represent other characters; for example, < and È show codes that stand for other characters (< and Ì).

✔ **Numeric entities:** Collections of numbers that represent characters. These are identified by a pound sign (#) that follows the ampersand. For example, < and È show a string of numbers (60 and 200) that stand for characters (< and Ì).

Table 12-1 illustrates that there are many more numeric entities than character entities. In fact, every character in the ISO-Latin-1 set has a corresponding numeric entity, but this is not true for all character entities.

As the amount and kind of information presented in Web format has grown, the need for a more extensive character entity set has become apparent. HTML 4.0 supports such an extended entity set, which includes

- ✔ Greek characters
- ✔ Special punctuation
- ✔ Letter-like characters
- ✔ Arrows
- ✔ Mathematical characters
- ✔ Special technical characters
- ✔ Playing card suits

Because the support for these other character sets is new to HTML 4.0, only browsers that support a full implementation of HTML 4.0 (Navigator 4.0 and Internet Explorer 4.0 and newer versions) can render the character entity codes found in these sets correctly.

The remainder of this chapter includes listings for all the character sets supported by HTML 4.0. Tables 12-1 through 12-8 include each character's name, applicable entity and numeric codes, and description. We begin with ISO-Latin-1 because it is fully supported by all current and most older browsers, and then continue with HTML 4.0's new character sets.

Table 12-1		The ISO-Latin-1 Character Set	
Char	**Character**	**Numeric**	**Description**
A-Z (capitals)		A - Z	A is $#65, B is $#66, and so on
a-z (lower case)		a - z	a is $#97, b is $#98, and so on
0-9 (numerals)		0 - 9	0 is $#48, 1 is $#49, and so on
			Em space, not collapsed
			En space
			Nonbreaking space
		&#00; - &#08;	Unused
		&#09;	Horizontal tab

Char	Character	Numeric	Description

		
	Line feed or new line

		&#11; - &#31;	Unused
		 	Space
!		!	Exclamation mark
"	"	"	Quotation mark
#		#	Number
$		$	Dollar
%		%	Percent
&	&	&	Ampersand
'		'	Apostrophe
(		(	Left parenthesis
)		)	Right parenthesis
*		*	Asterisk
+		+	Plus
,		,	Comma
-		-	Hyphen
.		.	Period (full stop)
/		/	Solidus (slash)
:		:	Colon
;		;	Semicolon
<	<	<	Less than
=		=	Equals
>	>	>	Greater than
?		?	Question mark
@		@	Commercial at
[		[	Left square bracket
\		\	Reverse solidus (backslash)

(continued)

Table 12-1 *(continued)*

Char	Character	Numeric	Description
]		`&#93;`	Right square bracket
^		`&#94;`	Caret
_		`&#95;`	Horizontal bar
`		`&#96;`	Grave accent
{		`&#123;`	Left curly brace
|		`&#124;`	Vertical bar
}		`&#125;`	Right curly brace
~		`&#126;`	Tilde
		`&#127;` - `&#159;`	Unused
	` `	` `	Nonbreaking space
¡	`&iexcl;`	`&#161;`	Inverted exclamation mark
¢	`&cent;`	`&#162;`	Cent
£	`&pound;`	`&#163;`	Pound sterling
¤	`&curren;`	`&#164;`	General currency
¥	`&yen;`	`&#165;`	Yen
¦	`&brvbar;`	`&#166;`	Broken vertical bar
§	`&sect;`	`&#167;`	Section
¨	`&uml;`	`&#168;`	Umlaut (dieresis)
©	`&copy;`	`&#169;`	Copyright
ª	`&ordf;`	`&#170;`	Feminine ordinal
«	`&laquo;`	`&#171`	Left angle quote, guillemet left
¬	`&not;`	`&#172;`	Not
	`&shy;`	`&#173;`	Soft hyphen
®	`&reg;`	`&#174;`	Registered trademark
¯	`&macr;`	`&#175;`	Macron accent
°	`&deg;`	`&#176;`	Degree
±	`&plusmn;`	`&#177;`	Plus or minus
2	`&sup2;`	`&#178;`	Superscript two

Char	_Character_	_Numeric_	_Description_
3	`&sup3;`	`&#179;`	Superscript three
´	`&acute;`	`&#180;`	Acute accent
µ	`&micro;`	`&#181;`	Micro
¶	`&para;`	`&#182;`	Paragraph
•	`&middot;`	`&#183;`	Middle dot
¸	`&cedil;`	`&#184;`	Cedilla
1	`&sup1;`	`&#185;`	Superscript one
º	`&ordm;`	`&#186;`	Masculine ordinal
»	`&raquo;`	`&#187;`	Right angle quote, guillemot right
¼	`&frac14;`	`&#188;`	Fraction one-fourth
½	`&frac12;`	`&#189;`	Fraction one-half
¾	`&frac34;`	`&#190;`	Fraction three-fourths
¿	`&iquest;`	`&#191;`	Inverted question mark
À	`&Agrave;`	`&#192;`	Capital A, grave accent
Á	`&Aacute;`	`&#193;`	Capital A, acute accent
Â	`&Acirc;`	`&#194;`	Capital A, circumflex accent
Ã	`&Atilde;`	`&#195;`	Capital A, tilde
Ä	`&Auml;`	`&#196;`	Capital A, dieresis or umlaut
Å	`&Aring;`	`&#197;`	Capital A, ring
Æ	`&AElig;`	`&#198;`	Capital AE diphthong (ligature)
Ç	`&Ccedil;`	`&#199;`	Capital C, cedilla
È	`&Egrave;`	`&#200;`	Capital E, grave accent
É	`&Eacute;`	`&#201;`	Capital E, acute accent
Ê	`&Ecirc;`	`&#202;`	Capital E, circumflex accent
Ë	`&Euml;`	`&#203;`	Capital E, dieresis or umlaut
Ì	`&Igrave;`	`&#204;`	Capital I, grave accent

(continued)

Table 12-1 *(continued)*

Char	Character	Numeric	Description
Í	Í	Í	Capital I, acute accent
Î	Î	Î	Capital I, circumflex accent
Ï	Ï	Ï	Capital I, dieresis or umlaut
Đ	Ð	Ð	Capital ETH, Icelandic
Ñ	Ñ	Ñ	Capital N, tilde
Ò	Ò	Ò	Capital O, grave accent
Ó	Ó	Ó	Capital O, acute accent
Ô	Ô	Ô	Capital O, circumflex accent
Õ	Õ	Õ	Capital O, tilde
Ö	Ö	Ö	Capital O, dieresis or umlaut
×	×	×	Multiply
Ø	Ø	Ø	Capital O, slash
Ù	Ù	Ù	Capital U, grave accent
Ú	Ú	Ú	Capital U, acute accent
Û	Û	Û	Capital U, circumflex accent
Ü	Ü	Ü	Capital U, dieresis or umlaut
Ý	Ý	Ý	Capital Y, acute accent
þ	Þ	Þ	Capital THORN, Icelandic
ß	ß	ß	Small sharp s, German (sz ligature)
à	à	à	Small a, grave accent
á	á	á	Small a, acute accent
â	â	â	Small a, circumflex accent
ã	ã	ã	Small a, tilde
ä	ä	ä	Small a, dieresis or umlaut
å	å	å	Small a, ring

Char	Character	Numeric	Description
æ	æ	æ	Small ae diphthong (ligature)
ç	ç	ç	Small c, cedilla
è	è	è	Small e, grave accent
é	é	é	Small e, acute accent
ê	ê	ê	Small e, circumflex accent
ë	ë	ë	Small e, dieresis or umlaut
ì	ì	ì	Small i, grave accent
í	í	í	Small i, acute accent
î	î	î	Small i, circumflex accent
ï	ï	ï	Small i, dieresis or umlaut
ð	ð	ð	Small eth, Icelandic
ñ	ñ	ñ	Small n, tilde
ò	ò	ò	Small o, grave accent
ó	ó	ó	Small o, acute accent
ô	ô	ô	Small o, circumflex accent
õ	õ	õ	Small o, tilde
ö	ö	ö	Small o, dieresis or umlaut
÷	÷	÷	Division
ø	ø	ø	Small o, slash
ù	ù	ù	Small u, grave accent
ú	ú	ú	Small u, acute accent
û	û	û	Small u, circumflex accent
ü	ü	ü	Small u, dieresis or umlaut
ý	ý	ý	Small y, acute accent
þ	þ	þ	Small thorn, Icelandic
ÿ	ÿ	ÿ	Small y, dieresis or umlaut

Table 12-2		Greek Characters	
Char	*Character*	*Numeric*	*Description*
Α	&Alpha;	&#913;	Capital letter alpha
Β	&Beta;	&#914;	Capital letter beta
Γ	&Gamma;	&#915;	Capital letter gamma
Δ	&Delta;	&#916;	Capital letter delta
Ε	&Epsilon;	&#917;	Capital letter epsilon
Ζ	&Zeta;	&#918;	Capital letter zeta
Η	&Eta;	&#919;	Capital letter eta
Θ	&Theta;	&#920;	Capital letter theta
Ι	&Iota;	&#921;	Capital letter iota
Κ	&Kappa;	&#922;	Capital letter kappa
Λ	&Lambda;	&#923;	Capital letter lambda
Μ	&Mu;	&#924;	Capital letter mu
Ν	&Nu;	&#925;	Capital letter nu
Ξ	&Xi;	&#926;	Capital letter xi
Ο	&Omicron;	&#927;	Capital letter omicron
Π	&Pi;	&#928;	Capital letter pi
Ρ	&Rho;	&#929;	Capital letter rho
Σ	&Sigma;	&#931;	Capital letter sigma
Τ	&Tau;	&#932;	Capital letter tau
Υ	&Upsilon;	&#933;	Capital letter upsilon
Φ	&Phi;	&#934;	Capital letter phi
Χ	&Chi;	&#935;	Capital letter chi
Ψ	&Psi;	&#936;	Capital letter psi
Ω	&Omega;	&#937;	Capital letter omega
α	&alpha;	&#945;	Small letter alpha
β	&beta;	&#946;	Small letter beta

Char	Character	Numeric	Description
γ	γ	γ	Small letter gamma
δ	δ	δ	Small letter delta
ε	ε	ε	Small letter epsilon
ζ	ζ	ζ	Small letter zeta
η	η	η	Small letter eta
θ	θ	θ	Small letter theta
ι	ι	ι	Small letter iota
κ	κ	κ	Small letter kappa
λ	λ	λ	Small letter lambda
μ	μ	μ	Small letter mu
ν	ν	ν	Small letter nu
ξ	ξ	ξ	Small letter xi
o	ο	ο	Small letter omicron
π	π	π	Small letter pi
ρ	ρ	ρ	Small letter rho
ς	ς	ς	Small letter final sigma
σ	σ	σ	Small letter sigma
τ	τ	τ	Small letter tau
υ	υ	υ	Small letter upsilon
φ	φ	φ	Small letter phi
χ	χ	χ	Small letter chi
ψ	ψ	ψ	Small letter psi
ω	ω	ω	Small letter omega
θ	ϑ	ϑ	Small letter theta
ϒ	ϒ	ϒ	Upsilon with hook
ϖ	ϖ	ϖ	Pi

Table 12-3		Special Punctuation	
Char	*Character*	*Numeric*	*Description*
•	`&bull;`	`&#8226;`	Bullet
...	`&hellip;`	`&#8230;`	Horizontal ellipsis
′	`&prime;`	`&#8242;`	Prime
″	`&Prime;`	`&#8243;`	Double prime
‾	`&oline;`	`&#8254;`	Overline
/	`&frasl;`	`&#8260;`	Fraction slash

Table 12-4		Letter-Like Characters	
Char	*Character*	*Numeric*	*Description*
℘	`&weierp;`	`&#8472;`	Script capital P
ℑ	`&image;`	`&#8465;`	Blackletter capital I
ℜ	`&real;`	`&#8476;`	Blackletter capital R
™	`&trade;`	`&#8482;`	Trademark
ℵ	`&alefsym;`	`&#8501;`	Alef

Table 12-5		Arrow Characters	
Char	*Character*	*Numeric*	*Description*
←	`&larr;`	`&#8592;`	Left arrow
↑	`&uarr;`	`&#8593;`	Up arrow
→	`&rarr;`	`&#8594;`	Right arrow
↓	`&darr;`	`&#8595;`	Down arrow
↔	`&harr;`	`&#8596;`	Left-right arrow
↵	`&crarr;`	`&#8629;`	Down arrow with corner left
⇐	`&lArr;`	`&#8656;`	Left double arrow

Char	Character	Numeric	Description
⇑	⇑	⇑	Up double arrow
⇒	⇒	⇒	Right double arrow
⇓	⇓	⇓	Down double arrow
⇔	⇔	⇔	Left-right double arrow

Table 12-6		**Mathematical Characters**	
Char	**Character**	**Numeric**	**Description**
∀	∀	∀	For all
∂	∂	∂	Partial differential
∃	∃	∃	There exists
∅	∅	∅	Empty set
Δ	∇	∇	Nabla
∈	∈	∈	Element of
∉	∉	∉	Not an element of
∋	∋	∋	Contains as member
π	∏	∏	n-ary product
Σ	∑	∑	n-ary sumation
-	−	−	Minus
*	∗	∗	Asterisk operator
√	√	√	Square root
∝	∝	∝	Proportional to
∞	∞	∞	Infinity
∠	∠	∠	Angle
∧	∧	ࢳ	Logical and
∨	∨	ࢴ	Logical or
∪	∪	∪	Union

(continued)

Table 12-6 *(continued)*

Char	Character	Numeric	Description
∫	`&int;`	`&#8747;`	Integral
∴	`&there4;`	`&#8756;`	Therefore
∼	`&sim;`	`&#8764;`	Tilde operator
≅	`&cong;`	`&#8773;`	Approximately equal to
≈	`&asymp;`	`&#8776;`	Almost equal to
≠	`&ne;`	`&#8800;`	Not equal to
≡	`&equiv;`	`&#8801;`	Identical to =
≤	`&le;`	`&#8804;`	Less than or equal to
≥	`&ge;`	`&#8805;`	Greater than or equal to
⊂	`&sub;`	`&#8834;`	Subset of
⊃	`&sup;`	`&#8835;`	Superset of
⊄	`&nsub;`	`&#8836;`	Not a subset of
⊆	`&sube;`	`&#8838;`	Subset of or equal to
⊇	`&supe;`	`&#8839;`	Superset of or equal to
⊕	`&oplus;`	`&#8853;`	Circled plus
⊗	`&otimes;`	`&#8855;`	Circled times
⊥	`&perp;`	`&#8869;`	Up tack
•	`&sdot;`	`&#8901;`	Dot operator

Table 12-7   Technical Characters

Char	Character	Numeric	Description
⌈	`&lceil;`	`&#8968;`	Left ceiling
⌉	`&rceil;`	`&#8969;`	Right ceiling
⌊	`&lfloor;`	`&#8970;`	Left floor
⌋	`&rfloor;`	`&#8971;`	Right floor
⟨	`&lang;`	`&#9001;`	Left-pointing angle bracket
⟩	`&rang;`	`&#9002;`	Right-pointing angle bracket

Table 12-8		Playing Card Symbols	
Char	*Character*	*Numeric*	*Description*
♠	&spades;	&#9824;	Black spade suit
♣	&clubs;	&#9827;	Black club suit
♥	&hearts;	&#9829;	Black heart suit
♦	&diams;	&#9830;	Black diamond suit

One thing to note about using this information: If you must frequently work with character or numeric entities in your documents, it's easier to use some kind of HTML editing tool to handle character replacements automatically. Or look for a file-oriented search-and-replace utility that you can use as a post-processing step on your files. You can find a variety of search and replace utilities if you look in the HTML Accessories category at

www.tucows.com

Appendix C covers HTML-related authoring and editing tools for a variety of platforms. If you want to be a serious Web developer or often need to use character codes in your pages, please check out the tools that are available for your platform. Such tools can save you time and effort and make you a happier, more productive webmaster.

Part IV
Shaping Your Design

The 5th Wave   By Rich Tennant

VISUAL WEB DEVELOPMENT TEAM

"Give him air! Give him air! He'll be okay. He's just been exposed to some raw HTML code. It must have accidently flashed across his screen from the server."

In this part . . .

Here, we cover some of the more advanced aspects of Web page design. To start, we show you how to combine what you've learned to approach and appreciate complex Web pages, and to create your own complicated Web confections. Next, you learn the ins and outs of building and using tables in your Web pages, for effects that can combine text and graphics in all kinds of interesting ways. Beyond tables come image maps, where you learn how to turn an ordinary graphical image into a Website navigation tool. After that, it's time to tackle the joys and sorrows of HTML frames, and what multiple frames can do for your Web site. In short, a whirlwind tour of some really snazzy stuff!

Chapter 13

Going High-Rise: Linking Complex Pages

● ●

In This Chapter

▶ Expanding your home page into a Web

▶ Touring the inside of your documents and local Web

▶ Jumping to remote sites

▶ Nesting lists

▶ Analyzing sophisticated Web pages

▶ Animating .GIFs

● ●

*J*ust for grins, let's get a little ahead of ourselves: Imagine you've worked up a trim, efficient home page, diligently honed by a disciplined use of the KISS (Keep It Simple, Sergeant) principle. It's nice, it's simple — it's only one screen. An urge to grow it bigger takes root: You want your site to compare favorably to all that wonderful stuff you've seen out there on the Web, right? That's pretty natural — and you don't have to kiss off the KISS principle, either. After all, *simple* is a relative term. (Ever suspect that some people have *very* simple relatives? Just kidding.)

Your single Web page can expand into a full blown *Web presence* (an ambitious term for a Web site that aspires to greater substance and complexity). But the more pages you add, the harder it gets for your users to find their way around. While you're growing a Web, your most important job is to make your users' journey through it as enjoyable as possible. Okay, pop quiz: *How do you do that?* Killer content? Fast-loading, appropriate graphics? Knockout organization? Easy navigation? Relevant links? Keeping It Simple, Schoolkids? *Right — all of the above.* You *have* been awake the whole time. (If you had to go back and brush up on the last 12 chapters, that's fine too; all quizzes here are open-book.) Now you get to put these principles to use.

This chapter helps you spin a complex Web without getting tangled up. Then it's virtual road-trip time as we visit some advanced Web sites and comment instructively on their elements and layout.

There's No Place Like Home

Home isn't only your home page, any more than it's only your home town. Your turf in cyberspace is more like a local system of planets orbiting your home page. Web surfers may arrive from afar to find the information you offer, but even a site of rare and fantastic beauty can put off users if navigating it is too hard. That's why you need a clear mental picture of your site as a fully developed system, well organized and free of drifting junk, *before* you start expanding things.

Organizing in style

If you pay close attention to your content, after a while it should start to gravitate toward an appropriate style of organization — in fact, it may demand a particular style. Hierarchical style, linear style, and interlinked combinations of these two styles are the standard organizational structures used in most Webs. These Web structures are illustrated in Figures 13-1, 13-2, and 13-3.

It's a straightforward process if you want to "webify" an existing linear document, but that's a one-way street. A random collection of ideas and concepts, wired up willy-nilly to each other, makes a godawful linear document, a reasonably awful Web page, and not much sense to the user. When you design and use links — whether within your site or among other Web documents — make sure they are relevant to the content, reflect the organization of your site, and enhance interconnectedness for easy navigation.

Hierarchical structure: So spreads the tree

The *hierarchical* (or *tree*) *structure* is the basis of most Web designs (see Figure 13-1). It's logical, familiar-looking to most computer users (think of hard-disk file trees or GUI help systems), and best of all, easy for users to navigate. It's even easier to use when you put a link back to the home page on each page. It's a reliable structure for your documents, especially if you're just starting your brilliant career as a webmaster.

Hierarchical information starts abstract and gets specific. A table of contents on your home page represents the most general *(root)* level of the tree structure, getting to the most detailed content as the tree branches out to its outermost leaves.

Figure 13-1:
A
hierarchical
structure
looks like a
family tree.

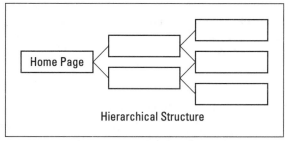

Hierarchical Structure

Your content dictates the divisions of the tree. If you try some sample "paths" to particular topics, it's easy to set them up as tree branches. For example, if you were building a hierarchical directory to organize information about a company's equipment, you might start at the most abstract level (say, *Equipment* just to be original). The branches would narrow down to specifics by progressively excluding characteristics.

So where would you put the hot red convertible on the Equipment tree? A sample "path" might start from *Equipment* (everything the company uses) and narrow down the characteristics as the tree branches out:

Equipment/Transportation/Cars/Convertibles/In "Howdy, Officer" Red

Our sample "path" could be expanded into a tree with ease, starting with the most general level and indenting our way down to specifics:

Equipment

> Office Furniture
>
> *Transportation*
>
> > Business Jets
> >
> > *Cars*
> >
> > > Minivans
> > >
> > > *Convertibles*
> > >
> > > > In Queasy Feeling Pink
> > > >
> > > > *In "Howdy, Officer" Red*

By sheer coincidence (yeah, right), that's exactly the way the "path" of a good old-fashioned DOS command used to work, showing the computer how to navigate the treelike directory structure from the general to the specific. Each level represents a choice: *Go here and not there.*

Here hyperlinks add a new wrinkle to the hierarchy: You can include interesting links between seemingly unrelated branches to better inform your users. For example, if the company has just painted its business jets Queasy Feeling Pink to match the pink convertibles, you could create a link to the Business Jets page. Your users could jump there with ease and read the exciting details.

Also, try providing multiple links to individual pages. If the company has started painting the office furniture pink, a link could help your users jump from Office Furniture to the Queasy Feeling Pink page. There they could see the color in all its glory, read *more* exciting details, and think about selling their stock (just kidding).

The hierarchical structure is reassuringly familiar to a typical user, works much like the index of a book (actively so, if you add some well-chosen links), and can also serve as a table of contents.

Linear structure: You've heard this line before

Simple and *booklike,* but also *rigid* and *confining,* are common descriptions of the linear structure (see Figure 13-2). If your information presents a series of steps or follows a process from start to finish, linear structure is a fitting choice for your document's organization. A linear structure keeps users on track and out of trouble. Here, you can make good use of links to "next page," "previous page," and "top or start page."

Figure 13-2:
Linear structure goes from start to finish, one step at a time.

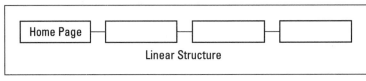

As with the hierarchical structure, effective use of links helps guide and orient your users. Be sure to put links to your home page (or to a starting point) on each page in a linear structure. Without such links, users who drop into the middle of your site can use only their browser's controls to bail out. Of course, if you trap them like this, they probably *will* talk about your site on the Net, but the talk won't be exactly flattering. (Not to put too fine a point on it, think *roast* and *flame-broil.*)

Careful placement of navigational clues *on each Web page you create* can stop the heartbreak of linklessness. For a characteristically modest example of a good navigational style, check out our LANWrights Web site at www.lanw.com.

The horror of the missing link

Hypertext linking is the most time-consuming part of HTML document development. Do it well, and your users will love you forever. Omit it or overdo it, and the consequences are too scary to imagine. (We get into them anyway, later in this chapter. Stay tuned.)

If you have extensive information on related subjects as you compose your text, put a few hyperlinks in it that can take users to specific paragraphs in other pages (*and back again to where they left off*). But don't get carried away; too much linkage can interrupt the flow of your text, making the train of thought hard to hang on to and the site easier to get lost in. A lost user is one you may have lost for good.

Keep in mind that readers can enter your Web space from somewhere other than your home page, so make sure to provide navigational clues for *jumped-in* users. You want them to find your home page (or other relevant pages) easily. Otherwise a user can feel about as welcome as a burglar. Imagine: You get an interesting URL by e-mail from some cohort who says, "Check out this page." You click and find yourself in the middle of the content, blundering around because nobody left you a link to the home page.

When you build a complex Web structure, always, always, *always* put a link to your home page on each page.

The WWW itself is a Web structure (see Figure 13-3), but it's also a loosely linked environment that allows fantastic freedom of movement and free-flowing design. Paradoxically, providing appropriate structure (without constraining users' freedom to explore) enables you to preserve that spontaneity and make good use of the Web's characteristics.

It's also a great idea to reproduce the URL for each page in its footer in small type. If you provide this data, users can return to any specific page in your Web by using that URL later on, even if they didn't add it to their bookmarks.

It's story (board) time, boys and girls!

As you may recall from Chapter 5, pencil and paper still have their uses. (You *did* sketch your home page, right? Excellent.) Time to pick them up again and draw your Web site's structure. For a schema on the scale of a personal Web page, pencil and paper should do nicely. Larger, more complex sites may require some more specialized and powerful tools. Read on for the details!

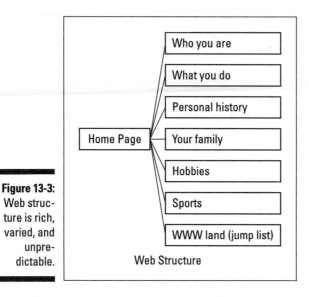

Figure 13-3:
Web struc-
ture is rich,
varied, and
unpre-
dictable.

First Things First — List 'em Out

Make a list of the major pieces of information you want to include in your Web site. These major points will probably turn into links on your home page and may be similar to the following:

- Who you are
- What you do
- Personal history
- Your family
- Hobbies
- Sports
- Your adventures in WWW land (jump list)

Sketch the Web

In the current example, it's good to start simple, with relatively few topics to consider. A combination of structures — hierarchical with some considered Web links — looks appropriate. This structure should look familiar, especially if you've done some file-management housework in your hard disk's directories.

Once you've got your sketch, use it to analyze your home page. You'll see some potential links that aren't readily apparent from looking at the HTML. For example, the "Who you are" page can be hyperlinked to the "What you do," "Personal history," and "Sports" pages; the "Your family" page is a natural to link with the "Hobbies" and "Sports" pages. And of course, remember to link all these secondary pages directly to the "Home Page." (We know, nag, nag, nag. But mark our words, you'll thank us for it someday.)

All a board — the whole story

A simple sketch of a Web site has its virtues — it fits so nicely on a cocktail napkin — but it can't provide enough information for you to fully visualize your site. Of course, you *could* try conjuring up a detailed mental picture of, say, eight separate pages — right down to all the elements and links specific to each one — in your head. (Hurts, doesn't it?) Save a little on aspirin; prepare a *storyboard* for your pages — a sequence of sketches that look like the Sunday funnies and show you how an event develops through time.

You've seen the results of storyboards — every movie, TV show, and comic book gets that treatment before any production takes place. Producing a set of Web pages is a lot like making a TV show, especially if you think of each Web page as a separate scene. Over time, you'll see an entire collection of Web documents and associated materials evolving from your work — resembling a whole season's worth of TV episodes. (And here you thought you were only doing a single show.)

Stick 'em up

To prepare a storyboard, you'll have to abandon the cocktail napkins, but the process is simple: Sketch the layout of each Web page separately, with the URLs for links written on each one. Some Web authors can diagram a small Web on a white marker board, using colored pens to show different types of links, forms, or other HTML elements.

For more complex Webs, use a sheet of paper (or a large index card) for each Web page, some string to represent links, and some push pins. Oh, yeah, you'll need a place you can spread out the sketches and move them around — say, a large bulletin board (no, not a BBS — an actual board covered with cork, like the ones in prehistoric times).

This method allows complex arrangements that you can change easily. (They don't even disappear if the power goes off. What a concept!) If you attach the text of each Web page to its layout sheet, the storyboard method is also invaluable for identifying potential hypertext links. Whenever you create a Web of more than a handful of pages, do a storyboard. It can save you much more time than it takes initially, and after you finish, you may find it has helped save your sanity as well.

Bringing out the power tools

Of course, some Web authors — practiced adepts of the information age — are more comfortable using software when things start getting complicated. We just happen to have some nifty Web-site management tools on the CD-ROM tucked into this book's back pocket. Some of them work like gang-busters for design and storyboarding, as well as for the maintenance and update phases after your site is fully realized. And here's a hot tip: Commercial software products like FrontPage 2000 or HotDog Pro often receive favorable mention in this category of tools.

Anchors Bring Moor to Your Documents

Okay, we *did* say it wasn't too terrible to create Web pages spanning up to three screens, *provided* your information demands extra room and you've already put the most important information on the first screen. Under pressure, we'll even admit that it might be okay to expand your home page to more than one screen — if you carefully drop your anchors and don't go overboard on images.

Intra or inter?

You can use two different *anchor tag attributes* for movement within your pages. Each has its own name and method:

- ✔ **Intradocument linking** provides viewers with links to specific parts within a particular Web page. Use the `name="text"` anchor to provide the destination for an `href="#label"` tag.

- ✔ **Interdocument linking** uses the standard `href="url"` tag to send users jumping from page to page.

If you want to mark a spot at the top of an HTML page so that you can link to that spot specifically later, you'd use code that looks something like this:

```
<a name="top"></a>
```

You don't even have to put any text between the `<a>...</a>` tag because you're just using the tag to mark a particular location in the document, not create a hyperlink. To make a link to this spot, you'd use this code:

```
<a href="#top">Back to top</a>
```

Notice the pound sign (#) before the word *top* in the `href=` attribute? This nifty mechanism lets the browser know that it needs to look within the current document for the spot named "top" and jump back there when the user clicks on the text `Back to top`. Cool huh? We think so, too.

When browsers hit the links

Normally, you must note the important distinction between in*ter*document and in*tra*document linking when you use a browser to follow links. Browsers can show some, ah, *interesting* quirks that you can either exploit or rein in, depending on your site's needs:

- To jump to a specific location within another page, you can combine both interdocument with intradocument linking. To do so, you'd use the `href="url#label"` tag.

- Normally, intradocument linking takes your viewers to places *other* than the default top-of-page. You can land them at the top of the page, safe and sound, if you put a named anchor there and the URL specifies this anchor as the destination of the link.

- Most browsers, when they follow an interdocument link, land your readers on the first line of a target document. If you want to make sure they get to that first line every time, you might want to place a named anchor that says *Go here and nowhere else.*

- If you put a named anchor near the bottom of a document, most browsers won't bring it up to the first line on-screen. (More about this shortly.)

Moral: A nice, tight, relevant linkage can often depend on a savvy use of anchors to bind the browser to your purpose.

Advanced intradocument linking

When you establish an intradocument link, setting an anchor with the `name="text"` attribute provides a destination for the link. If you think users may find a heading within a specific page immediately relevant or important, you can add an anchor tag next to it with a relevant `name` attribute and create a link to it.

Allow us to offer a self-effacing example of how you might use the `name="text"` attribute in anchor tags. Voilá — the LANWrights Corporate Overview page. An HTML line in this document that looks much like the following recurs in four locations, before each of that document's major headings, to speed users' transitions among them:

```
<center>
 <a href="#history">Corp History</a>
 <a href="#svcs">Services/Capabilities</a>
 <a href="#rate">Rates</a>
</center>
```

This HTML code creates a navigation bar for your intradocument text links and gives you a way to select major headings on the page that may not be visible on-screen just yet. This internal navigation bar is shown in Figure 13-4, just beneath the top-of-page logo.

Figure 13-4:
An internal navigation bar helps users jump around inside a document.

The unique quirks of intradocument linking

You are the captain of your fate, and the author of your page — the one who controls how your information is displayed and how your document is linked. Set your anchors correctly, and your users will go exactly where you say they should go. (For example, if a user selects the text that reads `Services/Capabilities` on the LANWrights page, the result is an instant jump to the "LANWrights Services/Statement of Capabilities" heading.) But beware: Computer programs are nothing if not literalists. If the browser can't find a named anchor, you get the default instead, which is to land at the top of the document. And browsers can get muddled looking for the anchor.

If you put an anchor near (or at) the very bottom of a document, for example, most browsers do *not* bring the named anchor to the first line on the screen. This is because the browser usually renders a full screen of text, and you've sent it looking for a piece of a full screen. Thus, if the anchor is near the bottom of a document, the link may drop you near the bottom of the screen, rather than the very bottom of the document itself.

Moral: Even absolute power has its limits.

Table of Contents links

You can use intradocument links and the `name="text"` attribute to create a really jumpin' table of contents (TOC) for long documents. Providing a linked TOC takes a little more time, but it's a great way to impress your users (provided, of course, that you remember to provide a link back to the TOC after each block of text in the destination document).

The following HTML code illustrates how to use the TOC links within a large document:

```
<!- Make this an anchor for return jumps.->
<p>
 <a name="toc">Table of Contents</a>
</p>

<!- This is the link to the section 1. below.->
<p>
 <a href="#sec1">Section 1.</a><br>
 <a href="#sec2">Section 2.</a><br>
 <a href="#sec3">Section 3.</a><br>
</p>

<!- This is a named anchor called "SEC1".->
<a name="sec1"></a>
 <h2>CFR Section 1.</h2>
<p>Text of section 1 is here.</p>

<!- This is a link back to the TOC at the top
     of the page->
<p>
 <a href="#toc">(TOC)</a>
</p>

<a name="sec2"></A>
 <h2>CFR Section 2.</h2>
<p>Text of section 2 is here.</p>

<p>
 <a href="#toc">(TOC)</a>
</p>

<a name="sec3"></A>
 <h2>CFR Section 3.</h2>
<p>Text of section 3 is here.</p>

<p>
 <a href="#toc">(TOC)</a>
</p>
```

Seeing the (TOC) after each text section may seem strange at first, but your users quickly become accustomed to this method of intradocument linking (see Figure 13-5). We recommend using this approach for longer, more complex documents or for a collection of related documents, but not for shorter pieces. A ubiquitous TOC in a short document may seem obtrusive to your users.

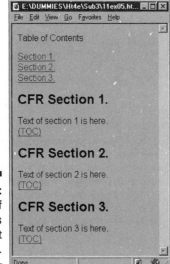

Figure 13-5:
Table of Contents and text links.

If you are thorough, consistent, and a stickler for uniformity, you can use this same general method to link just about anything to anything else within a single HTML document. It may look strange when written in HTML, but it works.

To keep the browser from becoming terminally confused, use the `"text"` part of each `name="text"` tag *only once per document*. Otherwise the browser gives up in frustration and deposits your users at the top of the page (the default for all unrecognized text anchors) yet again.

Such, O seeker, is the mystic secret behind creating hypertext links within a particular paragraph.

You should name named anchors with text starting with a character from the set {a-z, A-Z}. They should never be exclusively numeric, like `<a name="12">blah</a>`. Make sure to give anchors unique names within any single document. Anchor names are case-sensitive and space sensitive, so `name="Three Stooges"` is not the same as `name="ThreeStooges"` is not the same as `name="THREESTOOGES"`. You get the idea.

Jumping to Remote Pages

Yes, you too can amaze and amuse your users with the flashiest trick this side of teleportation — hypermedia links that take them from text in your pages directly to other Web sites (oh, yeah, and back again). Although you can't create `name="text"` anchors in text at remote sites, you may be able to use some of the anchors already in place there. If you find a linked TOC at another site, for example, you can reference the same links that it uses.

If you can link to any part of a remote page by using your browser, you can copy that link into the text of your Web pages. Just make sure you include the *full* URL in the `href="url"` tag you use to make the link.

Hypertext links to outside resources

Links to Web sites outside your own Web do require that you mind your *P*s, *Q*s, and URLs if they're going to work properly. Specifically, interdocument links to remote sites require *fully qualified URLs,* such as the following modest example:

```
<p>
URL: <a href="http://www.lanw.com/html4dum/
    html4dum.htm">
        http://www.lanw.com/html4dum/html4dum.htm</a>
<br>
Text - Copyright &copy; 1995-1999 Ed Tittel, &amp;
        Natanya Pitts.
<br>
Dummies Design and Art - Copyright &copy; 1995-1999
IDG Books Worldwide, Inc. 

<br>
Web Layout - Copyright &copy; 1995-1999
<a href="http://www.lanw.com/">LANWrights</a>
<br>
Revised - April 1, 1999
</p>
```

The two links (you can spot them by their `href` tags) connect the *HTML 4 For Dummies* home page to itself and to the LANWrights Web site. Wait a minute — why connect the page to itself? Doesn't it *know* where it is?

Well, yes, but there's method in the madness. Including the page's own URL as a link serves two purposes: (1) It shows the user the complete (and correct) URL for your page, and (2) it allows direct linking if users save this page's HTML source to their own computers.

All these tags and links make for rough sledding when you're trying to read the actual HTML source code for your page — unless you view them through a browser, that is. We illustrate this very cool technique in Figure 13-6.

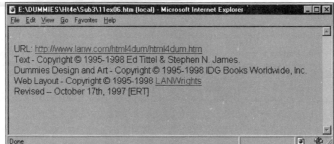

URL: http://www.lanw.com/html4dum/html4dum.htm
Text - Copyright © 1995-1998 Ed Tittel & Stephen N. James.
Dummies Design and Art - Copyright © 1995-1998 IDG Books Worldwide, Inc.
Web Layout - Copyright © 1995-1998 LANWrights
Revised -- October 17th, 1997 [ERT]

Figure 13-6:
External
links.

The browser identifies hypertext words by applying a different color, under-lining, or both. You can even specify which; use your browser's preference settings.

Jump pages

The term *jump page* refers to a Web page whose content is primarily a list of URLs that link to other Web pages, usually remote sites. HTML list tags are invaluable for creating visually pleasing (and easily understood) lists of links. Because their content is heavy on the hyperlinks, jump pages (also known as *hotlists*) look and function differently from basic Web pages. A hotlist is great for quick scanning and be-there-yesterday Web travel, but it's not really for general reading (unless your users like stories with seriously sparse descrip-tion, no characters, and no plot). Think of it as a cyberspaceport.

If you're going to have a hotlist on your site, set it apart by giving it some spe-cial visual treatment. Use icon images and spacer lines to separate the list into sections. Carefully choose the words you use for each hyperlink; they should, in effect, sum up or suggest the main point of the information to which the link itself refers.

When you type in the URLs for your links, we strongly recommend that you first link to the destination URLs by using your browser. Then highlight, copy, and paste the URLs directly into your HTML file to cut down on typos and syntax errors. (That sense of déjà vu does not deceive you; we've mentioned this before. It was relevant here too.)

A special <link>

The <link> tag provides information that links the current Web page to other Web pages or to other URL resources. When you want to be sure that your Web pages tell browsers and other software about themselves, put a <link> in the <head>...</head> section.

The <link> tag is primarily used these days to link style sheets to Web pages. Check out Chapter 18 for more information on this quick but powerful way to assign one style sheet to a multitude of Web pages.

Nesting Instinct (Lists within Lists)

The longer the Web page, the greater the risk that your users can space out from too much sameness. As you (no doubt) remember from Chapter 2, human memory is largely a filter. Most users automatically toss 90 percent of Web page content right out the airlock — and information-highway-hypnosis probably aggravates the old heave-ho. You want to keep visual diversity high by using text formatting. If you are preparing your Web site for the newer browser versions, you can break up visual monotony by using tables and frames (Chapters 14 and 16) to format your text.

On the Web (as in life), however, not everybody has the latest version of what works. Older versions of GUI browsers and text-only browsers understand the more basic HTML formatting: headings, emphasized text (bold, strong, font size), and indented lists. To offer some hospitality to users who have older browsers, try using a few features in your Web page that trace their lineage back to pre-Web antiquity. A classic example is the *nested list* — lists within lists that create the familiar, comforting outline form when displayed by most browsers. Figure 13-7 shows how a good old nested list looks (cookies and milk optional).

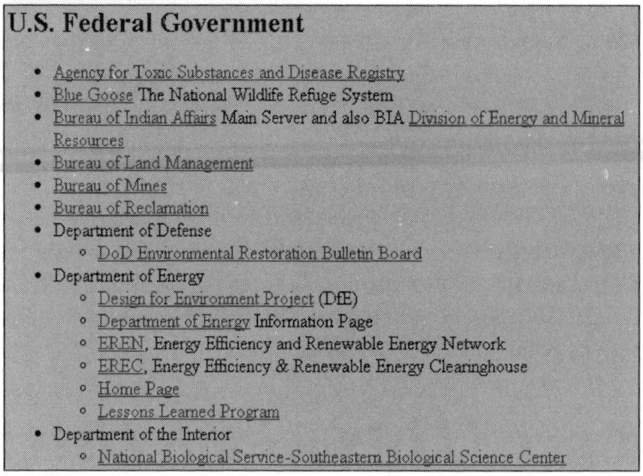

Figure 13-7:
Nested list
example.

The following HTML code created the browser display shown in Figure 13-7.
As you look through this HTML, remember that you see only a fragment, not
the whole thing:

```
<h2>U.S. Federal Government</h2>
<ul>
<li>
   <a href="http://atsdr1.atsdr.cdc.gov:8080/
     atsdrhome.html">Agency for Toxic Substances
     and Disease Registry </a>
</li>
<li>
   <a href="http://bluegoose.arw.r9.fws.gov/">
     Blue Goose </a> The National Wildlife Refuge
     System
</li>
<li>
   <a href="http://info.er.usgs.gov/doi/
     bureau-indian-affairs.html">Bureau of Indian Affairs</a>
     Main Server and also BIA <br>
   <a href="http://snake2.cr.usgs.gov/">
     Division of Energy and Mineral Resources</a>
</li>
<li>
   <a href="http://info.er.usgs.gov/doi/
     bureau-land-management.html">
     Bureau of Land Management</a>
</li>
<li>
   <a href="http://www.usbm.gov/">Bureau of Mines</a>
```

```
</li>
<li>
  <a href="http://info.er.usgs.gov/doi/
     bureau-of-reclamation.html">Bureau of Reclamation</a>
</li>

<li>Department of Defense
    <ul>
      <li>
        <a href="http://www.dtic.dla.mil/envirodod/
           envirodod.html"> DoD Environmental Restoration
           Bulletin Board</a>
      </li>
    </ul>
<li>Department of Energy
    <ul>
      <li>
        <a href=http://w3.pnl.gov:2080/DFE/home.html>
           Design for Environment  Project</a> (DfE)
      </li>
      <li>
        <a href="http://web.fie.com/web/fed/doe/">
        Department of Energy</A> Information Page
      </li>
      <li>
        <a href="http://www.eren.doe.gov/ee/ee.html">EREN</a>,
        Energy Efficiency and Renewable Energy Network
      </li>
      <li>
        <a href="http://www.nciinc.com/~erec">EREC</a>,
        Energy Efficiency & Renewable Energy Clearinghouse
      </li>
      <li>
        <a href="http://www.doe.gov">Home Page</a>
      </li>
      <li>
        <a href=http://venus.hyperk.com/trl/ll/ll.html>
           Lessons Learned Program</a>
      </li>
    </ul>
<li>Department of the Interior
    <ul>
        <li>
          <a href="http://www.nfrcg.gov/">
             National Biological Service-Southeastern
             Biological Science Center</a>
        </li>
    </ul>
</li>
</ul>
```

Pretty healthy fragment. Have another look: Carefully track the list *start tags* (`<ul>`) and *end tags* (`</ul>`). Directly under the U.S. Federal Government heading, you see a start tag; at the bottom of the listing, you see its end tag. Placing the tags this way indents all the items between the tags, fills 'em fulla bullets (one each), and marks them with `<li>` tags (as in *list item,* see?). This is a normal unordered list. But what about all items that are indented a second time and preceded by a box rather than a bullet, you ask? (Oh, a wiseguy, eh?)

Another pair of list tags (one pair each) contains each of those twice-indented sections. For example, the start tag for the second-level list appears immediately under the Department of Defense heading; its end tag occurs immediately before the Department of Energy heading. The text between them, `DoD Environmental Restoration Bulletin Board`, is marked with an `<li>` tag. Seeing that tag, the browser (in particular, Netscape Navigator) indents the item farther and places a box in front of it.

Some HTML 4.0-aware browsers keep track of the number of nests you use and change the bullets for each successive nesting. Bullet points become blocks or other symbols. You can also use the style tag to specify a symbol for each level in your list. It may be easier to visualize nested lists without the `<li>` lines:

```
<ul>Start level 1.
    <ul>Start level 2.
        <ul>Start level 3.
        </ul>End level 3.
    </ul>End level 2.
</ul>End level 1.
```

Nested lists are a good way to instruct a browser to indent certain lines of text without using the `<pre>...</pre>` or `<blockquote>...</block-quote>` tags (which have their own quirks). Along with indentations, your users must cope with bullets or numbers, but that's fine for lists, as in the earlier example. This sort of consistency makes them feel less alone in a strange and alien place.

Check your favorite browser developer's Web site to determine whether a version of their product understands the use of style tags in lists for changing the bullets and numbering. Such advances are happening all the time. Who knows what they'll think of next?

Analyzing Sophisticated Pages

Now it's time for a quick look at a complex Web page. In addition to inspecting our captive example, you may want to surf the Web looking for pages that strike your fancy. When you find one, view its source code to see how its author worked the underlying magic. The Web is one of the few places where you can easily look behind the curtain to see how an illusion is created; take full advantage of this opportunity. Ladies and gentlemen, all the way from its smash Broadway run . . .

The ...For Dummies home page

Hey, this example isn't about vanity (well, okay, not entirely). IDG Books' own ...*For Dummies* home page illustrates what you can accomplish if you use HTML 4.0 tags and your imagination (maybe you don't *need* frames anyway). It's eye-catching but not overdone (see Figure 13-8). Its information is arranged nicely and gives users multiple avenues of access. The graphics (logo and link images, or the client-side or CGI image maps) have neighboring text commands to make the site easy to navigate quickly, both graphically and textually. Users who want to "scan the site" can use the menu selections in the right-hand column to explore the site systematically. The right-hand column even includes a "search" function if a user wants to find any particular thing contained in the site and jump directly there. (Wow. Better than putting binoculars on a pogo stick.)

Figure 13-8:
The top of IDG Books' ...*For Dummies* home page.

The entire home page is less than two screens long. It makes liberal (but not frighteningly so) use of color and blank space to keep the text readable. The graphics load quickly, because each has been designed with only a few colors (under 16, in fact) and simple graphics components. Each link image or image map is repeated in text immediately to the right, a boon to users who don't have GUI browsers.

The footer contains much of the requisite information — not the page's URL, however — and makes much of the legal copyright notice that we professionals in the publishing world must hold so near to our hearts. (It *does* deflect a few legal slings and arrows.)

The HTML code for the *...For Dummies* home pages is HTML 4.0 compliant. It shows some interesting tricks that you may find useful. Its use of alt text with images ensures navigation even for non-GUI browsers. It also plays some interesting games with tables, arranging graphics and text elements pleasingly to minimize mnemonic heave-ho, and builds a seductively convenient right-hand column of menu selections. Behold:

```
<!— For brevity, we skipped lots of HTML in the head —>
<head>
 <title>...For Dummies Homepage</title>
</head>

<body bgcolor="#FFFFFF">
 <div align="center">
 <table border="0" width="544" height="124">
  <tr>
   <td colspan="2">
    <img src="http://www.dummies.com//images/mastb.gif"
         align="top" width="56" height="83">
    <img src="http://www.dummies.com//images/mast.side.b.gif"
         align="top" width="477" height="83"><br>
     The Knowledge Revolution Continues...
   </td>
  </tr>
 </table>
 </div>

 <div align="center">
 <table border="0" cellpadding="0" cellspacing="0"
        width="540">
  <tr>
   <td valign="top" colspan="2">
    <img src="http://www.dummies.com//images/spot1.gif"
         alt="In the Spotlight:" width="179" height="51">
    <font color="#808080" size="2">Friday,October 17, 1997
    </font>
```

```
</td>

<td valign="top" width="60"></td>

<td valign="top" rowspan="8" width="120">
 <img src="http://www.dummies.com//images/cag.bkg.gif"
     alt="Contents at a Glance" width="113" height="38">
 <a href="http://www.dummies.com/cgi/gatekeeper.plx:/
    search.html">
   <img src="http://www.dummies.com//images/cag_search.gif"
       alt="search" border="0" width="113" height="31">
 </a>
 <a href="http://www.dummies.com/cgi/gatekeeper.plx:/
    search.html">
    <img src="http://www.dummies.com//images/blue-
       bullet.gif"
        border="0" width="7" height="10">
     Search Books or Site
 </a>

 <a href="http://www.dummies.com/cgi/gatekeeper.plx:/
    dummies_books/">
  <img src="http://www.dummies.com//images/cag_books.A.gif"
      alt="books" border="0" width="113" height="31">
 </a>

 <img src="http://www.dummies.com//images/blue-bullet.gif"
     width="7" height="10">
 <a href="/cgi/dblookup.plx">
  Technology
 </a>
 <br>
 <img src="http://www.dummies.com//images/blue-bullet.gif"
     width="7" height="10">
 <a href="/cgi/dblookup.plx">
   Business/Personal
 </a>
 <br>
<!- and so on... ->
```

And that's what the wizard behind the curtain said. As you can see, the HTML arranges the "In The Spotlight" elements in the left-hand column and the "Contents at a Glance" elements in the right-hand column. Note the repeated use of the font tag to control type size, and the consistent use of ALT text to permit words to stand in for graphics where necessary. All these are elements of good design. (After some debate, we took the tail fins and extra chrome off.)

Animating .GIFs

Now, Igor, we give our creation life. One of the hidden capabilities of the GIF89a standard (as you'll recall from Chapter 7, and if you don't, please review it and *close that airlock*) is that it supports the inclusion of multiple images in a single shared file. You can also embed instructions in such a file's header that describe how its contents should be sequenced. This permits multiple images to act like the individual frames in a frame-by-frame animation. It's a crude, but effective, technique for building simple animations on your Web pages. Your creature, too, can shudder to life with hardly a twitch.

In fact, if you visit the *...For Dummies* Web site and look closely at the "In The Spotlight" graphic, you immediately realize it's an animated .GIF. It uses three versions of the same graphic, each with differently positioned light beams from a spotlight just above the upper left-hand corner of the image, to create the illusion of spotlights tracking across the image.

You can find a bevy of tools to assist in constructing animated .GIFs, including shareware and commercial software. Brian Hovis's GIF Animation page includes pointers to the vast majority of such tools, as well as an excellent tutorial that covers the details of constructing .GIF animations. You can get to all this material though this URL:

```
users.bendnet.com/brianhovis/anime.htm
```

Now, to reveal the secret in its grotesquely simple form: The process of creating an animated .GIF works like this:

1. **Create each of the graphics for the sequence as a separate .GIF file.**

2. **Determine the sequence of images.**

3. **Determine the timing.**

    You'll want to consider the start-up delay and the delay between images. You'll also need to decide if the animated .GIF should cycle through the sequence once or keep cycling (as the "In The Spotlight" image does on the *...For Dummies* page).

4. **Tell your software tool which images to grab and when to do it.**

5. **Let the tool create the animated .GIF for your page(s).**

Granted, such creatures do tend to be larger than the sum of their parts. An animated .GIF file will take up a bit more space than the sum of all the images that go into its animation sequence (to include the header information, of course). That's why the best animated .GIFs work with small, compact images, only a few colors, and as little complexity as possible. Otherwise these files may grow too large; users who must download them over slow connections may lead torchlight parades of flame mail.

Other sophisticated Web sites

We strongly urge you to explore the Web and view HTML source code for the many exciting sites that abound in Web space. You need to look not only at HTML source for a site's primary page but also at HTML source for each frame on those sites that use HTML frames. Try right-clicking on a frame and see what your browser lets you do. You may be surprised — newer browsers should show you the HTML source code for the frame you selected.

Chapter 14

Using HTML Tables Effectively

*I*n HTML, as in life, tables may seem prosaic, but they're handy for holding things. You can arrange everything from text to images on your pages, efficiently and attractively, in HTML tables. The 3.0 and later versions of both Netscape and Internet Explorer support them, as do the more recent versions of other, noncommercial browsers like Mosaic and Opera.

If your browser doesn't support tables, take it as a sign that upgrade time is here again.

Since the days of HTML 3.2, tables have become a standard element of Web documents. With HTML 4.0, proprietary extensions from Netscape and Microsoft have given way to official standards. This chapter heralds the New Age of HTML 4.0 Tables and gets you started using them.

First, Consider the Alternatives

The traditional approach to tabulating data, or organizing content on a page, is to use <table> tags. But before you walk down this road, please ask yourself this question: "Do I really have to use a table here?" You can use lists, images, preformatted text, or frames instead of tables. Each of these structures has its own good and bad points.

✔ **Lists:** Simple to implement and consistently well-rendered by every browser available. Lists are a sensible alternative to tables when you want to quickly and easily group information. However, they don't give you the formatting capabilities of tables, especially for images.

✔ **Images:** You can compose images in grids with borders and colors, but be warned that they may become static and difficult to change. They also get big and slow!

✔ **Preformatted text:** This is the original table markup and an option that will still work in a pinch without causing any concern over browser compatibility. But most browsers generally display preformatted text in a nonproportional font that looks terrible. Not recommended when look and feel are important.

✔ **Frames:** These complex constructs may offer an additional dimension to your Web site, but they're not really a replacement for tables.

The preceding alternatives notwithstanding, tables are great for many uses — presenting financial results, organizing lists of related elements (such as dates and birthdays), and giving rowdy elements a defined layout.

HTML <table> Overview

Table markup brings versatility to describing your content. HTML tables offer virtually limitless description possibilities because you can put almost any other HTML tag into a table cell.

For now, Keep It Simple, Stradivarius. We strongly recommend that you stick with basic table elements unless you're developing documents for a private Web server where you *know* your audience is using a particular browser. Sticking to a common denominator (common table elements) is the best way to ensure the widest audience for your work. As you wander awestruck through the rest of this chapter (well, we can hope), eagerly absorbing the basics (and some nifty uses) of HTML tables, pay particular attention to how table constructs nest within each other. If you goof up just one nesting order, your information won't display the way you expect it to look!

Every time you add another level to a table, indent the code to offset it from the previous level. Then, when you return to a higher level, decrease your indentation to match previous code at the same level. To demonstrate this healthful and sensible principle, we use this method in all of the examples in this chapter for your rapt perusal.

An obvious-but-important fact: A table is a visual device that's hard to read aloud to someone who can't see it. If your readership includes users who may be print-handicapped or otherwise visually impaired, provide an alternative form for your table data. Some browsers can produce Braille or convert text to speech, but most aren't able to handle the HTML <table> tag for such conversions. As one solution, many Web sites offer text-only implementations for tables as an alternative. You may want to consider doing the same if it's appropriate for your audience.

HTML Table Markup

The amazing fact is, you can put *any* HTML body element into a table cell. You can even nest multiple tables within a single cell — a fun but time-consuming activity that we don't recommend you try just now. So, if you think that some particular combination of table elements and other elements might work for your table, give it a try. Your idea may work better than you think, or it may not work at all — the only way to be sure is to experiment. Go for what works.

The parts of a <table>

The basic parts of a table are the <table>...</table> tag that surrounds all of a table's contents, the <tr>...</tr> (table row) tag that defines each row within a table, and the <td>...</td> (table data) tag that defines each cell within each row of a table.

Optional table tags include the <caption>...</caption> tag, which places contained text above or below a table as a label, and <th>...</th> (table header) tag, which you can use to label columns in a table. The following code snippet for a simple HTML table illustrates all these tags, in the most boring way we could imagine. (Hey, ya gotta play some scales before you jump to the jazzy stuff!)

```
<table>
<caption>The caption.</caption>
  <tr>
    <th> Header: row 1, column 1</th>
    <th> Header: row 1, column 2</th>
  </tr>
  <tr>
    <td> Cell: row 2, column 1</td>
    <td> Cell: row 2, column 2</td>
  </tr>
</table>
```

If you put the preceding table code in a Web page and viewed the result in your browser, you'd have the snazzola table depicted in Figure 14-1 — all bones, no meat. (Bleah.)

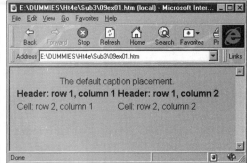

Figure 14-1: A basic table, complete with caption and headings.

If you're really feeling adventurous, take our first code sample, replace our less-than-exciting content with some of your own (text, images, or whatever you like), save the new code, and view it in your favorite browser. Voilà! You've created a table.

Regardless of how big or small your table is or what content you choose to include within its cells, you'll need to always include the following tags in every table you create:

- ✔ `<table>...</table>`
- ✔ `<tr>...</tr>`
- ✔ `<td>...</td>`

But wait. Once you've used this example, you've unlocked the basic concepts of table-tag layout and nesting techniques. Now that you have this potent knowledge, you can construct a basic table of your own. Before you go forth to rule the world, however, you need to know more about each of these tags and their attributes. Say no more; here it comes.

The table tag: <table> . . . </table>

The `<table>...</table>` tags are like a toy chest; they provide a container for all other table tags. Browsers (ever the sticklers for detail) ignore other table tags if they aren't contained inside `<table>...</table>` tags. The `<table>...</table>` tag accepts the following attributes: `align`, `border`, `cellpadding`, `cellspacing`, and `width`.

Always include the closing tag for tables. If you don't, your table may not show up at all; invisible tables aren't really very useful.

The table row tag: <tr> . . . </tr>

The <tr>...</tr> (as in *table row*) tags contain the information for all cells within a particular table row. Each tag represents a single row, no matter how many cells the row contains. The <tr>...</tr> tag accepts only the align and valign attributes — which, if you specify them, become default alignments that whip all the contents of all cells in the row into line.

The table data tag: <td> . . . </td>

The <td>...</td> (*table data*) tags hold the contents of each cell in a table. If those fussbudget browsers are going to recognize cells as cells, you have to put your cell data within these tags and then, in turn, nest the table data tag within a set of table row tags. Table data tags give your cells some friendly characteristics:

- ✔ You needn't worry about making each row contain the same number of cells because short rows are completed with blank cells on the right.
- ✔ A cell can contain any HTML tag normally used within the body (<body>...</body>) of an HTML document.

The <td> tag accepts the following attributes: align, bgcolor, colspan, height, nowrap, rowspan, valign, and width.

The table header tag: <th> . . . </th>

The *table header* tags (<th>...</th>) display text in boldface with a default center alignment. You can use a table header tag within any row of a table, but you'll most often find and use them in the first row at the top — or head — of a table. Except for their position and egotism, they act just like table data tags and should be treated as such.

The table caption: <caption> . . . </caption>

Captions are snobs; <caption>...</caption> tags will deign to exist anywhere inside a <table>...</table> tag but not inside table rows or cells (because then they wouldn't be *captioning* anything). Like table cells, captions will accommodate any HTML tags that can appear in the body of a document, but only those. By default, captions put themselves at horizontal dead center with respect to a table, wrapping their lines to fit within the table's width. The <caption>...</caption> tag pair accepts the align attribute if you ask it nicely.

Basic table attributes

Okay, here's where the incantations that create tables get a bit more complicated. You can use several attributes with the different table tags to determine how the table's parts and contents are displayed on-screen. Get to know these critters, use them innovatively, and they'll repay your attention by making your tables easier on the eye. Here's a quick overview of table attributes; next, we show you how to use them.

align=[left or center or right]

The `align` attribute works with all the various table tags to help you control how the browser horizontally aligns the table and its contents. Depending on which tag you add it to, the attribute has a different effect on the final display of the table.

- Use `align` with the `<caption>`...`</caption>` tag to specify how the table's caption should be aligned relative to the table itself. The default alignment for a caption is center.

- Use `align` with the `<table>`...`</table>` tag to set the table's alignment relative to the rest of the page. The default alignment for a table is left, so to center the table or force it to justify to the right, set the value of `align` to `center` or `right`.

- Use align with the `<tr>`...`</tr>`, `<td>`...`</td>`, or `<th>`...`</th>` tags to define how the content within table cells is aligned. When you set an alignment for a table row tag, the alignment applies to all the contents of all the cells or header cells in that row. When you set an alignment for a single table cell or table header, the alignment only applies to the content in that single cell or header cell. Finally, if you set the alignment for all the cells in a row and then set the alignment for a cell within that row, the setting you add to the cell overrides the setting for the row. Whew! Bet you didn't know one little attribute could do so much.

To show you the `align` attribute at work, we'll play with our original, plain vanilla table a bit. The HTML has been altered to align the table to the center, the caption to the right, the contents of the first row to the left, and the contents of the second row to the right. For good measure, the second cell on the second row has also been aligned to the center.

```
<table align=center>
<caption align=right>The caption.</caption>
  <tr align=left>
    <th> Header: row 1, column 1</th>
    <th> Header: row 1, column 2</th>
  </tr>
  <tr align=right>
    <td> Cell: row 2, column 1</td>
```

```
        <td align=center> Cell: row 2, column 2</td>
      </tr>
</table>
```

Figure 14-2 shows how the newly revised markup is displayed in a browser.

Figure 14-2:
The align
attribute
can change
how a table
and its
contents are
arranged.

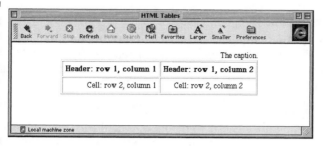

We've added a border to many of the screen shots in this chapter to make it easier to see each individual cell and the changes different attributes can effect on a table.

border [=number]

The border attribute only works with the <table>...</table> tag. Its job is to let the browser know whether you want a border around your table or not, and if so, how big you want that border to be. This attribute takes a numeric value — border=5 for example — that indicates how many pixels wide you want the border to be. If you don't want a border around your table, then specify border=0. If you don't specify a value, border defaults to a width of one (1) pixel.

If we change the first line of our plain-Jane table to <table border=5>, our table is now well-outlined, as shown in Figure 14-3.

Figure 14-3:
The border
attribute
can really
box up a
table.

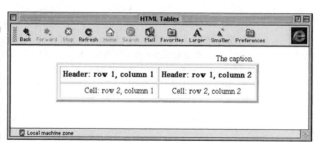

Tables without borders can provide a clean look and feel and help you control unruly text and graphics, but we've found the business of building tables to be both tedious and exacting. To make things a bit easier, we suggest you set the border on a table to one (1) while it's under construction so you can more easily see how the browser is interpreting your rows and columns. When you're done with construction and are satisfied with the results, simply change the one to a zero — and "Bye-bye, border."

cellpadding=number

Yet another attribute that you can only use with the `<table>...</table>` tags, `cellpadding` specifies the amount of space between a cell's perimeter and its contents. The default value for this attribute is one (1) pixel but you can make the value as large or small as you'd like.

This handy-dandy tool helps you put some space between the content in your cells, making them easier to read. Combined with cell spacing and a well-sized border, cell padding can enhance the visual impact of your tables.

Once again working with our basic table, we add a bit of white space within every cell by changing the opening table tag to `<table cellpadding=5>`. Check out the results for yourself in Figure 14-4.

Figure 14-4:
The cellpadding attribute keeps content from being too close for comfort.

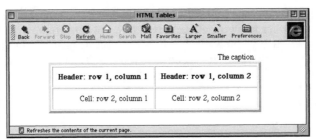

cellspacing=number

Use the `cellspacing` attribute within the `<table>...</table>` tag to determine the amount of space inserted between individual cells in a table. The default value is one pixel between cells. If we set the border on our basic table to 5 and change the cell padding to 5 using `<table border=5 cellspacing=5>`, the browser displays the HTML with a bit more space between the cells, as shown in Figure 14-5.

Figure 14-5:
The cellspacing attribute gives cells a bit of breathing room.

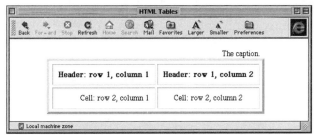

Unless you have your table border set to more than one pixel or the background colors of your table cells set to different colors, you won't be able to see a difference in the display of the cell spacing and the cell padding attributes.

width=[number or "percent%"]

When used with `<table>...</table>` tags, the `width` attribute sets the width of a table in absolute terms (a specific number of pixels) or as a percentage of a browser's display area. You can also use this attribute within `<th>...</th>` or `<td>...</td>` tags — to decree the width of a cell within a table as an absolute number of pixels or else assign it a percentage of the table's width. (Now, that's power!)

Until now, the display of our basic table has only taken up as much of the browser window as was necessary to show all its content. If we change the opening table tag so that its width is 75% (`<table width=75%>`), the table will take up 75% of the browser window's width, as shown in Figure 14-6. If we set the width to 100 (for 100 pixels) — `<table width=100>` — the table is forced to be exactly (or absolutely) 100 pixels wide, and the cell contents are wrapped to fit the specific size, as shown in Figure 14-7.

Figure 14-6:
Set a table's width to a percentage to set its size relative to the width of the browser window.

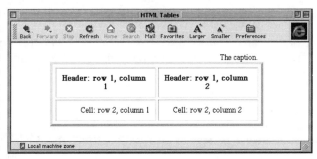

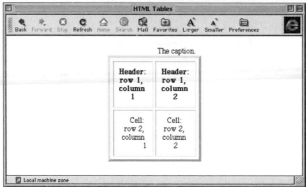

Figure 14-7:
Set a table's
width to a
pixel size to
specify
exactly how
big the table
should be.

To create tables that are more flexible and accommodate a wider variety of monitor sizes and browser window widths, we highly recommend that you use relative table widths — percentages instead of pixels. If you absolutely must create a table with an absolute width — pixels instead of percentages — don't make it any larger than 550 or 600 pixels. If you violate this restriction, users with smaller monitors may have to scroll horizontally to read your page, and in the Web world that's a no-no. In fact, it's sure to chase your users away in hordes.

valign=[top or middle or bottom]

Tuck the VALIGN (*vertical alignment*) attribute with the `<tr>...</tr>`, `<th>...</th>`, or `<td>...</td>` tags to vertically align the contents of the table to the top, middle, or bottom of the cell. In general, `valign` is a counterpart to `align`, so you'll often use them together. The default value for this attribute is `middle`. Ten-hut!

nowrap

When you use `nowrap` with a table cell or header (`<th>...</th>` or `<td>...</td>`), Web browsers will try to display all the text for that particular cell on a single line. This can sometimes produce weird results.

Using this attribute can create extremely wide cells (especially for people who like to write sentences even longer than this one). Be careful!

colspan=number

Spanning is a key component of HTML tables because it helps you overcome one of the most maddening characteristics of tables: their overwhelming desire to be symmetrical. By way of explanation, think about what might happen when you add another `<th>...</th>` tag to the first row of our basic table — but not to the second row — using this code:

```
<table border=1>
<caption>The caption.</caption>
  <tr>
    <th> Header: row 1, column 1</th>
    <th> Header: row 1, column 2</th>
    <th> Header: row 1, column 3</th>
  </tr>
  <tr>
    <td> Cell: row 2, column 1</td>
    <td> Cell: row 2, column 2</td>
  </tr>
</table>
```

Tables always want to be symmetrical, so the browser will automatically add an empty cell to our second row to serve as a balance for the new cell we added in the first row, as shown in Figure 14-8.

Figure 14-8:
Browsers
will
automatically
fill in cells if
your table
code isn't
symmetrical.

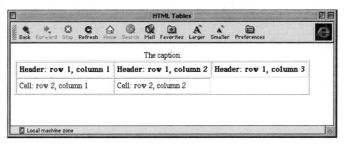

Not the prettiest picture we've ever seen. What to do, what to do? There's got to be a way to force one cell in a row to act as more than one cell. In fact, there is. Spanning allows you to create a single table cell that can span several rows or columns, depending on your needs. For example, to make the second column of our second row span two columns — act like two cells in one row — we only need change the table data tag to:

```
<td colspan=2> Cell: row 2, column 2</td>
```

Ta-da! As Figure 14-9 shows, the single cell now acts as two cells and spans across two columns, filling in the space where the empty cell created by the browser had previously been. It's not magic; it's HTML.

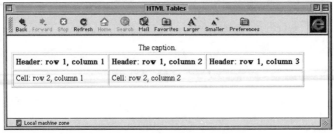

Figure 14-9:
The
colspan
attribute
helps one
cell act as
many.

rowspan=number

The rowspan attribute is similar to colspan in both form and function — as if their names didn't give that away. When you use rowspan with table data (<td>...</td>) or table header (<th>...</th>) tags, the cell spans multiple rows — as opposed to multiple columns. In the previous section, we used colspan=2 to force one cell to act as two in the same row in order to solve the dilemma created by the unbalanced table code example we used. In the same way, we can use rowspan=2 with the new table header cell (row 1, column 3) to force the cell to expand down into the second row and make the table symmetrical:

```
<th rowspan=2> Header: row 1, column 3</th>
```

Check out the results in Figure 14-10.

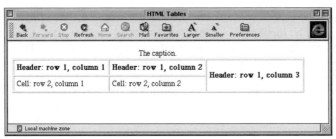

Figure 14-10:
The
rowspan
attribute
causes one
cell to
expand
down
several
rows.

bgcolor=color

Remember the bgcolor attribute that goes with the <body>...</body> tag? This is the same attribute, and it affects the background of table cells in the same way it affects the background of your entire HTML document. Simply add this attribute to any table cell or header to change its background color:

```
<td bgcolor="teal">...</td>
```

Build Your Own Tables

Building tables by hand is time-consuming, repetitive work, even if you make them out of data instead of wood. So be sure that a tabular form enhances your content. You can simplify your work by carefully planning the layout of your tabular data and by making use of search, replace, copy, and paste functions in your HTML/text editor. Before you start tagging your data to make it totally tabular (is there an echo in here?), consider . . .

Laying out tabular data for easy display

First, sketch how you want your table to look (give yourself room; it might be *bigger* than a cocktail napkin). Then create a small HTML table with only a few rows of data to test your layout; does the table appear the way you envisioned it? If you're using heads that span multiple columns or rows, you may need to adjust the space they take to fit your data. Finally, test your tables with several browsers to see how they look on each one. Finalize your design before you add the data you want the table to contain.

Multirow and multicolumn spans

Remember to build your tables by rows. If you use rowspan="3" in one table row (<tr>...</tr>), you must account for the extra two rows in the next two rows. For example, consider the following code morsel:

```
<table border>
  <tr>
    <td rowspan=3>Letters</td>
    <td>A</td>
  </tr>
  <tr>
    <td>B</td>
  </tr>
  <tr>
    <td>C</td>
  </tr>
</table>
```

The idea is to leave out a cell in each row or column that will be assumed ("spanned into," if you prefer) by the rowspan or colspan cell, as shown in Figure 14-11.

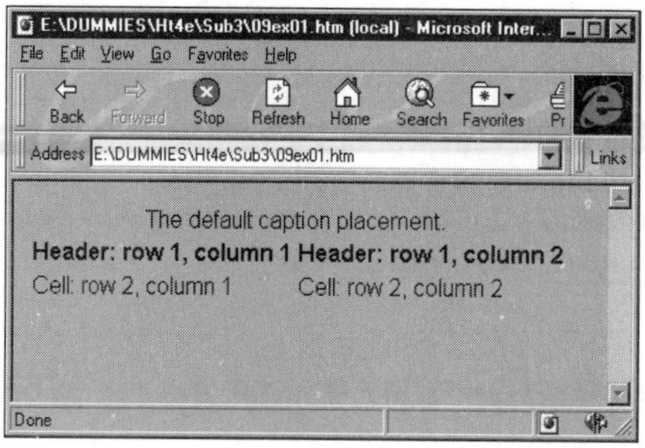

Figure 14-11: The `<rowspan>` tag, applied to Letters, creates a single left-hand column to match all three rows for `A`, `B`, and `C`.

Mixing graphics and tables to add interest

If you want to frighten off a visitor to your Web page, just pack a screen full of dense and impenetrable information — especially numbers. A long, unbroken list of numbers quickly drives away all but the truly masochistic. You can stop the pain: Put those numbers into an attractive table (better yet, *several* tables interspersed with a few well-chosen images). Watch your page's attractiveness and readability soar; hear visitors sigh with relief.

Individual table cells can be surprisingly roomy; you can position graphics in them precisely. If you are moved to put graphics in a table, be sure to:

- Select images that are similar in size and looks.
- Measure those images to determine their heights and widths in pixels (shareware programs like Paint Shop Pro and GraphicConverter do this automatically).
- Use HTML markup to position these images within their table cells.

We've made extensive use of this particular technique for better controlling graphics throughout the LANWrights Web site. Check out the top of the *HTML 4 For Dummies* book page at `www.lanw.com/books/ html4d4.htm`, shown in Figure 14-12.

A short and sweet table keeps the graphics in check and guarantees that the text will always sit nicely to its right.

Two more handy graphics-placement tips: (1) size your rows and columns of cells that contain images to accommodate the largest graphic, and (2) center all graphics in each cell (vertically and horizontally). Result: a consistent, coherent image layout.

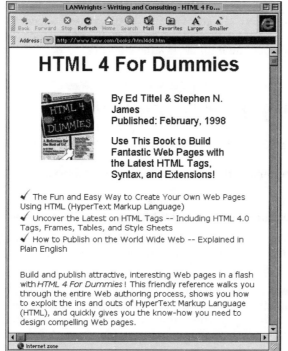

Figure 14-12:
Tables can
help keep
graphics
under
control.

Tools automate tedious markup

Most decent/recent HTML editors build tables for you. Many have table wizards that ask you how many rows and columns you'd like and then automatically generate the necessary HTML markup. In these same editors, you'll also find tools that make adding new rows, columns, spans, and background colors as easy as pie.

Likewise, Microsoft Excel now offers a "Save as HTML" option in the File⇨ Save menu. You can create your table in Excel — or easily transfer an existing Excel table to HTML — and then use this nifty function to make Excel create the necessary markup automatically.

Let's hear it for progress! So how come we made you learn the details of HTML table markup? Well, what can we say — we're sadists (just kidding).

Actually, none of these tools *fully* automates all the details that can appear within a table. Your artistic touch is still needed to create borders, cell padding, cell spacing, and so on. Besides, no automatic process really understands how to position graphics as precisely as a human designer can (take *that,* soulless machines!). Still, these tools simplify the initial and often tedious creation of table markup. Because you're going to have to tweak your tables by hand anyway, we figured the best way to get started was with a little "manual labor." (You'll thank us later. Honest.)

Some Stunning Table Examples

To find the best uses of tables on the Web . . . well, look around the Web.

We think these popular sites make excellent use of tables in their design:

- ✔ **CNET** — This entire site uses tables for all the complex layout. Often, tables are within tables within tables: `www.cnet.com`.

- ✔ **Yahoo!** — The most popular search engine on the Web uses tables to display their front page and all of the navigation items on all results pages: `www.yahoo.com`.

- ✔ **Dilbert Zone** — The only engineer on the planet to publicly disparage his boss and still keep his job (wait a minute — didn't he quit and become a cartoonist?). This daily dose of Dilbert is presented entirely by means of tables: `www.unitedmedia.com/comics/dilbert/`.

After you load these documents into your Web browser, take a look at each one's HTML source code (try View⇨Source from your menu bar). Observe how complex the markup is, and mark ye well when the markup looks haphazardly arranged (alas, if only they'd asked us . . .).

Chapter 15

The Map's the Thing!

. . . .

In This Chapter

▶ Using clickable maps

▶ Finding out what it takes to present maps

▶ Carving up maps for use

▶ Knowing the limitations of map use

▶ Mapping from the client side

. . . .

So you've already deciphered how to insert graphics into HTML documents using the `<img>` tag, eh? And we suspect you have seen other inscriptions that turn graphics into hypertext links within anchor tags (for example, `<a href=...><img scr=...></a>`). In this chapter, we show you how to take the next logical step — treating a graphic as a collection of selectable regions, each of which points to a different hypertext link or resource.

Where Are You? (Using Clickable Maps)

The geographical maps we grew up with identify land masses and divide them along boundaries into named regions — countries, counties, office parks, whatever. You can use graphics the same way on the Web, divvying up an image so its territories activate different hyperlinks. Users familiar with graphical interfaces have no trouble interacting with buttons, icons, and other kinds of interface controls. Graphical maps add this capability to a single image displayed on a Web page — in Web-speak, an *image map* or *clickable map*. We prefer the latter term because it suggests both the nature of these graphical elements and the way to use them:

  ✔ **Their nature:** Clickable maps break a graphic into discrete regions that function as a collection of individual hyperlinks. Normally the regional boundaries are obvious; users simply select whatever portion of the graphic attracts their interest.

  ✔ **Their use:** Users can select regions by putting the cursor inside the desired region and clicking the mouse. Then it's bon voyage!

Those who have bossed a computer around from a command prompt, word by word, are already hip to a fundamental limitation of clickable maps: They absolutely require a GUI browser. They don't work if you can't click 'em (or even see them). The image that represents the map isn't visible in a character-mode browser. Therefore, as a friendly gesture to users with text-only browsers, supplement your clickable maps by implementing alternate navigation methods that don't need pictures.

A typically modest example of a clickable map should save us a thousand words or so. Figure 15-1 shows the home-page graphic for *HTML For Dummies* (it appears in the file named ht4menum.gif in the /graphics subdirectory on the CD-ROM). This graphic features a set of buttons at the bottom, where each button contains a major access category for that set of *HTML For Dummies* pages. As part of a set of Web pages for the current edition of this book, it acts as the gateway to a page, or set of pages, for each category or topic mentioned. (All together now, "Wow. That is so *cool*. How do they *do* it?" Read on, MacDuff!)

Figure 15-1:
The *HTML For Dummies* home page (server version) includes a row of buttons on the bottom.

In this chapter, you see how to set up an image as a clickable map and how to use it to drive page navigation.

The approach that we used to build the identical graphic for the pages on the CD-ROM breaks the image into pieces. The top part of the graphic represents one piece (ht4logoi.gif), and each button has its own associated icon file. We did this because a local HTML file cannot use a server-side image map. This restriction exists because there's no server in the background to map the user's selection coordinates into a corresponding URL. Instead, each button's icon is directly linked to a URL, and clicking a graphical element automatically selects the right link. (Wanna see it again? Nothing up our sleeves. . . .)

Cosmic Cartography — Putting Maps on the Web

Because a clickable map is a mode of cybertransportation as well as a nifty picture, building one requires three different processes:

- ✔ **Creating (or selecting) a usable image:** This image can be an existing graphic or a custom-built one. Our *HTML For Dummies* button bar uses five custom-built icons, one for each button.

    If you create your own graphics, don't forget to eat and sleep.

- ✔ **Creating the *map file:*** This requires a step-by-step investigation of the image file inside a graphics program that gives you the *pixel addresses* (coordinates) of each point on the boundary that separates the regions you want to create. (The impatient, lazy, and/or efficient among you might want to use a map-building utility like the one we mention later in this chapter.)

    Our icons are all about the same size, so working through this process is easy: The image starts in the upper-left corner of the button bar (at vertical location 142, or about the middle of this 285-pixel-high image) and is consistently 143 pixels high. The individual buttons vary slightly in width, producing the following set of coordinates:

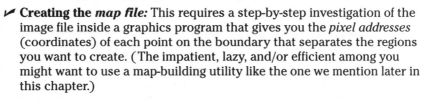

    Just that easy, just that simple. Unfortunately, the only way to produce this collection of numbers is to view the graphic inside a graphics program that shows pixel coordinates (we used Paint Shop Pro 5.00, a widely available shareware graphics program for Windows). The alternative, of course, is to use an image-map construction program. (You haven't peeked ahead yet, have you?)

    Well, okay, we'll tell you about using an image-map tool: It generates a map after you tell it what kind of shapes you're outlining. One example is Tom Boutell's excellent program, called Mapedit, which builds map files at your command. It's available for Mac, DOS/Windows, and UNIX. To find a suitable version, use "Mapedit" as a search string in your favorite Web search engine (a quick jump to Yahoo! turned up more than 40 sites that offer one or more versions of this program).

- ✔ **Establishing the right HTML information in your page:** You must link an image to both its map file and a CGI script that decodes map coordinates (and uses that information to select an appropriate link to follow).

Thus our immediate objective is a purposeful meander through the what-for and how-to of making image maps work in your HTML document. Later, we tear aside the veil of secrecy and build a complete back-end CGI script (one that translates the pixel coordinates for a user's map selection into a corresponding HTML link, *just like that*). But first things first; in this chapter, we cover the general techniques you need for constructing the image map and creating links between map regions and hypertext documents (or other resources). Trust us, that's plenty for now.

Thus, seeker, mark well when you have obtained the appropriate image, studied the image file for pixel addresses to use in creating map files, and established a convention to call the script that translates coordinates into links. Only then have you accomplished the epic labors that prepare you to set up a clickable map.

To hail this deed (and protect your sanity), we suggest you use the same name for the image map as for its related script: Thus, if the image is named ht4menum.gif, the script would be called `ht4menum.map`, or simply `ht4menum`. If your scripts reside in a CGI directory one level down from your HTML files, the URL for this script would then be `/cgi-bin/ht4menum.map`.

Warning: Different maps for different servers

The next quest is to define an appropriate format for your clickable-map-to-be. Wish we could report that all servers would be happy with just one format. No such luck. The awful truth is, no one image-map definition can meet the demands of all servers.

Et tu, CERN and NCSA?

Even the two most popular httpd servers — CERN and NCSA — differ on clickable map formats. In fact, even though they need more or less the same data to make a clickable map work, they need them in slightly different order and call them by slightly different names. Thus, for the truly stalwart, we've provided the gory details in "Building and Linking to CERN Map Files" and "Building and Linking to NCSA Map Files," later in this chapter.

Throughout this chapter, where specific differences between CERN and NCSA requirements exist, we fill you in. If you're not sure whether you're using an httpd server of either variety, you may want to investigate your server's requirements immediately, adjust our examples and recommendations to meet those requirements, and make sure you have your webmaster's contact info (an e-mail address, if not a phone number).

A Babel of servers

Some Web servers, especially if they're not UNIX-based, won't support either CERN or NCSA image-map formats; others support only their own proprietary image-map formats. Sometimes, though, a server's native platform can give you a good place to start and some sense of how large your audience may be. For example, the leading Macintosh Web server — WebSTAR — supports the NCSA image-map format, and Windows NT supports more than 20 Web servers.

To make a clickable map work, stay within the requirements of the server on which the map resides. If you don't know those requirements, contact your local webmaster — or at least, the system administrator for your Web server. That person should be able to set you straight right away and can probably help you find some useful information about how to build clickable maps for your system, above and beyond what we tell you here.

Your maps take shape (s)

As you assemble coordinates to build a clickable map, the process of identifying boundaries may remind you of high school geometry. Both CERN and NCSA image-map definitions recognize the following regions:

- **Circle:** (Specified by the coordinates for a point at the center and the number of pixels for the radius.) Use this to select a circular (or nearly circular) region within an image. To define a circle, you specify where its center is located and its radius. This usually takes the form of something like circle, x, y, radius, URL where circle is a keyword that denotes the shape, the x, y values specify the center's location, and radius defines its radius (in pixels). The URL identifies the Web document where a click in this region should take the user. Also, we hope it's obvious that the values for x, y, and radius should all be numbers.

- **Rectangle:** (Specified by the coordinates for the upper-left and lower-right corners.) Use this to select a square or rectangular region in your image. (This is the one we use in our button-bar map.) To define a rectangle, provide locations for the upper-left and lower-right corners. This usually takes the form of rectangle x1,y1, x2, y2, URL where rectangle is a keyword that denotes the shape, x1, y1 denotes the upper-left corner, and x2, y2 denotes the lower right corner. Here again, URL identifies the Web document where a click in this region should take the user.

- **Polygon:** (Specified by the coordinates for the point at the vertex of each edge. You remember *vertex* from geometry? We didn't either, but it sounded more exotic than *corner* or *intersection of endpoints*.) Simply put, vertices define the points where lines in a polygon come together to define a shape. This usually takes the form polygon x1, y1, x2, y2, ..., URL where one pair of xn, yn values is necessary for each vertex in the polygon. Once again, URL plays the same role: It identifies the Web document where a click in this region should take the user.

Use vertices to outline the boundaries of regularly or irregularly shaped regions that aren't circular or rectangular. Although it takes more effort, the more points you pick to define an outline, the more a region behaves as users expect it to when clicking inside or outside its borders.

✔ **Point:** (Specified by its *x* and *y* coordinates.) Use this only when a specific point is easy to select. (A point is usually too small a region on-screen and requires exact control to select — we recommend surrounding a point with a small circle or square so users can be a little sloppy.) We've never actually used a point reference in an image map, except as a vertex for a polygon or rectangle, or the center of a circle. This takes the form `point x, y, URL` where `point` is the keyword, and `x, y` denotes its location. Likewise, `URL` once again indicates the Web document where a click on the point should take the user.

Selecting boundaries for map regions determines the selection of the related links. Even though users may see a nicely shaped graphic to click, you know what really drives the selection: the areas you outline on top of that graphic. For image maps, the upper-left corner of an image resides at coordinates 0, 0, so you can reference any pixel location within an image region by counting to the right to determine the first pixel value (the x coordinate), and down to determine the second pixel value (the y coordinate).

The better a map's regions fit an image, the more the map behaves as users expect — and (given human nature) the more they'll like it! The moral of the story is: Take your time and, when in doubt, pick more points to outline something, rather than fewer. Even better, use a tool that follows your cursor movement to build the map for you. We mentioned Tom Boutell's Mapedit program earlier; other alternatives abound on the Web. Try out a couple; see what works for you.

For example, a Macintosh image-map tool called MapMaker is available at:

`www.kickinit.com/mapmaker/download.html`

Remember, Tom Boutell's outstanding PC-based image-map tool, Mapedit, is available at:

`www.boutell.com/mapedit/`

If you provide either tool with a URL for a graphic you want to map, the tool can guide you through the rest of the process using your very own Web browser. (Now if only we could find a power drill that did that . . .)

An outstanding general discussion on this topic, entitled "How to Create Clickable Image Maps For Your Web Pages" is available at:

`/spider4.spiderlink.com/develop/devimaps.htm`

Please read it for a slightly different take on this fascinating process.

Building and Linking to CERN Map Files

As promised, here's the first of two sections that grapple with the nuts and bolts of the most popular image-map formats. In this corner . . . the map files for CERN httpd servers, in a form that looks like this:

```
circle (x,y) r URL
rectangle (x1,y1) (x2,y2) URL
polygon (x1,y1) (x2, y2) (x3,y3) . . . (xn,yn) URL
point (x,y) URL
default URL
```

Okay, so it's a bit anticlimactic; the shapes are pretty much self-evident — except for the polygon, which identifies coordinates for individual points that trace a region's outline. If this sounds like connect-the-dots, you've got the concept! (Whoa, that was waaaay too easy.)

Don't forget to close your polygons; make sure that the last segment fills the gap between your last point and your first. (Here's a corny mnemonic to help you remember: "Always close the parrot cage or Polly gone.")

Another entry that might seem mysterious is the default URL: It's a fail-safe to prevent blunders by visitors who click randomly to see what happens (which, of course, no one *we* know ever does). You define a default so that nothing much happens if users click an undefined location in the map; they choose the fail-safe. A default can be a script that sends a message back — say, a paean to high-school nostalgia (*Click within the lines or stay after school!*) or maybe something kinder (*You have selected an area of the image that is not defined. Please try again.*).

A CERN map file for the button bar

Thus, for our button-bar example, the CERN map is as follows:

```
rectangle (0,142) (98,285) http://www.domain.com/html4dum/
          ftpstuff.htm
rectangle (99,142) (198,285) http://www.domain.com/html4dum/
          contents.htm
rectangle (199,142) (298,285) http://www.domain.com/html4dum/
          search4d.htm
rectangle (299,142) (398,285) http://www.domain.com/html4dum/
          contact.htm
rectangle (399,142) (499,285) http://www.domain.com/html4dum/
          whatsnew.htm
default http://www.domain.com/html4dum/contents.htm
```

Because the menu bar is a collection of rectangular buttons, defining its coordinates is easy. (Why do you think we picked this example?) Then we provide a default link to a `contents` page if somebody insists on staying outside the nice boxes we gave them to play in (can't have them wandering the halls). Notice, too, that we use absolute URLs (typing *carefully*). Absolute URLs make maps easier to debug and relocate.

Is my system ready for CERN map files?

To actually *use* a map file with the CERN httpd, your system must already have a program that handles image maps. The name of this program, which is included with the CERN httpd materials, is *htimage*. You must have htimage installed if you plan to use image maps on your system. After it's available, you must also know how to invoke it. For the purposes of this example, we've assumed it lives on the directory path `/cgi-bin/`. For details about how to do this on your system, contact your local webmaster or system administrator. For a sample file that explains how to use htimage on RightClick.Com's system, check out the Help file at:

```
www.rightclick.com/support/ihip.html
```

Building and Linking to NCSA Map Files

Behold NCSA, the *other* most-popular image-map format. Map files for NCSA servers, though they look much like those for CERN servers, do incorporate some sneaky differences. Have a look at this typical form that NCSA map files are likely to take:

```
circle URL x,y r
rect URL x1,y1 x2,y2
poly URL x1,y1 x2,y2 x3,y3 . . . xn,yn
point URL x,y
default URL
```

The shapes are the same as the CERN varieties and the same kinds of coordinates define them. But names are shorter, and URLs come first (instead of last) in the list of attributes. Here again, defaults work the same way: to provide a handler for people who click outside the image frame. But as you know, computers are literalists; they only read what's there, which gives minor differences in format a larger-than-life effect on compatibility.

An NCSA map file for the button bar

For the *HTML For Dummies* graphic, the NCSA map is as follows:

```
rect http://www.domain.com/html4dum/ftpstuff.htm (0,142)
       (98,285)
rect http://www.domain.com/html4dum/contents.htm (99,142)
       (198,285)
rect http://www.domain.com/html4dum/search4d.htm (199,142)
       (298,285)
rect http://www.domain.com/html4dum/contact.htm (299,142)
       (398,285)
rect http://www.domain.com/html4dum/whatsnew.htm (399,142)
       (499,285)
default http://www.domain.com/html4dum/contents.htm
```

Except for a change in the shape's name (`rect` instead of `rectangle`) and reordering the arguments (URLs first, and then coordinates), the map is nearly identical to the CERN variety.

Is my system ready for NCSA map files?

As with CERN, to use a map file with the NCSA httpd, a system must already have a program that handles image maps. The name of this program, which comes with the NCSA httpd materials, is *imagemap*. If it's not installed, you must have the program installed to use image maps on your system.

If you don't have imagemap yet, or need to check that you have the latest version, version information appears at

```
hoohoo.ncsa.uiuc.edu/docs/setup/admin/imagemap.txt
```

If the file date is more recent at NCSA, download the new file, rename it to `imagemag.c`, and recompile. Use the new version instead of the old one.

After you have imagemap available, you must then invoke it on the server. For our example, we've assumed it lives in the `/cgi-bin/` directory. For details about your particular Web server, contact your local webmaster or system administrator.

Final Touches

Fortunately, formatting your image map isn't all a matter of spotting and accommodating every niggling difference. No matter which type of Web server you use as host for your image maps, they all have a few things in common. This happy fact means you can add some classy touches and reasonably expect that most of your users will be able to appreciate them.

Creating and storing map files

Joyous news: You can create a map file with any plain text editor. Store the map file on the server in a special directory for your map definition files. Contact your system administrator or your webmaster to find out where this is and if you have *write* permission. If you don't, you must enlist the administrator's help to get those files installed. For our examples, we use the name, ht4menum.map, and store it in the http://www.domain.com/cgi-bin/ directory, with our other scripts.

Defining a clickable map in your HTML document

After you define a map and store it in the right location, you must bring all three of the magic elements together in an HTML file. Here's how:

```
<a href="http://www.lanw.com/cgi-bin/ht4menum.map">

<img scr="graphics/ht4menum.gif" ismap>

</a>
```

Here's what's going on in this series of statements:

- ✔ The opening anchor tag combines the htimage location, which handles the coordinate-to-URL translation, with a full URL for the map file. Even though you see no space between the name of the program (htimage) and the file specification, the server still knows what to do.

- ✔ The img tag points to the button-bar graphic but adds an ismap attribute to indicate that it's a clickable map.

- ✔ The closing anchor tag </a> indicates that the graphic specified by img is the target for the map file specified in the opening anchor tag.

There you are! After you make sure that all the right pieces are in place on your CERN server, you can try this, too.

Despite the existence of multiple image-map file formats, you need to create only one image-map file for each image map you use on your Web pages. Which kind should you use? Only your webmaster or system administrator knows for sure. But because *we* don't know what kind you'll use, we've told you about the two most common types in use. You may end up using neither, but if you're not using one or the other, your webmaster or system administrator should be able to explain the format to you or tell you how to obtain documentation about that format.

"The Map Is Not the Territory"

Alfred Korzybski didn't know about clickable images when he uttered this section's title (in *Manhood of Humanity: The Science and Art of Human Engineering,* in case you're ever asked about it on *Jeopardy!*). Give him a break; it was before computers. But as the twentieth century starts to show up in the rearview mirror, Korzybski's point takes on a new meaning: Because not all users can see an image map, be prepared to show the same set of selections in text that GUI users get in visual form.

Okay, you're game. How? First, consider that what you provide in an image map is a set of choices. You can add an equivalent set of text-based links (choices) near the image. Here's what the HTML for this looks like:

```
<a href="http://www.lanw.com/cgi-bin/html4dum.map">
<img border=0 align=top src="graphics/ht4menum.gif"
   alt="Navigation Bar" ismap></a><p>
<img align=middle width=130 height=0 src=graphics/space.gif
   alt=" ">
<b><a href="ftpstuff.htm">FILES</A> &#32;&#124;
<a href="contents.htm">CONTENTS</A> &#32;&#124;
<a href="search4d.htm">SEARCH</A> &#32;&#124;
<a href="contact.htm">CONTACT</A> &#32;&#124;
<a href="whatsnew.htm">NEW</A><BR>
<img align=middle width=240 height=0 src=graphics/space.gif
   ALT=" ">
<a href="navigate.htm">HOW TO NAVIGATE</a></b><p>
<a href="html4du2.htm">Click here for a non-imagemap
version</a>
```

As shown in Figure 15-2, this snippet of code creates a text bar (right beneath the graphic) that offers the same choices. Users with graphical browsers won't suffer from this redundancy, and character-mode browsers get a reasonable facsimile of what the graphically advantaged see in living color. We call this *mastering the art of compromise!*

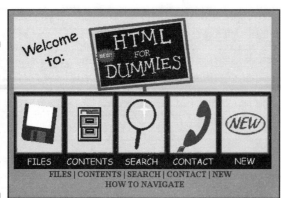

Figure 15-2:
A text-based bar combined with a button bar keeps everybody in the know.

Of Clickable Maps and URLs

Image links can sometimes play hob with relative URLs within HTML documents. One unforeseen side effect of following links through a map-reading script — to the map and back to the target page — can be a complete mangling of the context within which URLs are addressed. In English, this means it's a really, really, *really* good idea to use full URLs (instead of relative references) in documents that include clickable maps.

You would be wise (as well as cagey) to consider carefully before using any relative URL reference in documents with clickable maps. Test thoroughly to make sure everything works as it should. Avoiding trouble is, in general, the best way to prevent an encore of the URL Relative Reference Blues!

Client-Side Image Maps!

A *client-side image map* is a graphical navigation tool that runs within the users' browsers and requires neither a server nor a CGI map file to operate. (Whoa! No visible means of support! How do they *do* that?) Both Netscape's and Microsoft's Web browsers support client-side image maps. Creating one is as easy as building a server-side image map.

Building a client-side image map involves

- ✔ Defining the hot-spot areas of the image.
- ✔ Embedding the coordinates in an HTML document.

Possible area definitions include these familiar friends:

- **Point —** `<area shape="point" coords="x,y" href="URL1">`
- **Circle —** `<area shape="circle" coords="x,y,x2,y2" href="URL2">`
- **Rectangle —** `<area shape="rect" coords="x,y,x2,y2" href="URL3">`
- **Polygon —** `<area shape="poly" coords="x,y,x2,y2,x3,y3,..." href="URL4">`
- **Default —** `<area shape="default" href="URL5">`

You probably recognize all these types except for `circle`. A circle's area is defined by a central point and a point on the circle's edge (which, as we all fondly remember, defines its radius — and you thought you'd never *use* geometry). Coordinates are grouped together, separated by commas. The code for doing so unfurls thus:

Slam a set of `area` tags inside a `map` tag associated with a properly labeled `img` tag, and you've built a client-side image map. Notice that we name a client-side image map using the `name` attribute of the `map` tag and reference it with the `usemap` attribute in the `img` tag. Here's an example:

```
<img src="HT4MEMU.GIF" usemap="#h4dmap">
<MAP NAME="h4dmap">
  <area shape="rect" coords="0,142,98,285" href="http://www.
        domain.com/html4dum/ftpstuff.htm">
  <area shape="rect" coords="99,142,198,285" href="http://www.
        domain.com/html4dum/contents.htm">
  <area shape="rect" coords="199,142,298,285" href="http://
        www.domain.com/html4dum/search4d.htm">
  <area shape="rect" coords="299,142,398,285" href="http://
        www.domain.com/html4dum/contact.htm">
  <area shape="rect" coords="399,142,499,285" href="http://
        www.domain.com/html4dum/whatsnew.htm">
  <area shape="default" href="http://www.domain.com/html4dum/
        contents.htm">
</map>
```

Given all this flexibility, why use server-side image maps at all? Only one reason: Progress is never uniform. Which is to say, not all browsers support client-side image maps. But any graphical browser that can call a CGI can use a *server*-side image map. So be wary and au courant if you're switching to the client side of the street.

Character-mode browsers (or GUI browsers with graphics turned off) can't handle image maps of any kind. So, even if you do take the plunge into client-side image maps, always provide a text alternative, just as you would with a server-side equivalent. Either way, there has to be another way for the graphically disadvantaged to compensate!

Client-side image maps in action

In yet another revival of school-days skills, masters of the art of cut-and-paste can use simple map constructs just like this one in their own documents. No boxtops to send in, no library paste to eat. All you need is a file and your trusty cut-and-paste utility. Remember, client-side image maps don't need a map file (that information is included in the HTML) or a server (the client handles all map processing). If you want to see one in action, load up the front page of the example Web site from the book's CD-ROM and select "client-side image map version."

Special bulletin for Internet Explorer 3 for Macintosh users! You may find that HTML4DUM.HTM, which is on the CD-ROM, opens with graphics that appear cropped — that is, chopped so that only a part of the title graphic appears at the top of the page. To resolve this truncated expectation, choose the client-side version of the page by clicking the client-side link in the loaded HTML4DUM.HTM file, or open the HTML4DU2.HTM file.

Chapter 16

HTML Frames

*T*hat's right, you've been framed. And you may find you like it. *HTML frames* are so handy they're almost a crime: They delineate, outline, and give structure to HTML documents; they help move information coherently within and among themselves. But wait, there's more! The big fish decided they liked frames so much that they became standard in HTML 4.0. Best of all, today's exciting episode shows you — step by step — how you can use frames to make your Web pages get up and wail.

As you probably guessed, there's always more to learn about the incredibly cool powers of HTML. Frames are no exception; this chapter gives you a basic understanding of how they work, but practicality demands that we stop there. If you like what you see, and want to ferret out more down-and-dirty details about using frames, check out the following WWW sites:

```
www.htmlhelp.com/reference/html40/
home.netscape.com/assist/net_sites/frames.html
www.w3.org/tr/wd-html401
```

HTML Frames Overview

To frame a practical question: Do you really *need* to use the <frameset> tag? You could, of course, use a table to format your information into areas, complete with borders, on the browser screen. But remember: Tables are static and frames can be dynamic — you can scroll information within them, and users may find that appealingly easy to deal with.

Each frame works like a separate browser screen. Depending on the attributes you give it, a frame can act just like a standard browser screen, or it can be frozen into Elliot Ness untouchability.

With the approval of the HTML 4.0 standard, frames finally became part of the standard for HTML. This means that only state-of-the-art browsers (Versions 3.0 and later of just about any major browser) can handle frames properly, and that some of your users may not be able to appreciate their beauty and efficacy. Because both Netscape and Microsoft have implemented frames in their browsers, as long as you're sure users have a frames-compatible browser you can safely use frames on your site. But if your audience uses a wide variety of browsers, you may want to shy away from frames, or you may want to offer a non-framed version of the same materials so that users can pick which version of your pages they want to explore.

Frames have numerous uses, as in the following eye-catching instances:

- ✔ A Web page with a fixed logo at the top and a scrolling bottom section
- ✔ A page with a fixed top logo, a navigation bar and copyright notice at the bottom, and a scrolling middle section for displaying page contents
- ✔ A Web page with side-by-side frames that put a table of contents on the left and a scrolling text frame on the right
- ✔ A left frame filled with icons linked to different parts of a Web site, where whatever element is displayed in the right frame is based on a selection from the left frame

You find out how to set up these structures a bit later in this chapter. For now, note that frames are flexible without going all rubbery. They enable you to keep constant chunks of information on display while your users scroll happily through large amounts of text or dynamic content. But hold on there, pal. Before you jump ahead and start framing everything in sight, get to know the brass tacks — the HTML markup tags that make frames possible.

HTML Frame Tags

Welcome to HTML Tags for Frames Territory. Here's where we list 'em, discuss their proper syntax and use, and offer some pointers on their good and better uses. After that, it's all up to you and your good taste; hanging some nice frames around your Web site should make it feel homey for your visitors. So we start with basic groundwork (the structure of a document that includes frames) and then trot out the tags you use to make the frames.

No frames, please, we're text-only . . .

It's uncanny how the Web offers up slice-of-life lessons. One lesson is consistent: Where frames (and, for that matter, all HTML features) are concerned, *not everybody gets with the program at the same time.* Some of your visitors may (gasp) have no use for frames. If you're a nice person and want to provide something for frame-challenged browsers to display, you can use the `<noframes>` tag to include an alternative, nonframed HTML document. When you use the `<noframes>` tag, you must include the `<body>` tag within its embrace, like this:

```
<noframes>
<body>
The nonframed HTML code for
     your page goes here.
</body>
</noframes>
```

Details to follow, later in this chapter. Film at eleven.

The frame document structure

A frame document can simply be a normal HTML document in which you replace the `<body>`...`</body>` container with a `<frameset>`...`</frameset>` container that characterizes the HTML subdocuments — frames — that constitute the Web page. (Simply put: You use `<frameset>` instead of `<body>` as the box to put your content in.) The basic frame document starts within the following overall HTML, ah, *framework*. (Couldn't help it. The word seemed so appropriate.)

```
<html>
<head>
</head>
<frameset>
Your frame information goes here.
</frameset>
</html>
```

Frame syntax is uncannily similar to the syntax you use within HTML tables. In fact, you can think of frames as movable, dynamically updated tables. After you start using frame-related markup in your own pages, the syntax starts to look pretty straightforward. But it takes some practice to get used to the concepts involved.

<frameset>

The `<frameset>` tag is the main container for any frame. As we mentioned earlier, your basic, red-blooded frame document uses `<frameset>` instead of `<body>` to identify what's going on inside it. After that it gets only a little weird:

✔ The `<frameset>` tag follows immediately after the `</head>` tag.

✔ If any `<body>` tags appear before the `<frameset>` tags, the `<frameset>` tags are ignored, and what's a body stays a body.

✔ Between the outermost `<frameset>` . . . `</frameset>` tags, you can use only nested `<frameset>` tags, nested `<frame>` tags, or nested `<noframes>` tags to define any interior shenanigans.

To put all this into code perspective, every good frameset starts like this:

```
<frameset>

</frameset>
```

And you thought this was going to be hard. Okay, that's the big box o' frames. Next are the attributes you can put in it.

rows=" n " or " % " or " *, n " or " % " or " *, n " or " % " or " *, . . . "

(And just try reading *that* aloud.) The `rows` attribute determines two things: (1) the number of frames that appear vertically (stacked on top of each other) in the browser window and (2) the height of each frame. The `rows` attribute uses commas to separate the numbers that make up its list of values. The number of elements appearing there determines the number of frames shown up and down the screen. The total height of all the simultaneously displayed frames must equal the height of the browser window; the browser may adjust the `rows` height values to make them all fit. (Hint: If the text looks like a regiment of ants, you've probably got too many frames and too cramped a `rows` height.) `rows` values can be any valid mixture of the following elements:

✔ n: The direct approach — a fixed number of pixels. Seems simple, but take care: the size of the browser window can vary substantially from one user to another. When you use fixed-pixel values, it's good practice to use one or more relative values (described later in this chapter) with them. Otherwise, the user's browser could override your specified pixel value to ensure that the total height and width of all the frames equals 100 percent of the user's window. You might not want it to do that; a browser doesn't care about eyestrain. All it knows to do is follow orders and *display all defined frames,* even if mercilessly squashed together and crammed with unreadable text.

✔ value%: This value tells the browser, *Size this frame to a percentage of screen area, between 1 and 100.* If the total for all frames is greater than 100 percent, all percentages are reduced to fit the browser window (ants-in-travel-size-sardine-cans again). If the values total less than 100 percent, extra space is added to any relative-sized frames that happen to be hanging around (for example, the next item in this list).

> ✔ [value]*: A single asterisk * character designates a relative-sized
> frame. Browsers give such frames all remaining space left over after
> other allocations are satisfied. If you use multiple relative-sized frames,
> the remaining space is divided evenly among them.

If you place a value in front of the *, the frame gets that much more relative
space. For instance, an entry such as 3*, * allocates three times as much
space to the first frame (3/4 of the total on-screen space) as to the second
frame (which gets a measly 1/4).

Advanced math degrees aren't needed to use these different types of values,
but you do need to eyeball the on-screen results of your work carefully. Give
'em extra-severe scrutiny when you mix value types. Following are a couple
of examples, each a different way to stack frames on-screen.

> ✔ **Two vertically stacked frames:** The code looks like this for two equiva-
> lent value constructs:
>
> ```
> <FRAMESET ROWS="20%,80%">
> <FRAMESET ROWS="20%,*">
> ```
>
> ✔ **Three vertical frames:** A mere snippet of HTML code creates three verti-
> cal frames, using a fixed pixel value, a relative value, and a percentage
> value:
>
> ```
> <FRAMESET ROWS="100,*,20%">
> ```

COLS="n" or " % " or " *, n " or " % " or " *, n " or " % " or " *, ..."

The cols (for *columns*) attribute is as single-minded as the rows attribute; it
governs the number of frames that march horizontally across the browser's
screen, as well as the width of each frame.

The following quick example of HTML code displays two frames across the
screen; the first one (on the left) gets 20 percent of the available space and
the second (on the right) gets the rest:

```
<frameset cols="20%,*">
```

<frame>

If you're gonna do frames, go the whole correct route: A separate <frame>
tag must define each separate frame in your Web site. The <frame> tag has
no associated end tag; all by its lonesome, it defines contents, name, and
attributes for each frame. If you want to display four frames you'll need to
create four frames, so you need four <frame> tags. The first <frame> tag
defines the top left-most frame area. The second <frame> tag defines the
frame immediately to the right of the first frame, or if the edge of the browser
is reached, the frame in the next row. And so on, with no end tag in sight.

Within each frame that you create, you'll display another Web page. The following is an example of the syntax for a `<frame>` tag:

```
<frame src="yourstuf.htm" name="Your Frame">
```

You can modify the `<frame>` tag by using any of seven attributes. And here they are, one by one (we thought you'd never ask):

src="url"

The URL that identifies the `src` (for *source*) attribute points to the source material you want to appear in the frame. Aforesaid source material may be a link, an image, an HTML file, or any other legal URL. If you omit the `src` attribute, the frame appears blank and may cause the browser to display an error message.

name="window_name"

The `name` attribute assigns a name to a frame, which makes it easier to target the frame as a recipient of information. The `name` attribute is optional, and all name values must begin with an alphanumeric character.

frameborder="yes" or "no"

What's a picture without a border? The `frameborder` attribute allows you to decide for yourself. You can specify whether you want the frames within your frameset to have borders. Borders help your readers differentiate between frames, but they can also get in the way of a seamless page. Your specific implementation of frames is what determines the value you assign to this attribute.

marginwidth="value"

The `marginwidth` attribute accepts a value of one or more pixels to determine the exact width of the left and right margins of a frame. Margins must be one or more pixels wide to keep objects from touching the edges of a frame. (Of course, *some* wiseacres might want to specify margins that leave no space for a document's contents, but they're not allowed to. So there.) The `marginwidth` attribute is optional, but some margin is always gonna be there. If you omit this attribute, the browser sets its own margin widths (usually 1 or 2 pixels wide).

marginheight="value"

The `marginheight` attribute works like `marginwidth` — you specify one or more pixels for the height — except it controls the top- and bottom-edge margins of frames instead of the left and right margins. (And the height has to be more than zero — c'mon, you know the rules.)

scrolling="yes" or "no" or "auto"

Merrily they scroll along — but only if they need to. The optional scrolling attribute determines whether a frame displays a scroll bar. A value of yes forces the browser to display a scroll bar on that frame. A no value keeps scroll bars invisible. The scrolling attribute has a default value of auto, which means that scroll bars appear only when more content than fits in the window must be displayed. This is the (very sensible) default, and the wise will leave it in place under most circumstances. After all, you can't always determine what size window your users will tack up on their screens to display your framed pages; this way they get a scroll bar if they need one, nary a one if they don't.

noresize

By default, users can resize frames by dragging a frame edge to a new position. If you've got a good reason to say *Don't touch,* the noresize attribute sternly forbids a user to resize a frame by, ah, not letting them resize the frame. The noresize attribute is optional and not really a killjoy:

- ✔ If any frame adjacent to the edge of another frame isn't resizable, that entire edge can't move. This unmovable edge affects the resizing of any adjacent frames.

- ✔ If you want your viewers to stay aware of whose site it is and who's paying the bills, noresize can keep your logo or advertising space in view.

- ✔ We don't recommend using the noresize attribute willy-nilly for content frames, but not because it spoils the fun of tweaking them. Its restriction limits the extent to which users can tinker your hand-crafted frames (the results of all those display settings) into fitting their screens.

<noframes> . . . </noframes>

You say some of your users are surfing the Web with only the bearskin basics? Give 'em a break: Create some alternative content, put it between a starting <noframes> tag and an ending </noframes> tag, and presto! Frame-challenged browsers can appreciate at least the text part of your site's splendor, and frame-cognizant browsers ignore all tags and data between the <noframes> tags. (Almost lost 'em there. That was close.)

Putting it all together

So once you've added all the tags up, the basic code for a solid frameset with two horizontal frames — one right next to each other — looks like this:

```
<frameset cols="20%, *">
  <frame src="url" name="frame1">
  <frame src="url" name="frame2">

  <noframes>
    <body>
      <p>Users who can't view frames see this instead</p>
    </body>
  <noframes>

</frameset>
```

To create two vertical frames — one on top of the other — the opening
`<frameset>` tag would be:

```
<frameset rows="20%, *">
```

Of course you can add other attributes to the `<frame>` tags to tweak the final
look and feel of your display. Finally, don't forget that for each frame in your
frame document, you'll need a full-fledged Web document to display. So a two
frame frameset really requires three HTML documents to work:

- ✔ The Web page that defines the frameset
- ✔ The HTML page that will show up in the first frame
- ✔ The HTML page that will take up residence in the second frame

Targeting frames

The dilemma: You have a frame document with two vertical frames, a skinny
one on the left that serves as a navigation document and a wider one on the
right where the bulk of the content your users see shows up. You want to
create hyperlinks in the document that lives in the skinny frame on the left
that, when clicked, cause new Web documents to load in the wide frame on
the right. This is actually a common frame dilemma, as illustrated by the
layout of a Web-based training site shown in Figure 16-1.

Now you know by now that when you click a hyperlink, the document the link
is attached to replaces the one that you just clicked in. So how do you change
the nature of a hyperlink and force documents to show up in a different frame
than the one they were called from? Believe it or not it's as simple as adding a
single attribute to a hyperlink.

The `target` attribute gives you control over where the linked page or other
resource appears when a user clicks a link in your documents. Of course, you
can use the `target` attribute in the `<base>`, `<area>`, and `<form>` tags, but
the attribute really shines when you use it in the `<a>` (anchor) tag in conjunction with frames.

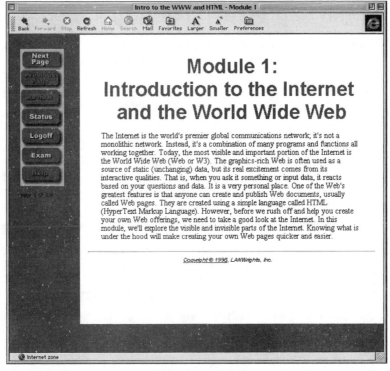

Figure 16-1:
Click a
button in the
right frame
and the
document
it links to
appears in
the left
frame. It's
magic.

So, how exactly does targeting work? Normally, when a user clicks a link, the browser displays the new document in a full browser window. Targeting enables you to change that first view: You can assign names to specific frames — remember the `name=` attribute — and decree that certain documents shall duly appear in the frame that bears the targeted name. (Control freaks, rejoice!)

In a prior section of this chapter, we explain how to use the `name` attribute to name a frame. Using the `target` attribute to, well, *target* the frame is just as easy: Insert the attribute and its corresponding value (the name of the frame, known inscrutably as the *frame name*) in the `<a>` tag. In the following example, the name of the targeted frame is — you guessed it — `frame name`:

```
<a href="url" target="frame name">Targeted Anchor</a>
```

The document referenced by this particular anchor tag will load in the frame defined by this tag:

```
<frame name="frame name">
```

Do you see a trend here? We thought we did.

Legal and predefined target names

Any valid frame name specified in a target attribute must begin with an alphanumeric character. Well, okay, the exceptions are a few predefined, special-purpose target names that begin with the underscore character (examples coming up). Any targeted frame name that begins with an underscore or a nonalphanumeric character (and *isn't* a special-purpose name) is ignored.

Special-purpose target names include _self, _blank, _parent, and _top. Of these values, _parent and _self can target particular files that share a parent/child relationship in the directory hierarchy. (Which would make 'em "family" values in that case. So to speak.) Use them to determine what the user sees when that fateful click selects the linked document:

- target="_self": Specifying the _self target always causes the linked document to load inside the frame in which the user has selected the anchor. This is how all links act by default, so you can imagine that every regular anchor has an invisible target="_self" attached to it. Aren't you glad you don't have to type that every time?

- target="_blank": Specifying the blank target causes the linked document to load inside a new browser window. This is an easy way to force the user's browser to launch another window. While this can be a useful attribute if you want to link to someone else's site but still make sure your site is immediately available to users — in the first browser window that never went away — don't over use it. Visitors to your site won't appreciate new browser windows popping up all the time.

- target="_parent": Specifying the _parent target makes the linked document load in the immediate frameset parent of the document. If the current document in which the _parent target appears has no parent, this attribute behaves like the _self value.

- target="_top": Specifying the _top target makes the linked document load in the full body of the window. If the current document is already at the top of the document hierarchy, then the _top target name behaves like _self. You can use this attribute to escape from a deeply nested frame. (Oxygen tank optional.)

If you get carried away using frames nested within frames nested within frames, or you link to someone else's framed site only to find their frames loading inside of yours — whew what a headache — you can use Target="_Top" to cancel out your frameset and revert back to a nice, simple, regular HTML page.

Framing Your Web

Your Web pages are like pictures waiting to be framed. Even if you provide pure text for your users, you can still use frames behind the scenes to help them navigate within your site.

One important feature of frames is that they let you keep important information on-screen constantly, while other portions of the screen change to reflect new content.

Okay, back to the drawing board: The first requirement for using frames successfully is to visualize your Web page as a collection of frames. Sketch it on a napkin, the back of an envelope, or whatever's handy in the trash can (except maybe that banana peel). As your rough-and-ready diagram takes shape, remember: You need one HTML document to define your sketched-out frame page *and* a separate HTML document for each frame in your sketch.

In the following example, watch closely as the multiple HTML documents needed to construct an image magically influence each resulting screen shot. At no time will our hands leave our sleeves — you will witness how using frames means creating more (generally smaller) HTML documents. Why the extra work? Two reasons: (1) each frame requires its own HTML document, and (2) such is the price we hardy Web pioneers must pay, slaving tirelessly to provide our users with the best possible Web sites . . .

Oh, well. With HTML documents, practice makes perfect. Which brings us to the eagerly-awaited example . . . .

HTML code for a three-frame page

The following HTML code sets up a top frame 150 pixels high and a bottom frame 100 pixels high. Top and bottom frames are nonscrolling; the bottom frame, a real party pooper, isn't resizable either. The middle frame is set to scrolling to illustrate the scroll bars.

```html
<html>
<head>
 <title>Three Frame Example</title>
</head>

<frameset rows="150, *, 100">
 <frame src="top.htm" name="top frame" scrolling="no">
 <frame src="middle.htm" name="middle frame"
        scrolling="yes">
 <frame src="bottom.htm" name="bottom frame"
        scrolling="no" noresize>
</frameset>

</html>
```

Such a three-frame setup is versatile enough to accommodate a hefty range of uses. Here's the HTML code for its top frame (titled `Top Frame` and coming soon to a Web page near you . . .). And check out that scintillating sample content that appears after the `</center>` end tag:

```
<html>
 <head>
  <title>Top Frame</title>
 </head>

<body>
 <center>
  <h2>Top frame text here.</h2>
 </center>

 <p>
    The text you are reading here is in a file named
    top.htm. The file is called by the following line
    in the main.htm document:<br>
      &lt;frame src="top.htm" name="Top Frame"
      scrolling="no"&gt;
 </p>
 </body>
</html>
```

Okay, next up is the HTML code for the middle frame. Nothing fancy, just a standard HTML document in which you can place any legal HTML tags and other information. (Speaking of which, we've included some, ah, dummy content that we have absolute confidence you can improve upon.)

```
<html>
 <head>
  <title>Middle Frame</title>
 </head>

<body>
 <center>
  <h2>Middle frame text here.</h2>
 </center>

 <p>
    The text you are reading here is in a file named
    top.htm. The file is called by the following line
    in the main.htm document:<br>
      &lt;frame src="middle.htm" name="Middle Frame"
      scrolling="no"&gt;
 </p>
 </body>
</html>
```

Finally, we get to the bottom of this: The following listing shows the HTML code for the bottom frame. This listing is another standard HTML document — but remember, the document is displayed within a fixed-height (100-pixel) frame that can't be resized. As for which content deserves to hang out there, calmly staring your readers in the face . . . that's up to you.

```html
<html>
 <head>
  <title>Bottom Frame</title>
 </head>

<body>
  <center>
   <h2>Bottom frame text here.</h2>
  </center>

<p>
     The text you are reading here is in a file named
     bottom.htm. The file is called by the following line
     in the main.htm document:<br>
        &lt;frame src="bottom.htm" name="Bottom Frame"
        NORESIZE &gt;
  </p>
 </body>
</html>
```

For fun, copy the code for the frameset and related pages into a text editor, save the four different files with the names we used, and then open `main.htm` in your Web browser to see the cool results. See, frames are both fun and simple; who could ask for more?

Your job as a Web page author is to make sure that any information you put in a frame is compact or short enough to fit the specified frame space, even when users resize their entire browser screens. If you can't make the information fit the frame, use relative values for the frame height and allow your users to resize as needed.

Of course, no proper exhortation would be complete without examples of framed sites in action. Got 'em right here. . . .

Two stunningly framed Web sites

Because frames are dynamic beasts, capturing them in a picture would not do them justice. So, load these URLs in your own frames-enabled browser to see the goods for yourself.

✔ DevEdge Online HTML Specification from Netscape:

```
developer.netwcape.com/library/documentation/htmlguid/
        index.htm
```

✔ Managing Your Web classroom materials from (ahem) our own LANWrights site:

```
www.lanw.com/training/myw/myw.htm
```

Part V
The Bleeding Edge

The 5th Wave   By Rich Tennant

"There's gotta be a more elegant way to prompt for credit card numbers."

In this part . . .

Part V is where we dare you to peek beyond the fringe of accepted standards and technologies, and take a look at what gonzo Web artists are working with — only they have to do it without a safety net! Here's where you learn what HTML forms are and how they work, where style markup makes it possible to give even humdrum text-only Web pages some color and pizazz, and where dynamic HTML lets you solicit input from your readers, and change your Web pages to match their moods on the fly! You find this part to be a real adventure, so buckle up before you dive in.

Chapter 17

Forms, Feedback, Scripting, and Beyond

*W*hen all the pieces come together properly, it's easy to see how the Web brings people and organizations together. At first glance, the Web might look pretty much like a one-way street — that is, an environment where webmasters communicate aplenty with Web users, with not much interaction coming back from users at all. But it doesn't have to be that way.

HTML Forms and Forthright Feedback

The essence of serving up useful information is relevancy and immediacy. But the best judge of the quality of your information is your audience. Wouldn't it be wonderful if your readers could give you feedback on your Web pages? Then, they could tell you what parts they like, what they don't like, and what other things they'd like to see included in your site.

Getting feedback is where HTML forms come into play. Up to this point in the book, we've talked about all the basics — and even a few advanced techniques — for communicating with an audience. In this chapter, you find out how to turn the tables and create HTML that lets your audience communicate with you!

As it turns out, HTML supports a rich variety of input capabilities to let you solicit feedback. In the pages that follow, you discover the tags to use, the controls and inputs they enable, along with some layout considerations for building forms. You also get to see some interesting example forms to help you understand what HTML forms look like and how they behave.

On the Limitations of Form (s)

HTML forms were established way back in the HTML 2.0 days — ancient history on the Web, but only a few years in how we measure time. With HTML 4.0, forms have gained some new capabilities and a bit of a face-lift, too. But even though forms give users the ability to communicate with Web authors and developers, you still find some important limitations in using them. You must be keenly aware of their abilities and limitations before you deploy forms on your site.

Beware of browser!

Most new browsers — Netscape Navigator or Communicator 4.0 (and higher) and Microsoft Internet Explorer (Windows 95 Version 3.0.3 and higher), plus NCSA Mosaic and its variants — already include HTML 4.0-level forms support, but other browsers do not. In fact, you won't know how well your favorite browser handles HTML 4.0 forms until you test your forms with it. If you follow our suggestions and test your pages against multiple browsers, you'll immediately observe different levels of robustness and capability when it comes to forms implementations.

The bottom line is that not all browsers support forms equally, but that support is pretty commonplace. Current or modern browser versions have no problem interacting with most form constructs. But don't be surprised if on older browsers, forms don't work that well or not at all.

 Assuming that the information your form solicits is important to you, consider adding an FTP URL to your page to let users download a file containing a text-only version of the form's content. Then they can download this file and complete with any text editor. If you include an e-mail address inside the form itself, they can e-mail it back to you, and you get feedback, even from users who can't deal with forms. That way nobody gets left out!

Sorry, servers . . .

Because the Web is a client/server environment, be aware that just because your browser supports forms doesn't automatically imply that the server installed at your site handles them. Unfortunately, keeping up with HTML advancements means that Web servers have to change right along with clients. In other words, your server may not support the input-handling programs necessary to process a form's input when it gets delivered. Or you may not be able to access the right input-handling programs on the server without help from an administrator, even if everything you need is already in place.

However, you'll find a silver lining in this potentially dark cloud: The most common implementations of the *httpd* server (the *http daemon* — the Web server software that handles requests for Web services, including forms, and responds as needed) come from NCSA and the W3C and run in the UNIX environment, among other platforms. Both of these industry groups have standardized forms-handling technology and offer useful, robust forms-handling capabilities.

These implementations are so common, in fact, that we assume your Web server works the same way that they do. This means that you may have to alter some of the approaches to CGI scripting and other programming that you might use to handle forms on your server, if our assumption is incorrect. If you're not using UNIX and the NCSA or CERN implementations of httpd, you'll want to investigate the particulars that your server's implementation requires and alter our instructions accordingly. This statement is particularly true for Windows NT, in which Perl is not a common language in the standard arsenal of server capabilities, and in which equivalent input-handling is available in a variety of alternate guises.

By this point in the evolution of the Web, you probably won't run into a Web server that does not offer some sort of support for forms, either through CGI, server-side includes, some native scripting language, or some other proprietary solution (like Microsoft Active Server Pages or its Internet Information Server API, also known as ISAPI).

What's in a Form?

When adding forms support to a Web page, you must include special tags to solicit input from users. You surround these tags with text to prompt user responses. You also include tags to gather input and ship it to your Web server, or to other servers that may offer services — like Gopher or Archie — that your form knows how to query. Here's how this works:

✔ On a particular Web page, you include tags to set up a form and solicit input from users. Some users work their way through this material and provide the information that you want. This essentially amounts to filling out the form that you supply.

✔ After users fill out your form, they can then direct their input to the program running on the Web server that delivered the form. In most cases, they select a particular control, called `submit`, to gather the data and send it to a specific input-handling program on your Web server.

✔ Assuming that the program is available (installed and running properly, that is), it accepts the input information. Then the program decodes and interprets the contents to guide its further actions.

✔ After the input is received and interpreted, the program can do pretty much anything it wants. In practice, this boils down to recognizing key elements in a form's content and custom-building an HTML document in response. Building a document isn't required but is a pretty common capability within the majority of forms-handling programs.

✔ This custom-built document is delivered to the user in response to the form's content. At this point, additional interaction can occur (if the "return page" includes another form), requested information can be delivered (in response to requests on the form), a simple acknowledgment issued, or so forth.

The information collected from a form can be

✔ Written to a file.

✔ Submitted to a database, such as Informix or Oracle.

✔ E-mailed to someone in particular.

Forms can also allow users to participate in building an evolving Web document, such as the Web site called WaxWeb, that allows users to dictate how a story plays out; in this case, the users collectively determine the outcome.

Thus, forms not only provide communication from users to servers, but also provide ongoing interaction between users and servers. This interaction is pretty powerful stuff and can add a lot of value to your Web pages.

Forms involve two-way communication

Most input-catching programs on the Web server rely on an interface between Web browsers and servers called the *Common Gateway Interface* (CGI). This interface codifies how browsers send information back to servers. It codifies formatting for user-supplied input, so that forms-handling programs know what to expect and how to deal with what they receive.

The action attribute in a <form> tag specifies a URL that indicates a specific CGI script or program that collects the form data that a user entered. Likewise, the method attribute describes the way in which input data is delivered to such a forms-handling program.

In this part of the chapter, we concentrate on the input side of HTML forms — building the *front end* of a form (the part that users see). If you've already built the front end and want to build the *back end* (the CGI or equivalent programs that your server uses to digest all that input from the forms), jump to the section in this chapter called "Interactivity, Multimedia, and Cold Feet."

Tag! You're a form . . .

HTML includes several different classes of forms tags (for the details on syntax and usage, go directly to Chapter 4; tell 'em the authors sent you). To begin with, all HTML forms occur within the <form> . . . </form> tags. The <form> tag also includes attributes that specify where and how to deliver input to the appropriate Web server.

All other forms-related tags and text must appear within the <form> . . . </form> tags. (Not just a good idea. It's the law.) These tags include methods for

✔ Specifying input (the <input> tag and its many attributes).

✔ Grouping related sets of form controls and fields using the <fieldset> . . . </fieldset> tags.

✔ Employing <button> . . . </button> tags to create forms controls. (Usually, this markup surrounds graphics of buttons, with alternate text defined by the value of the button's name attribute for non-GUI viewers.)

✔ Using <label> . . . </label> tags to identify form controls and fields.

✔ Using <legend> . . . </legend> tags to create captions for sets of related form controls (field sets, in other words).

✔ Setting up text input areas (the <textarea> . . . </textarea> tags).

✔ Selecting values from a predefined set of possible inputs (the <select> . . . </select> tags).

✔ Managing the form's content (using the submit attribute for input to deliver the content to the server, or the reset attribute to clear its contents and start over).

Though you can't reach out and touch your users (at least not yet), forms-input tags give you lots of ways to interact:

- ✔ Creating text input fields, called *text areas,* where users can type in whatever they want. Designers can choose either single- or multiline-text input fields and can govern how much text displays on-screen and how much text can be entered into any text area.

- ✔ Generating pull-down menus, often called *pick lists* because they require making one or more selections from a set of predefined choices.

- ✔ Creating custom buttons and graphical controls for incorporation into forms.

- ✔ Assigning all kinds of labels and captions to individual fields or buttons, or to groups of fields or buttons, as needed.

- ✔ Creating labeled checkboxes or radio buttons on-screen, which users can select to indicate choices. Checkboxes allow multiple selections and radio buttons allow just one selection.

These capabilities may sound mild-mannered, but when you combine them with the power to prompt users for input by using surrounding text and graphics, forms are actually a pretty super way to ask for information on a Web page. Which leads us back to the question we asked to kick off this section — *What's in a form?* Answer: *Almost anything you want!*

Now that you are suffused with these newfound powers, you get to use them to build an actual form. (Hey, sometimes you win.)

Using Form Tags

As many a Web-page designer (or housing contractor, for that matter) can tell you, it's wise to prepare the environment before you start to build. In this case, we're setting up your <form> environment to accommodate building a form within your Web page. You can add a form to an existing HTML document or build a whole separate document just to contain your form. We recommend that you add shorter forms (half a screen or less) to existing documents; the big-time forms that take up more than half a screen work best if they have their very own documents and don't have to share.

Setting the <form> environment

The two head-honcho attributes within the <form> tag are method and action. Together, these attributes control how your browser sends information to the Web server and which input-handling program receives the form's contents.

A method to our madness

`method` indicates how your browser sends information to the server when you submit the form. `method` takes one of two possible values: `post` or `get`.

Of these two methods, we prefer `post` because it's meticulous but practical: It causes a form's contents to be parsed one element at a time. `get`, on the other hand, joins all field names and their associated values into one long string — which works okay if it's a relatively *short* long string. As it happens, UNIX (and most other operating systems) put a practical, but inconvenient, limit on how long a single string can be; for UNIX, that's 255 characters (this sentence could just squeak by as a single string). It's not hard to imagine some heftier strings getting lopped off (*truncated*), losing important information en route.

For this reason, we use `post` as our only `method` for submitting forms in this book. We recommend that you do the same, unless you're dead certain that the number of characters in a form will never, *ever* exceed 255.

Lights, camera . . . action

`Action` supplies the URL for the CGI script or other input-handling program on the server that receives a form's input. This URL can be a full specification (absolute) or simply a relative reference. Either way, you need to make sure it points to the right program, in the right location, to do the job you expect.

You also need to make sure that the CGI script or program is executable and that it behaves properly. We reveal these secrets of the ages later in this chapter, apropos of testing HTML documents and related CGI programs.

Let's make an assumption . . .

To standardize handling input, we make two assumptions for all forms' syntax in this chapter:

- ✔ In every `<form>` tag, `method="post"`.

- ✔ For every `action`, `url="/cgi-bin/form-name"` — and when we discuss such creatures, we replace the placeholder `form-name` with the name of the form we're discussing (say, for the form named *get-inf.html*, we'd use `url="/cgi-bin/get-inf"`).

Okay, so it's a tad oversimplified for all possible cases; everybody's gotta start somewhere. These conventions make it easy to create sample HTML files to implement the forms in this chapter. (We've also put 'em on the CD-ROM that accompanies this book.)

Incoming! Taking aim with <input> tags

The <input> tag defines a basic form element. This tag takes at least two attributes — namely type and name. type indicates what kind of element should appear on the form. name assigns, well, a *name* to go with the input field (or with the value that corresponds to the <input> tag).

You use name to identify the contents of a field in the form information that is ultimately uploaded to the input-handling Web server. In fact, what the server receives is a series of name/value pairs. The name that identifies the value is the string supplied in the name="string" attribute, and the value is what the user enters or selects for that particular field. Read on — the section titled "A text-oriented <input> example" (catchy, eh?) contains an example that makes all this clear!

type-casting still works!

The type attribute can take any of the following values:

- ✔ button: Creates a button that has no specific use, except to call a script upon selection.

- ✔ checkbox: Produces an on-screen checkbox for users to make multiple selections.

- ✔ file: Allows users to upload a file, but for this to work, you must provide a list of acceptable file types using the accept attribute.

- ✔ hidden: Sort of a "stealth" attribute because it produces no visible input area. It passes data needed for other uses through the form. For example, this might be an ongoing series of forms based on an earlier interaction during which the user identifies himself or herself — a hidden field contains the name-value pair for that data but doesn't show it on the current form. (Some browsers display these fields at the bottom of a form, and each field has no accompanying label.)

- ✔ image: Designates a graphic as a selectable item in a form. You can use this to include icons or other graphical symbols.

- ✔ password: Same as the text type, but characters display as asterisks ("****") or some other masking character, to keep passwords from showing in clear text.

- ✔ radio: Nope, this attribute doesn't pick up FM. It creates a *radio button* for a range of selections, from which the user may select only one.

- ✔ reset: Creates a button labeled "reset" in your form. Include this so that users can clear a form's contents and start over (to err is human; to reset, a relief). Be sure to place it well away from other controls — you don't want them to clear the form by accident!

✔ submit: Creates a button labeled "submit" (by default, or whatever name you supply for the value attribute for submit) in your form. Not as tryannical as it sounds, the type submit tells the browser to bundle the form data and pass it all to the CGI script indicated by the action attribute. In plain English (remember that?) submit is the button readers use to send in the filled-out form, so a form is useless without an <input> field of type submit.

✔ text: Provides a one-line area for text entry. Use this for short fields only (as in the example that follows). For longer text fields, use the <textarea> . . . </textarea> tags instead.

These type attribute values provide a wide range of input displays and data types for form input. As you look at HTML forms on the Web (and in this book) with a new — dare we say more trained? — eye, you can see how effectively you can use these types.

Other <input> attributes

Most remaining attributes exist to modify or qualify the <input> attribute with text type as the default. Here's a list of the attributes du jour that we serve up elsewhere in the book, arrayed in alphabetical order for easy reference:

✔ align=(top|middle|bottom|left|right): For image elements, determines how the graphic is aligned on the form, vis-à-vis the accompanying text.

✔ checked: Makes sure that a certain radio button or checkbox is checked when the form is either visited for the first time or when it is reset. You can control default settings with the checked attribute of <input>.

✔ disabled: Renders an input element unusable (but it will still display on-screen).

✔ maxlength="number": Sets the maximum number of characters that a value in a text element can contain.

✔ readonly: Neither the contents of the control, nor the control itself, may be modified by the user. Any information already present in this control will be automatically submitted with the form. If combined with hidden, provides a way to pass "invisible" data along with other form input.

✔ size="number": Sets the number of characters that a text element can display without scrolling.

✔ src="url": Provides a pointer to the graphic for an image.

✔ tabindex="number": Specifies an element's position in the tabbing order so that field-to-field transitions when the user strikes the tab key can be explicitly controlled (default is by order of appearance).

✔ usemap="filename": Identifies a client-side image map to be used to solicit user input.

✔ value="value": Supplies a default value for a text or hidden element or supplies the corresponding value for a radio button or checkbox selection. You can use this to determine the label of a submit or a reset button, like value="Submit to Admin" for a submit or value="Clear Form" for a reset.

If you'd like to belabor these items (and related design concepts) some more, see Chapter 4 and have a browse through Part IV.

A text-oriented <input> example

That's it for the <input> tag by itself. Here's where we observe it in its natural habitat, a relatively simple survey form:

```
<html>
<head>
<title> Contact Information</title>
<!- the name of this form is usr-inf.html ->
</head>
<body>
<h3>Reader Contact Information</h3>
<p>Please fill out this form, so we'll know how to get in
touch with you. Thanks!
<form method="POST" action="/cgi-bin/usr-inf">
<p>Please enter your name:
<p>First name: <input name="first" type="TEXT" size="12"
          maxlength="20">
MI: <input name ="MI" type="TEXT" size="3" maxlength="3">
Surname(last name): <input name="surname" type="TEXT"
          size="15" maxlength="25">
<p>
<p>Please give us your mailing address:
<p>Address 1: <input name="adr1" type="TEXT" size="30"
          maxlength="45">
<p>Address 2: <input name="adr2" type="TEXT" size="30"
          maxlength="45">
<p>City: <input name="city" type="TEXT" size="15"
          maxlength="30">
<p>State: <input name="state" type="TEXT" size="15"
          maxlength="15">
   ZIP&#47;Postal Code: <input name="zip" type="TEXT"
          size="10" maxlength="10">
<p>Country: <input name="country" type="TEXT" size="15"
          maxlength="15">
<p>
<p>Thank you! <input type="SUBMIT"> <input type="RESET">
</form>
<address>
Sample form for <i>HTML for Dummies</i> Version
          3.1<br>10/16/97 http://www.noplace.com/HTML4D/usr-
          inf.html
</address>
</body></html>
```

Figure 17-1 shows this HTML form on display. Note the positions of the one-line text boxes immediately after field names and the ability to set these boxes on individual lines (as with `Address1` and `Address2`) or together — as with `First name`, `Middle initial (MI)`, and `Last name (Surname)`. These options make it easy to build simple forms that people can actually use (what a concept!).

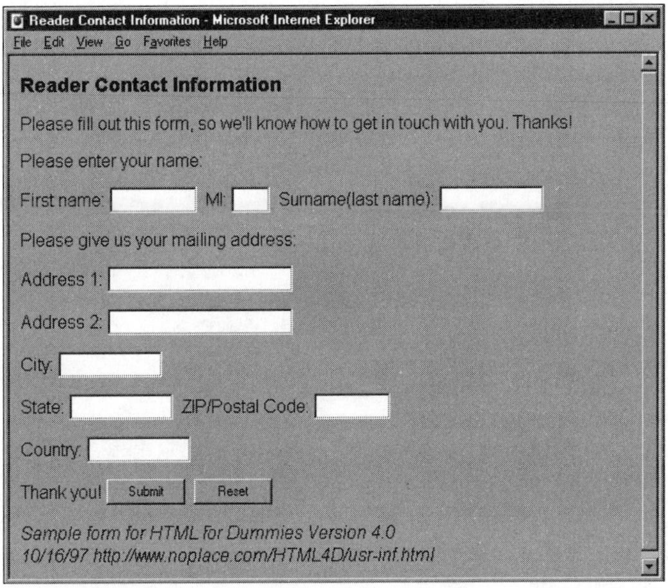

Figure 17-1:
The "Reader
Contact
Information"
form
on-screen.

Being <select>ive

The `<select>` . . . `</select>` pair works much like a list, except it builds a selectable list of `<option>` elements instead of the `<li>` list items. Within the `<select>` tag, the following attributes can occur:

- ✔ `disabled`: Renders an element unusable but still viewable.

- ✔ `tabindex="number"`: Identifies an element's position in the tabbing order defined for the page. The idea is to put some explicit controls on the field-to-field transitions that happen when the user strikes the Tab key with a finger or 8-pound sledgehammer (just kidding). The default setting is by order of appearance).

- ✔ `name="text"`: Provides the name that is passed to the server as the identifying portion of the `name-value` pair for this element.

- ✔ `size="number"`: Controls the number of elements that the pick list displays. Of course, you *could* define more than this number of elements, but keeping the list to a reasonable size makes it more manageable on-screen.

✔ multiple: Indicates that multiple selections from a list are possible; if this flag isn't present in a ⟨select⟩ statement, your users can select only a single element from the pick list.

Building a ⟨select⟩ field for your form doesn't take much work. In the following tasty example, you see how easy it is to construct a list of spices from which a user can select and order:

```
<html>
<head>
<title>&lt;select&gt; Spices</TITLE>
  <!- the name of this form is sel-spi.html ->
  </head>
  <body>
  <h3>This Month's Spicy Selections!</h3>
<p>Spice up your life.  Order from this month's special
        selections.
<br> All items include 2 oz. of the finest condiments, packed
        in tinted glass bottles for best storage.
<hr>
  <form method="POST" action="/cgi/sel-spi">
<p>
  <fieldset>
  <legend>Pepper Selections:</legend>
  <select name="pepper" size="4" multiple>
<option>Plain-black
<option>Malabar
<option>Telicherry
<option>Green-dried
<option>Green-pickled
<option>Red
<option>White
</select>
<p>Please pick a button to indicate how the pepper<br>
        should be delivered:
<br>Ground <input type="RADIO" name="grind" value="ground">
<br>Whole <input type="RADIO" name="grind" value="whole">

<br></fieldset>

<p>

<hr>

<p>Imported and Domestic Oregano:

<select name="oregano" size="4" multiple>

<option> Italian-whole

<option> Italian-crumbled

<option> Greek-whole
```

```
   <option> Indian

   <option> Mexican
   <option> Organic-California
   </select>
   <p>Thanks for your order! <input type="SUBMIT" value="Send
       Order">
<input type="RESET">
   </form>
<address>
Sample form for <i>HTML For Dummies</i> Version 3.1<br>
3/17/97 http://www.noplace.com/HTML4D/spc-ord.html
</address></body></html>
```

Figure 17-2 shows what nice results you can get from using <select> elements to provide options for your users to pick from. (Lunch, anyone?)

Notice the radio buttons for specifying whole or ground pepper. By giving both radio buttons the same name attribute, we indicate that the user can choose only one option.

<textarea> to wax eloquent (or wane profane)

The <textarea> . . . </textarea> tags may not give you total artistic freedom at last, but at least you can use 'em to create input elements of nearly any size on a form. Any text that appears between these opening and closing tags dutifully appears within the text area you've defined on-screen. If you leave the text area unmodified, the tags supply the default value delivered by the form. They've got it covered.

<textarea> takes these attributes:

- cols="number": Specifies the number of characters that can fit onto any one row of the text area; this value also sets the width of the text area on-screen.

- disabled: Makes the element unusable even though it still displays.

- name="text": Provides the identifier part of the all-important name-value pair delivered to the server.

- readonly: When set, this value prevents users from modifying the text area; any information contained therein will automatically be submitted with the form.

- rows="number": Specifies the number of lines of text that the text area will contain.

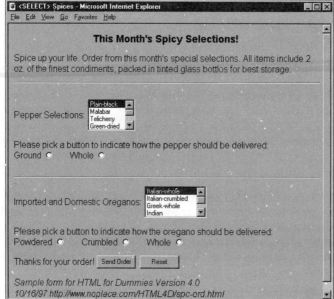

Figure 17-2:
`<select>`
creates
scrolling
pick lists of
choices for
users to
select.

✔ `tabindex="number"`: Identifies this element's position in the tabbing order defined for fields on the page so that field-to-field transitions when the user strikes the tab key can be explicitly controlled (default is by order of appearance).

The example that follows shows how you can use a text area to provide your users with space for free-form feedback (whoa, you *are* brave) or specific information as part of a survey-style form:

```html
<html>
<head>
<title>&lt;textarea&gt; On Display</title>
   <!- the name of this form is txt-ara.html ->
</head>
   <body>
   <h3>The Widget Waffle Iron Survey</h3>
<p>Please fill out the following information so that we
   can register your new Widget Waffle Iron.
<hr>
   <form method="POST" action="/cgi/txt-ara">
<fieldset><legend>Model Number</legend>
   <select name="mod-num" size="3">
   <option>102 (Single Belgian)
   <option>103 (Double Belgian)
   <option>104 (Single Heart-shaped)
   <option>105 (Double Heart-shaped)
   <option>204 (Restaurant Waffler)
   <option>297 (Cone Waffler)
```

```
      </select>
</fieldset>
   <hr>
   <b>Please complete the following purchase
         information:</b><br>
<p>Serial number: <input name="snum" type="TEXT" size="10"
   maxlength="10">
   <p>Purchase Price: <input name="price" type="TEXT" size="6"
   maxlength="10">
   <p>Location: <input name="location" type="TEXT" size="15"
   maxlength="30">
   <hr>
   <b>Please tell us about yourself:</b>

<p>Male <input name="sex" type="CHECKBOX" value="male">
   Female <input name="sex" type="CHECKBOX" value="female">
   <p>Age:
   under 25 <input name="age" type="CHECKBOX" value="lo">
   25-50 <input name="age" type="CHECKBOX" value="med">
   over 50 <input name="age" type="CHECKBOX" value="hi">
<p>
<hr>
   Please share your favorite waffle recipe with us. If we
like it, we'll include it in our next Widget Waffler cook
book! Here's an example to inspire you.
<p><textarea name="recipe" rows="10" cols="65">
   Banana Waffles
   Ingredients:
   2 c. waffle batter (see Widget Waffler cookbook for recipe)
   2 ripe bananas, peeled, sliced 1/4" thick
   1 tsp. cinnamon
   Preparation:
   Mix ingredients together.
   Preheat Widget Waffler (wait 'til light goes off).

   Pour 1/2 c. batter in Waffler (wait 'til light goes off).
   Keep browned waffles warm in oven until ready to serve.
   </textarea>
<p>Thank you! <input type="SUBMIT" value="Register now">
<input type="RESET">
</form>
<address>
Sample form for <i>HTML For Dummies</i> Version 3.1<br>
3/17/97 http://www.noplace.com/HTML4D/wfl-srvy.html
</address></body></html>
```

The screen that results from this HTML document appears in part in Figure 17-3. Notice the use of checkboxes for survey information, coupled with the text input area for recipes. May all your free-form feedback be at least as delightful. (So what time's breakfast?)

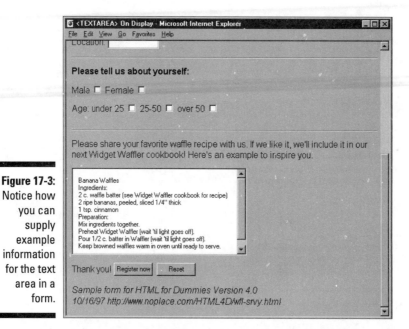

Figure 17-3:
Notice how
you can
supply
example
information
for the text
area in a
form.

If you've read this whole section, you've seen most of the nifty little tricks —
we like to call them *widgets* — that work within forms, but you can't really
appreciate what forms can do until you've browsed the Web to look at what's
out there. Our examples barely scratch the surface with a fork; there's a lot
more to see. Or is that taste?

Form Good Habits and Attitudes

Whenever you create an HTML form, it's especially important to test it against
as many browsers as you possibly can. Don't be utterly taken in by the graphical side of the Web force; many users still favor character-mode browsers
such as Lynx, and they'll miss your site if you miss accommodating them.

Ultimately, the HTML rules regarding layout-versus-content apply to forms: If
you can create a clear, readable layout and make a form interesting to your
users, you'll probably be a lot happier with the information returned than if
you spend extra hours tuning and tweaking graphics elements and precise
placement of type, widgets, and fields. Remember, too, that a form's just the
front end; a pretty grille and fancy headlights don't make up for befuddled
users or underpowered data collection.

Soon (in this selfsame chapter!) you tackle the demanding-but-rewarding task of building CGI scripts and other input-handling programs for your server. If you're a real glutton for CGI punishment . . . ah, *enlightenment,* check out our in-depth books on the subject:

- ✔ *CGI Bible* by Ed Tittel, Mark Gaither, Sebastian Hassinger, and Mike Erwin. IDG Books Worldwide, Inc., Indianapolis, IN, 1997. ISBN 0-7645-8016-7.

- ✔ *Web Programming Secrets with HTML, CGI, and Perl,* by Ed Tittel, Mark Gaither, Sebastian Hassinger, and Mike Erwin, IDG Books Worldwide, Inc., Indianapolis, IN, 1996. ISBN 156884-848-X.

Coming up, we scrutinize some tools you can use to automate the form and background CGI script-creation process, and then sail bravely into regions of the map labeled *Here be Dragons and Geeks.*

Interactivity, Multimedia, and Cold Feet

The old century is history, the Web rules, and now you fearlessly bestride Chapter 17. The time is right to go beyond HTML markup and simple graphics, plunging (briefly but brazenly) into interactivity and multimedia. You (yes, *you*) can add dynamic features to your Web documents in multiple arcane ways with minimal extra work, and — what luck — we discuss many of them in this very section. We know the Web is more than just markup and pretty pictures; we're not skeered, nope, not us.

We'll do no more than a reasonable amount of programming (a sudden chill invades the air . . .). Not to worry. First, we walk up to the longest-standing extension to the Web — CGI — and kick the tires. CGI can be a complicated beast to operate, and it often involves programming, but we're not gonna let that scare us off, nosiree. Then we move unflinchingly into other extensions — Java, JavaScript, VRML, Shockwave, ActiveX, and RealAudio. We know they aren't all that simple either — and here they come, even as we speak.

Specify CGI and Gate-a-Way with It

Building HTML forms and handling user interaction through Web pages requires action on both sides of the client-server connection. In this book, we concentrate mainly on the client side, It's time to slip quietly across the network connection from client side to server side; here dwells the *Common Gateway Interface (CGI).*

Along the way, we show you the history and foundations of CGI and cover the basic details of its design and use. We also introduce you to the issues surrounding your choice of a scripting or programming language for CGI, and we introduce you to some prime examples of that species. And hey, kids! You get these programs — and the code to run them — on the CD-ROM that comes with this book. We hope you befriend them and use them on your Web pages.

You've ventured to the client side (and come back alive) if you've read Chapter 15's account of clickable image-map files. If this present section seems too much like pidgin geekspeak, skip ahead for the skinny on "How to Cheat at CGI."

A CGI program lets Web pages communicate with applications on the server to provide customized information or to build interactive exchanges between clients and servers.

If you read the previous paragraphs carefully, you've noticed one important element of CGI programs: They run on the Web server, not on the client side (where you run your browser to access Web-based information). You can't use our CGI programs on your own machine unless it can run Web server software (usually called an HTTP daemon, or more simply, httpd) at the same time that it runs your browser.

On Windows NT, Macintoshes, and UNIX machines, running both a Web server and a browser is quite doable; on Windows 3.*x* and Windows 95 computers, it's a bit trickier. For the latter machines, the Quarterdeck inexpensive WebServer software package fits the bill nicely: It supports CGI Version 1.1 and enables you to work both sides of the client/server street with ease. For more information on this product, visit Quarterdeck's Web site at www.qdeck.com.

Common Gateway: This way to server side

Gateway scripts, or programs, add a powerful capability: true interaction between browsers and servers across the Web. It's a power limited only by your imagination and the tools at hand. Gateway scripts supply the underlying functions that enable you to work Web magic — perform searches on Web documents, parley with databases that can accept and process data from your forms, get hold of the strategic market intelligence, and customize your Web pages in response to user input.

If you build Web pages, you must manage all this interaction across the Web. That means building the front-end information (and display) that users see and interact with. It also means paying practical attention to the back-end programming — how else can your system accept, interpret, and respond to all that user input you've sweated to get? This coordination does require some effort and some programming, but if you're willing to take the time to learn CGI, you'll be limited only by the amount of time and energy you have for programming your Web pages.

For more rich rewards from a little investment of time in programming and learning, take a gander at Chapter 19 on Dynamic HTML.

CGI scripts/programs: Watch your language

Whether you call your server-side creation a *program* or a *script*, here's a trade secret: This distinction often describes the tools you actually use to build the monster. Scripts get built with scripting languages, and programs with programming languages. The distinction can be useful:

- ✔ A **scripting language** creates a set of actions and activities that must be performed in the prescribed order each time a script is executed. Like a script read by an actor, scripts are often said to be *interpreted.*

- ✔ Statements written in a **programming language** are transformed, by a special program called a compiler, into equivalent computer instructions in an *executable* form that the computer can, well, *execute.*

Both these approaches work equally well with the Web's Common Gateway Interface. But let's keep it simple, sport — we'll use *CGI programs* to mean any code creature you conjure up. You can call them whatever you want (though they don't answer to "Fido," "Ralph," or "Hey, you").

CGI retains a fairly pervasive presence on the Web. UNIX-based CERN and NCSA Web servers use it to mediate interaction between servers and programs. Because UNIX was the original Web platform, it sets the model (yet again) for how the Web handles user interaction. Although you can find other platforms that support Web servers — such as Windows NT or the Macintosh OS — they, too, must follow the standard set for the CERN and NCSA implementations of httpd. Regardless of whether they conform to the CERN or NCSA models, all Web servers must provide CGI capabilities — either the real McCoy or a set of functions to match what CGI can do.

What's going on in a CGI program?

You can think of a CGI program as an extension of the core WWW server services. In fact, CGI programs are like worker bees that do the dirty work on behalf of the server. The server serves as an intermediary between the client and the CGI program. It's good to be queen bee — all those workers jump at your behest. (Whoa. Imagine having a behest!)

The server invokes CGI programs based on information that the browser provides (as in the `<form>` tag, where the `action` attribute supplies a URL for the particular program that services the form). The browser request sets the stage for a series of information hand-offs and exchanges:

- ✔ The browser makes a request to a server for a URL, which actually contains the name of a CGI program for the server to run.

- ✔ The server fields the URL request, figures out that it points to a CGI program (usually by parsing the filename and its extension or through the directory where the file resides), and fires off the CGI program.

- ✔ The CGI program performs whatever actions it's been built to supply, based on input from the browser request. These actions can include obtaining the date and time from the server's underlying system, accumulating a counter for each visit to a Web page, searching a database, and so on.

- ✔ The CGI program takes the results of its actions and returns the proper data back to the server; often the program formats these results as a Web page for delivery back to the server (if the Content-Type is `text/html`).

- ✔ The server accepts the results from the CGI program and passes them to the browser, which renders them for display to the user. If this exchange is part of an ongoing, interactive Web session, these results can include additional forms tags to accept further user input, along with a URL for this or another CGI program. Thus, the cycle begins anew.

This method is a rather disjointed way to have a conversation over the Web, but it does allow information to move both ways. The real beauty of CGI programs is that they extend a simple WWW server in every conceivable direction and make that server's services more valuable. As you see later in this chapter, Dynamic HTML can do all that too, except it does its work on the client side (preferring not to rely on client-server and server-client "conversations").

CGI input: What's in this stuff anyway?

A request for a CGI program is encoded in HTML in a basic form as shown in this example:

```
<a href="http://www.hal.com/hal-bin/silly-quote.pl"> Silly
Quote</a>
```

The URL declaration says to execute the `silly-quote.pl` CGI program on the `www.hal.com` WWW server from the hal-bin directory. This request has no additional input data to pass to the CGI program. (The clue is that no ? is appended to the URL — see the explanation of the question mark argument later in this chapter.) The result of the CGI program is a Web page created on the fly and returned to the browser.

The information gathered by an HTML form or requested by a user (with a search request or other information query) passes to CGI programs in one of two ways:

✔ As an appendage to a CGI program's URL (most commonly, for WAIS requests or other short information searches). This way uses the method="get" option.

✔ As a stream of bytes through the UNIX default standard input device (stdin) in response to the action setting for an HTML <form> tag. This way is best used with the method="post" option.

In the next section, you see how forms create special formats for information intended for use in CGI programs. Also, you see how those programs use and deliver that information.

Short and sweet: Extended URLs

Most search engines use what's called a *document-based query* to obtain information from users. You can tinker up such a query by tacking some special characters onto the end of the search engine's URL (just that easy, just that simple). Document-based queries are intended to solicit search terms or key words from a browser and then deliver them to a CGI program that uses them to search a database or a collection of files. Such simplicity makes document-based queries so good for soliciting small amounts of input from users and why you see them in so many Web pages.

Document-based queries depend on three ingredients for their successful operation:

✔ The <isindex> tag within the <head> section of an HTML document enables searching of the document by the browser.

✔ A special URL format is generated by adding the query text to the URL, with terms added at the end, delimited by question marks.

✔ Including special arguments in your underlying CGI program processes the query.

Here's how the process actually works:

✔ The <isindex> tag in the <head> of the document causes the browser to supply a search widget that allows the user to enter keywords. A widget is a generic bit of software that performs a particular task; in this case, the widget handles packages and sends search requests. These keywords are bundled into an HTTP request and passed to the named CGI program. If the CGI program finds no arguments appended to the

URL, it returns a default page that delivers the search widget to the browser. This sometimes happens with the first search request because a complete search widget may not be included on every Web page.

✔ At the prompt, users enter a string they want to search for and then press Enter (otherwise the string goes to the CGI program).

✔ The browser calls the same URL as before, except it appends the search string following a question mark. So, if the search engine program's URL is

```
wwww.HTML4d.com/cgi-bin/searchit
```

and the string to be searched for is `tether`, then the new URL becomes

```
wwww.HTML4d.com/cgi-bin/searchit?tether
```

✔ The server receives the URL exactly as formatted and passes it to the searchit program, with the string after the question mark passed as an argument to search it.

✔ This time, the program performs an actual search and returns the results as another HTML page (instead of the default prompt page that was sent the first time).

Every part of this operation depends on the others: The browser activates the `<isindex>` tag that allows the query to be requested and entered. Then the browser appends the query string to the URL and passes on the query as an argument to the search program. The search program uses the query value as the focus of its search operation and returns the search results to the browser via another custom-built HTML document. (Gads. They all get along. Maybe there's a lesson in there somewhere.)

Gabby and thorough: Input stream

As you build an HTML form, you have important definitions to make, including the assignment of names and associated values to your variables or selections. When users fill out HTML forms, they actually instruct the browser to build a list of associated name-value pairs for each selection made or for each field they fill in.

Your garden-variety `name=value` pairs take a distinctive form:

```
name=value&
```

The equal sign (=) separates the name of the field from its associated value. The ampersand (&) separates the end of the value's string from the next item of text information in a completed form. For `<select>` statements where multiple choices are allowed, the resulting list has multiple name=value pairs where the name remains the same, but the value assignment changes for each value chosen. Complex, maybe, but versatile.

Reading through forms information delivered to a CGI program's standard input (stdin) is a matter of checking certain key environment variables (which we cover in the next section) and then parsing (separating into individual words or units or information) the input data. This reading consists of separating name=value pairs and using the names, with their associated values, to guide subsequent processing. The easiest way to do this, from a programming perspective, is to first parse and split out name=value pairs by looking for the ending ampersand (&), and then divide these pairs into their name and value parts by looking for the equal sign (=).

Here are some Perl code fragments that you can use to parse a form's input data. (It assumes that, in keeping with our recommendation, you use method="post" for passing data.)

```perl
# this reads the input stream from the Standard Input
# device (STD) into the buffer variable $buffer, using
# the environment variable CONTENT_LENGTH to know how
# much data to read
read(STDIN, $buffer, $ENV{'CONTENT_LENGTH'});
#Split the name=value pairs on '&'
@pairs = split (/&/, $buffer);
# Go through pairs and determine the name and value for
# each named form field
for each $pair (@pairs) {
# Split name from value on "="
($name, $value) = split(/=/,$pair);
# Translate URL syntax of + for blanks
$value =~ tr/+/ /;
# Substitute hexadecimal characters with their normal
            equivalents

$value =~ s/%([a-fA-F0-9][a-fA-F0-9])/pack("C",hex($1))/eg;
# Deposit the value in the FORMS array, associated to name
$FORM($name) = $value;
```

A shell game with CGI environment variables

As part of the CGI environment, the httpd server's software version and configuration are of interest, as are the multiple variables associated with the server. You can use the following shell program to produce a complete listing of such information. This program is a valuable testing tool to use when you install or modify a Web server (even if it won't mount the Continental kit):

```
#!/bin/sh
echo Content-type: text/plain
echo
echo CGI/1.1 test script report:
echo
echo argc is $#. argv is "$*".
echo
echo SERVER_SOFTWARE = $SERVER_SOFTWARE
echo SERVER_NAME = $SERVER_NAME
echo GATEWAY_INTERFACE = $GATEWAY_INTERFACE
echo SERVER_PROTOCOL = $SERVER_PROTOCOL
echo SERVER_PORT = $SERVER_PORT
echo REQUEST_METHOD = $REQUEST_METHOD
echo HTTP_ACCEPT = $HTTP_ACCEPT
echo PATH_INFO = $PATH_INFO
echo PATH_TRANSLATED = $PATH_TRANSLATED
echo SCRIPT_NAME = $SCRIPT_NAME
echo QUERY_STRING = $QUERY_STRING
echo REMOTE_HOST = $REMOTE_HOST
echo REMOTE_ADDR = $REMOTE_ADDR
echo REMOTE_USER = $REMOTE_USER
echo CONTENT_TYPE = $CONTENT_TYPE
echo CONTENT_LENGTH = $CONTENT_LENGTH
```

This same UNIX shell script is widely distributed around the Net. We found the present version in the NCSA hoohoo collection at

```
hoohoo.ncsa.uiuc.edu/cgi-bin/test-cgi
```

Running this script on a Web server (in this case, the NCSA Web server hoohoo) produces the following output:

```
CGI/1.1 test script report:
argc is 0. argv is .
SERVER_SOFTWARE = NCSA/1.5.2
SERVER_NAME = hoohoo.ncsa.uiuc.edu
GATEWAY_INTERFACE = CGI/1.1
SERVER_PROTOCOL = HTTP/1.0
SERVER_PORT = 80
REQUEST_METHOD = GET
HTTP_ACCEPT = application/vnd.ms-excel,
application/msword, application/vnd.ms-powerpoint,
image/gif, image/x-xbitmap, image/jpeg, image/pjpeg,
*/*
HTTP_USER_AGENT = Mozilla/2.0
(compatible; MSIE 3.02; Win32)
HTTP_REFERER =
PATH_INFO =
PATH_TRANSLATED =
SCRIPT_NAME = /cgi-bin/test-cgi
QUERY_STRING =
REMOTE_HOST = max2-54.ip.realtime.net
REMOTE_ADDR = 205.238.153.54
```

```
REMOTE_USER =
AUTH_TYPE =
CONTENT_TYPE =
CONTENT_LENGTH =
ANNOTATION_SERVER =
```

Each capitalized variable name (to the left of the equal marks) and its associated output are environment variables that CGI sets. These variables are always available for use in your programs (such a deal).

Two environment variables are especially worthy of note:

- ✔ The QUERY_STRING variable is associated with the GET method of information-passing (as is common with search commands) and must be parsed for such queries or information requests.

- ✔ The CONTENT_LENGTH variable is associated with the POST method of information-passing (as is recommended for forms or other lengthier types of input data). The browser accumulates the variable while assembling forms data to deliver to the server; the variable then tells the CGI program how much input data it must read.

But wait! There's more! The environment variables also identify other handy items such as the name of the remote host and its corresponding IP address, the request method used, and the types of data that the server can accept. (Well, okay, these values might seem a little abstruse now, but the more you tinker with CGI programs, the more uses you're likely to find for them. Just don't forget to eat.)

Forming up: Input-handling programs

When you create a form in HTML, each input field has an associated unique name. Filling out the form usually associates one or more values with each name. As shipped from the browser to the Web server (and on to the CGI program the URL targets), the form data is a stream of bytes, consisting of name=value pairs separated by ampersand characters (&).

Each of these name=value pairs is URL-encoded, which means that spaces are changed into plus signs (+) and some characters are encoded into hexadecimal. Decoding these URLs is what caused the, ah, *interesting* translation contortions in the Perl code sample we lassoed into the preceding section.

If you visit the NCSA CGI archive, you can find links to a number of input-handling code libraries that can help you build forms. You can find all this information at

```
ftp://ftp.ncsa.uiuc.edu/Web/httpd/Unix/ncsa_httpd/cgi/
```

The common input-handling code libraries include

- ✔ **Bourne Shell:** The AA Archie Gateway contains calls to sed and awk to convert a `GET form` data string into separate environmental variables. (`AA-1.2.tar.Z`)
- ✔ **C:** The default scripts for NCSA http includes C routines and example programs for translating the query string into various structures. (`ncsa-default.tar.Z`)
- ✔ **Perl:** The Perl CGI-lib contains a group of useful Perl routines to decode and manage forms data. (`cgi-lib.pl.Z`)
- ✔ **TCL:** The TCL argument processor includes a set of TCL routines to retrieve forms data and insert it into associated TCL variables. (`tcl-proc-args.tar.Z`)

Most of the work of reading and organizing forms information is already widely and publicly available in one form or fashion, which is great for you. This simplifies your programming efforts because you can concentrate on writing the code that interprets the input and builds the appropriate HTML document that's returned to your reader as a response.

Options for coding CGI

In this section, we give three different CGI programs the third degree. We include their code and a great deal of associated information on the CD-ROM. Each of these programs is available in three versions: AppleScript (for use on an Apple httpd server), Perl (for use on any system that supports a Perl interpreter/compiler), and C (for use on any system that supports a C compiler). Ladies and gentlemen, choose your weapons!

Build Your Own CGI Juggernaut

Before we launch you into these excellent examples, we'd like to encourage you to use them in your own HTML documents and CGI programs (we're giving away the license to this code, so you can use it without restrictions). We first conclude the discussion portion of this chapter with an investigation of why we chose to implement each of these programs in three forms and how you can choose a suitable language to write your CGI programs.

You can build your CGI programs with just about any programming or scripting language that your Web server supports. Nothing can stop you from ignoring all options that we cover here and using something completely different.

Nevertheless, we can think of good reasons why you should consider using these options — and equally good reasons why you should ignore other options. We cheerfully concede that you'll find probably as many opinions on this subject as there are CGI programmers, but we ask that you consider care-fully before deciding on a CGI language that may demand considerable time and effort to learn before you can actually *use* it to turn the Web on its ear.

For example, we include the NCSA `test-cgi` script earlier in this chapter. It's written in the basic C shell (a command language common on many UNIX systems) and makes an adequate scripting language for many uses. Never-theless, we don't think that UNIX shells are suitable for heavy-duty CGI programming because they mix UNIX system commands freely within their own syntax.

The problem with CGI programming under UNIX is that it depends on the standard input (stdin) and standard output (stdout) devices as the methods for moving data between Web servers and browsers. Each new UNIX process automatically creates its own stdin and stdout; get enough of those puppies running, and UNIX shells can get confused about where the input comes from and where the output goes.

This confusion can be a side effect of running system commands or of spawn-ing tasks (or having one running program start up another program to perform a specific task and report its results back to the original program when it finishes). Whatever the cause, this confusion can lose the input or output for CGI programs. That's the main reason we don't recommend shell scripts of any kind for heavier-duty CGI applications (for example, forms-processing versus query-handling). Always get the right tool for the job.

On the plus side, Perl offers straightforward access to UNIX system calls and capabilities within a tightly structured environment. Perl includes the posi-tive features of languages like C, Pascal, awk, sed, and even Basic, and it offers powerful string-handling and output-management functions. Perl is emerging as the favorite of many Web programmers; certainly it's our favorite CGI gurus' language of choice (though even they don't use it to order a capuccino). Best of all, Perl implementations are already available for UNIX, DOS, Windows NT, Macintosh OS, and the Amiga, with numerous other imple-mentations under way. We've had excellent luck moving Perl from one platform to another with only small changes.

We include C because it's a powerful programming language and remains a tool of choice in the UNIX environment. What features and functions it doesn't offer as built-ins are readily available in the form of system APIs (Application Programming Interfaces — the set of routines used to invoke system functions and other kinds of prepackaged functionality within a program) and code libraries. C is also portable (barring the use of system APIs, which can change from one system to another). One version of C is available for just about every platform, and multiple implementations are available for popular platforms and operating systems. We're especially fond of the GNU C and the related GNU Tools from the Free Software Foundation that Richard Stallman pioneered.

If you use a Macintosh as a Web server, AppleScript is pretty much your only option. Even so, it has proven to be a worthwhile tool for building CGI programs and is widely used in the Macintosh Web community. If you're a real Macophile, have a look at Appendix C for some excellent pointers on Macintosh tools and technologies for the Web.

Whatever language you choose for your CGI programs, be sure it provides good string-handling capabilities and offers reasonable output controls. Because you'll be reading and interpreting byte-stream input and creating HTML documents galore, look for these important capabilities. Also, we recommend that you pick a language that's already in wide use among the savvy folk of the Web community. You're likelier to find lots of related modules, libraries, and code widgets that may save you programming time and make your job easier. But hey — it's your choice!

We're convinced that anything short of an all-CGI volume barely scratches the surface, but for Pete's sake, we've got other fish to fry here as well. For more information, consult your favorite search engine and use "CGI" or "CGI script" as your search string. You'll turn up tons of useful references, but we'll save you at least some hassle by mentioning a pair of tomes largely devoted to CGI programming: *CGI Bible* and *World Wide Web Programming Secrets with Perl and CGI*, both by (ahem) Ed Tittel, Mark Gaither, Sebastian Hassinger, and Mike Erwin, and both available from IDG Books Worldwide, Inc. (Coincidence? We think not. In fact, we can safely say you won't find two CGI books anywhere that your authors like more. And did we mention that they make great gifts . . . ?)

In the following sections, we examine three different CGI programs. Their code and a great deal of associated information are on the CD-ROM. Each program is available in three versions: AppleScript (for use on an Apple httpd server), Perl (for use on any system that supports a Perl interpreter/compiler), and C (for use on any system that supports a C compiler).

Example 1: What time is it?

This short Perl program accesses the system time on the server and writes an HTML page with the current time to the user's screen. This program has filenames beginning with "time" in the CGI subdirectory on this CD-ROM.

Example 2: Counting page visits

This AppleScript program establishes a counter that tracks the number of times a page is visited. This kind of tool can provide useful statistics for individuals or organizations curious about how much traffic their pages actually receive. This program has filenames beginning with "counter" in the CGI subdirectory on this CD-ROM.

Example 3: Decoding clickable map coordinates

This C program can distinguish whether the right or left side of a graphic is selected (as well as defining a default to handle when the graphic isn't selected at all). It shows how a script handles the definitions inside an image map file. This program has filenames beginning with ismapper in the compressed CGI files available from the FTP subdirectory on this CD-ROM.

Installing and using CGIs

Most Web servers are configured to look for CGI programs in a particular directory that's under the server's control. Normal users (including you) probably won't be able to copy CGI scripts into this directory without obtaining help from their friendly neighborhood systems administrator or webmaster. Before you can install and use any CGI program on a particular server, you want to talk to one of these individuals (if not both), tell them what you want to do, and ask for their help and advice in making it happen.

Don't be nonplussed or surprised if this process takes some time: Systems administrators and webmasters tend to be chronically busy people. You may have to wait a while to get their attention and then discuss your needs with them. Consider the following as you interact with your webmaster:

- Make your initial approach to your webmaster by e-mail or a phone call and briefly explain what you want to do. (For example, say something like "I want to include a counter CGI on my home page to track visitors.") Among other things, you may discover that the wiz already has a CGI available for that very purpose on your server and will simply tell you how to include its reference in the CGI invocation of your home page. (You may not have to use our code at all! But backup is such a comfort.)

- Most webmasters are responsible for the safe and proper operation of the server and/or the Web site on which you want to run a CGI program. Don't be offended if you hear one say, "Well, I need to look it over first to make sure that it's okay before you can use it." It's the mark of a pro, trying to make sure that nobody introduces software that could cripple or compromise the system (saves on headaches and awful language). Don't take it personally when this happens — webmasters are just doing their jobs, and asking for a review shows you that they care about what happens on their (and your) server, which is actually a good thing!

- Finally, the systems administrator or webmaster can show you how to install and use CGIs more quickly and efficiently than if you try to figure it out for yourself. Be ready to wait your turn to get some time with this person and be ready to listen and learn when your turn comes. You won't be disappointed!

As the sample CGI programs in this chapter illustrate, you'll find as many ways to skin the proverbial CGI as ideas and approaches about how to implement them. We sincerely hope that you can use the tools that we include on this CD-ROM, where you can find C, Perl, and AppleScript versions for all three programs. In Chapter 15 of the book, we extend our coverage of server-side Web activities as we investigate search engines, Webcrawlers, and other interesting server-side services.

How to Cheat at CGI

If CGI doesn't exactly give you a warm, fuzzy feeling, you're not alone. CGI can be difficult, especially if you're not a programmer and don't really want to be. But before you throw out the virtual CGI baby with the cyber-bathwater, let us show you how to cheat at CGI! Here, as promised, are the crib notes.

The secret is to use a forms-designing application to create your forms and the background CGIs *automatically*. O'Reilly PolyForm is one great application for this. Answer a few simple questions, click a few buttons, follow the instructions of the semi-intelligent program wizard, and *poof!* Out comes a form and matching CGI application. No messy code lists, no contortions, no infomercials. And it really, really works!

Find out more about PolyForm by visiting `polyform.ora.com`. Unfortunately for the Apple end of the stick, PolyForm is only available for Windows computers. Diligent searching didn't turn up any worthwhile Mac or UNIX software that provides similar features, but take heart, Mac stalwarts: the Web is changing all the time. If you find some candidates for the Mac Answer to PolyForm, let us know.

Java

Java has been hot for some years now (they must have a mug-warmer under there). It's a Web-enabled programming language that got its start as the brains for kitchen appliances. No, really! Amazing but true (though we haven't found any coffeemakers that run it . . .). Java is not only hot, it's cool — programs written in it can be executed on the client side of the Web communications link. You don't have to go bothering the server — a setup opposite to that of standard CGI. (If that little tidbit of information got you excited enough to change your shorts, you just might be a Web programmer.)

Sun Microsystems, Inc. developed Java as a platform-independent, client-executable, have-your-cake-and-eat-it-too programming language. Any browser that supports Java on any platform can access Java resources. Java resources can be just about anything, such as audio, video, animation, interactive applications, multimedia, and more.

Java is a programming language based on C; thus you need to be a programmer to do much with Java. But you can find a handful of good programming environments that simplify the applet creation process, such as Symantec Visual Café and Microsoft J++, but you still need to be a programmer at heart to get any real use out of these.

If Java sounds just like your kind of café latte, then you need to get more information straight from the coffee makers themselves — JavaSoft (a division of Sun Microsystems) at `java.sun.com`. To see some great examples of Java in action, go visit the Gamelan Java Directory:

```
www.gamelan.com.
```

JavaScript

JavaScript (also called LiveScript) is a scripting language that Netscape developed. JavaScript is not a CGI replacement, nor does it have anything to do with Java. It's just a plain-text scripting code that you can use to add a bit of zip to stale HTML documents. It's also a key ingredient in Dynamic HTML (see Chapter 19) as well as a Captain Neato scripting language in its own right.

JavaScript is not as complex and difficult as Java, but it is still a programming language. If you'd like to see what is really involved with adding JavaScript to your Web pages, visit the Netscape JavaScript site at

```
home.netscape.com/eng/mozilla/3.0/handbook/javascript/
```

To see some live examples of JavaScript, take a peek at these sites:

```
jrc.livesoftware.com/
www.c2.org/~andreww/javascript/
www.gamelan.com/pages/
```

You may discover a sudden urge to add this type of enhancement to your Web site.

VRML

VRML *(Virtual Reality Modeling Language)* is a tool for creating three-dimensional graphical worlds. This programming language is complex enough to frighten most neophytes. But here's a peek behind the curtain: Most VRML programmers use GUI modeling tools to create their worlds, letting the tool write that gnarly VRML code automatically. No fools they.

VRML worlds are big on realism and even bigger on certain dreamlike qualities. Visitors navigate them by walking or flying around. They can explore in, around, above, below, and often *through* objects in VRML space. A VRML world can be anything from a single boxy room with text "hanging" on the walls to fully rendered planets with interactive multimedia behind every turn.

Of course, planets can be a little hard to cram through wires. Creating any world takes a lot of resources, and a VRML world is no exception — it requires a lot of powerful hardware, a high-end video card, and a large communications pipeline for a VRML world of reasonable size to be brought from design to final completion.

Many online sites have used VRML to spice up their content, but we figure it's got some evolving to do before the bang quite justifies the bucks. Waiting 30 minutes for a 5MB VRML file to download, only to see a blocky room with distorted pictures and funky colored wallpaper, is still anticlimactic. VRML may realize more of its potential quality and excitement in a few years, especially if large-budget science-fiction movies exert an influence. (*Use VRML, Luke . . .*)

If you want to learn more about VRML and gain an understanding of the tools and equipment involved, visit the VRML Repository at `www.sdsc.edu/vrml/`.

After you create a VRML world, you don't need a lot of high-end hardware to distribute it to your users, just a regular Web server with the right MIME extensions defined. The viewers of your site must have a VRML-enabled browser and a 256-color graphics display to gain entry into your virtual world.

For complete details on VRML, including the technical specs, the latest specification details, and sample sites, visit `www.vrml.org`.

We discuss VRML in a bit more detail in *The 60 Minute Guide to VRML* from IDG Books Worldwide, Inc.

Shockwave

Shockwave is the Web delivery mechanism and technology that Macromedia created to distribute Director productions over the Internet. Macromedia Director is the premier multimedia interactive CD-ROM authoring tool. With Shockwave, Web authors can add many special effects, interactive applications, and multimedia excitement to their Web sites. Shockwave presentations often include audio, video, animations, interaction, and more.

To create a Shockwave file, you must have the Director Multimedia Studio software. Unfortunately, this bad boy is very, very expensive. But if you are a multimedia genius or an artistic sensation, you may find the heavy-duty price tag reasonable. After the initial sticker shock and the intense learning curve for creating worthwhile Director presentations, creating a Shockwave version is simple — just run it through a converter and presto! It's ready for Web consumption.

After you have a Shockwave presentation, you don't need anything other than a Web server and a properly defined MIME extension to serve it over your site. However, your viewers still need to get the Shockwave plug-in from Macromedia to see your heartfelt presentations. To learn more about Shockwave and Directory, visit the Macromedia Web site: www.macromedia.com. While there, be sure to download the Shockwave plug-in and then go exploring in the gallery to see what others are doing with Shockwave.

Shockwave can enhance your site with rich results so quickly that, frankly, it's shoc . . . no, we won't go there. But you can.

ActiveX

ActiveX is a programming technique, standards, and environment for creating interactive Internet and intranet-based Web applications. With ActiveX, adding multimedia effects, interactive objects, and sophisticated high-impact applications is within the grasp of any webmaster. ActiveX is, in theory, platform-independent; however, in practice, it only functions within the Windows operating systems. Future plans for ActiveX include porting this technology to the Macintosh OS and other non-Microsoft systems.

Microsoft developed ActiveX as a way to extend the power of the BackOffice products to the world of the Internet/intranet. They have created a system that enables cross-platform software interoperability across a network.

Creating your own ActiveX applications is as easy as writing any other program, but it does require solid programming knowledge and experience. You can use almost any of the popular programming languages to create ActiveX applications. But, if you are not a programmer, you can easily license prebuilt applications from vendors to distribute over your own site.

A lot of technobabble and programming-speak is associated with ActiveX. You can get tools to help you create your own ActiveX controls, but even they require that you have a solid understanding of programming. So, we're gonna skip the finely detailed high-technese explanation of ActiveX (other than what we've already said), and send you out to explore the depths of this nifty technology on your own. Unless, of course, you're already there.

You can learn about ActiveX in the following ways:

ActiveX's Web site:

`www.microsoft.com/activex/.`

ActiveX's mailing lists:

- ✔ To subscribe: Send an e-mail message to `Listserv@listserv.msn.com` with a blank subject line and a message body of "subscribe ActiveXControls and your name," "subscribe ActiveXScript your name," or "subscribe ActiveXSearch your name."

- ✔ To unsubscribe: Send an e-mail message to `Listserv@listserv.msn.com` with a blank subject line and a message body of "signoff ActiveXControls," "signoff ActiveXScript," or "signoff ActiveXSearch" respectively.

Cruise 'n' peruse the archives of these lists by visiting these sites:

`microsoft.ease.lsoft.com/archives/activexcontrols.html`

`microsoft.ease.lsoft.com/archives/activexscript.html`

`microsoft.ease.lsoft.com/archives/activexsearch.html`

You can also participate in ActiveX Newsgroups hosted on the public news server "`msnews.microsoft.com`":

`microsoft.public.activex.*` (more than 30 subgroups)

To see some great examples of ActiveX in action, visit one of these sites:

`www.microsoft.com/activex/gallery/`

`www.activex.com/`

`www.techweb.com/activexpress/`

RealAudio

Adding audio to a Web site is easy, just like to a sound file. But to add streaming on-demand and live audio, you should use RealAudio from Progressive Networks. This proprietary technology enables users with modems as slow as 14.4 Kbps to access audio over the Internet. The audio is often FM radio quality or better.

Hundreds (maybe thousands) of RealAudio sites are scattered around the world, providing music, news, and entertainment over the Internet. Just think; with RealAudio, now you can host that underground radio program you've been dreaming about since you were 12. (Say what? You haven't? Well, maybe now you can.)

The only way to get a good feel for what RealAudio can do is to download the player, power it up, and explore it yourself. We use RealAudio everyday to listen to news briefs, catch live concerts, and even sports events. Go for the gusto and find out more at www.realaudio.com.

By the way, Progressive Networks has also moved into the video market. The current release of RealPlayer 5.0 can access both audio and video streams. RealPlayer is not as good as television, but it is a great leap forward. While you are at their Web site, read up on it and get the player!

So after the gosh-wow, then what? Thereby hangs another epic tale. For practicality's sake (and for now), your intrepid authors must stop short of dropping you right into the cockpit. Before you put these extensions to use, take some time to study up. They're not what anybody would call entry-level or sandbox stuff — and even you veterans of the present tome's expert guidance should tread lightly.

Authoring environments continue to proliferate, each one with some unique, idiosyncratic aspects. This chapter is for planting your feet on a good, solid Square One: adding preexisting media files of these types to your site — using standard HTML markup — and listing some online and print resources that can boost you to the intermediate and advanced levels of Web enhancement.

Chapter 18

Style Is Its Own Reward

· ·

· ·

Style sheets represent one of the most exciting new additions to HTML 4.0 and the Web. Style sheets allow authors to specify layout and design elements — such as fonts, colors, indentation, and precise control over how elements appear on a Web page — for an entire Web site. Neither users' whims — nor misconfigured browsers — can mangle the display of style-dependent Web documents.

A style sheet's specification combines with users' personal settings to make sure an HTML document displays "properly." You must understand that the term *properly* is determined by a document's creator, not its viewer — if you don't believe us, ask any artist how she feels about her work!

Style sheets are important enough that the W3C has devoted an entire section of its Web site to this topic. You can find style-sheet information there, plus a collection of links for further study. Look them up at `www.w3.org/pub/WWW/Style/`.

Before you dive into this chapter expecting to find out how to create and use style sheets, please understand that we don't tell you how to make style sheets of your own in this book! Style sheets are more than complex; they're quite advanced and difficult to wrap your brain around. Not that we think you can't tackle them successfully, it's just that creating style sheets isn't for beginners. The real reason we don't cover them in depth here is that we'd have to write a whole book on the subject to do them complete justice. In fact, we've done just that — it's called *The HTML Style Sheets Design Guide,* by Natanya Pitts, Ed Tittel, and Stephen N. James (Coriolis Group Books).

Instead, we give an introduction to the concept of style, describe Cascading Style Sheets (CSS), and show you an example style sheet, complete with comments, so you can get a taste of what style sheets are and how they work. We hope our introduction to this new Web technology gives you an idea of what style sheets can do and shows you what direction your site can follow after you master the fundamentals of HTML style.

Of Styles and Style Sheets

If you've worked with desktop publishing applications, you should be familiar with the concept of a style sheet or template. If not, the idea isn't that complicated, so bear with us. (If you belong to the cognoscenti on this subject, see the sidebar "Background investigation reveals . . .")

A style sheet defines design and layout information for documents. Usually, style sheets also specify fonts, colors, indentation, kerning, leading, margins, and even page dimensions for any document that invokes them.

In the publishing world, style sheets are indispensable. Style sheets enable numerous people to collaborate. All participants can work at their own systems, independently of other team members. When the pieces of a project are brought together, the final product derives a consistent look and feel (or design and layout, if you prefer "typographically correct" language), because a common template — what style sheets are often called in the print industry — ensures a common definition for the resulting final document.

Consistency is a highly desirable characteristic in final products for both print and electronic (online) documents. The W3C has therefore made a gallant effort to incorporate such consistency on the Web by introducing style sheets. With the use of Web style sheets, an entire site can look nearly the same on every platform, within any browser that supports style sheets. For Web authors who want to create consistent documents, this promises a vast improvement over the current, somewhat more chaotic, status quo.

A second issue that arises out of proprietary non-SGML-compliant HTML extensions is *browser envy*. Since Netscape introduced proprietary markup in 1994, other vendors — such as Microsoft and NCSA — introduced gimmicks and flashy additions to their own browsers. All this work has been expended in hopes that those browsers that can display proprietary Web documents correctly will draw the largest customer bases. This conflict has spawned some exciting and eye-catching HTML, but it has caused more harm than good. Incompatible HTML, stifled competition, and narrow-minded browser development is just some of the fallout from this battle.

Background investigation reveals . . .

As you no doubt know, HTML is both a subset and a superset of SGML. If you don't know what this means, take a quick look online at www.w3.org/pub/WWW/MarkUp/.

Scroll down to the SGML link in the Related Resources section (or read the introductory chapters in this book). The Document Type Definitions (DTDs) that define how HTML works are written using a Backus-Naur Format (BNF) grammar notation. For more information, please visit

```
cuiwww.unige.ch/db-research/
    Enseignement/analyseinfo/
    AboutBNF.html
```

These original DTDs were designed to keep HTML within the confines of SGML. But recently, HTML's DTDs have been modified to allow non-SGML functionality. For many standards-obedient programmers and designers, this violates proper programming and design. For those interested in extending HTML's capabilities, it's a breath of fresh air (and function).

Web-based style sheets offer a promising solution to this situation. Style sheets allow proper separation of a document's structure and content from its form and appearance. With the implementation of style sheets, HTML can return to handling document structure and content (and get back to being proper SGML); style sheets can handle document form and appearance.

The separation of form and content allows authors and users to influence the presentation of documents without losing software or device independence. It also lessens the need for new HTML tags, either proprietary or standard, to support more sophisticated layout or appearance controls. Every possible layout or design element in a document can be defined by an attached — that is, linked — style sheet. This reduces the pressure to add tags and controls directly to HTML, when this capability becomes a matter of style.

Cascading Style Sheets (CSS1)

Today, the first version of the CSS standard, known as CSS1, is not quite an official standard, but it is so nearly complete that any forthcoming changes promise to be minor and cosmetic, rather than sweeping or major. Instead of exploring its details completely, we discuss its key concepts to help you appreciate its capabilities. We also use a style sheet in the sample Web site included on our CD-ROM to heighten your appreciation of their use.

One of CSS1's fundamental features is its assumption that multiple, related style sheets can *cascade,* which means that authors can attach preferred style sheets to Web documents, yet readers can associate their own personal style sheets to those same documents, to correct for human or technological handicaps. Thus, a print-handicapped reader could override an author's type distinctions between 10 and 12 point sizes, accommodating that reader's need for 40-point type. Likewise, local limitations on resolution or display area might override original layouts and type styles.

Basically, CSS contains a set of rules to resolve style conflicts that arise when applying multiple style sheets to the same document. Because conflicts are bound to arise, some method of resolution is essential to make the content of a document appear properly on a user's display.

The specifics of these rules depend on the assignment of a numeric weight to represent the relative importance of each style item. You accomplish this by assigning a value between 1 (least important) and 100 (most important) for a particular style element when it's referenced in a style sheet.

To prevent users' preferences from being completely overridden by a document's author, never set style-item weights to the maximum setting of 100. Keeping the settings low enables users to override settings at will, which is especially helpful for visually handicapped users who may require all characters to be at least 36 point, or who may demand special text-to-speech settings.

After all the referenced style sheets and their alterations are loaded into memory, the browser resolves conflicts by applying the definition with the greatest weight and ignoring other definitions.

For example, assume that a document's author creates a style for a level-1 heading, <H1>, using the color red and assigns that rule a weight of 75. Further assume that the reader has defined a style for <H1>, colored blue with a weight of 55. In that case, a CSS-enabled browser uses the author's definition, because it has the greater weight.

You can incorporate CSS into a Web document using one or more of four methods. The following code fragment illustrates all four of these methods:

```
<HEAD>
  <TITLE>title</TITLE>
  <LINK REL=STYLESHEET TYPE="text/css"
    HREF="http://www.style.org/cool" TITLE="Cool">

  <STYLE TYPE="text/css">

    @import "http://www.style.org/basic"

    H1 { color: blue }

  </STYLE>

</HEAD>
<BODY>
```

```
<H1>Headline is blue</H1>
<P STYLE="color: green">While the paragraph is green.
</BODY>
```

You see all four CSS implementation methods:

- ✔ Using the `<LINK>` tag to link an external style sheet (line 3 of the preceding listing).
- ✔ Using `<STYLE>` inside the `<HEAD>` section (lines 5 through 8).
- ✔ Importing a style sheet using the CSS @import notation (line 6).
- ✔ Using the `STYLE` attribute in an element inside the `<BODY>` section (line 12).

Other benefits of the CSS implementation of style sheets include

- ✔ **Grouping:** You can group multiple style elements or definitions together as follows:

```
H1 {font-size: 12pt; line-height: 14pt; font-family:
        Helvetica}
```

- ✔ **Inheritance:** Any nested tags inherit the style-sheet definitions assigned to the parent tag, unless you explicitly redefine the same elements. For example, in the HTML line

```
<H1>The headline <EM>is</EM> important!</H1>
```

if you define `<H1>` to display in red, then the text enclosed by `<EM>` also displays in red, unless you specifically assign `<EM>` another color.

- ✔ **Alternative Selectors:** Post-HTML 2.0 includes `CLASS` and `ID` attributes for most HTML tags. You can use these to define subsets or alternative sets of tags defined by a style sheet. For example:

```
<HEAD>
 <TITLE>Title</TITLE>
 <STYLE TYPE="text/css">
   H1.punk { color: #00FF00 }
 </STYLE>
</HEAD>
<BODY>
 <H1>Not green</H1>
 <H1 CLASS=punk>Way too green</H1>
</BODY>
```

- ✔ **Context-Sensitive Selectors:** CSS also supports context-based style definition. This is best described using an example:

```
<STYLE>
 UL UL LI    { font-size: small }
 UL UL UL LI { font-size: x-small }
</STYLE>
```

Following this notation, the second and third nested unnumbered lists (`<UL>`) use increasingly smaller font sizes.

✔ **Comments:** You can add comments inside a style sheet using the common C language syntax: `/* comment */`.

Style's Got Pros and Cons

The CSS1 standard includes some amazing features and capabilities, most of which mean little until you see them in action. Not every aspect of CSS1 is perfect, but to incline you further toward a positive outlook on style sheets, consider these other benefits of CSS1:

✔ The viewer can turn style sheets on and off.

✔ Style element definitions replace nonstandard tags.

✔ You can hide most complicated presentation markup within style sheets, instead of embedding it in documents, which results in cleaner HTML markup.

✔ You can use one style sheet for multiple HTML documents, making it easier to create consistent styles across a collection of pages.

✔ Both authors and readers can create new, previously impossible Web layouts.

Before you get too excited, though, we feel compelled to bring you back to earth by pointing out that CSS1 lacks a few items that you may consider important:

✔ **No absolute enforcement.** Any user has the option to turn off styles or use a style sheet with higher weights. Authors do not have absolute control over the display of their creations on other systems.

✔ **No multiple columns or overlapping frames.** Styles cannot define overlapping `<frame>`s, or assign the number of columns in a `<table>` layout. In other words, such definitions must still be hard-coded in HTML documents and cannot be tweaked in a style sheet.

✔ **No query language.** Users have no way to figure out what a style looks or acts like by asking for a definition from some kind of all-knowing style-sheet facility. Inspection is the only way to get that information.

A Bit of Speculation

You may find these other stylish things of interest. The W3C's goal is to create a platform-independent method to control the appearance of a Web document. With CSS1, the W3C took a big step in that direction, but other issues remain unresolved.

✔ Some parties have voiced interest in creating a public style-sheet server, where standard, general-use style sheets can reside. Doing so would encourage users to use widely accepted and broadly compatible style sheets. Although creating a core set of style sheets as a basis for most Web creations is a good idea, this kind of forced conformity can provoke a style-sheet standards battle among industry leaders (think Beta versus VHS). Also, the load placed on a "worldwide style-sheet server" could be overwhelming, even with lots of mirror sites — further diminishing bandwidth available on the Internet.

✔ A second, often-discussed issue is the extra lag or transfer time associated with long, complex style sheets. It's not hard to imagine a style sheet (`<link>`ed or included in the `<head>`) as big as 50K, especially if an author is "layout happy." Although authors should practice restraint, using common style sheets or the same style sheet over an entire Web site shouldn't significantly increase the time needed to transfer and view Web pages. After a `<link>`ed or `@import`ed style sheet is cached, it can be quickly recalled whenever needed.

✔ A third and extremely important issue is media-specific style sheets. Most Web content is designed for presentation through a graphical browser viewed on a computer monitor. The influences of the Web are quickly expanding beyond pixel-based displays, however. Print, fax, Braille, audio, and other media must also be considered for Web content.

Ideas for implementing media-specific style sheets include on-the-fly style cascades, standardized formats available on Web servers, and native browser support for alternate media. These areas of style-sheet standardization are sure to attract a lot of attention in upcoming months.

CSS1 has made a significant impact on the Web, even before the standard has become final. Stay tuned to your favorite Web developer or Internet news provider for the latest updates and implementations. As always, for the latest style-sheet specification information, turn to the W3C's style-sheet pages at `www.w3.org/Style`.

Chapter 19

Dynamic HTML

• •

• •

*H*TML 4.0 has sprouted lots of interesting capabilities and features, including new and improved markup and Cascading Style Sheets. Fans of the cutting edge will also find some exciting Web functionality that's become a common, everyday occurrence on the Web in the last couple of years: *Dynamic HTML* (just plain ol' *DHTML* to its friends).

Unfortunately, this new frontier is not free of conflict. In the past some major industry players — Microsoft and Netscape Communications, to be specific — had different visions of what Dynamic HTML should be and how it should work. While it's not that difficult to create DHTML that works well in the most current versions of the major browsers, older browsers may be less cooperative. No big surprise; that's business-as-usual on the Web — but caveat emptor: DHTML compatibility issues lie in wait for the unwary!

What's So Cool about DHTML?

For the moment, set aside concerns over compatibility and look at the basic concepts behind DHTML. You may as well get a line on what the fuss is all about; here we put DHTML in perspective and evaluate the impact it can have on the Web in general — or maybe on your Web pages in particular.

The essence of DHTML seems simple enough at first. With DHTML you can create Web pages that can change — almost as if by magic — *after* they have been sent to the browser from the server. *How is this amazing feat accomplished?* you might wonder. In a nutshell, scripting (combined with regular

HTML) provides the Web browser with the instructions it needs to automagi-cally alter a Web page on the client side — without extra help from the server — according to user activities. (See, we told you it was cool. . . .)

With DHTML, you can coax your Web pages into performing all kinds of nifty tricks, including these:

- **May I see a menu?** DHTML provides great support for hierarchical menus, where clicking a selection on one menu causes another submenu to pop up. When Web designers can create a user interface that's famil-iar to anyone who's used a GUI application like MS Word, a Web browser, and so on, that's attractive because it's so familiar to the users.

- **Shazam, here's everything.** Imagine the power to change a page on the client side in response to user selections (no matter how they're han-dled). This means your users can interact with Web documents more quickly; plus, they don't have to request a new page from a server across the Internet and wait for it to arrive. Users get what they need quickly, like it, and spread the word. (Read: business advantage.)

  DHTML enables Web page designers to package everything needed for interactivity *in a single document that may be sent to users all at once,* instead of a little bit at a time. Some experts say we may see current Web-site architecture (lots of simple, static HTML documents) replaced by fewer, but more complex, DHTML documents. Simple text may be more informative, but bells and whistles get immediate attention.

- **Styles on parade.** Because HTML supports style sheets (CSS1 and CSS2), and DHTML can operate on style sheets as well as HTML documents, page designers can even change styles dynamically. Font selections, sizes, and text color can all change in response to user actions on a Web page. For example, the contents of a Web-site map could be presented in 4- or 5-point black type — say, to fit as much information as possible onto a single screen. Then when a user selects an item for examination, that item could change to appear on-screen in a more readable, 8- or 9-point type, perhaps in multiple festive colors. As a viewer moves from page to page, DHTML can reflow text around each new focal point, keep-ing it at the current center of attention. (Imagine the possibilities that spring from applying such handling to whatever focuses a user's atten-tion. Magic lamps, anyone?)

- **Help yourself.** Microsoft announced in 1996 that it would switch its Windows Help environment from proprietary code to HTML. Because a help system needs access to topic indexes, multiple displays, and pre-cise positioning of elements on-screen, DHTML is an ideal technology to use. As an added bonus, such documents work equally well from a CD-ROM, a hard disk, or across the Web.

In fact, that's just a small chunk of DHTML capabilities; think *cornucopia*. Well, okay, the company that controls DHTML may not control the universe. But the extraordinary power and potential inherent in DHTML aren't lost on Microsoft and Netscape — or on the W3C. All three have made a commitment to the development of DHTML capabilities that will benefit developers and users alike.

DHTML's Pieces and Parts

It takes more than HTML tags to make a Web page *dynamic*. Other technologies get to play, too, including these:

- **Scripting** commands tell a browser how to change a document dynamically.
- **Style sheets** help a browser figure out how to display the many iterations possible any DHTML document can go through.
- **A document object model (DOM)** helps the browser recognize the many different elements in a document (*elements* refer to individual tags and their content) — and change those elements as directed by scripting commands.

But heed, O seekers: Before ye venture forth into DHTML, be ye up to speed on HTML. To fully grok the ins and outs of DHTML, first add a working knowledge of these three technologies to your repertoire. They hold the secret of bringing your Web pages to life.

Scripting your pages

Just as a movie script (with assistance from the director, of course) dictates action in a film, scripts included in dynamic Web pages direct a page's dynamic activities. Even the simplest rollover requires a short, sweet script to do its thing.

No, it's not an aerobic exercise for lazy dogs. In Web parlance, a *rollover* is a common Web-page addition that swaps one image for another when a user rolls the mouse pointer over the original image. To make the switch, the underlying script must include specific instructions to do the following:

1. Detect when a user rolls the mouse pointer over a specific image.
2. Rewrite the value for the `src=` attribute for the `<img>` tag that defines the graphic so the new value points to the location of a new image.

3. Detect when a user moves the mouse off that image.

4. Rewrite the value of `scr=` to point back to the location of the original image.

The code that passes all these instructions to the computer can't be written in just any ol' language; the browser needs its instructions written in a special *computer scripting language.* (Could that be why they're called *scripts?* Eureka!) A wide variety of scripting languages is available, but the two most common ones used for DHTML are JavaScript — also called ECMAScript — and VBScript.

Both Navigator and Internet Explorer support JavaScript. If you're running Internet Explorer on a Win32 platform, IE also supports VBScript. To enable as many browsers as possible — on the widest range of platforms — to view your pages, we suggest using JavaScript instead of VBScript.

Both JavaScript and VBScript are complete programming languages. If you want to learn to write your own scripts, you'll need to learn the semantics for one or both languages. (Don't make that face. What if it froze that way?) Admittedly, it takes some time to learn how to script — but it's not impossible by a long shot. Besides, we know a couple of really great books to help you learn how to script DHTML pages. Try the *JavaScript Bible,* 3rd Edition, by Danny Goodman (IDG Books Worldwide, Inc., 1998) and *JavaScript for Dummies*, 2nd Edition, by Emily Vander Veer (IDG Books Worldwide, Inc., 1997).

If you don't really *need* another hobby but you still want to tuck some scripts into your Web pages to make them dynamic, good news: You may have an honorable alternative to learning scripting. You can use *canned* scripts, which are scripts written by others that you can plug right into your pages and use. Various Web sites offer hundreds — if not thousands — of scripts just waiting for you to pick them up and use them on your pages. We found three chock-full sites that are also good learning resources for would-be script writers:

✔ www.scripting.com

✔ www.webcoder.com

✔ javascript.internet.com/

Events and the users who love them

In the previous list of steps, a script had to swap one image for another. Did you notice that Steps 2 and 4 required that the browser detect when a user moved the mouse pointer over a graphic? We're sure you did. The big question you're probably asking is: *How does the browser know when a user does something on a Web page?*

Well, it isn't psychic, but a browser is designed to be "smart" in certain ways. Browsers that can understand and implement scripts are also smart enough to recognize events. An *event* can represent a user action *or response*. When a Web developer creates a named set of events, he or she can instruct a Web document to respond in a specific way when the browser recognizes a particular event. In fact, without events a browser wouldn't know when it was supposed to run any script on a Web page. Events act as triggers for scripts, telling them when to run.

For example, when a user's cursor stays in position over an object or crosses an object on a Web page, the document can tell the browser to recognize this user action as a *mouseover*. When a mouseover occurs, the browser can display a specific response (such as a short, descriptive pop-up window that identifies a navigation button or an active region on an image map). Likewise, *mousedown* represents what happens when a user clicks the left-hand mouse button when the pointer rests on a particular object on a page. Here again, a document can be instructed to respond to a user event in a specific fashion (say, by activating a link or making a rude noise).

Here's a quick look behind the scenes of a hierarchical menu: When the user clicks a higher-level menu entry, the response to that event is the redrawing of the screen to show the lower-level menu next to the higher-level menu entry that's been clicked.

Web-page developers can associate any kind of script with a user event, which means all kinds of interesting things can happen when the browser recognizes those events. Imagine your page showing explanatory messages, looking up terms in a glossary and displaying them elsewhere on-screen (or in a pop-up window), opening a text-entry box to solicit and handle user input, or making an even ruder noise (just kidding). Remember, too, that all this activity happens purely on the client side of the Web connection. It means your Web page acts like any other local application — which can open a whole other box of delights (or can of worms, depending on whom you ask).

So the browser recognizes events that then trigger scripts that then tell the browser how to adjust the display or behavior of the already-downloaded Web page. See a cycle forming here? We do too.

Adding a touch of style to your pages

DHTML gives you unprecedented stylistic power (insert lightning flash and maniacal laughter here). Well, no, it won't change the weather, but DHTML provides an ongoing opportunity to control positioning of elements on your Web page. You can use (and manipulate) standard CSS1 or CSS2 style sheets to control how and where elements appear on your Web page. Precisely. Directly. Even (dare we say it?) consistently.

Of course you remember our old friends CSS1 and CSS2 from their starring roles in Chapter 18. If not, you can get reacquainted anytime.

Style sheets include a capability to place elements in precise positions at the same time they begin to appear on-screen. You can specify various units of measure, both relative and absolute. For example, you could determine where to put that snazzy stegosaurus graphic by specifying an absolute pixel count relative to the upper-left-hand corner of the user's display window, or by specifying dimensions and location relative to other elements — paragraphs, other images, and so forth — on the page.

Style sheets also make it possible for you to organize and address elements in layers. The idea is to associate on-screen elements not only with x and y coordinates for horizontal and vertical positioning, but also with a z coordinate for layer number, treating the screen as if it were a surface on which you could stack things (memos, photos, pizzas, whatever). Because you can assign attributes to HTML elements (such as transparency or clipping), you can micromanage any overlapping elements and use their attributes to create all kinds of cool effects.

To hobnob with this rich and powerful set of page controls, drop in next door at Chapter 18. For the ultimate resource on the subject, consult the W3C's draft specification for "Cascading Style Sheets Level 2" (CSS2) at

```
www.w3.org/TR/REC-CSS2
```

Adding awareness with the DOM

There's one last piece to the DHTML puzzle: awareness (in this case, the browser's, though yours is always a good resource too). In fact, without this piece, DHTML just wouldn't work. The *Document Object Model* (DOM) is a component of a Web browser that allows it to recognize the different elements in a page as unique entities that can be manipulated by a script.

Imagine, for example, loading a Web page from a browser's point of view. As the browser starts to load the page, it no longer just sees tags as mere switches that turn formatting On or Off. Instead, the browser puts each tag and its content — now identified as an element — into a miniature database that contains all the pieces and parts of that page. These elements are the objects in the document; the browser's database is a model for how they all fit together. Hence the name — Document Object Model. (It's like a model kit that contains all the parts and instructions that the browser needs to snap the page together *just like that.*)

Once a browser has a DOM stored for a Web page, that browser is able to follow the instructions in a script to recognize and change anything about the different elements on the page — for example, these:

- ✔ Element attributes and their values
- ✔ Element content
- ✔ Actual elements themselves

So the script that drives a rollover to switch `image1.gif` with `image1a.gif` tells the browser to find the first image tag in its database — usually by assigning that image a unique identifier using the `ID=` attribute. Next, the script tells the browser to rewrite the tag that reads `<img id=rollover src=image1.gif>` to read `<img id=rollover src=image1a.gif>`. When the browser rewrites the tag, it knows it must then display a specific change to the page — namely, `image1a.gif` rendered in place of `image1.gif`.

The major problems associated with creating DHTML pages stem from differences in the way Internet Explorer (IE) and Navigator implement the DOM. IE incorporates built-in support for all the elements in HTML 4.0 so it can recognize and change anything about any element in a page. But the Netscape Navigator DOM only recognizes a small subset of the elements in HTML 4.0, so it can only access and change the elements that belong to that subset (not all elements, as IE can). This makes it easy to create a DHTML page that works fine in IE but not so fine in Navigator.

For a vigorous rundown on the ins and outs of these DOM differences, scrutinize at the later section in this chapter that's devoted to the purpose. It's titled "Drafting inclusive DOM requirements." You'll find out more about DOMs than you ever wanted to know.

DHTML à la Microsoft

The Microsoft view of DHTML has four principal components:

- ✔ **An HTML *Document Object Model* (or *DOM*).** This model creates a data structure for an entire HTML document. Every element in the document can be addressed by instance, name, type, or position.
- ✔ **A method to control how elements are positioned.** Microsoft supports most of the CSS1 specification and some of the CSS2 specification for controlling where elements may sit on a page (and behave themselves).
- ✔ **A set of multimedia controls.** Designed for animation, graphical displays, channel filtering, and other capabilities, these controls make it easier to incorporate interactive multimedia — and to integrate the fancy stuff with other content that just sits there.

✔ **A method to associate databases (or other orderly collections of data) with HTML documents.** Called *data binding*, this capability permits a single Web document to manage multiple views of a single data set. If, for example, viewers are gazing raptly at a massive stock portfolio, data binding enables them to display stocks by ticker symbol, date of purchase, absolute value, and so on. (Gee. Sounds like fun . . .)

Beyond these four components, Microsoft has also created a Scripting Object Model for Internet Explorer (starting with Version 4.0). The idea is to let developers use whatever scripting language they choose to control page elements within the Microsoft browser. Previously Microsoft supported only Visual Basic, Scripting Edition (usually known as VBScript) and Jscript (Microsoft's version of the popular JavaScript language originally defined by Netscape and Sun Microsystems).

DHTML and the multimedia wish list

While it's not exactly science fiction, the Microsoft concept of multimedia for DHTML is pretty ambitious. It offers support for what amounts to a "wish list" of advanced on-screen display controls — the sort of razzle-dazzle tech that developers have labored mightily to produce in customized form, but which we haven't seen widely deployed in many commercial products yet.

Microsoft obviously imagines a visible and audible garden of delights. Supported visual capabilities include animated color washes and textures, font-morphing and transitions, screen shifts similar to those used for transitions in movies (such as fades, wipes, bleeds, and other common scene-shifting techniques), plus support for compact, scalable graphics displayed using a simple vector format. (In short, nearly anything a high-end TV commercial can do.)

For audio effects, Microsoft offers support for defining, creating, precisely mixing, and making smooth transitions among multiple channels of sound. Imagine a capability that works much like a multichannel audio mixer, not only mixing and blending sounds and voiceovers, but also associating audio effects with user-triggered events and overlaying them on other audio streams — or replacing them as needed. New art forms, anyone?

By offering this support, Microsoft is attempting to prepare the way for the introduction and management of multiple data streams — animation, video, and audio — in the Web pages of the near future. The idea is to encourage designers to make such elements part of a truly interactive, dynamic environment. (As Shakespeare might have written, but didn't, "O brave new world, that hath such Web sites in it!")

So far, the Microsoft DOM has deeply influenced the W3C's work to standard-ize DHTML, up to and including significant attention to element positioning and controls. Not taken up, however, is the topic of multimedia support. Microsoft data-binding technologies (discussed in the next section) also remain to be addressed in the W3C's work on DHTML. But give it time. Even now, however, data binding is worth a closer look.

Data binding in DHTML (however you look at it)

The built-in database support that Microsoft includes with its version of DHTML is called *data binding*. This technology enables a Web page designer to associate documents with specific sets of data so the page can display a default organization for any data while it's loading. Thereafter, freedom reigns — users can employ whatever controls the designer gives them to sort and sift the data. The beauty of this approach is that *all data resides on the client side of the Web connection*. Thus, when users operate on the data or reorganize it, all such operations occur locally without grabbing any data from the server. Result (in theory, at least): less server traffic, faster data tweaks, happier users.

Under the hood, the capability to reorganize and reformat data on the fly requires users to have access to some kind of local data-management applica-tion — say, Excel or Access — to carry out the operations that appear on a Web page. If such tools are handy (say, at a user's workstation), local perfor-mance is pretty fast — and search or edit operations on the client side are easy to support. Then, in effect, most of the work's already been done and another application handles it. (If this approach sounds remarkably like the old idea of helper applications for Web browsers, that's no accident.)

Both multimedia controls and data binding are Microsoft proprietary tech-nologies that don't work in Navigator or other browsers. Use these sparingly, or not at all, if you need to reach the broadest possible audience.

Summing up the Microsoft DHTML story

Microsoft and its adherents have already made effective use of DHTML tech-nology and have created some astonishing Web documents built around their (trademarked) brand of DHTML. If you visit Microsoft's own Web site at www.microsoft.com (using IE, of course) and observe how its page naviga-tion and pull-down menus work, you'll see a compelling demonstration of DHTML at work.

But you'll find even zippier capabilities when you visit some of the other pages built along the same lines. For example, because a browser builds a hierarchical model of a document's elements as they arrive, this hierarchy can be scanned, reorganized, and categorized as needed. Some sites can use this capability to construct "active" tables of contents (whose elements act as hyperlinks to associated documents), build graphical site maps on the fly, and create other infrastructure amenities (such as an index) without having to construct them in advance — and all automatically.

Dynamic HTML has a fun side and a business side. Those seduced by the fun side have used it to build online, Web-based versions of games such as Battleship, Mines, and Tetris. On the business side, some creative designers have used DHTML to craft interactive, self-modifying screen forms to dazzle the customer. Try this one on for size: An order for a shirt automatically pops up a subwindow that asks for collar size and sleeve length. Or how about "smart" requisition forms that calculate their own totals and figure sales taxes, delivery charges, and whatever else the customer needs to know to pay up? (Sorry, there isn't one that'll do Form 1040 for you. But we can dream.)

The Microsoft approach appears to offer powerful, flexible interactivity to Web page designers. Although learning this technology is not a trivial job, the rewards seem to justify the effort. Table 19-1 lists some places to observe Microsoft's version of DHTML in action, and to learn more about its ways and habits.

Table 19-1	Microsoft Dynamic HTML Resources
Description	*URL*
Dynamic HTML home page	`msdn.microsoft.com/workshop/author/dhtml/default.htm`
DHTML Overview document	`msdn.microsoft.com/workshop/author/dhtml/default.htm`
Event Handling in IE 4.0	`msdn.microsoft.com/workshop/author/dhtml/reference/events.asp#om40_event`

Netscape Does DHTML

As is so often the case when giants battle for market share, similar concepts lead to different executions — and the contestants slug it out in the marketplace until the rest of us get headaches. The Netscape vision of DHTML is similar to Microsoft's, but Netscape takes it in a significantly different direction. (Hint: A Web-page designer who wants to build DHTML that works with both Microsoft *and* Netscape browsers had best get a LARGE bottle of aspirin.)

While the central DHTML concept remains consistent — building a Web page that can interact with users entirely on the client side — the Netscape approach to DHTML comes across as less dynamic than Microsoft's in the eyes of most outside observers (including the W3C). To get a sense of why it looks that way, take a closer look at the elements of Netscape's DHTML vision.

In the Netscape view, dynamic HTML capability has three primary components:

- ✔ **HTML markup**, including Netscape extensions, especially those for addressing document layers through the `<div>` tag, plus dynamic font controls

- ✔ **Java and JavaScript**, used in tandem with proprietary Netscape Java-Accessible Style Sheets (JASS) or CSS

- ✔ **An object model for HTML documents**, that differs substantially from the Microsoft DOM

The most obvious distinction between Netscape and Microsoft weighs heavily in Microsoft's favor: Microsoft incorporated standard style sheets (CSS) and standard HTML 4.0 markup into its DHTML. Navigator 4.0 versions and later do as well but earlier versions only supported Netscape's proprietary `<layer>` tag and JASS. Also, the Microsoft vision of the DOM is much closer to the W3C's DOM standard. Even so, the Netscape concept has some real strengths.

Netscape dynamic HTML as <layer> cake

Netscape bases its implementation of DHTML on the `<layer>` tag. Not only does this tag provide the mechanism that divvies up HTML content into layers, it also provides methods to impose order on these layers. A designer gets some client-side flexibility here: A user can tell a browser to manipulate a layer's precedence, visibility, and display characteristics. A familiar *x, y, z* coordinate model (good ol' high school geometry) defines precise points of reference for HTML elements and objects. That means you can control their precise positioning on a Web page — not only horizontal and vertical position on the "surface" of the page, but also (so to speak) who upstages whom as you shuffle elements in front of and behind each other.

Anything you can do with <layer> and its attributes, you can do with <div> and CSS properties. The basic concepts are the same, but the actual implementations are different. In a move towards standards compliance, Netscape has included support in its most current version of Navigator for layers that use the <div> tag, but if you want your Dynamic HTML pages to work in older versions of Navigator, you'll have to use the <layer>_tag.

A layering model is common to many high-end graphics programs such as Adobe Photoshop. Of course, a discussion about layering can get into quite a few layers itself, so let's keep ours few and tasty. Suffice to say that layering displays only those elements that meet two specific conditions:

✔ Their visibility attributes are set to require their display.

✔ Their position places them within the frame of the current display area for the page.

As HTML markup goes, <layer> is a powerful and highly descriptive tag, replete with numerous attributes and associated values. Some of its most noteworthy attributes are as follows:

✔ background: Used as in the <body> tag to set a background graphic for a designated layer.

✔ bgcolor: Used as in the <body> tag to set a background color for a designated layer.

✔ clip: Defines what area of a layer is viewable on-screen.

✔ name: Provides a unique identifier for each defined layer, so that scripts can refer to it in the process of controlling layer transitions, selections, and access.

✔ visibility: Indicates whether a layer is currently visible or invisible (that is, whether it appears on-screen — invisible things are kinda hard to work with).

✔ width: Sets right margin controls for text-wrap and *padding* (the white space between the rightmost character and the edge of the layer's clip boundary). Padding actually helps a page's legibility.

Taken as a whole, the layer mechanism gives page designers a great way to break up content into mutually exclusive sets of data, text, and graphics and to switch among the sets as needed. This functionality provides the foundation for the entire Netscape approach to DHTML.

Java-Accessible Style Sheets (JASS)

Java-Accessible Style Sheets (or *JASS,* as in the early word for jazz) let page designers access any object with a `name` attribute while an HTML document is loading on the client side. The JASS specification has quietly faded away and works only with JavaScript in older versions of Netscape. Once again, stick with CSS when styling your Web pages. Netscape's support isn't as complete as Microsoft's, but it will get you by.

They said it couldn't be done, but somebody did it anyway. Shelly Powers wrote a great article for Netscape titled "Adding Dynamic Content for Multiple Browsers and Versions." This piece does a good job of describing how designers can build just the kind of ambidextrous Web pages that can use DHTML but work equally well for both kinds of users. You can find this article at the following site:

```
www.netscapeworld.com/nw-05-1997/nw-05-dynamic.html
```

The Netscape object model: If you build it . . .

will enough of them come? The Netscape object model (like the Microsoft DOM) seeks to organize and address elements within an HTML document. But its notation is completely different from Microsoft's: Individual elements can only be addressed by assigning them unique names. The object references look much different, not everything is guaranteed to be accessible unless it has a name, and naming things one by one takes time. For these reasons, Netscape's object model has not been widely adopted outside the Netscape developer community.

Rounding out the Netscape vision of DHTML

Though the Netscape vision of DHTML differs from (and is arguably less dynamic than) Microsoft's, Netscape's approach still offers similar capabilities and functionality. Seeing the effects that this technology can produce provides the most compelling demonstration of its features and benefits. Table 19-2 includes further information resources on the Netscape view of DHTML, plus some great examples of this technology at work.

Table 19-2	Netscape DHTML Resources and Examples	
Category	*Description*	*URL*
Overview	Dynamic HTML Overview	`developer.netscape.com/docs/manuals/communicator/dynhtml/index.htm`
	Compelling Content	`www.netscapeworld.com/nw-07-1997/nw-07-webmaster.html`
Ads	Online fashion mall	`www.fashionmall.com`
Animations	Taboca ArtworK	`www.taboca.com/layer/`
	Sinfomic Layers Demo	`www.sinfomic.fr/Demo/`
	Games Mix-a-Pol	`www.xnet.com/~april/mix/`
	Web Design Group Tutorial	`www.htmlhelp.com/reference/css/`

The W3C's Role in DHTML

Imagine a referee trying to paste together a comprehensive rulebook and use it for a rowdy game that's already in progress, while caught between two giants who are playing by different rulebooks. That's roughly the W3C's position between these two main DHTML contenders. Today, the W3C is organized in terms of several activity domains. Its User Interface (UI) domain covers three areas of concern:

- HTML markup and specifications
- Cascading Style Sheets
- An inclusive W3C Document Object Model

Since Dynamic HTML interweaves all three of these topics, DHTML also falls within the UI domain at the W3C.

The W3C has said that it will not issue a DHTML specification but instead will continue to create specs for the component pieces of DHTML. So far, the W3C's main contribution to DHTML is its definition of a Document Object Model that accommodates this upstart technology.

The W3C does seem committed to implementing a standard for a complete, thoroughgoing head-knocker of a DOM. Proprietary DOMs included in vendor-specific browsers will have to comply with this specification to be considered W3C-compliant. In addition to HTML and CSS, the new DOM description keeps one eye on the emerging Extensible Markup Language (XML), but more about that in a minute. For now, it's enough to note that XML represents a powerful, open-ended middle ground between HTML and SGML; to accommodate it, the W3C's proposed DOM must itself be flexible and open-ended.

In late 1998, the W3C issued its final recommendation for a level-1 implementation of a standard DOM. The working group responsible for the DOM continues to work to improve the DOM and its capabilities, aiming primarily for a level-2 implementation. As always, the W3C keeps its eyes on the prize of a quality standard that works well for everyone. But for now, what's been defined is what you get: the only true (dare we say legitimate?) standard for a Document Object Model.

You can learn more about the W3C's work in this area — and read the relevant specifications for yourself — if you visit this Web page:

```
www.w3.org/DOM/.
```

However elegant additional levels of this specification might be, implementing a standard DOM remains a tall order. ("Hey, all we've got to do is to get those giants to play by the same rules." "Right. *You* tell them.") Let's see how healthy the definition looks right now.

Drafting inclusive DOM requirements

The W3C's DOM document includes a classic three-part structure: (1) a set of requirements for a workable DOM, (2) a summary of issues that affect core document structure and navigation, and (3) a discussion of structure and navigation specific to HTML and XML.

Though still a relative youngster among markup languages, *XML* (*Extensible Markup Language*) has monster potential: It's a tool for creating not only documents, but entire custom markup languages. The good news for the adventurous is that familiarity with HTML is a pretty decent springboard to XML. In fact, the W3C plans to incorporate HTML into the XML family sooner rather than later — which is a tale for another time (say, a little later on in the twenty-first century).

The DOM requirements show the current direction of the W3C's thinking about document object models. We paraphrase these requirements in the following list to make them easy to digest with a minimum of chewing; our apologies to the experts who worked so hard on the details that we're about to so cheerfully ignore.

Here's our fast-snack summation of the current requirements. (You want fries with that?)

According to the W3C, a Document Object Model must have the following characteristics:

✔ Common core of functionality across all document types

✔ Consistent document representation, so that same document read from Web or from hard disk creates same object hierarchy

✔ Language neutrality and platform independence

✔ No requirement for complete graphical user interface (for example, search engines or user agents may see only text and nothing else)

✔ Openness to other document-manipulation tools and techniques

✔ Security and reliability, so that (1) only valid documents can be produced as output from the model, and (2) multiple users can access the model without disrupting data integrity or concurrency

✔ Support for external user agents and internal scripts

The rest of the working draft blooms into a wealth of subdocuments and sections, each of which addresses various topics. For practicality's sake, we'll stick to the elements that pertain to dynamic HTML.

Malleable elements, squashy documents

The W3C DOM centers around the capability to address (and operate on) any element in a document that's represented according to the model. Thus, if a document is getting worked over by a browser, a script, or a program that generates documents on-the-fly, the program should be able to access and change any element within the document — even the associated style information and the governing DTDs. In effect, the document becomes putty in the designer's hands.

The specification also covers a set of *core primitives* — no, not underground Neanderthals, but commands assumed to be available when you want to do simple-but-indispensable stuff (say, getting and altering document elements and attributes). Examples of the species include operators like `get` and `set`, plus more elaborate phrasings like `get first`, `get next`, `get where`, `type=xx`, and so on.

The W3C event model

Sometimes you've got to redefine the basics. "Event," for example. The W3C DOM includes an *event model* designed to support user interaction. The definition expects the document to respond to user input and selections even while its components are still being downloaded (sort of like fielding a question while dancing on one foot and putting on the other shoe).

This specification calls for a series of messages and status codes that indicate what kinds of events are occurring (*both shoes are on and I'm looking for a tie*), and provides a platform-neutral way to tell the browser what the user is up to at any given moment (*getting no clicks just now, boss — user seems pacified*). The model also covers responses to user interactions; these include assigning default actions, overriding defaults, and taking a conditional action based on both the document's content and user's input. (You *could* get your document to respond to an error with a rude noise. Though of course we'd never suggest such a thing . . .)

A bid for control of the DTD

At the *Document Type Definition* (*DTD*) level, the model gives the DOM control of detecting — or assigning — a governing DTD. In effect, the DOM gets final sayso over what a document is or isn't. If a document comes complete with a handy, explicit DTD, the DOM can incorporate it and use it. Then the DOM can navigate and manipulate the DTD it swallowed, in much the same way as it would the document itself.

For example, the DOM should be able to use specific methods to request document validation. That's the method of choice for making sure a particular document passes muster according to its corresponding DTD — *and* according to the markup language it's written in. The DOM may not be able to fetch a newspaper (at least not yet), but it does seek to deliver well-formed, complete documents to a Web site.

But wait, there's more! Aside from the numeric error codes associated with HTTP, current HTML and CSS implementations have no consistent capabilities to report or handle errors. (Not even an *I'm sorry, Dave.*) The DOM spec not only calls for a consistent error-handling mechanism that works throughout the Web environment (the nerve!), it also defines a set of messages to report and log errors as they occur. A proper DOM could keep track of error-status information and report a document's error status any time you asked for it. Now, *that* would be industrial-strength error-handling — and a mighty improvement.

Finally, the DOM does its best to capture and deliver descriptive information about documents to the browser:

✔ The DOM states its assumptions about the DTDs governing HTML when a document arrives with no SGML preamble. (*No identity, huh? We'll give you one . . .*)

✔ The DOM requires that documents supply *metadata* (data about data) to describe themselves. Metadata can include information about a document's author, its creation and modification dates, and any associated data packages (such as cookies) that want in, too.

✔ The DOM defines mechanisms to obtain information about a user's browser and display environment, which would enable the Web page designer to query this information and take local conditions into account.

✔ The DOM requests local checks to determine exactly which MIME types are supported, so it can decide what kinds of data the local browser can handle.

The W3C specification for the DOM aims at one primary target: to deliver a document's contents, structure, and properties for easy inspection and manipulation, and to support on-the-fly modification of such documents. No muss, no fuss, minimum frou-frou, and *here's the info!* Since the spec also calls for a consistent event model (Consistency! Hmmph! The very idea!), as well as the capability to recognize and respond to events, the total concept is a thoroughly dynamic view of user interaction. In effect, it's a new vision of HTML documents, in which they readily transform themselves to fit their user's desktops and respond to user input and events. These capabilities should make the Web much more of a bustling two-way street in the future. (Smog optional.)

What's Ahead for DHTML?

To be sure, the W3C is kowtowing to neither Microsoft nor Netscape as purveyors of The One True DHTML. The W3C's documents and specifications, however, indicate that they're leaning more heavily toward Microsoft than toward Netscape. The main differences between the W3C and Microsoft are three W3C desiderata:

✔ An insistence on platform independence and language neutrality

✔ A broader notion of events and error handling

✔ A firm insistence on openness and standardization

Does this mean Microsoft has "won" the game? We think not; for one thing, the game is far from over. The W3C has always had a broader vision of the Web than does Microsoft (or, for that matter, the other major players). Helpful as its own DOM guidelines have been, Microsoft's vision seems to treat all operating systems as equal — and Windows operating systems as "more equal than others." (Coincidence? We think not.) Although the W3C actually tries to create a level playing field for all operating systems, Microsoft remains deeply involved in the evolution and refinement of this technology. We believe they'll continue to influence the course of DHTML while the W3C builds its standards.

Both Netscape and Microsoft swear they plan to adhere to all relevant standards, including those that will govern DHMTL, as soon as the W3C defines them. (Imagine those giant players promising the ref: "_No rough stuff, honest . . ._") Though standards will struggle closer to clarity, the issues surrounding them will probably stay chaotic for years to come.

But chaos is always a fairly safe prediction for modern life. We want to go out on a limb and make some predictions about where DHTML may lead, starting with a short list of fairly likely outcomes. Then, dessert: some far out, but way cool, possibilities that could happen, but may have relevance only in our own twisted minds!

So let's start with the most probable results the Web will see from the W3C's work on DHTML:

- ✔ You'll start seeing lots of dynamic buttons, hierarchical menus, navigation tools, and layered animation on a Web site near you. They may be there already. Pray they come in peace.

- ✔ Element positioning and rendering are already included in the Cascading Style Sheet specifications (CSS1 and CSS2) and will continue there, regardless of what DHTML does.

- ✔ We may have an early winner for the "notation-of-choice award" for using the DOM. Ladies and gentlemen, presenting the dot notation — that same humble device used to reference document elements and attributes — you've also seen it querying documents for information by element type, instance, and order of occurrence.

- ✔ _Full Dynamic HTML_ — the power to change a document's content and element attributes at any time, on the client side (once that information is available to the browser) — will become très chic.

Less likely, but full of possibility, are some kickier capabilities that DHTML may yet deliver:

- ✔ Document validation will become a standard requirement for all HTML, XML, and CSS documents, to make sure they can be fully dynamic and fit within the DOM.

✔ Self-modifying forms, surveys, tests, and questionnaires will define basic mechanisms for users to supply data via the Web, and to add custom functionality to intranet Web servers.

✔ Tools to manipulate style sheets and DTDs will emerge and become an integral part of the Web designer's toolkit. This will increase power and flexibility of Web pages by an order of magnitude.

✔ Visual scripting tools will become the rage, permitting designers to create interactive, script-driven Web pages the same way that such tools as Symantec's Visual Café, or Microsoft's Visual J++ already can.

✔ Web designers will pay a lot more attention to building *pages* that behave like applications, rather than trying to construct entire Web sites that behave like applications.

Yeah, and Super Bowl XXXIX might be broadcast live from the moon. (Hey, stranger things have happened.) But before any of these modest predictions can run the gauntlet of time and subsequent events, an awful lot of work still needs doing. The specifications underway at the W3C have to work their way to consensus and become formal Recommendations or Specifications. Web-browser developers have to take up the challenge of all the functionality that the W3C designers demand (and suggest). And finally, we all have to learn to work within this new framework without too much future shock. It promises to be a real adventure! (Spacesuit optional.)

Part VI
The Part of Tens

The 5th Wave   By Rich Tennant

"Gotta hand it to our Web page designer - she found a way to make our pie charts interactive."

In this part . . .

*H*ere, we cover the do's and don'ts for HTML markup, help you rethink your views on document design, and help you catch potential bugs and errors in your pages. Enjoy!

Chapter 20

Ten HTML Do's and Don'ts

*B*y itself, HTML is neither excessively complex nor overwhelmingly difficult. As some high-tech wags (including a few rocket scientists) have put it, *This ain't rocket science!* Nevertheless, a few important do's and don'ts can make or break the Web pages you build with HTML. Consider these humble admonishments as guidelines to help you make the most of HTML without losing touch with your users or watching your page blow up on the pad.

If some of the fundamental points that we made throughout this book seem to be cropping up here too (especially regarding proper and improper use of HTML), it's no accident. Heed ye well the prescriptions and avoid ye the maledictions. But hey, we know they're your pages and you can do what you want with them. Your users will decide the ultimate outcome. (We'd *never* say, "We told you so!" Nope. Not us.)

Never Lose Sight of Your Content

So we return to the crucial question of payload: the content of your page. Why? Well, as Darrell Royal (legendary football coach of the University of Texas Longhorns in the '60s and '70s) is rumored to have said to his players, "Dance with who brung ya." In normal English, we think this means that you should *stick to the people who've supported you all along* and give your loyalty to those who've given it to you.

We're not sure what this means for football, but for Web pages it means keeping faith with your users and keeping the content paramount. If you don't have strong, solid, informative content, users quickly get that empty feeling that starts to gnaw when a Web page is content-free. Then they'll be off to richer hunting grounds on the Web, looking for content. To satisfy their hunger, then above all, *place your most important content on the site's major pages.* Save the frills and supplementary materials for the secondary pages. The short statement of this principle for HTML is, "Tags are important, but *what's between the tags* — the content — is what really counts."

For a refresher course on making your content the very best it can possibly be, take a spin through Chapter 2.

Structure Your Documents and Your Site

Providing users with a clear road map and guiding them through your content is as important for a single home page as it is for an online encyclopedia. When longer or more complex documents grow into a full-fledged Web site, a road map becomes even more important. This map ideally takes the form of (yep, you guessed it) a flow chart that shows page organization and links. If you like pictures with a purpose, the chart could appear in graphic form on an orientation page for your site.

We're strong advocates of top-down page design: Don't start writing content or placing tags until you understand what you want to say and how you want to organize your materials. Then start the construction of any HTML document or collection of documents with a paper and pencil (or whatever modeling tool you like best). Sketch out the relationships within the content and the relationships among your pages. Know where you're building before you roll out the heavy equipment.

Good content flows from good organization. It helps you stay on track during page design, testing, delivery, and maintenance. And organization helps your users find their way through your site. Need we say more? Well, yes: Don't forget that *organization changes over time.* Revisit and critique your organization and structure on a regular basis, and don't be afraid to change either one to keep up with changes in your content or focus.

Keep Track of Those Tags

While you're building documents, it's often easy to forget to use closing tags, even when they're required (for example, the </a> that closes the opening anchor tag <a>). Even when you're testing your pages, some browsers can be a little too forgiving; compensating for a lack of correctness and leading you into a false sense of security. The Web is no place to depend on the kindness of strangers; scrutinize your tags to head off possible problems from other browsers that may not be quite so understanding (or lax, as the case may be).

As for the claims some vendors of HTML authoring tools make ("You don't even have to know any HTML!"), all we can say is, *Uh-huh, surrre*. HTML itself is still a big part of what makes Web pages work; if you understand it, you can troubleshoot with a minimum of teeth-gnashing. Also, ensuring that your page's inner workings are correct and complete is something only *you* can do for your documents, whether you build them yourself or a program builds them for you.

We could go on ad infinitum about this, but we'll exercise some mercy and confine our remarks to the most pertinent:

- ✔ **Keep track of tags yourself while you write or edit HTML by hand.** If you open a tag — whether it be an anchor, or a text area, or whatever — create the closing tag for it right then and there, even if you still have content to add. Most HTML editors will do this for you.

- ✔ **Use a syntax-checker to validate your work as part of the testing process.** These are automatic tools that find missing tags for you and also find other ways to drive you crazy along the way! Use these whether you build pages by hand or with software assistance. Here's the URL for the W3C's own HTML validator: http://validator.w3 .org/.

- ✔ **Try to obtain and use as many browsers as you possibly can when testing your pages.** This not only alerts you to missing tags; it can also point out potential design flaws or browser dependencies (covered in a section later in this chapter). This exercise also emphasizes the importance of alternate text information. That's why we always check our pages with Lynx (a totally character-mode browser).

- ✔ **Always follow HTML document syntax and layout rules.** Just because most browsers don't require tags like <html>, <head>, and <body> does not mean you can omit them; it just means the browsers don't give a hoot if you do. But browsers per se are not your audience. Your users (and, for that matter future browsers) may indeed care — the spiders will, for sure — and we don't expect any asteroids to fall on your head (metaphorically speaking, of course) because of improperly structured HTML.

Although HTML isn't exactly a programming language, it still makes sense to treat it like one. Therefore, following formats and syntax helps avoid trouble, and careful testing and rechecking of your work ensures a high degree of quality, compliance with standards, and a relatively trouble-free Web site.

Make the Most from the Least

More is not always better, especially when it comes to Web pages. Try to design and build your pages using minimal ornaments and simple layouts. Don't overload pages with graphics; add as many levels of headings as you can fit, and make sure your content is easy to read and follow. Make sure any hyperlinks you include connect your user to useful information that adds value to your own info. Gratuitous links are no one's friend; if you're tempted to link to that webcam that shows a dripping faucet, resist, resist.

Remember that structure and images exist to *highlight* content. The more elaborate your structure — or the more bells, whistles, and dinosaur growls dominate a page, the more they distract your visitors from your content. Therefore, use structure and graphics sparingly, wisely, and as carefully as possible. Anything more can be an obstacle to content delivery. Go easy on the animations, links, and layout tags, or risk having your message (even your page) devoured by a hungry T. Rex.

Build Attractive Pages

When users visit Web pages with a consistent framework that focuses on content — and supplements (but doesn't trample) that content with graphics and links — they're likely to feel welcome. Making those same Web pages pretty and easy to navigate only adds to the site's basic appeal, and makes your cybercampers even happier. If you need inspiration, cruise the Web and look for layouts and graphics that work for you. If you take the time to analyze what you like about them, you can work from other people's design principles without having to steal details from their layouts or looks (which isn't a good idea anyway).

As you design your Web documents, start with a fundamental page layout. Pick a small-but-interesting set of graphical symbols or icons and adopt a consistent navigation style. Use graphics sparingly (yes, you've heard this song before), and make them as small as possible — reducing size, number of colors, shading, and so on, while still retaining their eye appeal. When you've worked up simple, consistent navigation tools for your site, label them clearly and use them throughout. You can make your pages appealing, informative, and powerfully inviting if you're willing to invest the time and effort.

Avoid Browser Dependencies

When you're building Web pages, the temptation to view the Web in terms of your favorite browser is hard to avoid. That's why you should always remember that users view the Web in general (and your pages in particular) from many different perspectives — through many different browsers.

During the design and writing phases, you'll probably ping-pong between HTML and a browser's-eye view of your work. At this early point in the process, we recommend switching from one browser to another, testing your pages among a group of browsers (including at least one character-mode browser). This helps balance how you imagine your pages and helps keep you focused on content.

During testing and maintenance, you must browse your pages from many different points of view. Make sure to work from multiple platforms; try both graphical and character-mode browsers on each page. Such testing takes time but repays that investment with pages that are easy for everyone to read and follow. It also helps viewers who come at your materials from a platform other than your own, and helps your pages achieve true independence from any one platform or browser. Why limit your options?

If several pages on your site will use the same basic HTML, create a single template for those pages. Test the template with as many browsers as you can find. Once you're sure the template is browser-independent, use it to create other pages. Thus will you attain the knowledge that every page looks good, regardless of which browser a visitor might be using, and be on your way to true enlightenment.

Think Evolution, Not Revolution

Over time, Web pages change and grow. Keep a fresh eye on your work, and keep recruiting fresh eyes from the ranks of those who haven't seen your work before, to avoid a process we call "organic acceptance."

This concept is best explained by the analogy of your face and the mirror: You see it every day, you know it intimately, so you aren't as sensitive as someone else to the impact of changes over time. Then you see yourself on video, or in a photograph, or through the eyes of an old friend. At that point, changes obvious to the world are obvious to you as you exclaim, "I've gone completely gray!" or "My spare tire could mount on a semi!" or "Who the heck is *that?*"

As with the rest of life, changes to Web pages are usually evolutionary, not revolutionary. They proceed with small daily steps; big radical leaps are rare. Nevertheless, you must remain sensitive to the supporting infrastructure and readability of your content as your pages evolve. Maybe the lack of on-screen links to each section of your Product Catalog didn't matter when you had only three products — now that you have 25, it's a different story. You've heard of form following function; in Web terms, the structure of your site needs to adapt to follow changes in the content. If you regularly reevaluate your site's effectiveness at communicating its contents, you'll know when it's time to make changes, whether large or small.

This is where user feedback is absolutely crucial. If you don't get feedback through forms or other means of communication, you should go out and aggressively solicit info from your users. If you're not sure how you're doing, then consider: If you don't ask, you won't be able to tell.

Navigating Your Wild and Woolly Web

Users who view the splendor of your site don't want to be told *You can't get there from here;* aids to navigation are vital amenities for a quality Web site. In Chapter 7, for example, we introduce the concept of a *navigation bar* — a consistent graphical place to put buttons that help users get from A to B. By judicious use of links and careful observation of what constitutes a "screenful" of text, you can help your users minimize (or even avoid) having to scroll. Text anchors can make it easy to move to "previous" or "next" screens, as well as to "top," "index," and "bottom" in any document. Just that easy, just that simple, or so it appears to the user.

We believe pretty strongly in the *low scroll* rule: That is, users should have to scroll *no more than one* screenful in either direction from a point of focus or entry without encountering a navigation aid to let them jump (not scroll) to the next point of interest.

We don't believe that navigation bars are always required, nor that the names for controls should always be the same. We do believe that the more control you give users over their reading, the better they like it. The longer a document gets, the more important such controls become; they work best if they occur about every thirty lines in longer documents (or in a separate, always visible frame, if you use HTML frames).

Beat the Two-Dimensional Text Trap

Conditioned by centuries of printed material and the linear nature of books, our mind-sets can always use adjustment. The nonlinear potentials of hypermedia give the Web a new definition of what constitutes a document. Of course, the temptation is to pack your page full of these capabilities till it resembles a Pony Express dynamite shipment and gallops off in all directions at once. To avoid this, judge your hypermedia according to whether they (1) add interest, (2) expand on your content, or (3) make a serious — and relevant — impact on the user. Within these constraints, this kind of material can vastly improve any user's experience of your site.

Stepping intelligently outside old-fashioned linear thinking can improve your users' experience of your site and make your information more readily available to your audience. That's why we encourage careful use of document indexes, cross-references, links to related documents, and other tools to help users navigate within your site. Keep thinking about the impact of links as you look at other people's Web materials; it's the quickest way to shake free of the linear trap imposed by Gutenberg's legacy. (The printing press was high-tech for its day, but that *was* 500 years ago!) If you're looking for a model for your site's behavior, don't think about your new trifold four-color brochure, however eye-popping; think about how your customer-service people interact with new customers on the telephone (*What can I do to help you today?*).

Overcome Inertia through Constant Vigilance

Finally, when dealing with your Web materials postpublication, remember that the human tendency is to goof off after a big job. Maintenance may not be nearly as heroic, inspiring, or remarkable as creation, yet it represents the bulk of the activity that's needed to keep a living document alive and well. Sites that aren't regularly maintained often become ghost sites; users stop visiting them when developers stop working on them. Never fear — a little work and attention to detail will keep the tumbleweeds away from your pages.

If you start with something valuable and keep adding value, a site appreciates over time. Start with something valuable and leave it alone, and a site soon becomes stale and loses value. Consider your site from the viewpoint of a master aircraft mechanic: Correct maintenance is a real, vital, and ongoing accomplishment, without which you risk a crash. A Web site, as a vehicle for important information, deserves the same regular attention; the work of maintaining it requires discipline and respect.

Keeping up with constant change translates into creating (and adhering to) a regular maintenance schedule. Make it somebody's job to spend time on the Web site regularly; check to make sure the job's getting done. If someone is set to handle regular site updates, changes, and improvements, normally they start flogging other participants to give them things to do when scheduled site maintenance rolls around. The next thing you know, everybody's involved in keeping information fresh — just as they should be. This keeps your visitors coming back for more!

Chapter 21

Ten Design Desiderata

In This Chapter

▶ Establishing standard layout and graphical elements

▶ Using graphics, multimedia, and hypermedia effectively

▶ Asking for, utilizing, and responding to user feedback

▶ Hearing some familiar sage advice yet again (a little review never hurts)

*1*t's that familiar refrain from other chapters: Before you can design and build a Web site that works, you have to know exactly what you wish to communicate (the content) and to whom (the audience). Remember that content is your site's king, queen, and big kahuna, and must always remain so. Nevertheless, we'd like to suggest a bevy of design desiderata to consider when you lay out your Web pages. Consider the principles in this chapter as Big Kahuna Content's court and cabinet: As long as they play a supporting, not a starring, role, they'll add value and appeal without getting you in too much trouble.

Create Standard Layout Elements

As you build or renovate your site, focus your first design efforts on a common layout for your pages. The elements of this common layout may include text links, graphical controls, or a combination of both, as well as frequently used icons (or other graphical conventions such as logos) and styles for page headings and footers. Ambitious designers may have to build style sheets to keep it all straight; regardless of complexity, it's up to you to govern layout and typography for your site's pages. If you choose to use HTML frames, you can establish a set of *framing rules* to lay out common page areas and elements.

Headings can incorporate text, navigation, graphics, and other information that works best if it's consistent on all pages. Footers should include contact information and a unique URL for reference, preceded by a horizontal rule or graphical line (or packaged in their own compact frames).

Whatever your final layout looks like, make it as attractive as you can (without making it distracting) and apply it consistently. From the users' points of view, these reassuring touches help create a welcome feeling of familiarity across your pages and make it easier to navigate around your site.

For some solid examples of good-looking, consistent site layout, have a look at the family of CNET sites, including www.cnet.com, www.builder.com, and www.news.com.

Build a Graphical Vocabulary

Web sites speak in pictures partly because it saves a lot of words. If you use graphics for navigation, keep icons or buttons as small and simple as possible. The smaller the graphic (in file size, not necessarily in number-of-pixels), the faster it downloads. That saves your users time on their way to your content.

Building a small, consistent set of graphical symbols (what we call a *vocabulary*) also improves browser efficiency: Most browsers cache graphics so they don't have to download them after they first appear in a particular session. It's much faster to reuse an existing graphic than to download a new one. An added benefit of keeping a graphics vocabulary small is that users can quickly become accustomed to your graphical conventions and don't have to work through making sense of a new set of graphics on each new page. Result: Content is easier to see.

Supply alt text definitions for graphical elements when you reference them. This keeps users with character-mode browsers (or users who surf with graphics turned off) from being left in the lurch. Such graphical elements should be simple enough that a single word or short phrase can substitute for, yet still deliver, the same meaning and impact as the graphic itself does.

Use White Space

While content may be the acknowledged potentate of Web pages, you can have too much of a good thing. Nothing obscures words like too many other words. Even though it's laudable to limit the scrolling a user has to do, don't muddle the text by eliminating headings and paragraph breaks; try dropping in a little empty space.

White space is the term used by page designers to describe the space on a page that's unoccupied by things like graphics and type. Even if your background is navy blue, you'll still have "white" space (well, okay, *blue* space in this case). The human eye needs to rest now and then; a certain amount of white space is critical for it to function well. In general, the more complex the images or content, the more positive the effect of white space on a page.

Be sure to give your content and images room to breathe by leaving *at least 20 percent of any screen* unoccupied. You can build white space into your documents by (1) using alignment attributes to place your graphics, (2) using headings to separate regions of text and graphics, or (3) building a style sheet that controls line spacing and white space for all kinds of tags. Whatever method you use, give readers plenty of room to follow your lead through your pages!

Format for Impact

HTML includes a variety of character tags — whether descriptive (`<em>`, `<strong>`, `<cite>`, and so on) or physical (`<i>`, `<b>`, `<tt>`, and so on). These tools can give you ways to set particular words apart from the others in a sentence or paragraph. You can employ larger fonts and text styles to give your headings a presence and look different from ordinary text. When you use these controls, however, remember that emphasis and impact are relative terms. In fact, the *less* often you use such tags, the more impact they have. In the wake of Cascading Style Sheets, we think working with `style` attributes may often make more sense than using such tags to achieve a consistent look throughout your site. The tags work well if you have a really unique-but-relevant item to include — say, a snippet of text that mimics a newspaper:

```
900 Bags of T. Rex Chow Missing from Local
Warehouse
```

City officials were stunned Tuesday to find the Hungry Dino Pet Food Store's main distribution center opened like a sardine can . . .

Character-handling can be a nice effect, whether descriptive, stylistic, or physical — but overusing it can blunt any document's overall impact. Be sure to use such controls only where impact is critical. Also too much **boldface**, *italicized*, or <u>underlined</u> text can be difficult to read on a computer screen. Be kind to your users (and their eyes) by limiting your use of character formatting wherever possible. Keep It Simple, Smarty.

While you're deciding how to emphasize your chosen text elements, be aware that certain browsers provide wider options for descriptive tags than for physical tags, and that style definitions have the widest latitude of all. Physical tags are often associated with certain fonts (for example, mono-spaced Courier is typical for <tt>). Browsers often display descriptive tags (such as <b>) the same way they display physical tags (such as <strong>) — in fact, those two particular tags produce the same effect in most browsers: boldface text. Some browsers (especially the graphical ones) provide other options for representing descriptive tags — such as different fonts or text colors.

Style tags give designers complete control over text appearance and layout, but can be overridden by savvy users or may not be supported by older browsers. Bottom line: Consider which aspect of your text — appearance or emphasis — is more important to your message. If it's appearance, use a physical style; if it's emphasis, use a logical one or a style definition.

Enhance (Don't Curb) Content with Graphics

If a picture is worth a thousand words, are a thousand words worth a picture? (All together, now: *Which thousand words? Which picture?*) When you combine text and graphics in your Web pages, emphasize the relationship between the two. Graphics can be useful for diagramming complex ideas, representing physical objects or other tangible phenomena, and for compressing large amounts of content into a small space. But text that surrounds a graphic image needs to play off the image itself, to use it as a point of reference, and to refer back to key elements or components as they're discussed. Thus, the methods you use to identify graphical elements — such as labels and captions — can be almost as important as the graphic itself. Careful integration of text and graphics enhances the content. (Have a look back at that "newspaper" snippet. Imagine it illustrated with a simple graphic — say, a Volkswagen half squashed by a reptilian footprint . . .)

Graphics can pull double duty, both enhancing the look and feel of your page and adding significant content. Some graphics that work overtime to play both roles include navigational aids (such as buttons and arrows) as well as diagrams and charts. If you do use a graphic to provide content as well as splash of color, include appropriate alternative text as well.

The rules for using graphics also apply to any other hypermedia you add to your Web pages. Beyond their novelty, effects such as sound (including music), animation, or video can deliver striking content. To create the greatest impact without distraction, they must be carefully — often sparingly — integrated with your text.

The Web offers unprecedented expressive options — for example, educators have new ways to engage students' interest. Instead of using pure text to explain, say, a leitmotif (a musical phrase with a specific referent), a teacher could define, and then discuss, a musical phrase from a symphony or string quartet as a leitmotif, setting up a hyperlink that plays the phrase on command. (A beginners' version could highlight the sequence of notes on a musical staff as the musical file plays.) Likewise, a discussion of film-editing techniques (such as dissolves), could include actual examples excerpted from the work of classic directors.

If you plan to quote the creative work of others in your Web site, make sure you know — and heed — any applicable copyright restrictions before you do so. Getting written permission is often a good idea. Just assuming you can use a creative work without asking is usually a bad idea.

Whatever materials appear in or through your Web pages, they should be solidly integrated and share a common focus. This applies as strongly to hypermedia as it does to text, but all the Web's possibilities to enhance content should be fully exploited.

Make Effective Use of Hypermedia

The key ingredient in effective use of hypermedia (linked pages, graphics, and other Web elements) is *relevance.* How well does the linked document relate to the content on the page that links to it? If (for example) you make a link to the Dallas Cowboys Web page from a page about the Wild West just because they both mention cowboys, you'll lose your readers in a heartbeat. A link to a site about Buffalo Bill or Jesse James, on the other hand, would be right on target. (Moral: Rein in those free associations, pardner.)

In addition to making effective hyperlinks, a Web designer must also understand the potential bottlenecks that some users face. Not all browsers come to your site with identical capabilities or settings. The more a user must interact with hypermedia to fully appreciate a page, the fewer users will be equipped to get the whole point.

Effective use of hypermedia, therefore, implies asking your users for *informed consent* before inflicting the whole cornucopia of effects on them. For graphics, this means preparing thumbnails of large images, labeling them with file sizes, and using the miniature on-screen versions as hyperlinks so users can request to download a full-sized image. Users who decide to pull down a full-color image of *The Last Supper* cannot complain when they already know it's a 1.2MB file that may take several minutes to download. By the same token, "decorating" your Web page by putting 2MB-worth of photorealistic T. Rex smack in the middle of every visitor's screen — without asking permission — means committing every visitor to a long wait, even those who merely wanted information. (Irritating? You ain't *seen* ferocious yet . . .)

This principle applies equally to sounds, video, and other kinds of hypermedia that travel (a) in very large files and (b) very slowly over phone lines. Remember to ask for informed consent from your users, and you can be sure that only those individuals who can stand the wait will be subjected to delivery delays.

Aid Navigation wherever Possible

The Web can be a confusing place for new or infrequent visitors. The more you can do to help your users out, the more likely they are to return to your pages, time and time again. Put some steering gear on that Web page — outlines, tables of contents, indexes, or search engines — so your users can not only find their way around your materials, but also recognize your site as friendly territory.

Form Good Opinions

We think no Web site is complete without an interactive HTML form to ask users for their feedback. Feedback not only gives you a chance to see your work from somebody else's perspective, but also serves as a valuable source of input and ideas to enhance and improve your content. This is akin to asking for directions when you're lost. Remember, "Assuming isn't knowing; nothing beats knowing, and you can't know if you don't ask."

Know When to Split

As pages get larger, or as your content grows oversized, you may come to a point where a single, long document would function better as a collection of smaller documents.

How can you decide when it's time to split things up? Weigh the convenience of a single page against the lengthy download that may tag along with it. A single, long document takes longer to download and read than any individual smaller one, but each time a user requests an individual document, it may have to be downloaded on the spot. The question then becomes *One long wait or several short ones?*

The answer lies in the content. If your document is something that's touched quickly and then exited immediately, delivering information in small chunks makes sense. The only people who suffer delays are those who choose to read many pages; in-and-outers don't have to wait much. If your document is something designed to be downloaded and perused in detail, it may make sense to keep large amounts of information within a single document — and to let your readers know you've set it up that way.

By using your materials frequently yourself (make sure you test them over a slow link as well as a fast one) and by asking users for feedback, you should be able to strike a happy medium between these extremes. The happier the medium, the happier the users — and the more receptive they may be to your content.

Add Value for Value

Obtaining feedback from users is incredibly valuable and makes HTML forms all the more worthwhile. But you're missing half the benefit if it's good *only* for you; *responding* to that feedback in a visible, obvious way can make the experience as good for the respondents as it should be for you.

Publicly acknowledging feedback that causes change is a good idea, whether for reasons good or ill. On many sites (and maybe on yours, too) a "What's New" page that links to the home page is a good place to make such acknowledgments. We also believe in acknowledging strong opinions by e-mail or letter — it's often a relatively flame-retardant way to let respondents know that you heard what they said and to thank them for their input.

If you cultivate your users as allies and confederates, they help you improve and enhance your content. These improvements, in turn, could lead to improved business or maybe just to improved communications. Either way, by giving valuable information and acknowledging the value of other people's contributions, you create a superior site. And the more superior sites exist, the greater the total value of the Web itself!

Chapter 22

Ten Ways to Exterminate Web Bugs

*A*fter you put the finishing touches on a set of pages, and before you post them on the Web for all the world to see, it's time to put them through their paces. Testing is the royal road to controlling your content's quality. Thorough testing should include a content review, a complete analysis of HTML syntax and semantics, checks on every possible link, and a series of sanity checks to make doubly sure that what you built is what you really wanted. Read on for some gems of testing wisdom (torn from a wealth of Web adventures) — as we undertake to rid your Web pages of bugs, errors, gaucheries, and lurking infelicities.

Make a List and Check It — Twice

Your design should include a road map that tells you what's where in every individual HTML document in your site, and the relationships among them. If you're unusually perceptive, you diligently kept this map up-to-date as you moved from design to implementation (and in our experience, things always change when you go down this path). If you're merely as smart as the rest of us, don't berate yourself — go forth and update thy map now. Be sure to include all intra- and interdocument links.

Such a road map can act as the foundation for a test plan. Yep, that's right — effective testing isn't random. Investigate and check every page and every link systematically. You want to make sure that everything works as you think it does — and that what you built has some relationship (however surprising) to what you designed. Your site's road map also defines your list of things to check; as you go through the testing process, you'll check it (at least) twice. (Red suit and reindeer harness optional.)

Master the Mechanics of Text

By the time any collection of Web pages comes together, you're typically looking at thousands of words, if not more. Yet the number of Web pages published without even a cursory spelling check is astonishing. That's why we suggest — no, demand — that you include a spelling check as a step in testing and checking your materials. (Okay, we don't have a gun to your head. But you *know* it's for your own good.) Many HTML development tools have their own spell-check utilities built right in. Even if you only use these tools occasionally and hack out the majority of your HTML by hand, take advantage of their HTML-aware checkers before you post your documents to the Web. (For a handy illustration of why this matters, try keeping a log of the spelling and grammar errors you encounter during your Web travels. Be sure to include a note on how those gaffes reflect on the people who created the page.)

You can use your favorite word processor to spell-check your pages. Before you check them, add HTML markup to your custom dictionary, and pretty soon, the program becomes almost pukeless — getting indigestion only on URLs and other strange strings that occur from time to time in HTML files.

If you'd prefer the fashionably up-to-date approach, try out one of the several HTML-based spell-checking services now available on the Web. We like the one at the Doctor HTML site, which you can find online at www2.imagiware.com/RxHTML/.

If Doctor HTML's spell-checker doesn't work for you, visit one of the search engines available at www.yahoo.com, and use *web page spell check* as a search string. Choose the *Computers and Internet> Information and Documentation> Data Formats> HTML> Validation and Checkers* category to find a list of spell-check tools (as well as few other really cool testing and maintenance tools) made specifically for Web pages.

One way or another, persist till you root out all typos and misspellings. Your users, intent on your content, may not know to thank you for your impeccable use of language — but if they don't trip over any errors while exploring your work, they'll have a higher opinion of your pages (and of the pages' creator). Even if they don't know why. Call it stealth diplomacy.

Lack of Live Links — a Loathsome Legacy

In an unscientific and random sample we undertook as a spot check, users told us that their positive impressions of a particular site are proportional to how many working links they find there. The moral of this survey: Always check your links. This is as true after you publish your pages as it is before they're subject to public scrutiny. Nothing is more irritating to users than when a link to some Web resource on a page that they're dying to read produces the dreaded 404 Server not found error, instead of "the good stuff."

Link checks are as indispensable to page maintenance as they are to testing. If you're long on twenty-first-century street smarts, you'll hire a robot to do the job for you: They work incredibly long hours (no coffee breaks), don't charge much, and faithfully check every last link in your site (or beyond, if you let them loose).

We're rather fond of a robot named MOMspider, created by Roy Fielding of the W3C. Visit MOMspider at www.ics.uci.edu/WebSoft/MOMspider. This spider takes a bit of work to use, but you can set it to check only local links, and it does a bang-up job of catching stale links before users do. If you don't like this tool, try a search engine with *link check* or *robot* as your search term. You'll find lots to choose from! The best thing about robots is that you can schedule them to do their jobs at regular intervals: They always show up on time, always do a thorough job, and never complain (though we haven't yet found one that brings homemade cookies).

Another hint: If a URL points to one page that immediately points to another, that doesn't mean you should leave that link alone. If your link-checking shows a pointer to a pointer, do yourself (and your users) a favor by updating the URL to point *directly* to the content's real location. You save users time, reduce bogus traffic on the Internet, and generate good cyberkarma.

If you must leave a URL active even after it has become passé, you can instruct newer browsers to jump straight from the old page to the new one by including the following HTML command in the old document's <HEAD> section:

```
<meta http-equiv="refresh" content="0"; url="newurlhere">
```

This nifty line of code tells a browser (if sufficiently new) that it should refresh the page. The delay before switching to the new page is specified by the value of the content attribute, and the destination URL by the value of the url= attribute. If you must build such a page, be sure to include a plain-vanilla link in its <body> section, too, so that users with older browsers can follow the link manually, instead of automatically. Getting there may not be half the fun, but it's all of the objective.

Look for Trouble in All the Right Places

You and a limited group of users should test your site before you let the rest of the world know about it. This process is called *beta-testing*, and it's a bona fide, five-star *must* for a well-rounded Web site, especially if you're building it for business use. When the time comes to beta-test your site, bring in as rowdy and refractory a crowd as you can possibly find. If you have picky customers (or colleagues who are pushy, opinionated, or argumentative), be comforted to know that you have found a higher calling for them: Such people make ideal beta-testers. Provided you can get them to cooperate.

They use your pages in ways you never imagined possible. They interpret your content to mean things you never intended in a million years. They drive you crazy and crawl all over your cherished beliefs and principles. Before your users do.

These colleagues also find gotchas, big and small, that you never knew were there. They catch typos that the word processors couldn't. They tell you things you left out and things that you should have omitted. They give you a whole new perspective on your Web pages, and they help you to see them from extreme points of view.

The results of all this suffering, believe it or not, are positive. Your pages emerge clearer, more direct, and more correct than they would have been if you tried to test them all by yourself. (If you don't believe us, of course, you *could* try skipping this step. And when real users start banging on your site, forgive us if we can't watch.)

Covering All the Bases

If you're an individual user with a simple home page or a collection of facts and figures about your private obsession, this particular step may not apply. But go ahead and read along anyway — it just might come in handy down the road.

If your pages express views and content that represent an organization, then chances are oh, *about 100 percent* that you should subject your pages to some kind of peer-and-management review before publishing them to the world. In fact, we'd recommend that you build reviews into each step along the way as you build your site — starting by getting knowledgeable feedback on such ground-zero aspects as the overall design, writing copy for each page, and the final assembly of your pages into a functioning site. These reviews help you avoid potential stumbling blocks. If you have any doubts about copyright matters, references, logo usage, or other important details, you may want to get the legal department involved (if you don't have one, you may want to consider a little consulting investment).

It may even be a good idea to build a sign-off process into reviews so that you can prove that responsible parties reviewed and approved your materials. We hope you don't have to be that formal about publishing your Web pages, but it's far, far better to be safe than sorry. (So is this process best called *covering the bases,* or covering, ah, something else? You decide.)

Use the Best Tools of the Testing Trade

When you grind through your completed Web pages, checking your links and your HTML, remember that automated help is available. If you visit the HTML Validation and Checkers corner at Yahoo! (as mentioned earlier), you'll be well on your way to finding computerized assistance to make sure your HTML is pure as a whistle, clean as the driven snow, and standards-compliant as, ah, *really well-written HTML.* (Do we know how to mix a metaphor, or what?)

Likewise, it's a good idea to investigate the Web spiders discussed earlier in the chapter; use them regularly to check the links in your pages. (Spiders? Ewww! Relax; it's another name for *robot.*) These faithful creatures will get back to you if something isn't current, so you know where to start looking for links that you need to fix. And while you're at it, make link-checking part of your maintenance routine. The most painless way to go about it is to schedule and use a spider at regular intervals! (Arachnophobia — what's that?)

Foster Feedback

Even after you publish your site, the testing isn't over. (Are you having flashbacks to high school and college yet? We know we are.) You might not think of user feedback as a form (or consequence) of testing, but it represents the best reality-check that your Web pages are ever likely to get. That's why it's a good idea to do everything you can — including offering prizes or other tangible inducements — to get users to fill out HTML forms on your Web site.

That's also why it's even better to read *all* the feedback that you do get. Go out and solicit as much as you can handle (don't worry; you'll soon have more). But the best idea of all is to carefully consider the feedback that you read and then implement the ideas that actually bid fair to improve your Web offerings.

Make the Most of Your Audience

Asking for feedback is an important step toward developing a relationship with your users. Even the most finicky and picky of users can be an incredible asset: Who better to pick over your newest pages and to point out those small, subtle errors or flaws that they revel in finding? Your pages will have contributed mightily to the advance of human society by actually finding a legitimate use for the universal human delight in nitpicking. And your users develop a real stake in boosting the success of your site. Working with your users can mean that some become more involved in your work, helping guide the content of your Web pages (if not the rest of your professional or obsessional life). Who could ask for more? Put it this way: You may yet find out, and it could be remarkably helpful.

Part VII

Appendixes

The 5th Wave — By Rich Tennant

IF BOB DYLAN HAD DESIGNED WEB PAGES

"His text content is fantastic, but lose those harmonica WAV files."

In this part . . .

The appendixes in this part are many and magnificent. In Appendix A, you find a concise overview of HTML syntax and markup codes. Its worthy successor, Appendix B, provides a glossary to help explain and defuse all the techno-babble we were unable to avoid in the rest of the book. Appendix C explores some powerful and useful HTML tools that we keep in our Webmaster's toolbox, and present for your consideration. Finally, Appendix D closes the show, by detailing all the neat programs and examples that we include on the CD-ROM that comes with this book. These appendixes are kind of like the instructions that come with a Christmas bicycle: You don't always have to read them, but they're handy to keep around for when you need 'em! Just remember, when it comes to building your own Web pages "some assembly is required!" Have fun!

Appendix A

HTML 4 Tags

● ●

Keeping track of the bountiful bevy of HTML tags can often be a trick, even for experienced webmasters. To make your HTML coding life a bit easier, we've included Table A-1. Every tag is listed with its name, a short description, and a quick reference to the chapter in the book that describes that tag.

Tags that are in italics have been *deprecated* in HTML 4.0. The standards committee, W3C, plans to stop supporting deprecated tags in future versions of HTML.

Table A-1	HTML Tags in Alphabetical Order		
Tag	*Name*	*Chapter*	*Function*
<!— —>	comment	8	Identifies a comment within a page
A	anchor	3	Identifies text or objects (images, et cetera) in a Web page as an anchor for a hyperlink
ABBR	abbreviation	10	Identifies text as an abbreviation
ACRONYM	acronym	10	Identifies text as an acronym
ADDRESS	address	8	Specifies addressing information
APPLET	Java applet	17	Includes a Java applet in a Web page
AREA	image map area	15	Defines a single region within a client-side image map
B	boldface	9	Specifies that text should be displayed in bold
BASE	base URL	8	Identifies the base URL for a document
BASEFONT	base font	9	Specifies a basic font for displaying the entire document

(continued)

Table A-1 *(continued)*

Tag	Name	Chapter	Function
BDO	bi-directional option	9	Changes the direction in which the browser reads the text on the page
BIG	big	9	Specifies that text should be displayed one size bigger than the surrounding text
BLOCKQUOTE	block quote	10	Identifies a block quotation
BODY	body	8	Identifies the document body
BR	line break	10	Inserts a line break into the page
BUTTON	button	17	Inserts a button into the page
CAPTION	table caption	14	Identifies a table caption
CENTER	center	9	Specifies that text should be centered on the page when displayed
CITE	citation	10	Identifies a citation
CODE	code	10	Identifies text as computer code
COL	column	14	Identifies a column in a table
COLGROUP	column group	14	Identifies a column group in a table
DD	definition description	14	Describes the description for a definition term in a definition list
DEL	deleted text	10	Marks text as deleted from a document
DFN	definition	10	Identifies text as a defined term
DIR	directory list	11	Identifies a directory list
DIV	division	8	Identifies a generic block element within a document
DL	definition list	11	Identifies a definition list
DT	definition term	11	Identifies a definition term within a definition list
EM	emphasis	10	Identifies text as emphasized
FIELDSET	field set	17	Identifies a collection of controls within a form as a group

Tag	Name	Chapter	Function
FONT	font	9	Specifies type face, size, and color information for text within a document
FORM	form	17	Identifies an input form
FRAME	frame	16	Identifies a frame within a frame set
FRAMESET	frame set	16	Identifies a set of frames
H1	first level heading	8	Identifies text as a level one heading
H2	second level heading	8	Identifies text as a level two heading
H3	third level heading	8	Identifies text as a level three heading
H4	fourth level heading	8	Identifies text as a level four heading
H5	fifth level heading	8	Identifies text as a level five heading
H6	sixth level heading	8	Identifies text as a level six heading
HEAD	head	8	Identifies the document header
HR	horizontal rule	9	Inserts a graphical vertical line in the page
HTML	HTML	8	Identifies the document as an HTML document
I	italic	9	Specifies that the enclosed text should be rendered in italics
IFRAME	inline frame	16	Creates a frame within a standard, non-framed HTML page
IMG	image	6	Inserts an image into a Web page
INPUT	input	17	Identifies a form input control such as a radio button or text field
INS	inserted text	10	Marks text as having been inserted into the document
KBD	keyboard text	10	Identifies contents as text to be entered by the user

(continued)

Table A-1 *(continued)*

Tag	Name	Chapter	Function
LABEL	label	17	Assigns a label to form field
LEGEND	field set caption	17	Assigns a caption to a group of form controls in a fieldset
LI	list item	11	Identifies an item in a list
LINK	link	18	Defines a link between the current document and other documents
MAP	image map	15	Identifies a client side image map
MENU	menu list	11	Identifies a menu list
META	meta data	8	Specifies information about the Web page used by the browser and search engines but not seen by the user
NOFRAMES	no frames	16	Specifies information seen by users with browsers that don't support frames
NOSCRIPT	no script	17	Specifies information seen by users with browsers that don't support scripting
OBJECT	object	17	Inserts one of several different kinds of non-text objects into a Web page
OL	ordered list	11	Identifies a numbered list
OPTGROUP	option group	17	Identifies a group of options within a form selection list
OPTION	menu option	17	Identifies a single option in a form drop down (selection) list
P	paragraph	10	Marks enclosed text as a paragraph
PARAM	object parameter	17	Specifies parameters for embedded applets and objects
PRE	preformatted text	10	Specifies that the enclosed text and white space should be rendered exactly as in the HTML

Tag	Name	Chapter	Function
Q	short quotation	10	Identifies a short quotation
S	strike-through text	9	Specifies that the enclosed text should be displayed by the browser as struck text
SAMP	sample	10	Identifies the enclosed text as sample data
SCRIPT	script	17	Inserts a client-side script into a Web page
SELECT	select	17	Identifies a drop-down list within an HTML form
SMALL	small	9	Specifies that the enclosed text should be rendered one size smaller than the text surrounding it
SPAN	span	8	Identifies a generic inline element within a document
STRIKE	strike-through text	9	Specifies that the enclosed text should be displayed by the browser as struck text
STRONG	strong emphasis	10	Identifies the enclosed text as strongly emphasized text
STYLE	style	8	Inserts a style sheet into a Web page
SUB	subscript	10	Specifies that the enclosed text should be displayed by the browser as subscript
SUP	superscript	10	Specifies that the enclosed text should be displayed by the browser as superscript
TABLE	table	14	Identifies a table
TBODY	table body	14	Identifies the body of a table
TD	table data cell	14	Identifies a single cell within a table
TEXTAREA	text area	17	Identifies a multi-row and column text box in a form
TFOOT	table footer	14	Identifies the footer of a table

(continued)

Table A-1 *(continued)*

Tag	Name	Chapter	Function
TH	table header cell	14	Identifies a table cell that acts as a column header
THEAD	table head	14	Identifies the header of a table
TITLE	title	8	Identifies the title of an HTML document
TR	table row	14	Identifies a row within a table
TT	teletype text	9	Specifies that the enclosed text should be rendered as text from a typewriter
U	underlined text	9	Specifies that the enclosed text should be underlined in the browser's display
UL	unordered list	11	Identifies a bulleted list
VAR	variable	10	Identifies the enclosed text as a variable

Appendix B

Glossary

● ●

absolute: When used to modify pathnames or URLs, a full and complete file specification (as opposed to a relative one). An absolute specification includes a host identifier, a complete volume, and path specification.

anchor: In HTML, an anchor is a tagged text or graphic element that acts as a link to another location inside or outside a given document, or it may be a location in a document that acts as the destination for an incoming link. The latter definition is most commonly how we use it in this book.

animation: A computerized process of creating moving images by rapidly advancing from one still image to the next.

anonymous ftp: A type of Internet file access that relies on the File Transfer Protocol service, where any user can typically access a file collection by logging in as anonymous and supplying his or her username as a password.

Archie: An Internet-based archival search facility, based on databases of file and directory names taken from anonymous ftp servers around the Internet.

ASCII (American Standard Code for Information Interchange): A binary encoding method for character data that translates symbols, letters, and numbers into digital form.

attribute: In HTML tags, an attribute is a named characteristic associated with a specific tag. Some attributes may be required, while others may be optional. Some attributes may also take values (if so, the syntax is `attribute="value"`) or not, depending on the particular tag and attribute involved (Chapter 6 provides tag information, including attributes, in alphabetical order).

authoring software: In the context of HTML, authoring software refers to programs that understand HTML tags and their proper placement. Some such programs can even enforce HTML syntax rules; others can convert from word-processing or document-formatting programs to HTML.

back end: The server-side of client/server is called the back end because it is usually handled by programs running in obscurity on the server, out of sight (and mind) for most users.

Backus-Naur Format (BNF grammar): A representational notation developed to completely and formally describe computer programming languages.

bandwidth: Technically, bandwidth is the range of electrical frequencies a device can handle; more often, it's used as a measure of a communications technology's carrying capacity.

body: The body is one of the main identifiable structures in any HTML document. It is usually trapped between the head information and the footer information.

bookmark: A reference from a saved list of URLs kept by the Netscape Web browser. Bookmarks allow quick loading of a Web site without retyping the URL. Bookmarks work the same as Microsoft Internet Explorer favorites.

browser: A Web access program that can request HTML documents from Web servers and render such documents on a user's display device (see **client**).

bugs: Small verminous creatures that sometimes show up in software in the form of major or minor errors, mistakes, and gotchas. Bugs got their name from insects found in antiquated tube-based computers of the late 1950s and early 1960s that were attracted to the glow of the filament in a tube.

C: A programming language developed at AT&T Bell Laboratories, C remains the implementation language for UNIX and the UNIX programmer's language of choice.

case-sensitive: Means that the way computer input is typed is significant; for instance, HTML tags can be typed in any mixture of upper- and lowercase, but because HTML character entities are case sensitive, they must be typed exactly as reproduced in this book.

CERN (Conseil Européen pour la Recherche Nucléaire): Agency that established the High-Energy Physics Laboratory in Geneva, Switzerland, now known as the birthplace of the World Wide Web. CERN is commonly used as a name for the laboratory itself.

character entity: A way of reproducing strange and wonderful characters within HTML, character entities take the form `&string;` where the ampersand (&) and semicolon are mandatory metacharacters, and string names the character to be reproduced in the browser. Because character entities are case sensitive, the string between the ampersand and the semicolon must be reproduced exactly as written in Chapter 7 of this book.

character mode: When referring to Web browsers, character mode (also called textmode) means that such browsers can reproduce text data only. They cannot produce graphics directly without the assistance of a helper application.

clickable map: An image in an HTML file that offers graphical Web navigation. The file contains linked regions that point to specific URLs when a user clicks them.

client: The end-user side of the client/server arrangement; typically, "client" refers to a consumer (rather than a provider) of network services; a Web browser is therefore a client program that talks to Web servers.

client/server: A model for computing that divides computing into two separate roles, usually connected by a network: The client works on the end-user's side of the connection and manages user interaction and display (input, output, and related processing); the server works elsewhere on the network and manages data-intensive or shared-processing activities, such as serving up the collections of documents and programs that a Web server typically manages.

client-side image map: The same as a server-side image map, except that the hot-spot definitions are stored within the HTML document on the client side, rather than in a map file stored on the server.

common controls: For designing HTML documents, most experts recommend using a set of consistent navigation controls throughout a document (or collection of documents) to provide a consistent frame of reference for document navigation.

Common Gateway Interface (CGI): The specification that governs how Web browsers communicate with and request services from Web servers; also the format and syntax for passing information from browsers to servers via HTML forms or document-based queries. The current version of CGI is 1.1.

computing platform: A way of designating what kind of computer someone is using, this term encompasses both hardware (type of machine, processor, and so on) and software (the operating system and applications).

content: For HTML, content is its raison d'être; although form is important, content is why users access Web documents and why they come back for more.

convention: An agreed-upon set of rules and approaches that allows systems to communicate with one another and work together.

Cougar: The official nickname for the HTML 4.0 specification.

CSS1 (Cascading Style Sheets Level 1): A style sheet standard that lets authors attach preferred style sheets to Web documents, while allowing readers to associate their own personal styles to those same documents.

DARPA (Defense Advanced Research Projects Administration): A U.S. Department of Defense agency that supplied cash and some of the expertise that led to development of the Internet, among other interesting things.

default: In general computer-speak, a selection made automatically in a program when the user specifies no explicit selection. For HTML, the default is the value assigned to an attribute when none is supplied.

dial-up: A connection to the Internet (or some other remote computer or network) made by dialing up an access telephone number.

directory path: Device and directory names needed to locate a particular file in a given file system; for HTML, UNIX-style directory paths usually apply.

DNS (Domain Name Service): See **domain names.**

document: The basic unit of HTML information, a document refers to the entire contents of any single HTML file. Since this doesn't always correspond to normal notions of a document, we refer to what could formally be called HTML documents more or less interchangeably with Web pages, which is how such documents are rendered by browsers for display.

document headings: The class of HTML tags that we refer to as <h*>. Document headings allow authors to insert headings of various sizes and weights (from 1 to 6) to add structure to a document's content. As structural elements, headings identify the beginning of a new concept or idea.

document structure: For HTML, this refers to the methods used to organize and navigate within HTML documents or related collections of documents.

DoD (Department of Defense): The folks who paid the bills for and operated the earliest versions of the Internet, and one of the more prominent institutions to adopt SGML.

domain names: The names used on the Internet as part of a distributed database to translate computer names into physical addresses and vice versa.

DOS (Disk Operating System): The underlying control program used to make most Intel-based PCs run. Microsoft's MS-DOS is the most widely-used implementation of DOS, and provides the scaffolding atop which its 3.*x* versions of Windows run. See also **OS.**

DTD (Document Type Definition): A formal SGML specification for a document, a DTD lays out the structural elements and markup definitions that can then be used to create instances of documents.

Dynamic HTML: HTML technologies that enable a user to change Web pages on the fly without requesting a new document from the server.

e-mail: An abbreviation for electronic mail, e-mail is the preferred method for exchanging information between users on the Internet (and other networked systems).

encoded information: A way of wrapping computer data in a special envelope to ship it across a network. Data-manipulation techniques change data formats and layouts to make them less sensitive to the rigors of electronic transit. Encoded information must usually be decoded by its recipient before it can be used.

error message: Information delivered by a program to a user, usually to inform him or her that things haven't worked properly, if at all. Error messages are an ill-appreciated art form and contain some of the funniest and most opaque language we've ever seen (also, the most tragic for their unfortunate recipients).

Ethernet: The most commonly used local-area networking technology in use today, Ethernet was developed at about the same time (and by many of the same people and institutions) involved in building the Internet.

FAQ (Frequently Asked Questions): Usenet newsgroups, mailing list groups, and other affiliations of like-minded individuals on the Internet will usually designate a more senior member of their band to assemble and publish a list of frequently asked questions in an often futile effort to keep from answering them quite as frequently.

Favorites: References from a saved list of URLs kept by the Internet Explorer Web browser. Favorites allow quick loading of a Web site without retyping the URL. Favorites work the same as Netscape Navigator's bookmarks.

file extension: A three-or-more-character suffix after a period character at the end of a filename in DOS, Windows, or UNIX. File extensions are generally required by computers to tell DOS or Windows what program should be used to open the file. On a Macintosh, file extensions are not needed and are generally used for DOS/Windows compatibility.

footer: The concluding part of an HTML document, the footer should contain contact, version, date, and attribution information to help identify a document and its authors.

forms: In HTML, forms are built on special markup that lets browsers solicit data from users and then deliver that data to specially designated input-handling programs on a Web server. Briefly, forms provide a mechanism to let users interact with servers on the Web.

front end: In the client/server model, the front-end part refers to the client side; it's where the user views and interacts with information from a server; for the Web, browsers provide the front end that communicates with Web servers on the back end.

FTP (sometimes ftp; File Transfer Protocol): An Internet file transfer service based on the TCP/IP protocols, FTP provides a way to copy files to and from FTP servers elsewhere on a network.

gateway: A type of computer program that knows how to connect to two or more different kinds of networks and to translate information from one side's format to the other's and vice versa. Common types of gateways include e-mail, database, and communications.

.GIF: An abbreviation for CompuServe's Graphic Interchange Format, GIF is one of a set of commonly used graphics formats within Web documents, because of its compressed format and compact nature.

Gopher: A program/protocol developed at the University of Minnesota, Gopher provides for unified, menu-driven presentation of a variety of Internet services, including WAIS, Telnet, and FTP.

graphics: In HTML documents, graphics are files that belong to one of a restricted family of types (usually .GIF or .JPEG) that are referenced via URLs for inline display on Web pages.

GUI (Graphical User Interface): Pronounced "gooey," GUIs make graphical Web browsers possible; they create a visually oriented interface that makes it easy for users to interact with computerized information of all kinds. Microsoft Windows and the Mac OS are operating systems that use GUIs.

heading: For HTML, a markup tag used to add document structure. Sometimes the term refers to the initial portion of an HTML document between the `<head>` . . . `</head>` tags, where titles and context definitions are commonly supplied.

helper applications: Today, browsers can display multiple graphics files (and sometimes other kinds of data); sometimes, browsers must pass particular files — for instance, motion picture or sound files — over to other applications that know how to render the data they contain. Such programs are called helper applications because they help the browser deliver Web information to users.

hexadecimal: A numbering system composed of six letters and ten numbers that is to condense binary numbers. In HTML, hexadecimal numbering is used with tags and their attributes to denote what colors should comprise backgrounds and other elements in a Web page.

hierarchical structure: A way of organizing Web pages using links that make some pages subordinate to others (see **tree structured** for another description of this kind of organization).

hotlist: A Web page that consists of a series of links to other pages, usually annotated with information about what's available on each link. Hotlists act like switchboards to content information and are usually organized around a particular topic or area of interest.

HTML (HyperText Markup Language): The SGML-derived markup language used to create Web pages. Not quite a programming language, HTML nevertheless provides a rich lexicon and syntax for designing and creating useful hypertext documents for the Web.

http or HTTP (hypertext teleprocessing protocol, also known as HyperText Transfer Protocol): The Internet protocol used to manage communication between Web clients (browsers) and servers.

httpd (http daemon): The name of the collection of programs that runs on a Web server to provide Web services. In UNIX-speak, a daemon is a program that runs all the time listening for service requests of a particular type; thus, an httpd is a program that runs all the time on a Web server, ready to field and handle Web service requests.

hyperlink: A shorthand term for hypertext link, which is defined below.

hypermedia: Any of a variety of computer media — including text, graphics, video, sound, and so on — available through hypertext links on the Web.

hypertext: A method of organizing text, graphics, and other kinds of data for computer use that lets individual data elements point to one another; a non-linear method of organizing information, especially text.

hypertext link: In HTML, a hypertext link is defined by special markup that creates a user-selectable document element that can be selected to change the user's focus from one document (or part of a document) to another.

image map: A synonym for clickable image, this refers to an overlaid collection of pixel coordinates for a graphic that can be used to locate a user's selection of a region on a graphic, in turn used to select a related hypertext link for further Web navigation.

Information Superhighway: The near-mythical agglomeration of the Internet, communications companies, telephone systems, and other communications media that politicians seem to believe will be the "next big thing" in business, academia, and industry. Many people believe that this highway is already here, and that it's called "the Internet."

input-handling program: For Web services, a program that runs on a Web server designated by the action attribute of an HTML <form> tag; its job is to field, interpret, and respond to user input from a browser, typically by custom-building an HTML document in response to some user request.

Internet: A worldwide collection of networks that began with technology and equipment funded by the U.S. Department of Defense in the 1970s. Today, it links users in nearly every country, speaking nearly every known language.

Internet service provider (ISP): A company or organization that provides a variety of Internet services for a fee.

IP (Internet Protocol; see TCP/IP): IP is the specific networking protocol of the same name used to tie computers together over the Internet; IP is also used as a synonym for the whole TCP/IP protocol suite.

ISO (International Standards Organization): The granddaddy of standards organizations worldwide, the ISO is made up of standards bodies from countries all over the world. Most important communications and computing standards — like the telecommunications and character code standards mentioned in this book — are the subject of ISO standards.

Java: An object-oriented, platform-independent, secure, and compact programming language designed for Web application deployment. Java was created by Sun Microsystems but is supported by most system vendors.

.JPEG or .JPG: .JPEG stands for Joint Photographic Experts' Group, an industry association that defined a highly compressible format for images designed for complex color still images (like photographs). .JPEG files usually take the extension .JPEG (except DOS or Windows 3.*x* machines, which are limited to the three-character .JPG equivalent). Today, .JPEG is one graphics format of choice for Web use, particularly for complex images.

Kbps (Kilobits per second): A measure of communications speed, in units of 2^{10} bits per second (2^{10} = 1024, which is just about 1,000 and explains the quasi-metric "K" notation).

KISS (Keep It Simple, Sweetheart): Our kinder, gentler version of a self-explanatory philosophy (Keep It Simple, Stupid!) that's supposed to remind us to "eschew obfuscation" but is easier to understand!

LAN (Local-Area Network): One of many communications technologies used to link computers together in a single location or on a campus.

linear text: Shorthand for old-fashioned documents that work like this book: by placing one page after the other, ad infinitum, in a straight line. Even though such books have indexes, pointers, cross-references, and other attempts to add linkage, such devices can be employed only by manipulating the physical book (rather than by clicking your mouse).

link: For HTML, a link is a pointer in one part of a document that can transport users to another part of the same document, or to another document entirely. This capability puts the "hyper" into hypertext. In other words, a link is a one-to-one relationship/association between two concepts or ideas, similar to "cognition" (the brain has triggers such as smell, sight, and sound that cause a link to be followed to a similar concept or reaction).

list element: An item in an HTML list structure tagged with <li> (list item) tag.

list tags: HTML tags for a variety of list styles, including ordered lists `<ol>`, unordered lists `<ul>`, menus `<menu>`, glossary lists `<dl>`, or directory lists `<dir>`.

listserv: An Internet e-mail handling program, typically UNIX-based, that provides mechanisms to let users manage, contribute and subscribe to, and exit from named mailing lists that distribute messages to all subscribed members daily. A common mechanism for delivering information to interested parties on the Internet, this is how the HTML working group communicates amongst its members, for instance.

Lynx: A widely used UNIX-based character-mode Web browser, useful for checking a Web page before "going live" with it.

Macintosh: A type of PC created by Apple Computer in 1984 that first commercially introduced the graphical user interface (GUI), complete with a mouse, icons, and windows. Microsoft Windows uses design elements similar to those of the Macintosh operating system. The Mac operating system is the most popular alternative to Windows.

MacWeb: A Macintosh-based graphical-mode Web browser implemented by MCC (see **MCC**).

maintenance: The process of regularly inspecting, testing, and updating the contents of Web pages; also, an attitude that such activities are both inevitable and advisable.

majordomo: A set of Perl programs that automate the operation of multiple mailing lists, including moderated and unmoderated mailing lists, and routine handling of subscribe/unsubscribe operations.

map file: Pixel coordinates that correspond to the boundaries of regions that users might select when using a graphic for Web navigation. This file must be created by using a graphics program to determine regions and their boundaries, and then stored on the Web server that provides the coordinate translation and URL selection services.

markup: A way of embedding special characters (metacharacters) within a text file that instructs a computer program how to handle the file's contents.

markup language: A formal set of special characters and related capabilities used to define a specific method for handling the display of files that include markup; HTML is a markup language that is an application of SGML and used to design and create Web pages.

Mbps (Megabits per second): A measure of communications speeds, in units of 220 bits per second (2^{20} = 1,048,576, which is just about 1,000,000 and explains the quasi-metric "M" notation).

metacharacter: A specific character within a text file that signals the need for special handling; in HTML the angle brackets (< >), ampersand (&), pound sign (#), and semi-colon (;) can all function as metacharacters.

MIME (Multipurpose Internet Mail Extensions): Http communications of Web information over the Internet rely on a special variant of MIME formats to convey Web documents and related files between servers and users. The same technology is used to convey attached files with e-mail messages.

modem: An acronym for modulator/demodulator, a modem is a piece of hardware that converts between analog forms for voice and data used in the telephone system and digital forms used in computers. In other words, a modem lets your computer communicate using the telephone system.

Mosaic: A powerful graphical Web browser originally developed at NCSA, now widely licensed and used in several browser implementations.

.MPEG or .MPG: An acronym for Motion Picture Experts' Group, .MPEG is a highly compressed format designed for moving pictures or other multiframe-per-second media (like video). .MPEG not only provides high compression ratios (up to 200 to 1), but it also updates only elements that have changed on screen from one frame to the next, making it extraordinarily efficient. .MPEG is the file extension that denotes files using this format, but .MPG is the three-letter equivalent used on DOS and Windows 3.x systems (which can't handle four-letter file extensions).

MPPP (Multilink Point-to-Point Protocol): An IP protocol that allows combined use of multiple physical connections between two computers, to create a "larger" virtual link between two machines.

multimedia: A method of combining text, sound, graphics, and full-motion or animated video within a single compound computer document.

navigation: In the context of the Web, navigation refers to the use of hyperlinks to move within or between HTML documents and other Web-accessible resources.

navigation bar: A way of arranging a series of hypertext links on a single line of a Web page to provide a set of navigation controls for an HTML document or a set of HTML documents.

NCSA (National Center for Supercomputing Applications): A research unit of the University of Illinois at Urbana, where the original Mosaic browser was built, and where NCSA httpd code is maintained and distributed.

nesting: In computer terms, one structure that occurs within another is said to be nested; in HTML, nesting happens most commonly with list structures that may be freely nested within one another, regardless of type.

netiquette: A networking takeoff on the term *etiquette,* netiquette refers to the written and unwritten rules of behavior on the Internet. When in doubt whether an activity is permitted or not, ask first, and then act only if no one objects (check the FAQ for a given area, too; often it states the local rules of netiquette for a newsgroup, mailing list, and so on).

newbies: A term that describes individuals who are new to various computer environments or applications.

numeric entity: A special markup element that reproduces a particular character from the ISO-Latin-1 character set. A numeric entity takes the form &#nnn; where nnn is the one-, two- or three-digit numeric code that corresponds to a particular character (Chapter 7 contains a complete list of these codes).

on-demand connection: A dial-up link to a service provider that's available whenever it's needed (on demand, get it?).

online: A term that indicates information, activity, or communications located on, or taking place in, an electronic, networked computing environment (like the Internet). The opposite of online is offline, which is what your computer is as soon as you disconnect from the Internet.

OS (operating system): The underlying control program on a computer that makes the hardware run and supports the execution of one or more applications. DOS, UNIX, and OS/2 are all examples of operating systems.

packet: A basic unit (or package) of data used to describe individual elements of online communications; in other words, data moves across networks like the Internet in packets.

pages: The generic term for the HTML documents that Web users view on their browsers.

paragraph: The basic element of text within an HTML document, using a paragraph character (¶) as the markup tag to indicate a paragraph break in text (the closing ¶ tag is currently optional in HTML).

path, pathname: See **directory path.**

PC (personal computer): Today, PC is used as a generic term to refer to just about any kind of desktop computer; its original definition was as a product name for IBM's 8086-based personal computer, the IBM/PC. Even though a PC is technically any type of desktop computer, many people still use it to refer to IBM-compatible machines only.

PDF (Portable Document Format): Adobe's rich, typographically correct document format, used to provide multiplatform document access through its Acrobat software as a more powerful alternative to HTML.

Perl: A powerful, compact programming language that draws from languages like C, Pascal, sed, awk, and BASIC, Perl is the language of choice for CGI programs, partly owing to its portability and the many platforms on which it is currently supported, and partly owing to its ability to exploit operating system services quickly and easily.

physical character tags: Any of a series of HTML markup tags that specifically control character styles — bold (`<b>`) and italic (`<i>`) — or typeface (`<tt>`) for typewriter font.

RAM (Random-Access Memory): The memory used in most computers to store ongoing work and that also provides space to store the operating system and any applications that are actually running at any given moment. When you turn off or restart your computer, any contents stored in RAM disappear forever.

relative: When applied to URLs, relative means that in the absence of the tag, the link is relative to the current page's URL in which the link is defined. This makes for shorter, more compact URLs and explains why most local URLs are relative, not absolute.

Request for Comment (RFC): Numbered documents maintained by the IETF that contain the standards, procedures, and specifications of protocols, plus descriptions of Internet environments, addressing schemes, and capabilities.

resource: Any HTML document, capability, or other item or service available via the Web. URLs point to resources.

return: In text files, a return (short for *carriage return,* a term left over from the typewriter era) causes the words on a line to end and makes the display pick up at the leftmost location on the line below. As used in this book, it means: *Don't hit the Enter or Return key in the middle of a line of HTML markup or a URL specification.*

robot: A special Web-traveling program that wanders widely, following and recording URLs and related titles for future reference in search engines.

ROM (Read-Only Memory): A form of computer memory that allows values to be stored only once; after the data is initially recorded, the computer can only read the contents. ROMs are used to supply constant code elements like bootstrap loaders, network addresses, and other more or less unvarying programs or instructions. The contents of ROM remain even after the computer is switched off.

router: A special-purpose piece of Internet-working gear that makes it possible to connect networks together, a router is capable of reading the destination address of any network packet. It can forward the packet to a local recipient if its address resides on any network that the router can reach, or on to another router if the packet is destined for delivery to a network that the current router cannot access.

screen: The glowing part on the front of your computer monitor where you see the Web do its thing (and anything else your computer might like to show you).

scripting language: A special kind of programming language that is read and executed by a computer at the same time (which means that the computer figures out what to do with it when it appears in a document or at the time that it's used. JavaScript and Perl are common scripting languages associated with Web use).

search engine: A special Web program that can search the contents of a database of available Web pages and other resources to provide information that relates to specific topics or keywords supplied by a user.

search tools: Any of a number of programs (see Chapter 16) that can permit HTML documents to become searchable, using the `<isindex>` tag to inform the browser of the need for a search window, and behind-the-scenes indexing and anchoring schemes to let users locate particular sections of or items within a document.

server: A computer on a network whose job is to listen for particular service requests and to respond to those that it knows how to satisfy.

service provider: An organization that provides individuals or other organizations with access to the Internet. Service providers usually offer a variety of communications options for their customers, ranging from analog telephone lines, to a variety of higher-bandwidth leased lines, to ISDN and other digital communications services.

SGML (Standard Generalized Markup Language): An ISO standard document definition, specification, and creation mechanism that makes platform and display differences across multiple computers irrelevant to the delivery and rendering of documents.

shareware: Software, available by various means, that users can run for free for a trial period. When that trial period expires, users must register and purchase the software, or they must discontinue its use.

singleton tag: An HTML tag that does not require the use of a closing tag.

SLIP (Serial Line Interface Protocol): A relatively old-fashioned TCP/IP protocol used to manage telecommunications between a client and a server that treats the phone line as a "slow extension" to a network.

SMTP (Simple Mail Transfer Protocol): An underlying protocol and service used for Internet-based electronic mail.

specification: A formal document that describes the capabilities, functions, and interfaces for a specific piece of software, a markup language, or a communications protocol.

spider (Web spider, Webcrawler): A Web-traversing program that tirelessly investigates Web pages and their links, while storing information about its travels for inclusion in the databases typically used by search engines.

stdin (UNIX standard input device): The default source for input in the UNIX environment, stdin is the input source for CGI programs as well.

stdout (UNIX standard output device): The default recipient for output in the UNIX environment, stdout is the output source for Web browsers and servers as well (including CGI programs).

superstructure: In HTML documents, we refer to superstructure as the layout and navigational elements used to create a consistent look and feel for Web pages belonging to a document set.

syntax: Literally, the formal rules for how to speak, we use syntax in this book to describe the rules that govern how HTML markup looks and behaves within HTML documents. The real syntax definition for HTML comes from the SGML Document Type Definition (DTD).

syntax checker: A program that checks a particular HTML document's markup against the rules that govern its use; a recommended part of the testing regimen for all HTML documents.

tag: The formal name for an element of HTML markup, usually enclosed in angle brackets ($<$ $>$).

TCP/IP (Transmission Control Protocol/Internet Protocol): The name for the suite of protocols and services used to manage network communications and applications over the Internet. *TCP,* a reliable, connection-oriented protocol, usually guarantees delivery across a network; *IP* is the specific networking protocol that ties computers together over the Internet. (IP also serves as a synonym for the whole TCP/IP protocol suite.)

technophobe: Literally, someone who's afraid of technology, this term is more commonly applied to those who don't want to understand technology, but simply to use it!

Telnet: The Internet protocol and service that lets you take a smart computer (your own, probably) and make it emulate a dumb terminal over the network. Briefly, Telnet is a way of running programs and using capabilities on other computers across the Internet.

template: Literally, a model to imitate, we use the term template in this book to describe the skeleton of a Web page, including the HTML for its heading and footer, and a consistent layout and set of navigation elements.

terminal emulation: The process of making a full-fledged, standalone computer act like a terminal attached to another computer, terminal emulation is the service that Telnet provides across the Internet.

test plan: The series of steps and elements to be followed in conducting a formal test of software or other computerized systems; we strongly recommend that you write — and use — a test plan as a part of your Web publication process.

text controls: Any of a number of HTML tags, including both physical and logical markup, text controls provide a method of managing the way that text appears within an HTML document.

thumbnail: A miniature rendering of a graphical image, used as a link to the full-size version.

title: The text supplied to a Web page's title bar when displayed, used as data in many Web search engines.

TMP directories: Special working directories, normally associated with Microsoft Windows operating systems, where temporary files are created and manipulated while programs are executing.

transparent .GIF: A specially rendered .GIF image that takes on the background color selected in a browser capable of handling such .GIFs. This makes the graphic blend into the existing color scheme and provides a more professional-looking page.

tree structure(d) (see hierarchical structure): Computer scientists like to think of hierarchies in graphical terms, which makes them look like upside-down trees (single root at the top, multiple branches below). File systems and genealogies are examples of tree-structured organizations that we all know, but they abound in the computer world. This structure also works well for certain Web document sets, especially larger, more complex ones.

UNIX: The operating system of choice for the Internet community at large, and the Web community, too, UNIX offers the broadest range of tools, utilities, and programming libraries for Web server use.

UNIX shell: The name of the command-line program used to manage user-computer interaction, the shell can also be used to write CGI scripts and other kinds of useful programs for UNIX.

URI (Uniform Resource Identifier): Any of a class of objects that identify resources available to the Web; both URLs and URNs are instances of URIs.

URL (Uniform Resource Locator): The primary naming scheme used to identify Web resources, URLs define the protocols to use, the domain name of the Web server where a resource resides, the port address to use for communication, and a directory path to access named Web files or resources.

URL-encoded text: A method for passing information requests and URL specification to Web servers from browsers, URL encoding replaces spaces with plus signs (+) and substitutes special hex codes for a range of otherwise unreproducible characters. This method is used to pass document queries from browsers to servers (for the details, please consult Chapter 12).

URN (Uniform Resource Name): A permanent, unchanging name for a Web resource, URNs are seldom used in today's Web environment. They do, however, present a method guaranteed to obtain access to a resource, as soon as the URN can be fully resolved (it sometimes consists of human or organizational contact information, rather than resource location data).

Usenet: An Internet protocol and service that provides access to a vast array of named newsgroups, where users congregate to exchange information and materials related to specific topics or concerns.

V.32: CCITT standard for a 9.6-Kbps, two-wire, full-duplex modem operating on a regular dial-up or two-wire leased lines.

V.32bis: Newer, higher-speed, CCITT standard for full-duplex transmission on two-wire leased and dial-up lines at rates from 4.8 to 14.4 Kbps.

V.34: The newest high-speed CCITT standard for full-duplex transmission on two-wire leased and dial-up lines at rates from 4.8 to 28.8 Kbps.

V.42: CCITT error correction standard that can be used with V.32, V.32bis, and V.34.

V.42bis: CCITT data compression standard, capable of compressing files on-the-fly at an average rate of 3.5:1. It can yield speeds of up to 38.4 Kbps on a 9.6 Kbps modem, and up to 115.2 Kbps on a 28.8 modem. If your modem can do this, try to find an Internet service provider that also supports V.42bis. This feature pays for itself very quickly.

WAIS (Wide-Area Information Service): A collection of programs that implement a specific protocol for information retrieval, able to index large-scale collections of data round the Internet. WAIS provides content-oriented query services to WAIS clients and is one of the more powerful Internet search tools available.

Web pages: Synonym for HTML documents, we use Web pages in this book to refer to sets of related, interlinked HTML documents, usually produced by a single author or organization.

Web server: A computer, usually on the Internet, that plays host to httpd and related Web-service software.

Web site: An addressed location, usually on the Internet, that provides access to the set of Web pages that correspond to the URL for a given site; thus a Web site consists of a Web server and a named collection of Web documents, both accessible through a single URL.

white space: The "breathing room" on a page, this refers to parts of a display or document unoccupied by text or other visual elements. A certain amount of white space is essential to make documents attractive and readable.

World Wide Web (WWW or W3): The complete collection of all Web servers available on the Internet, which comes as close to containing the "sum of human knowledge" as anything we've ever seen. Shorthand terms for the World Wide Web include WWW, the Web, and W3; we also use web (lowercased) in this book to refer to a related, interlinked set of HTML documents.

WYSIWYG (What You See Is What You Get): A term used to describe text editors or other layout tools (like HTML authoring tools) that attempt to show their users on-screen what final, finished documents will look like.

Appendix C

Tools of the Trade

● ●

In This Appendix

▶ Finding an HTML tool for every platform

▶ Identifying exactly the right HTML editor

▶ Authoring systems for the Web

▶ Using non-HTML tools for HTML purposes

● ●

Stone-age HTML was created using only simple text editors, with each and every tag composed by hand. Today, a mere eight years later, hand-coding HTML is no longer the only way to do it, although some authors — ourselves included — still prefer this approach. The latest generation of HTML editors declares that you can "build Web pages without knowing HTML." Amazing . . . or maybe not.

HTML editors are intended to make Web page creation easier, but editors that claim to do "all the work for you" make us a little nervous. Imagine someone gives you a word processor that claims to know English grammar and writes your documents for you. You wouldn't expect that word processor to write the way you prefer, and you wouldn't stake your reputation on its output without checking and tweaking the results. (We wouldn't, anyway.) You should be just as demanding, careful, and skeptical about your HTML authoring program as your word processor. Fortunately for you, we're demanding, careful, and skeptical people, too!

And just because an HTML editor may make creating your Web pages easier, this doesn't mean it's the only tool you'll need to publish and maintain your Web site. Nope, one tool just won't do the trick. Instead you'll need an entire collection — fondly referred to in the "biz" as a webmaster's toolbox. In addition to your HTML editor, you'll need an FTP tool to upload your files to a Web server, as well as validation and maintenance tools to help you check your pages twice and keep them ship-shape. This appendix reviews and recommends the latest HTML authoring tools — as well as other tools you'll find in any professional webmaster's well-stocked toolbox. You may be surprised to find that some of these tools may already be on your system quietly waiting to help you create stupendous Web pages.

We've told you what kinds of tools you need, and in this chapter, we recommend some of our favorites. Until you see a good toolbox in action, you can't truly understand how all these products can work together to create and maintain HTML pages. We devote the remaining sections of the chapter to a good, hard look at the different webmaster tools — editors, FTP tools, and maintenance tools — organized by type. The first of those sections — HTML Editors — is further divided by platform — Windows, Mac, and UNIX — and for each platform, we list the best tool, the most popular tool, and a good inexpensive — okay cheap — tool. The remaining sections just list quality tools since many are available on multiple platforms or are Web-based. So roll up those virtual sleeves and get ready to build your very own webmaster's toolbox.

Keep in mind that shareware editors aren't as multifunctional as those that cost real money. If you write a lot of HTML and manage a large site (or more than one site), you may need to invest in an editor that can handle many different tasks. Most of the major software players, including companies like Adobe Systems, Symantec Corp., and Microsoft, have jumped into the HTML editor fray.

Making an HTML Editor Work for You

Although this book explains how to create and maintain HTML pages with nothing more complicated than a pocket knife and a ball of string, we don't think you should snub all HTML editors. But we do want you to understand that they are just tools, and like every other tool you use, they are no substitute for knowledge, only a helping hand when you apply what you know. Because HTML editors seem to have multiplied as quickly as rabbits, we'd like to give you a few tips on how to locate and choose a good one.

At the very least, an HTML editor should:

- Be easy to understand and use.
- Accurately preview HTML without using an external browser.
- Comply with HTML 4.0.
- Upgrade as HTML changes.
- Support image map creation.
- Check local links for accuracy.
- Support HTML validation and spell checking.
- Enable you to see and tweak your HTML code directly.

An exceptional HTML editor also:

- ✔ Provides site map information.
- ✔ Checks external links for accuracy.
- ✔ Provides pixel-level control over object and text placement.
- ✔ Accommodates CGI scripts, Java applets, and scripting.

Keep in mind that there are two different kinds of HTML editors: helpers and WYSIWYG editors. An HTML helper does exactly what it sounds like: It helps you create HTML but doesn't do all the work for you. Usually a helper displays "raw" HTML — tags and all (shocking though this may seem) — and such tools often color tags to help you differentiate them from your content; they usually include an HTML-aware spell check system that knows your tags aren't just misspelled words, and they also incorporate other functionality to make HTML development easier and more fun. In our opinion, no webmaster's toolbox is complete without a good HTML helper.

WYSIWYG stands for "What You See is What You Get" and editors that fall into this category usually create HTML for you and hide its R-rated nakedness from you along the way. These tools look much like word processors or page layout programs and are designed to do quite a bit of the work for you. While WYSIWYG editors can make your life easier and can save you from hours of endless coding — after all, you do have a life — once again we stress that you don't want to let this kind of editor substitute for your own know-how. Instead, use WYSIWYG editors for initial design work on your pages — with a WYSIWYG editor you can create a complex table in under a minute flat — and use your helper to refine and tweak your HTML code directly.

Often the best, most popular, and least expensive HTML editor for a particular platform is neither helpers nor editors but may be a combination of the two. As we review our selections for each platform in this category, note that both kinds of editors may be listed.

While we believe that the different tools we list here are of high quality and are part of a great many different webmaster's toolboxes, we do know that our opinions and needs may not match yours exactly — no, as hard as we try we can't read your mind (yet). If you find yourself still looking for bliss, you can find more information on the latest and greatest Web page development tools on many WWW sites. Our favorite is TUCOWS — The Ultimate Collection of Windsock Software — at www.tucows.com. The developers of the TUCOWS site review all the tools they list, and if a tool isn't up to snuff, it doesn't get listed; it's as simple as that. TUCOWS has been around for a long time — in Web years that is — and we've never known it to lead us astray.

Why you should know HTML

There's a boat-load of reasons why you should know HTML, despite what any HTML-editor marketing gadfly may tell you. We could write an entire book about this, but never mind. Here's a brief rundown of our arguments instead:

✔ You must know what HTML can and can't do. HTML has many capabilities, but just as many limitations. If you don't know HTML, you won't be completely aware of either side of this puzzle. For instance, even with the latest HTML 4.0 markup, you can't be sure that a complicated table, image, or text format will look exactly as you expect it to. You must contend with many variables — different browser types and versions, user preferences, and more. On the flip side, if your editor doesn't support the latest HTML attributes, you wouldn't know anything about them, much less be able to use them in your pages. Generally, ignorance is a bad thing. This statement is doubly true for HTML.

✔ You need to know HTML to identify problems and fix them. To figure out what's wrong with a page, you must know what's right. Your pages may look great in an editor or even in your browser of choice, but chances are they won't always be that way. Broken links, corrupted files, and new tags and interpretations can all change the way HTML looks. If you can't identify errors or changes because you can't recognize them for what they are, you won't be able to troubleshoot your pages without the help of a professional, and we don't come cheap (but we can be had!).

✔ You must know HTML to know what tags to use. What's the difference between <strong> and <b>? They look the same, but one is logical and the other is physical. One conveys meaning while the other creates only a textual effect. If you don't know HTML, you simply see boldface text. Another more extreme example is using <pre> to create columnar data instead of the <table> tag because you don't know about table markup. Although you can build a page in a variety of ways, usually there's only one best way. If you know HTML, you can figure out the best way to meet your needs.

✔ You need to know HTML to implement the latest cool stuff. That HTML editor you invested so much time and money in may not support frames, but what if you want frames on your pages? If you know HTML, the solution is simple: Dust off your text editor and code them by hand. If you don't know HTML, you must wait until a new version of the editor — presumably, one that supports frames — is released. In short, if you don't know the HTML tags, your pages are limited to the ones that your editor supports.

We know that you bought *HTML 4 For Dummies* because you are interested in learning HTML and therefore won't fall prey to the attractive promises of the many editors out there and give up learning HTML because you think you can skip it. Take it from us, you need to know HTML, even if your editor does 99 percent of the work.

Windows Web authoring systems

It seems like every programmer and company is trying to produce a better mousetrap for Windows Web authoring. Some of them we surveyed appear to be well-constructed and low on bugs, but we decided it's more fun to cover the cheesy, buggy ones instead. (If you believe that, we have a deal for you on some swampland in . . . never mind.) We wouldn't waste your time or ours by discussing anything but the best of what we could find. The following sections describe the (most widely acknowledged) best in this category.

Best of Breed: Macromedia Dreamweaver

Unlike many other HTML editors, Dreamweaver is relatively new on the scene. Released for the first time in early 1998, Macromedia is quickly becoming the professional webmaster's tool of choice. The folks at Macromedia, best known for their Director multi-media authoring system, went to great lengths to research the needs of established Web professionals and create a product that would meet all their needs. Dreamweaver is a WYSIWYG tool that can help you build the simplest of pages but also includes tools for creating Dynamic HTML — motion and more on the screen — even if you don't know the first thing about scripting. For a first-hand look at a high-end Web site Dreamweaver was used to create, visit www.dhtmlzone.com and take a look at the tutorial portion of the site. You'll be amazed, we promise.

Although Dreamweaver is a WYSIWYG tool, it comes with built-in support for another popular HTML editor, Allair's HomeSite. HomeSite is an advanced HTML helper that allows you to manipulate your HTML code by hand as well as manage your Web site. HomeSite is an extremely feature-rich HTML editor for both the beginner and the professional. You edit the HTML directly but can instantly get a browser view by clicking a tab.

HomeSite color-codes the HTML to help you in your editing. It uses drag-and-drop and right mouse-click menus. The integrated spell checker and global search and replace can check your spelling and update entire projects, folders, and files simultaneously. You can use the image and thumbnail viewers to browse image libraries directly in your editor.

HomeSite even has customizable toolbars and menus. Add to that an extensive online help system to access documentation on HTML and other popular scripting languages, and you have an impressive system. But there's even more. HomeSite helps you with your project management, provides for link verification, internally validates your HTML, and opens and uploads your files to your remote Web server.

You can open a Web page in both Dreamweaver and HomeSite, and the changes you make to it in one program are automatically registered in the other. This two-in-one combination of a WYSIWYG tool and a helper is a direct reflection of what the pros have figured out — you don't need just one kind of HTML editor, you need both. Finally Dreamweaver and HomeSite both create solid HTML that plays by the official HTML 4.0 rules so you don't have to worry about the quality of your HTML. If you create code by hand and Dreamweaver is concerned about its validity, it will warn you that you've made a booboo and will correct it for you if you so desire. About the only thing it doesn't do is make you coffee in the morning.

With all this functionality, rest assured the Dreamweaver doesn't come cheap. It's priced in the $300 range, but that price includes a HomeSite license, quality documentation, tutorials, and an all-around tool that you can use for many aspects of Web development. Also, Macromedia is loyal to its customers, and once you buy a copy of Dreamweaver, upgrades will be available at minimal cost. Plus you have all the power of an established multi-media company behind the product. What more can you ask for?

To find out more about Dreamweaver, point your Web browser at `www.macromedia.com/software/dreamweaver/`.

Most Popular: Microsoft FrontPage 2000

FrontPage 2000 is Microsoft's commercial Web authoring system for Windows 95/98 and NT. Since Microsoft bought FrontPage from Vermeer Technologies, Inc., in January 1996, Microsoft has made FrontPage its premier personal Web authoring, publishing, and maintenance tool for Windows. As we predicted, this product has become the most widely used tool of its kind on the Internet.

Within FrontPage, each Web site is in its own project folder so you can develop and manage multiple sites. Enhanced drag-and-drop features let you drag Microsoft Office files into the FrontPage Explorer or move hyperlinks, tables, and images within the FrontPage Editor. The "Verify all links" feature automatically verifies that all hyperlinks are valid — within and outside your Web site. This feature even corrects all link errors within your site for you. FrontPage 98 also supports database connectivity, ActiveX controls, Java applets, plus VBScript and JavaScript creation and insertion, tables, frames, and HTML 4.0, plus Microsoft's version of Dynamic HTML. Phew!

As if all of this isn't enough, the FrontPage Bonus Pack includes a powerful image editor to create and edit graphics for your Web documents. It includes more than 500 tools and effects and works with PhotoShop-compatible plug-in products, such as Kai's Power Tools from MetaTools, Inc. Image Composer includes more than 600 royalty-free Web-ready images. You may also download the free Microsoft GIF Animator to animate your own Image Composer images and make your Web site really jump on the screen.

As a bonus for Microsoft Office users, the FrontPage interface also allows you to use any document created with Microsoft Office 97 or 2000 because it works like other Office applications. FrontPage uses the shared spelling checker, global Find and Replace, and the Microsoft Thesaurus. Now you can't quite say "Use FrontPage to create my Web site" into your PC's microphone, walk off, have an espresso, and come back to view the finished work. But if you apply the knowledge of planning and preparation from earlier chapters in this book, you should be able to have an outstanding Web site created, tested, and running on your ISP's Web server in very little time by using FrontPage.

For more information about FrontPage 2000, check out the Microsoft Web site at `www.microsoft.com/frontpage/`.

Good 'n' Cheap: HotDog Express

Sausage Software is the purveyor of HotDog Express, currently available in Version 1.5. Like its predecessors, HotDog continues to grab massive accolades from users and editors alike. Although HotDog Pro — the bigger, badder, and more expensive version of this little gem — has more bells and whistles and is more widely used, most of the really smart people we know who use an HTML editor use HotDog Express.

Not only does HotDog Pro assist with the HTML editing process and help you produce flawless HTML, it's smart enough to recognize if it's got the latest set of extensions installed and goes out and downloads them for you if it's not in synch with the most current set. We've heard of smart programs before, but this is the only HTML editor we know of that's got the brains to recognize it needs an HTML DTD tune-up, and then goes out and grabs the changes for itself! This makes it a snap to keep with changes to draft HTML standards and DTDs, and to track release of standards as soon as they go official. And if all this wasn't enough, this quality shareware tool is available for less than $50.

To find out more about HotDog Express and download a working copy, visit `www.sausage.com`.

Macintosh Web authoring systems

You can download a plethora of excellent HTML authoring tools for the Macintosh from numerous online sites. Most of these Macintosh products ship with very good to pretty good documentation, and some even have online or balloon help. (For non-Mac heads, balloon help is pop-up information that takes the form of cute little balloons that appear when you run your mouse over a portion of the program's interface.) Thankfully, these tools are easy to learn because they use familiar Macintosh word-processing or text-editor models and the Macintosh menuing system.

Best of Breed: Macromedia Dreamweaver

Once again Dreamweaver wins hands down as the best Web development tool for the Macintosh. All that can be said about the Windows version of this excellent tool can also be said for the Macintosh version. Macromedia is truly Mac user friendly and has committed to continued development of this product. That cute little iMac has definitely won hearts at Macromedia.

Instead of working with HomeSite, Dreamweaver for the Macintosh interacts directly with the most popular HTML text editor available, BBEdit. Almost a legend in the Mac world and the preferred tool for any Mac programming nerd, BBEdit is also a powerful tool for Web page development. As a helper, BBEdit is HTML aware and supports tag color-coding, site management, HTML validation, HTML-aware spell checking, and more. You can launch BBEdit directly from Dreamweaver, and any changes you make in a document open in both applications will be reflected in the other. This close relationship with BBEdit is one of the reasons that Dreamweaver has become so popular with Macintosh Web gurus. If you've used BBEdit and appreciate its power as part of your Web arsenal, then you'll love Dreamweaver. If you've never used either and you're a Mac Web head, we recommend you acquire them both immediately. Once again, Dreamweaver for the Mac is not an inexpensive solution, also weighing in at about $300, but also once again worth every cent. It's an investment you'll never regret.

To read more about Dreamweaver visit
`www.macromedia.com/software/dreamweaver/`.

Most Popular: Claris Home Page

From the makers of the ever-popular Claris Works, the Claris Home Page site designer is for novice and expert Web authors alike. In addition to supporting basic and advanced Web page creation, this tool permits users to create dynamic Web pages without having to know everything about coding such documents. This package includes lots of built-in programming features that perform all the complicated HTML work behind the scenes.

In addition, Claris Home Page offers numerous advanced features, such as support for Java applets, multimedia plug-ins, and HTML forms. And, after you construct your documents, Home Page can publish your finished product to any designated Web server. Check this product out at `www.claris.com/products/claris/clarispage/clarispage.html`.

Good 'n' Cheap: BBEdit Lite

As its name suggests, BBEdit Lite is a limited version of the BBEdit package we raved about earlier in our discussion of Dreamweaver. From the folks at Bare Bones Software, BBEdit Lite is a Macintosh text editor that comes complete with a set of HTML extensions to make Web page development easier.

These HTML extensions for BBEdit Lite are quite extensive and provide a well-rounded HTML authoring system. Tools of this kind can cause an editor to open a standard text file and save it with HTML tags automatically. The two sets of extensions for BBEdit Lite — BBEdit HTML Extensions by Charles Bellver and BBEdit HTML Tools by Lindsay Davies — come with the editor so you don't have to do any extra installation along the way.

While BBEdit Lite doesn't include all the functionality that its big brother BBEdit does, you'll find that using BBEdit Lite gives you access to most, if not all, of the HTML authoring functions you'll ever need, even for the most complex Web pages. It will also addict you to the BBEdit way of life, and we predict that soon you'll be using the full-blown version of BBEdit. It's all a conspiracy, didn't you know? Seriously though, to download a copy of BBEdit Lite, simply point your Web browser at `www.barebones.com`.

UNIX Web authoring systems

Outstanding new HTML authoring tools for UNIX-based systems continue to find their way onto the Web. Some are still under testing, but the current crop looks promising, especially certain graphical editing tools. For those of you who happen to like text-only, EMACS is still alive and well, and supports numerous HTML modes that can liven it up considerably. To top things off, you can convert or filter almost any file type into or out of HTML using one of the myriad HTML utility programs available for UNIX.

The UNIX mindset is one of sharing resources; so nearly all UNIX-based HTML authoring systems are freeware. Even commercial UNIX packages typically offer a freeware version for download and evaluation. But free and shareware UNIX HTML authoring tools aren't supported the same way as recently released commercial products. Thankfully, they don't cost much, either. These tools are usually easy to figure out because they use familiar text editor metaphors or they act as add-ins to your own UNIX text editors. Either way, if you've ever used any kind of editor, you can learn one of these HTML tools easily.

Best of Breed: HoTMetaL Pro

HoTMetaL Pro is SoftQuad's commercial HTML editor. HoTMetaL requires you to edit a document with its embedded HTML codes visible, and then hands the code off to your browser for display. It supports all HTML 4.0 tags and can handle definitions for custom markup (which makes it easy to extend for the occasional bit of proprietary markup that is sometimes needed). HoTMetaL can open lots of document formats — Lotus WordPro/AmiPro; Microsoft Word for Macintosh, Windows, and DOS; RTF (Rich Text Format); and WordPerfect for DOS, Windows, and Macintosh — and convert them to HTML.

HoTMetaL performs both syntax checking and HTML validation. With syntax (rules) checking turned on, HoTMetaL helps you enter only valid HTML. If you select HTML validation, it checks your document for conformance to your choice of any of a number of HTML DTDs. It also provides a list of all nonstandard tags in your document to alert you to possible incompatibilities with browsers that don't support such markup.

To find out more about HoTMetaL, visit the Web site at `www.sq.com/products/hotmetal`.

Most Popular: EMACS Modes and Templates

The old tried-and-true UNIX EMACS editor has several add-in macro systems (modes) available to help you create HTML documents. These modes vary in their features but generally are basic in their approach. They save you from typing each tag in its entirety and provide pick lists from which you can choose the markup you want.

EMACS users will understand this section, and everyone else will think it's written in E-Greek. But then, EMACS is a foreign language to most non-UNIX computer users.

Various EMACS macro packages are available for editing HTML documents. The first and oldest is Marc Andreesen's html-mode.el. It was written while he was at the University of Illinois. (Andreesen was the primary designer of Mosaic and Netscape Navigator.) Heiko Muenkel at the University of Hannover, Germany, added pull-down menus (hm — html-menus.el) and template handling (tmpl-minor-mode.el), which is up to Version 4.15.

Nelson Minar of the Santa Fe Institute wrote and continues to improve html-helper-mode.el, which supports Lucid EMACS menu bar and font-lock capabilities and runs under GNU EMACS, Epoch, and Lucid EMACS.

Generally speaking, the various forms of HTML mode display text and HTML tags alike in fixed-size fonts. By using the hilit.el package, tags and references can be colored differently from text. The HTML modes do not support in-line graphics. More recent versions of HTML mode can call a Mosaic or Navigator process to display pages in a browser view, however.

All these HTML modes work primarily from direct keyboard commands that create paired begin/end HTML tags with an entry point available between the tags. You can select a segment of text, and tags will be inserted around it. None of these modes checks the validity of tags or suggests possible tag usage. However, html-helper-mode and tmpl-minor-mode provide templates for entering multiple fields inside link tags.

For EMACS users, these modes may be just the thing for creating HTML documents. Using them should make HTML tagging easier and less prone to error than manual tag entry. You must still know what tags to use, however, and where to use them. You can obtain information and copies of Muenkel's and Minar's packages, respectively, at

```
www.tnt.uni-hannover.de/~muenkel/software/own/
            hm--html.menus/
www.santafe.edu/~nelson/tools/
```

Good 'n' Cheap: A.S.H.E.

A.S.H.E. — A Simple HTML Editor — was written using the C language, Motif, and NCSA HTML Widgets. It is a stand-alone, unchecked, plain-text HTML editor. The emphasis in A.S.H.E. is Simple. If you understand the UNIX environment, you can learn A.S.H.E. fairly quickly. A.S.H.E. provides active hyperlinks, supports multiple windows, prints text or postscript, and offers automatic file backup. The menu bar is well-designed with File, Edit, HTML, Styles, and Lists menus. It provides a unique user Message Area while displaying the HTML code in a browser screen view. Unfortunately, it only works under Motif on Sun workstations and requires the NCSA HTML Widget library. A.S.H.E provides simple but adequate HTML assistance for users of Motif. If that sounds like it's up your alley, please give it a try!

The A.S.H.E. beta version was created by John R. Punin, Department of Computer Science. Rochester Polytechnic Institute, Troy, New York (e-mail:). You can download it from

```
ftp://ftp.cs.rpi.edu/pub/puninj/ASHE/ASHE-1.1/src/
           ashe-1.1.tar.Z
```

Lists of UNIX helper and filter programs are available at

```
www.utoronto.ca/webdocs/HTMLdocs/UNIXTOOLS/unixdocman.html
www.w3.org/hypertext/WWW/Tools/Word_proc_filters.html
```

The Doctor Is In: Page Checkups

So you've written a bunch of HTML, and you think you're done. Not by a long shot — at least, not if you want to avoid being a laughing stock on the Web. Before all these great tools were available, an occasional misspelled word or broken link was acceptable, but now you have no excuse for such boo-boos. Before you post pages for public display, you must perform three important checks:

- ✔ HTML validation
- ✔ Spelling
- ✔ Links to other pages

Lots of different tools can do one or more of these jobs; many are available for free on the Web. You can find a number of stand-alone utilities as well, not to mention those already embedded in HTML editors. As we said, you no longer have a valid excuse for mistakes.

HTML validation: Bad code is bad news

A majority of browsers are forgiving of markup errors. Most don't even require an `<html>` tag to identify an HTML page, and instead look only for an .HTML or .HTM suffix to identify a document as readable. Just because the real world is that way doesn't make it right. You may see a day when browsers can't afford to be so forgiving, and that day is drawing closer as HTML becomes more complicated and precise. It's better to get it right from the beginning and save yourself a bunch of trouble later on.

HTML validation is built into many HTML editors, and although not many standalone HTML validation applications exist, the W3C has put together a free, Web-based validation system available at `validator.w3.org`.

This validation tool lets you choose which HTML DTD (version) you want to check your document against and will provide you with a variety of different outputs depending on your preference. You can choose a terse output that only lists the line numbers in your document with boo-boos and a brief description of the error, or a verbose output that goes into great detail about why each and every error is an error and even includes links to the relevant information in the HTML specification.

We strongly recommend that you don't ever, ever, ever — have we made our point yet — post a page on the Web without running it through this validator. If your HTML is correct, your pages will look better on a variety of Web browsers, and your users will be happier — even if they don't know exactly why.

Of cars hew kin spill (but spell-check those pages anyway)

What is the biggest problem with checking HTML pages for spelling errors? The tags themselves are misspellings, according to Webster's and most other dictionaries. Sitting and clicking the ignore key for each and every new tag can make spell checking tedious. After your eyes glaze over, you're more apt to miss real misspellings. Once again, many editors include HTML-aware spell checkers that skip markup and check just the text. Because so many editors support this option, few stand-alone utilities are available, or any dedicated online spell checkers that we could find.

Dr. HTML is an HTML checking tool that performs several different checks, including spell checks, on any HTML document or on an entire site. To investigate this utility and try its analytical skills, please visit this Web site:

```
www2.imagiware.com/RxHTML/
```

Regardless of how you do it, even if it means cutting and pasting text from a browser to a word processor, you must check your pages for spelling errors. Bad spelling is often considered to be an indicator of intelligence and abilities, and we wouldn't want anyone to underestimate you.

Don't lose the connection: Link checking

If you think spelling errors are embarrassing, here's something that's even worse: broken hyperlinks. Hyperlinks make the Web what it is; if you have broken links on your site, that's borderline blasphemous. Seriously, if your text promises a link to a great resource or page but produces the dreaded 404 Object Not Found error when that link is clicked, users will be disappointed and may not ever revisit your site. The worst broken link is one that points to a resource in your own pages. You can't be held responsible for what others do to their sites, but you are 100 percent accountable for your own site. Don't let broken links happen to you!

As with the other checks, many HTML editors include built-in local link checkers, and some editors even scour the Web for you to check external links. In addition, a majority of Web servers also offer this feature. Checking external links isn't as simple as it sounds because a program is involved that must work over an active Internet connection to query each link. This can be processor intensive, and you should check external links only during off-peak hours, like early morning, to avoid tying up other Web servers as well. A number of scripts and utilities are available on the Web to help you test your links. In the following sections, we share some of our favorites.

MOMSpider

MOMSpider was one of the first link checkers available to Web authors. This link checker is written in Perl and runs on virtually any UNIX machine. The nice thing about MOMSpider is that it needn't reside on the same computer as the site it checks, so even if you don't serve your Web from UNIX, you can still check links from MOMSpider on a remote system.

Anyone who has some knowledge of Perl can easily configure MOMSpider to create custom output and to check both internal and external links on a site. Don't fret; if you don't know Perl, you can easily find a programmer who can adjust a MOMSpider in his or her sleep for a nominal fee. Many ISPs run a MOMSpider on your site for a low monthly fee and will cheerfully handle the configuration and implementation for you.

To find out more about MOMSpider, visit the official site at

www.ics.uci.edu/pub/websoft/MOMspider/

Web Walker

Web Walker is a simpler, annotated version of MOMSpider that non-Perl users can implement themselves with just a little study. Once again, it must run on a UNIX server with Perl installed, but the program itself is heavily commented to help you configure it without calling in a programmer. If you feel adventurous and want to try your hand at a little programming, give Web Walker a shot.

Point your browser at the Web Walker page for more information:

```
info.webcrawler.com/mak/projects/robots/active/html/webwalker.html
```

Web-Site Garage: An all-around checker

We stumbled across a great Web site not too long ago that adds a powerful punch to your Web arsenal: Web-Site Garage. This Web-based Web page checking tool is a gem that you can't afford to be without. This site checks your HTML, spelling, download time, and many other aspects of the mechanics under the hood of your Web pages to help you fine tune your code. The site analyzes a page and flags code that may potentially cause problems in particular browsers or Web graphics that can be made smaller. You can find out how long a page may take to download over a variety of connections and find out if your pages are accessible or not. To drive your page in for an inspection and tune-up, visit www.websitegarage.com.

Other Useful Tools and Utilities

You'll find helpful tools and utilities to create Web pages in the most unexpected places sometimes. The word processor on your computer right now may double as an HTML editor — or a converter in the very least. Other application-like page layout programs and database tools may also have HTML functionality, even if their primary focus isn't creation of Web pages. Finally, there are certain utilities whose only purpose in life is to convert documents from a particular format — such as RTF — into HTML. While you may be able to live without some of these tools in your webmaster's toolbox, you'll find that they can be quite useful at times and are worth a second look.

Word processors as HTML editors

If you're joined at the hip to Microsoft Word, Corel WordPerfect, or Lotus Word Pro, you may want to try their built-in HTML editing and site management features. These features provide adequate HTML assistance but aren't really in the same ballpark with better stand-alone WYSIWYG Web development and HTML editing systems. If you already own one of these word processing programs, however, their Web functionality is free. For now, you may want to use your favorite one for text and for Web development.

For example, Word 97 for Windows has a nice WYSIWYG editing window with a good number of functions in its toolbar. This program is adequate for a word processor turned Web document editor. However, who knows what Microsoft will do in the long-term with both Word 97 and FrontPage contending for the role of Web document development systems. Why worry about that now? If you own one, try it out for Web development.

Keep in mind that word processors may not create HTML that is 100 percent standard; instead Web pages these tools create can be erratic and clumsy. If you have long documents that have been developed in a particular word processor that need to be converted to HTML, it may be easier to do a first-stage conversion in the processor itself but to do any final clean up and tweaking in a full-fledged HTML editor.

See the following sites for their respective information on Microsoft Word 97 for Windows, Corel WordPerfect 8.0 for Windows, and Lotus Word Pro 97 for Windows:

```
www.microsoft.com/office/
wp.novell.com/products/wordperfect/cwps7/
www2.lotus.com/wordpro.nsf
```

Filters and file converters for Windows

Automatically converting existing text documents into HTML is supported by several of the current crop of HTML editors, word processors, and page layout programs. They work quickly and easily. For example, if you use Word for Windows, simply open a standard Word document; then save the file in HTML format via the Save As command, and it's converted. Most of the text formatting that really counts, including headings, is transformed into HTML. However, you may have files saved in a particular format for a specific application that doesn't support this automatic conversion. If that's the case, then you may need a stand-alone converter to help you along.

The following two stand-alone converters are examples of the numerous converters available on every conceivable computer platform to convert virtually every file format to HTML and sometimes back again. HTML Transit imports and converts a large number of file formats, whereas WebMaker is designed specifically to convert FrameMaker files. If you have many highly formatted files that you want to convert to HTML for Web display, check into these two systems.

HTML Transit

HTML Transit, from InfoAccess, Inc., reads the structure of the source document, recognizing elements such as headings, subheads, bullets, images, and so on. HTML Transit then creates a default template based on this structure that becomes the foundation for one-button generation of HTML documents. HTML Transit offers direct translation of all major word processing formats and all major graphics formats.

HTML Transit is based on over a decade of electronic publishing experience by InfoAccess (formerly OWL International), which produced the industry's first commercially available hypertext product ten years ago. Their $45,000 GUIDE Professional Publisher was the model for HTML Transit's template-based architecture.

With a well-formatted word processor or page layout file and HTML Transit, you may not need an HTML "editor" at all. Although HTML Transit is a bit expensive, it may be just what you're looking for. Have a look for yourself at

```
www.infoaccess.com/
```

WebMaker 3.5

WebMaker 3.5 from the Harlequin Group Limited is a new and promising FrameMaker converter and, with its low price, is quite a deal for FrameMaker users. WebMaker is a powerful, easy-to-use Web publishing solution for the creation of full-featured Web pages from FrameMaker documents. WebMaker's conversion capabilities convert FrameMaker documents and books to HTML complete with graphics, tables, and equations.

WebMaker takes full advantage of the layout styles you apply in FrameMaker to let you define specialized layout styles for Web publishing. Customization and hyperlinking are accomplished and automated easily and produce fast, predictable results. After you complete the conversion, you can use the conversion template you create over and over again to automatically convert documents to HTML in the format you've specified. No additional work is required no matter how many pages, documents, or books you decide to convert.

WebMaker is available for Windows at

```
www.harlequin.copm/webmaker/Welcome.html
```

Appendix D

About the CD-ROM

● ●

*I*n this section of the book, we explain what you find on the *HTML 4 For Dummies* CD-ROM. In a nutshell, it contains the following goodies:

- ✔ A collection of Web documents built specifically to help you find your way around the book's materials.

- ✔ A hotlist of all URLs mentioned in the book to make it easy for you to access any of the Web resources we mention.

- ✔ Copies of all the HTML examples, easily accessible by chapter.

- ✔ A hyperlinked table of contents for the book to help you find your way around its many topics and treasures.

- ✔ A collection of Common Gateway Interface (CGI) programs, built especially for you, to help add functionality to your own Web server (and to provide what we hope are sterling examples of the art of CGI programming).

How to Use the Web Pages and Examples

Regardless of what platform and operating system you run, you can view all the material in the book straight from the CD-ROM. To do so, however, you must have a Web browser installed on your system. We did not include browser software on the disc, but you can download evaluation versions of Netscape Navigator at `www.netscape.com` or Internet Explorer at `www.microsoft.com/ie/`. To browse the CD-ROM contents, just do the following:

1. **Launch your Web browser.**

2. **Using the Open File command in your browser's File menu, open the file `\html4Fd2\html4dum.htm\` from the CD-ROM.**

This page serves as the home page for the CD-ROM; it connects you to all other files. Although you won't be able to edit any of the files on the disc itself, you can make changes and save them elsewhere. If you modify any examples or templates, save them to your local drive before you do so. The simplest way to do it is to copy the `html4Fd2` folder to your hard drive, which transfers the entire directory structure from the CD-ROM to your computer. (You'll need about 2MB of drive space to accommodate it, so we suggest you check first.)

The HTML 4 For Dummies Files

The top level of the *HTML 4 For Dummies* CD-ROM directory includes the following items:

- ✔ The `html4fd2` folder
- ✔ Folders containing installers for shareware, freeware, and trial programs
- ✔ A License Agreement text file
- ✔ A Read Me file

The `html4Fd2` folder contains all the Dummies HTML files; the software folders are chock-full of trial versions that introduce you to some of the best HTML editors in the business (they're software, so you don't have to invite them out to dinner). License.txt includes some important end-user information, and Readme.txt is a text-only version of this appendix (just in case your book grows legs and happens to wander away somewhere).

To give you an idea of what's in each folder, we cover the files within them according to their home directory — and subdirectory when necessary. The `html4Fd2` directory contains the majority of *HTML 4 For Dummies* files. Nearly every file in this directory ends with the extension `.htm`, indicating that it is an HTML document.

All in all, the best way to explore the *HTML 4 For Dummies* Web pages is to fire up your browser and point it at the file named `html4dum.htm` (the home page for the whole collection). For a complete, linked, graphical overview of all the files on the CD-ROM, open `menu.htm` and behold! Table D-1 lists and describes the remaining top-level HTML.

Table D-1	The html4Fd2 Directory File Listing
File	*Description*
contact.htm	List of e-mail, home-page, and biography page links for the authors
copy.htm	Important copyright information
etbio.htm	Ed Tittel's biography page
html4dum.htm	The *HTML 4 For Dummies* home page
menu.htm	A bird's-eye view of the entire page collection
npbio.htm	Natanya Pitts' biography page
wayfind.htm	HTML navigation information

The html4Fd2 directory has seven subdirectories whose names are a good indication of what you find within them.

- ✔ **contents:** contains files listing the book contents by chapter

- ✔ **examples:** contains files listing the book examples by chapter

- ✔ **graphics:** contains all the graphics used with the *HTML 4 For Dummies* Web pages

- ✔ **h4dftp:** contains compressed versions of all the Dummies files

- ✔ **cgi-bin:** contains AppleScript, C, and Perl CGI scripts

- ✔ **templates:** contains a collection of templates to get you started

- ✔ **urls:** contains files that list the book's URLs by chapter

For you list enthusiasts who need to know more about the files lurking within the subdirectories, the following list unveils them in greater detail:

- ✔ **html4Fd2/contents:** The file default.htm within the contents of the subdirectory includes a hyperlinked listing of all the chapter titles. Click a chapter title to view a list of its contents. The other files in the subdirectory are named chnncont.htm (where nn is a two-digit number between 0 and 9) and are keyed to the chapters of the book. ch01cont.htm contains the contents listing for Chapter 1. The easiest way to navigate through these pages is to choose a chapter from default.htm to view a chapter's contents. To return to the list of chapter titles, choose "Book Contents" from the bottom image map (or text provided for navigation).

✔ **html4Fd2/examples:** The file `default.htm` within the contents of the subdirectory includes a hyperlinked listing of all the chapter titles. The examples folder is further broken down into subfolders that contain the individual HTML example documents for each chapter. Click a chapter title in `default.htm` to view a listing of the examples included for the chapter. To view a specific example, click the example name. Each example includes the code listing from the book and shows the final rendering of the example by a Web browser when possible.

Note: The easiest way to navigate through these pages is to choose a chapter from `default.htm` to view a listing of the chapter's examples and select the example you would like to see. When you finish with a particular example, press the Back button in your browser windows to return to the list of examples by chapter. To return to the list of chapter titles, choose `"Book Examples"` from the bottom image map (or text navigation).

✔ **html4Fd2/graphics:** This is the graphics subdirectory for the graphics used in the HTML documents for the *HTML 4 For Dummies* pages themselves. As its name implies, this folder houses all the `.gif` image files in our Web page. If we used an image on a Web page (except in the templates pages) you can find it here. All we can say further is *Help yourself!*

✔ **html4Fd2/h4dftp:** To make transferring our file collections easier, we included a Web page where you'll find links to download a compressed version of the CGI, `html4fd2`, and template folders. Each one is available as a `.zip` (PC), `.sea.hqx` (Macintosh), and `.tar` (UNIX) archive; you should be able to get at them regardless of what operating system you use.

✔ **html4Fd2/cgi-bin:** This folder contains three subfolders (`AppleScript`, `C`, and `Perl`), each of which holds unarchived versions of the CD-ROM's CGI files.

✔ **html4Fd2/templates:** For your pleasure and convenience, we include a few simple templates to get you started on your HTML authoring adventures. The folder's main page, `default.htm`, gives you a complete rundown on each template. The `graphics` subdirectory within the `templates` folder contains all the graphics we used in creating the templates. As we said before, *Help yourself!*

✔ **html4Fd2/urls:** The file `default.htm` within the `urls` subdirectory includes a hyperlinked listing of all the chapter titles. Click a chapter title to view a list the URLs we included in it. The other files in the subdirectory are named `chnnurls.htm` (where nn is a number between 0 and 9) and are keyed to the chapters of the book. The easiest way to navigate through these pages is to choose a chapter from `default.htm` to view a chapter's URLs. To return to the listing of chapter titles, choose `"Book URLs"` from the bottom image map (or text provided for navigation).

The Software

In addition to the nifty files, examples, and scripts described in the previous section, we also include a small software collection on the CD-ROM. Heft and try out these evaluation and shareware versions of webmaster tools that might fit your needs. Fear not the compatibility dragon; the disc is a multi-platform hybrid format. You have access to only those packages that can run on the platform you currently use (clever, eh?). To see the other tools, you must load the disc into a computer that uses a different OS (of course it has to be one of the platforms the disc itself supports . . . but you knew that).

System Requirements

Make sure that your computer meets the minimum system requirements listed in this handy section. If your computer doesn't match up to most of these requirements, you may have problems using the contents of the CD-ROM. Avoid the heartbreak of obsolescence; look before you load.

- ✔ A PC with a 486 or faster processor, or a Mac OS computer with a 68030 or faster processor.
- ✔ Microsoft Windows 3.1 or later, or Mac OS system software 7.5 or later.
- ✔ At least 24MB of total RAM installed on your computer. For best performance, we recommend that Windows 95-equipped PCs and Mac OS computers with PowerPC processors have at least 32MB of RAM installed.
- ✔ At least 10MB of hard drive space available to install all the software from this CD-ROM. (You need less space if you don't install every program.)
- ✔ A CD-ROM drive — double speed (2x) or faster.
- ✔ A monitor capable of displaying at least 256 colors or grayscale.
- ✔ A modem with a speed of at least 28,800 bps.

If you need more information on the basics, check out *PCs For Dummies,* 6th Edition, by Dan Gookin; *Macs For Dummies,* 6th Edition, by David Pogue; *Windows 98 For Dummies, Windows 95 For Dummies,* or *Windows 3.11 For Dummies,* 4th Edition, all by Andy Rathbone (all published by IDG Books Worldwide, Inc.).

If You've Got Problems (Of the CD Kind)

We tried our level best to compile programs that work on most computers with the minimum system requirements. Alas, your computer may differ, and some programs may not work properly for some reason. (Check the label. Was your system reverse-engineered from a UFO?)

The two likeliest problems are (1) you may not have enough memory (RAM) for the programs you want to use, or (2) you may have other programs running that are affecting installation or running of a program. If you get error messages like `Not enough memory` or `Setup cannot continue`, try one or more of these methods and then try using the software again:

- ✔ **Turn off any antivirus software that you have running on your computer.** Installers sometimes mimic virus activity and may make your computer incorrectly believe that it is being infected by a virus.

- ✔ **Close all running programs.** The more programs you're running, the less memory is available to other programs. Installers also typically update files and programs; if you keep other programs running, installation may not work properly.

- ✔ **In Windows, close the CD-ROM interface and run demos or installations directly from Windows Explorer.** The interface itself can tie up system memory or even conflict with certain kinds of interactive demos. Use Windows Explorer to browse the files on the CD-ROM and launch installers or demos.

- ✔ **Have your local computer store add more RAM to your computer.** This is, admittedly, a drastic and somewhat expensive step, but be of good cheer: More RAM is almost always a good thing. However, if you have a Windows 95 PC or a Mac OS computer with a PowerPC chip, adding more memory can really help the speed of your computer and enable more programs to run at the same time.

If you still have trouble installing the items from the CD-ROM, please call the IDG Books Worldwide Customer Service phone number: 800-762-2974 (outside the United States: 317-596-5430).

Index

• E •

• Y •

• Z •

FREE

IDG Books/PC WORLD CD Wallet

and a Sample Issue of

PC WORLD

PC WORLD

Break the 56K Barrier — How Modems Promise Higher-Speed Web Access

Best Big Monitors! We Rate 27 Leading Models—Priced Right

Put Your Small Office on the Net — Best Connections for Lowest Cost

3RD ANNUAL

BEST FREE STUFF ONLINE

Plus: Tips for Smart Downloading
The Scoop on Online Discounts
How to Try Before You Buy

GREAT FREEWARE, SITES, SHAREWARE, SERVICES— AND WHERE TO FIND THEM

THE #1 MONTHLY COMPUTER MAGAZINE

How to order your sample issue and FREE CD Wallet:

✉ Cut and mail the coupon today!

☎ Call us at 1-800-825-7595 x434
Fax us at 1-415-882-0936

☞ Order online at
www.pcworld.com/resources/subscribe/BWH.html

ORDER TODAY!

...For Dummies is a registered trademark under exclusive license to IDG Books Worldwide, Inc., from International Data Group, Inc.

FREE GIFT/SAMPLE ISSUE COUPON

Cut coupon and mail to: PC World, PO Box 55029, Boulder, CO 80322-5029

YES! Please rush my FREE CD wallet and my FREE sample issue of PC WORLD! If I like PC WORLD, I'll honor your invoice and receive 11 more issues (12 in all) for just $19.97—that's 72% off the newsstand rate.

NO COST EXAMINATION GUARANTEE.
If I decide PC WORLD is not for me, I'll write "cancel" on the invoice and owe nothing. The sample issue and CD wallet are mine to keep, no matter what.

PC WORLD

Name _____

Company _____

Address _____

City _____ State _____ Zip _____

Email _____

Get the Most from Your PC!

Every issue of PC World is packed with the latest information to help you make the most of your PC.

- Top 100 PC and Product Ratings
- Hot PC News
- How Tos, Tips, & Tricks
- Buyers' Guides
- Consumer Watch
- Hardware and Software Previews
- Internet & Multimedia Special Reports
- Upgrade Guides
- Monthly @Home Section

YOUR FREE GIFT!

As a special bonus with your order, you will receive the IDG Books/ PC WORLD CD wallet, perfect for transporting and protecting your CD collection.

SEND TODAY
for your sample issue
and FREE IDG Books/PC WORLD CD Wallet!

How to order your sample issue and FREE CD Wallet:

✉ Cut and mail the coupon today!
Mail to: PC World, PO Box 55029, Boulder, CO 80322-5029

☎ Call us at 1-800-825-7595 x434
Fax us at 1-415-882-0936

☛ Order online at www.pcworld.com/resources/subscribe/BWH.html

PC WORLD

IDG Books Worldwide, Inc., End-User License Agreement

READ THIS. You should carefully read these terms and conditions before opening the software packet(s) included with this book ("Book"). This is a license agreement ("Agreement") between you and IDG Books Worldwide, Inc. ("IDGB"). By opening the accompanying software packet(s), you acknowledge that you have read and accept the following terms and conditions. If you do not agree and do not want to be bound by such terms and conditions, promptly return the Book and the unopened software packet(s) to the place you obtained them for a full refund.

1. **License Grant.** IDGB grants to you (either an individual or entity) a nonexclusive license to use one copy of the enclosed software program(s) (collectively, the "Software") solely for your own personal or business purposes on a single computer (whether a standard computer or a workstation component of a multiuser network). The Software is in use on a computer when it is loaded into temporary memory (RAM) or installed into permanent memory (hard disk, CD-ROM, or other storage device). IDGB reserves all rights not expressly granted herein.

2. **Ownership.** IDGB is the owner of all right, title, and interest, including copyright, in and to the compilation of the Software recorded on the disk(s) or CD-ROM ("Software Media"). Copyright to the individual programs recorded on the Software Media is owned by the author or other authorized copyright owner of each program. Ownership of the Software and all proprietary rights relating thereto remain with IDGB and its licensers.

3. **Restrictions on Use and Transfer.**

    (a) You may only (i) make one copy of the Software for backup or archival purposes, or (ii) transfer the Software to a single hard disk, provided that you keep the original for backup or archival purposes. You may not (i) rent or lease the Software, (ii) copy or reproduce the Software through a LAN or other network system or through any computer subscriber system or bulletin-board system, or (iii) modify, adapt, or create derivative works based on the Software.

    (b) You may not reverse engineer, decompile, or disassemble the Software. You may transfer the Software and user documentation on a permanent basis, provided that the transferee agrees to accept the terms and conditions of this Agreement and you retain no copies. If the Software is an update or has been updated, any transfer must include the most recent update and all prior versions.

4. **Restrictions on Use of Individual Programs.** You must follow the individual requirements and restrictions detailed for each individual program in the "About the CD" section of this Book. These limitations are also contained in the individual license agreements recorded on the Software Media. These limitations may include a requirement that after using the program for a specified period of time, the user must pay a registration fee or discontinue use. By opening the Software packet(s), you will be agreeing to abide by the licenses and restrictions for these individual programs that are detailed in the "About the CD" section and on the Software Media. None of the material on this Software Media or listed in this Book may ever be redistributed, in original or modified form, for commercial purposes.

5. **Limited Warranty.**

IDGB warrants that the Software and Software Media are free from defects in materials and workmanship under normal use for a period of sixty (60) days from the date of purchase of this Book. If IDGB receives notification within the warranty period of defects in materials or workmanship, IDGB will replace the defective Software Media.

(b) **IDGB AND THE AUTHOR OF THE BOOK DISCLAIM ALL OTHER WAR-RANTIES, EXPRESS OR IMPLIED, INCLUDING WITHOUT LIMITATION IMPLIED WARRANTIES OF MERCHANTABILITY AND FITNESS FOR A PARTIC-ULAR PURPOSE, WITH RESPECT TO THE SOFTWARE, THE PROGRAMS, THE SOURCE CODE CONTAINED THEREIN, AND/OR THE TECHNIQUES DESCRIBED IN THIS BOOK. IDGB DOES NOT WARRANT THAT THE FUNC-TIONS CONTAINED IN THE SOFTWARE WILL MEET YOUR REQUIREMENTS OR THAT THE OPERATION OF THE SOFTWARE WILL BE ERROR FREE.**

(c) This limited warranty gives you specific legal rights, and you may have other rights that vary from jurisdiction to jurisdiction.

6. **Remedies.**

(a) IDGB's entire liability and your exclusive remedy for defects in materials and workmanship shall be limited to replacement of the Software Media, which may be returned to IDGB with a copy of your receipt at the following address: Software Media Fulfillment Department, Attn.: *HTML 4 For Dummies,* 2nd Edition, IDG Books Worldwide, Inc., 7260 Shadeland Station, Ste. 100, Indianapolis, IN 46256, or call 800-762-2974. Please allow three to four weeks for delivery. This Limited Warranty is void if failure of the Software Media has resulted from accident, abuse, or misapplication. Any replacement Software Media will be warranted for the remainder of the original warranty period or thirty (30) days, whichever is longer.

(b) In no event shall IDGB or the author be liable for any damages whatsoever (including without limitation damages for loss of business profits, business interruption, loss of business information, or any other pecuniary loss) arising from the use of or inability to use the Book or the Software, even if IDGB has been advised of the possibility of such damages.

(c) Because some jurisdictions do not allow the exclusion or limitation of liability for consequential or incidental damages, the above limitation or exclusion may not apply to you.

7. **U.S. Government Restricted Rights.** Use, duplication, or disclosure of the Software by the U.S. Government is subject to restrictions stated in paragraph (c)(1)(ii) of the Rights in Technical Data and Computer Software clause of DFARS 252.227-7013, and in subparagraphs (a) through (d) of the Commercial Computer–Restricted Rights clause at FAR 52.227-19, and in similar clauses in the NASA FAR supplement, when applicable.

8. **General.** This Agreement constitutes the entire understanding of the parties and revokes and supersedes all prior agreements, oral or written, between them and may not be modified or amended except in a writing signed by both parties hereto that specifically refers to this Agreement. This Agreement shall take precedence over any other documents that may be in conflict herewith. If any one or more provisions contained in this Agreement are held by any court or tribunal to be invalid, illegal, or otherwise unenforceable, each and every other provision shall remain in full force and effect.

Installation Instructions

For Mac OS users

1. **Insert the CD into your CD-ROM drive.**

   The *HTML 4 For Dummies CD* icon appears on your desktop.

2. **Double-click the *HTML 4 For Dummies CD* icon.**

   A window that reveals the contents of the CD opens.

3. **Read the Read Me First file and the License Agreement file by double-clicking their icons.**

To view the examples and templates on the CD, including the *HTML 4 For Dummies* Web page, open your Web browser and, with its Open or Open File command, open this file on the CD: HTML4DUM.HTM. This file is in the H4D4E folder at the root level of the CD (H4D4E/HTML4DUM.HTM).

To install any of the software included on the CD, double-click the folder for the program you want, and then run the program's setup or installation file.

For Windows 98/95 users

1. **Insert the CD in your CD-ROM drive.**

   Wait a few seconds while your CD-ROM drive reads the CD.

2. **Double-click the My Computer icon on your desktop and then double-click the icon for your CD-ROM drive.**

   A window that reveals the contents of the CD opens.

3. **Please read the ReadMe file (readme.txt) and End User License file (license.txt) by double-clicking their icons.**

To view the examples and templates on the CD, including the *HTML 4 For Dummies* Web page, follow the instructions listed for the Mac in the previous section, "For Mac OS users." To install any of the programs included on the CD, double-click the folder for the program you want, and then run the program's setup or installation file.

For more information about the CD, check out the "About the CD" appendix.

IDG BOOKS WORLDWIDE BOOK REGISTRATION

Register This Book and Win!

We want to hear from you!

Visit **http://my2cents.dummies.com** to register this book and tell us how you liked it!

- ✔ Get entered in our monthly prize giveaway.

- ✔ Give us feedback about this book — tell us what you like best, what you like least, or maybe what you'd like to ask the author and us to change!

- ✔ Let us know any other ...*For Dummies*® topics that interest you.

Your feedback helps us determine what books to publish, tells us what coverage to add as we revise our books, and lets us know whether we're meeting your needs as a ...*For Dummies* reader. You're our most valuable resource, and what you have to say is important to us!

Not on the Web yet? It's easy to get started with *Dummies 101*®*: The Internet For Windows*® *98* or *The Internet For Dummies*®, 5th Edition, at local retailers everywhere.

Or let us know what you think by sending us a letter at the following address:

...*For Dummies* Book Registration
Dummies Press
7260 Shadeland Station, Suite 100
Indianapolis, IN 46256-3917
Fax 317-596-5498

™

BESTSELLING
BOOK SERIES